AutoCAD 2019:
A Power Guide for Beginners and Intermediate Users

CADArtifex

The premium provider of learning products and solutions
www.cadartifex.com

AutoCAD 2019: A Power Guide for Beginners and Intermediate Users

Published by
CADArtifex
www.cadartifex.com

Copyright © 2017 CADArtifex

This textbook is copyrighted and the CADArtifex reserves all rights. No part of this publication may be reproduced, stored in a retrieval system, transmitted, transcribed, stored in a retrieval system or translated into any language, in any form or by any means, electronic, mechanical, photocopying, recording, scanning or otherwise without the prior written permission of the Publisher.

NOTICE TO THE READER
The publisher and the author make no representations or warranties with respect to the accuracy or completeness of the contents of this work/text and specifically disclaim all warranties, including without limitation warranties of fitness for a particular purpose. Publisher does not guarantee any of the products described in the text or perform any independent analysis in connection with any of the product information contained in the text. No warranty may be created or extended by sales or promotional materials. This work is sold with the understanding that the publisher is not engaged in rendering legal, accounting, or other professional services. Neither the publisher nor the author shall be liable for damages arising herefrom. Further, readers should be aware that Internet Websites listed in this work may have changed or disappeared between when this work was written and when it is read.

Examination Copies
Textbooks received as examination copies in any form such as paperback and eBook are for review only and may not be made available for the use of the student. These files may not be transferred to any other party. Resale of examination copies is prohibited.

Electronic Files
The electronic file/eBook in any form of this textbook is licensed to the original user only and may not be transferred to any other party.

Disclaimer
The author has made sincere efforts to ensure the accuracy of the material described herein, however the author makes no warranty, expressed or implied, with respect to the quality, correctness, accuracy, or freedom from error of this document or the products it describes.

www.cadartifex.com

Dedication

First and foremost, I would like to thank my parents for being a great support throughout my career and while writing this book.

Heartfelt thanks goes to my wife and my sisters for their patience and support in taking this challenge and letting me spare time for it.

I would also like to acknowledge the efforts of the employees at CADArtifex for their dedication in editing the content of this textbook.

Content at a Glance

Chapter 1. Introduction to AutoCAD .... 17 - 56
Chapter 2. Creating Drawings - I .... 57 - 108
Chapter 3. Working with Drawing Aids and Layers .... 109 - 162
Chapter 4. Creating Drawings - II .... 163 - 214
Chapter 5. Modifying and Editing Drawings - I .... 215 - 272
Chapter 6. Working with Dimensions and Dimensions Style .... 273 - 340
Chapter 7. Editing Dimensions and Adding Text .... 341 - 372
Chapter 8. Modifying and Editing Drawings - II .... 373 - 388
Chapter 9. Hatching and Gradients .... 389 - 400
Chapter 10. Working with Blocks and Xrefs .... 401 - 434
Chapter 11. Working with Layouts .... 435 - 462
Chapter 12. Printing and Plotting .... 463 - 494
Chapter 13. Introducing 3D Basics and Creating 3D Models .... 495 - 546

INDEX .... 547 - 554

Table of Contents

Dedication 3

Preface 13

Chapter 1. Introduction to AutoCAD .... 17 - 56

- Installing AutoCAD 18
- Getting Started with AutoCAD 18
- Starting a New Drawing File 23
- Working with Various Components of a Drawing 26
    - Application Menu 26
    - Quick Access Toolbar 27
    - Ribbon 27
    - InfoCenter 29
    - Command Line Window 30
    - ViewCube 31
    - Navigation Bar 33
    - Status Bar 33
- Starting a New Drawing File by using the Create New Drawing dialog box 40
    - Starting a New Drawing file from Scratch 40
    - Starting a New Drawing file by using a Template 41
    - Starting a New Drawing file by using a Wizard 41
- Changing the Color Scheme 45
- Changing the Background Color 46
- Working with Workspaces 47
    - Switching between Workspaces 47
    - Creating a New Workspace 47
- Working with Sheet Sets 48
    - Creating an Example Sheet Set 48
    - Creating an Existing Drawing Sheet Set 52
- Opening a Drawing File 53
- Saving a Drawing File 54
- Summary 56
- Questions 56

Chapter 2. Creating Drawings - I .... 57 - 108

- Setting up Drawing Units 57
- Setting Drawing Limits 61
- Specifying Grid and Snap Settings 62
- Understanding Coordinate Systems 65
    - Cartesian Coordinate System 66
    - Polar Coordinate System 69
- Creating a Drawing 72
- Drawing a Line 72

6 Table of Contents

- Example 1 74
- Hands-on Test Drive 1 77
- Example 2 77
- Hands-on Test Drive 2 79
- Drawing a Circle 80
  - Drawing a Circle by Defining Center Point and Radius 80
  - Drawing a Circle by Defining Center Point and Diameter 81
  - Drawing a Circle by Defining 2 Points 82
  - Drawing a Circle by Defining 3 Points 83
  - Drawing a Circle by Defining Tangent, Tangent, Radius 84
  - Drawing a Circle by Defining Tangent, Tangent, Tangent 85
- Drawing an Arc 86
  - Drawing an Arc by Defining 3 Points 86
  - Drawing an Arc by Defining Start, Center, and End Points 87
  - Drawing an Arc by Defining Start Point, Center Point, and Angle .. 88
  - Drawing an Arc by Defining Start Point, Center Point, and Length .. 89
  - Drawing an Arc by Defining Start Point, End Point, and Angle 89
  - Drawing an Arc by Defining Start Point, End Point, and Direction .. 90
  - Drawing an Arc by Defining Start Point, End Point, and Radius 90
  - Drawing an Arc by Defining Center Point, Start Point, and End Point .. 91
  - Drawing an Arc by Defining Center Point, Start Point, and Angle .. 91
  - Drawing an Arc by Defining Center Point, Start Point, and Length .. 92
  - Drawing an Arc by using the Continue Tool 92
- Canceling, Erasing and Restoring Objects 93
- Navigating 2D Drawing 94
  - Zoom 94
  - Zoom Realtime 94
  - Zoom All 95
  - Zoom Window 96
  - Zoom Previous 96
  - Zoom Extents 96
  - Zoom In 97
  - Zoom Out 97
  - Pan 98
- Tutorial 1 98
- Tutorial 2 102
- Hands-on Test Drive 3 107
- Hands-on Test Drive 4 107
- Summary 108
- Questions 108

Chapter 3. Working with Drawing Aids and Layers .... 109 - 162
- Working with Ortho Mode 109
- Example 1 110
- Working with Polar Tracking 112
- Example 2 114
- Working with Object Snap 117

Working with Object Snap Tracking 119
Working with Layers 121
    Creating a New Layer 122
    Setting the Current Layer 123
    Assigning Color to a Layer 125
    Assigning Linetype to a Layer 125
    Assigning Lineweight to a Layer 127
    Turning a Layer On or Off 128
    Freezing a Layer 128
    Locking or Unlocking a Layer 129
    Deleting a Layer 130
    Setting Transparency of a Layer 130
    Restricting a Layer for Plotting 130
    Freezing a Layer in New Viewports 131
    Freezing the New Layer in All Viewports 131
    Toggle Override Highlight 131
Assigning Objects to a Layer 133
    Tutorial 1 134
    Tutorial 2 148
    Hands-on Test Drive 1 161
    Summary 161
    Questions 161

Chapter 4. Creating Drawings - II .... 163 - 214
Drawing a Rectangle 163
    Drawing a Rectangle by Specifying Diagonally Opposite Corners 164
    Drawing a Rectangle by Specifying its Area and One Side 165
    Drawing a Rectangle by Specifying Dimensions 166
    Drawing a Rectangle at an Angle 167
    Drawing a Rectangle with Chamfer 168
    Drawing a Rectangle with Fillets 169
    Drawing a Rectangle with Elevation 170
    Drawing a Rectangle with Thickness 171
    Drawing a Rectangle with Width 172
Drawing a Polygon 173
    Inscribed Polygon 173
    Circumscribed Polygon 174
Drawing a Polyline 174
    Procedure for Drawing a Polyline with Line Segments 175
    Procedure for Drawing a Polyline with Line and Arc Segments 176
    Procedure for Drawing a Polyline with Width 178
    Procedure for Drawing a Polyline with Halfwidth 179
Drawing an Ellipse 180
    Procedure for Drawing an Ellipse by Using the Axis, End Tool 180
    Procedure for Drawing an Ellipse by Using the Center Tool 181
Drawing an Elliptical Arc 182
Drawing a Spline 183

8 Table of Contents

- Drawing a Spline by Using the Spline Fit Tool 184
- Drawing a Spline by Using the Spline CV Tool 186
- Drawing Donuts 188
- Drawing Construction and Ray lines 189
  - Procedure for Drawing Construction Lines 190
  - Procedure for Drawing Ray Lines 194
- Drawing Points and Defining Point Style/Size 195
  - Procedure for Drawing Reference Points 195
  - Procedure for Defining the Point Style and Point Size 195
- Tutorial 1 197
- Tutorial 2 204
- Tutorial 3 209
- Hands-on Test Drive 1 213
- Hands-on Test Drive 2 213
- Summary 214
- Questions 214

Chapter 5. Modifying and Editing Drawings - I .... 215 - 272

- Working with Object Selection Methods 216
  - Window Selection Method 216
  - Cross Window Selection Method 216
- Invoking a Selection Method within a Command 217
  - Window Selection Method 217
  - Cross Window Selection Method 217
  - All Selection Method 218
  - Cross Polygon Selection Method 218
  - Window Polygon Selection Method 218
  - Fence Selection Method 219
  - Last Selection Method 219
- Trimming Drawing Entities 220
- Extending Drawing Entities 221
- Working with the Array 223
  - Procedure for Creating a Rectangular Array 224
  - Procedure for Creating a Polar/Circular Array 225
  - Procedure for Creating a Path Array 227
- Mirroring Drawing Entities 228
- Filleting Drawing Entities 229
- Chamfering Drawing Entities 232
  - Procedure for Creating a Chamfer by Distance distance Method 233
  - Procedure for Creating a Chamfer by Angle distance Method 234
- Offsetting Drawing Entities 235
- Moving Drawing Objects 237
- Copying Drawing Objects 238
- Rotating Drawing Objects 239
- Scaling Drawing Objects 240
- Stretching Drawing Objects 242

Lengthening Drawing Objects 243
　　　　Procedure for Lengthening Object by Specifying Delta Value 243
　　　　Procedure for Lengthening Object by Specifying Percentage 244
　　　　Procedure for Lengthening Object by Specifying Total Length 245
　　　　Procedure for Lengthening Object by Dragging 245
　　Tutorial 1 246
　　Tutorial 2 250
　　Tutorial 3 257
　　Hands-on Test Drive 1 270
　　Hands-on Test Drive 2 270
　　Hands-on Test Drive 3 271
　　Summary 271
　　Questions 271

Chapter 6. Working with Dimensions and Dimensions Style .... 273 - 340
　　Working with Components of a Dimension 274
　　Creating New Dimension Style 276
　　Modifying Existing Dimension Style 300
　　Overriding Dimension Style 301
　　Applying Dimensions 302
　　　　Applying the Linear Dimension 304
　　　　Applying the Aligned Dimension 306
　　　　Applying the Angular Dimension 308
　　　　Applying the Arc Length Dimension 311
　　　　Applying the Radius Dimension 311
　　　　Applying the Diameter Dimension 312
　　　　Applying the Jogged Radius Dimension 313
　　　　Applying the Jogged Linear Dimension 314
　　　　Applying the Ordinate Dimension 315
　　　　Applying Baseline Dimensions 317
　　　　Applying Continue Dimensions 319
　　　　Applying Multiple Dimensions 320
　　Tutorial 1 322
　　Hands-on Test Drive 1 336
　　Hands-on Test Drive 2 337
　　Hands-on Test Drive 3 337
　　Hands-on Test Drive 4 339
　　Summary 340
　　Questions 340

Chapter 7. Editing Dimensions and Adding Text .... 341 - 372
　　Editing Dimensions by using DIMEDIT Command 342
　　　　Procedure for Specifying the New Dimension Text/Value 342
　　　　Procedure for Rotating the Dimension Text 342
　　　　Procedure for Restoring the Dimension Text to Original Position 343
　　　　Procedure for Changing the Oblique Angle of Extension Lines 343
　　Editing Dimensions by using DIMTEDIT Command 344

Editing Dimensions by using DDEDIT Command 345
Editing Dimensions by using Dimension Grips 346
    Procedure for Changing the Position of Dimension Text 346
    Procedure for Changing the Space between Dimension Line and Object 347
    Procedure for Changing the Position of Extension Lines 347
Editing Dimensions by using PROPERTIES Palette 348
Editing Dimensions by using Editing Tools 349
    Procedure for Editing Dimensions by using the Trim Tool 349
    Procedure for Editing Dimensions by using the Extend Tool 350
    Procedure for Editing Dimensions by using the Stretch Tool 351
Adding Text/Notes 352
    Creating and Modifying a Text Style 352
    Adding Text by using the Single Line Tool 353
    Adding Text by using the Multiline Text Tool 355
Editing the Single line and Multiline Text 357
Converting the Single line Text to the Multiline Text 358
Tutorial 1 358
Tutorial 2 367
Hands-on Test Drive 1 371
Summary 371
Questions 371

Chapter 8. Modifying and Editing Drawings - II .... 373 - 388

Editing Objects by using Grips 373
    Stretching Objects by using Grips 374
    Moving Objects by using Grips 374
    Rotating Objects by using Grips 375
    Scaling Objects by using Grips 376
    Mirroring Objects by using Grips 376
Editing Objects by using PROPERTIES Palette 377
Matching Properties of an Object 377
Identifying Coordinates of a Point 379
Tutorial 1 380
Hands-on Test Drive 1 386
Hands-on Test Drive 2 387
Summary 388
Questions 388

Chapter 9. Hatching and Gradients .... 389 - 400

Creating the Hatches 390
Creating the Gradients 393
Tutorial 1 395
Hands-on Test Drive 1 398
Hands-on Test Drive 2 399
Summary 400
Questions 400

Chapter 10. Working with Blocks and Xrefs .... 401 - 434
    Creating a Block 402
    Inserting a Block in the Drawing 407
    Creating a WBlock 410
    Inserting a WBlock in the Drawing 412
    Editing a Block 413
    Making a Dynamic Block 415
    Working with External References (Xrefs) 419
    Tutorial 1 423
    Hands-on Test Drive 1 433
    Summary 434
    Questions 434

Chapter 11. Working with Layouts .... 435 - 462
    Getting Started with Paper Space/Layout 436
    Understanding Different Components of a Layout 436
    Setting up the Sheet/Paper Size of a Layout 437
    Adding, Renaming, and Deleting a Layout 439
    Working with Viewports 440
        Editing a Viewport 441
        Deleting a Viewport 442
        Creating Viewports 442
    Accessing the Model Space within a Viewport 448
    Clipping a Viewport 449
    Locking the Object Scale in a Viewport 450
    Controlling the Display of Objects in a Viewport 451
    Controlling Layers Properties for Viewports 451
        Viewport Freeze 452
        Viewport Color 452
    Switching to the Model Space 453
    Creating Viewports in the Model Space 454
        Viewport Configuration 454
    Joining Two Viewports 455
    Restoring Viewports 455
    Tutorial 1 455
    Hands-on Test Drive 1 460
    Hands-on Test Drive 2 461
    Summary 462
    Questions 462

Chapter 12. Printing and Plotting .... 463 - 494
    Configuring a Plotter (Output Device) 463
    Creating a Plot Style 466
    Setting up a Default Plot Style 471
    Plotting a Drawing 473
    Tutorial 1 480
    Tutorial 2 484

12 Table of Contents

Hands-on Test Drive 1 493
Hands-on Test Drive 2 493
Summary 494
Questions 494

Chapter 13. Introducing 3D Basics and Creating 3D Models .... 495 - 546

Invoking the 3D Modeling/3D Basics Workspace 496
Creating 3D Primitives 497
    Creating a 3D Solid Box 498
    Creating a 3D Solid Cylinder 499
    Creating a 3D Solid Cone 501
    Creating a 3D Solid Sphere 501
    Creating a 3D Solid Pyramid 502
    Creating a 3D Solid Wedge 503
    Creating a 3D Solid Torus 504
Creating 3D Models 505
Working with World Coordinate System (WCS) 506
Working with User Coordinate System (UCS) 507
Setting Work Plane to Predefined Orthographic View 512
Working with Dynamic UCS 513
Controlling the Display of the UCS 514
Creating an Extrude Feature 515
Converting a Closed Sketch into a Region 517
Creating a Revolve Feature 518
Creating a Sweep Feature 519
Creating a Loft Feature 521
Working with Presspull Tool 524
Creating a 3D Wall-like Polysolid 526
Performing Boolean Operations 527
    Combining Solid Bodies 527
    Subtracting Solid Bodies 527
    Intersecting Solid Bodies 528
Checking Interference between Bodies 529
Copying Edges of a Solid Feature 530
Performing Modifying Operations 532
Tutorial 1 532
Hands-on Test Drive 1 543
Hands-on Test Drive 2 544
Hands-on Test Drive 3 545
Summary 545
Questions 546

INDEX .... **547 - 554**

Preface

AutoCAD, the product of Autodesk Inc., is one of the biggest technology providers to engineering, architecture, construction, manufacturing, media, and entertainment industries. It offers complete design, engineering, and entertainment software that let you design, visualize, simulate, and publish your ideas before they are built or created. Moreover, Autodesk continues to develop the comprehensive portfolio of state-of-art 3D software for global markets.

AutoCAD delivers a comprehensive set of productivity tools/commands that allow you to create stunning designs, speed up the documentation work, and add precision to your engineering and architectural drawings. AutoCAD is very comprehensive in its ability to create 2D and 3D drawings. With AutoCAD, you can share your designs with your clients, sub-contractors, and colleagues in smart new ways.

AutoCAD 2019: A Power Guide for Beginners and Intermediate Users textbook is designed for instructor-led courses as well as for self-paced learning. It is intended to help engineers, designers, and CAD operators interested in learning AutoCAD for creating engineering and architectural 2D drawings as well as 3D Models. This textbook is a great help for new AutoCAD users and a great teaching aid in a classroom setting. This textbook consists of 13 chapters, total 554 pages covering major workspaces of AutoCAD such as Drafting & Annotation and 3D Modeling. This textbook teaches you how to use AutoCAD software to create, edit, plot, and manage real world engineering and architectural 2D drawings as well as 3D Models.

This textbook not only focuses on the usage of the tools/commands of AutoCAD but also on the concept of design. Every chapter of this book contains tutorials that instruct users step-by-step how to create mechanical designs and drawings with ease. Moreover, every chapter ends with hands-on test drives that allow the users of this textbook to experience themselves the ease-of-use and powerful capabilities of AutoCAD.

Who Should Read This Textbook

This textbook is written with a wide range of AutoCAD users in mind, varying from beginners to advanced users and AutoCAD instructors. The easy-to-follow chapters of this book allow you to understand different design techniques and AutoCAD tools/commands easily.

What Is Covered in This Textbook

AutoCAD 2019: A Power Guide for Beginners and Intermediate Users textbook is designed to help you learn everything you need to know to start using AutoCAD 2019 with easy to understand, step-by-step tutorials. This book covers the following:

*Chapter 1, "**Introduction to AutoCAD**,"* introduces system requirements for installing AutoCAD and explains how to start a new drawing file. It also introduces screen components, workspaces, and sheet sets of AutoCAD. Additionally, it explains how to change the color scheme, background color, and open and save drawing files in AutoCAD.

*Chapter 2, "**Creating Drawings - I**,"* introduces how to set drawing units, drawing limits, and grid and snap settings. It also introduces various coordinate systems used in AutoCAD and explains how to create a line, circle, and arc entities in AutoCAD. Additionally, it introduces how to cancel, erase, undo, and navigating 2D drawing.

*Chapter 3, "**Working with Drawing Aids and Layers**,"* introduces Ortho mode, Polar Tracking, Object Snap, and Object Snap Tracking. It also explains how to specify grids and snaps settings. Additionally, it explains how to work with layers and assigning objects to layers.

*Chapter 4, "**Creating Drawings - II**,"* introduces how to create rectangles, polygons, polylines, ellipses, elliptical arcs, splines, donuts, construction lines, ray lines, and points. It also introduces how to define point style/size.

*Chapter 5, "**Modifying and Editing Drawings - I**,"* introduces various object selection methods and how to trim and extend drawing entities. It also explains how to create arrays, mirror, fillet, chamfer, offset, move, copy, rotate, scale, stretch, and lengthen drawing entities.

*Chapter 6, "**Working with Dimensions and Dimensions Style**,"* introduces various components of a dimension, how to create a new dimension style, modify the existing dimension style, and override dimension style. It also explains how to apply various types of dimensions such as linear dimension, aligned dimension, angular dimension, diameter dimension, radius dimension, jogged dimension, ordinate dimension, and baseline dimension.

*Chapter 7, "**Editing Dimensions and Adding Text**,"* introduces how to modify dimensions by using the DIMEDIT command, DIMTEDIT command, DDEDIT command, dimension grips, Properties palette, and editing tools such as Trim, Extend, and Stretch. It also introduces how to add text/notes to drawings, create and modify text style, and add text by using the Single Line and Multiline Text tools. Moreover, it also introduces how to edit single line and multiline texts, and how to convert the single line text to the multiline text.

*Chapter 8, "**Modifying and Editing Drawings - II**,"* introduces how to edit drawing entities by using the grips and the Properties palette. It also introduces matching the properties of an object with the other drawing objects. Moreover, it also explains how to identify the coordinates of a point in a drawing.

*Chapter 9, "**Hatching and Gradients**,"* introduces how to create different types of hatch patterns and gradients in enclosed areas of a drawing.

*Chapter 10, "**Working with Blocks and Xrefs**,"* introduces how to create and insert a Block and WBlock in a drawing. It also explains how to edit Blocks and make Dynamic Blocks. Moreover, it also explains how to work with external reference files (Xrefs).

Chapter 11, "**Working with Layouts**," introduces how to get started with a Paper space/layout and introduces different components of a layout (Paper space). It also explains how to set up sheet/paper size of a layout, how to add, rename, and delete a layout. Moreover, it also explains how to work with viewports, access the Model space within a viewport, clips a viewport, lock the object scale in a viewport, control the display of objects in a viewport, and control layer properties of a viewport. Additionally, it explains how to switch between the Model space and layout, and how to create viewports in the Model space.

Chapter 12, "**Printing and Plotting**," introduces how to configure a plotter (output device) in AutoCAD. It also explains how to create a plot style and set up the default plot style for plotting/printing. Additionally, it introduces how to plot/print drawings in AutoCAD.

Chapter 13, "**Introducing 3D Basics and Creating 3D Models**," introduces about creating 3D Models in the 3D Modeling workspace. It introduces how to create various 3D primitives such as box, cylinder, sphere, cone, and torus. Also, explains about World Coordinate System (WCS) and User Coordinate System (UCS). It also introduces how to set the work plane to predefined orthographic view, work with Dynamic UCS, and control the display of UCS. Besides, it introduces how to create an extrude, revolve, sweep, loft, and 3D wall-like polysolid features of a 3D model. It also introduces how to perform various boolean operations, check interference, and copy edges of a solid feature.

Icons/Terms used in this Textbook
The following icons and terms used in this textbook:

Note
Note: Notes highlight information which requires special attention.

Tip
Tip: Tips provide additional advice, which increases the efficiency of the users.

Flyout
A flyout is a pop-up in which a set of tools is grouped together, see Figure 1.

Drop-down List
A drop-down list is a pop-up in which a set of options is grouped together to perform a task, see Figure 2.

Field
A field allows you to enter a new value, or modify the existing value, as per your requirement, see Figure 2.

Check box
A check box allows you to turn on or off the use of a particular option. It is used to select an appropriate option to turn it on, see Figure 2.

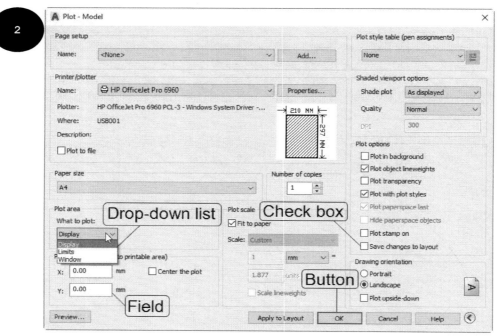

Button
A button appears as a 3D icon and is used to confirm or discard an action. It is also used to turn on or off the uses of a particular option or command.

How to Contact the Author
We welcome your valuable feedback and suggestions. Please E-mail us at *info@cadartifex.com*. You can also login to our website *www.cadartifex.com* and write your comments about the textbook.

Thank you very much for purchasing **AutoCAD 2019: A Power Guide for Beginners and Intermediate Users** textbook. We hope that the information and concepts introduced in this book will help you to accomplish your professional goals.

CHAPTER 1

Introduction to AutoCAD

In this chapter, you will learn the following:

- Installing AutoCAD
- Getting Started with AutoCAD
- Starting a New Drawing File
- Working with Various Components of a Drawing
- Starting a New Drawing File by using the Create New Drawing dialog box
- Changing the Color Scheme
- Changing the Background Color
- Working with Workspaces
- Working with Sheet Sets
- Opening a Drawing File
- Saving a Drawing File

Welcome to the world of Computer-aided design (CAD) with AutoCAD. AutoCAD, the product of Autodesk Inc., is one of the biggest technology providers to engineering, architecture, construction, manufacturing, media, and entertainment industries. It offers complete 3D design, engineering, and entertainment software that let you design, visualize, simulate, and publish your ideas before they are built or created. Moreover, Autodesk continues to develop the comprehensive portfolio of state-of-art CAD software for global markets.

AutoCAD delivers a comprehensive set of productivity tools/commands that allow you to create stunning designs, speed up the documentation work, and add precision to your engineering and architectural drawings. AutoCAD is very comprehensive in its ability to create 2D and 3D drawings. With AutoCAD, you can share your designs with your clients, sub-contractors, and colleagues in smart new ways.

Due to the capabilities available with AutoCAD to create 2D and 3D drawings, AutoCAD used across a wide range of industries by engineers, architects, project managers, graphic designers, and other professionals.

Installing AutoCAD

If you do not have AutoCAD installed in your system, you first need to get it installed. However, before you start installing AutoCAD, you need to check the system requirements and make sure that you have a system capable of running AutoCAD adequately. Below are the system requirements for installing AutoCAD 2019.

1. **Operating Systems:** Microsoft® Windows® 7 SP1 with Update KB4019990(32-bit & 64-bit), Microsoft Windows 8.1 with Update KB2919355 (32-bit & 64-bit), and Microsoft Windows 10 Anniversry Update (64-bit only, version 1607 or higher).
2. **Processor**: Basic processor 2.5-2.9 GHz and recommended processor 3+ GHz.
3. **RAM:** Basic memory 8 GB and recommended memory 16 GB.
4. **Display Card:** Basic 1 GB GPU with 29 GB/s Bandwidth and DirectX 11 compliant and recommended 4 GB GPU with 106 GB/s Bandwidth and Directx 11 compliant.
5. **Disk Space:** 6.0 GB.

For more information about the system requirement for AutoCAD 2019, visit *AutoCAD website at https://knowledge.autodesk.com/support/autocad/learn-explore/caas/sfdcarticles/sfdcarticles/System-requirements-for-AutoCAD-2019-including-Specialized-Toolsets.html*

Once the system is ready, install AutoCAD using the AutoCAD DVD or the downloaded AutoCAD data.

Getting Started with AutoCAD

Once the AutoCAD 2019 installed on your system, start it by double-clicking on the **AutoCAD 2019** icon available on the desktop of your system. As soon as you double-click on the **AutoCAD 2019** icon, the system prepares for starting AutoCAD by loading all required files. Once all the necessary files are loaded, the initial screen of AutoCAD 2019 appears, see Figure 1.1.

If you are starting AutoCAD for the first time after installing the software, the **Sign in** window appears, see Figure 1.2. In this window, enter your E-mail and then click on the **NEXT** button. The **Welcome** page of the **Sign in** window appears, see Figure 1.3. In this **Welcome** window, enter your password and then click on the **SIGN IN** button. The initial screen of AutoCAD 2019 appears, refer to Figure 1.1.

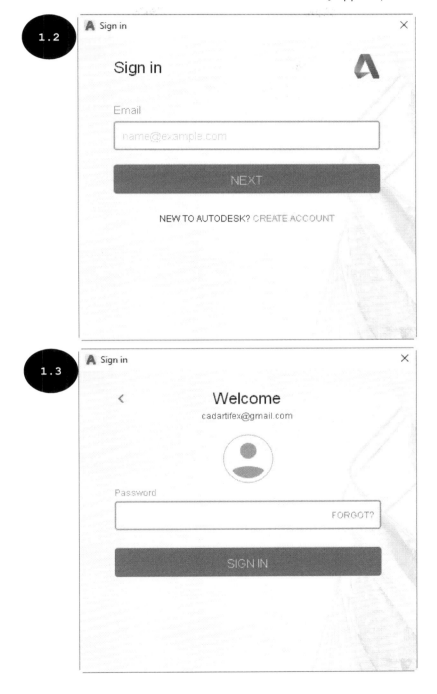

Chapter 1 > Introduction to AutoCAD

The initial screen of AutoCAD allows you to start a new drawing, open an existing drawing, learn about various featured topics, and so on. The initial screen of AutoCAD is provided with **CREATE** and **LEARN** pages, see Figure 1.4. By default, the **CREATE** page is activated. As a result, the initial screen of AutoCAD allows you to create a new drawing, open an existing drawing, and so on, see Figure 1.4. To activate the **LEARN** page, click on the **LEARN** option at the bottom of the initial screen of AutoCAD. The **LEARN** page provides access to learning resources such as What's New, Getting Started videos, Learning tips, and Online Resources, see Figure 1.5.

The various components of the CREATE page in the initial screen of AutoCAD are discussed next.

Get Started
The options in the **Get Started** section are used to start a new drawing file and open an existing drawing file. The options are discussed next.

Start Drawing
The **Start Drawing** option/icon of the **Get Started** section is used to start a new drawing file with the default drawing template (*acad.dwt*). For doing so, click on the **Start Drawing** option/icon in the **Get Started** section. A new drawing file with default template (*acad.dwt*) gets started and appears in a new tab with the default name '**Drawing 1**', see Figure 1.6. Note that in this figure, the background color of the drawing area has changed to white and the display of grids has been turned off for better clarity. You will learn about changing the background color and grid settings later in this chapter. Also, the various components of a new drawing file are discussed later in this chapter.

1.6

Templates
The **Templates** drop-down list of the **Get Started** section displays a list of all the available drawing templates, see Figure 1.7. To invoke this drop-down list, click on **Templates** in the **Get Started** section. Note that by default, the **acad.dwt** drawing template is selected in the **Templates** drop-down list. As a result, on clicking **Start Drawing** in the **Get Started** section. A new drawing file with the *acad.dwt* drawing template gets invoked. Click on the required template in the **Templates** drop-down list to start a new drawing file with the specified drawing template.

The **Create New Sheet Set** option in the **Templates** drop-down list is used to create a new sheet set. A sheet set is used to manage multiple drawings (sheets) of a project in a tree view, see Figure 1.8. It helps in plotting, publishing, opening, e-transmitting, and zipping many drawing files easier and faster. You will learn more about creating a sheet set later in this chapter.

Open Files
The **Open Files** option in the **Get Started** section is used to open an existing drawing file. For doing so, click on the **Open Files** option. The **Select File** dialog box appears. In this dialog box, browse to the location where the drawing file is saved. Next, select the drawing file to be opened and then click on the **Open** button in the **Select File** dialog box. The selected drawing file gets opened in AutoCAD.

Open a Sheet Set
The **Open a Sheet Set** option in the **Get Started** section is used to open an existing sheet set file. To open an existing sheet set file, click on the **Open a Sheet Set** option. The **Open Sheet Set** dialog box appears. This dialog box displays the list of all the existing sheet sets. Select the required sheet set and then click on the **Open** button.

Get More Templates Online
The **Get More Templates Online** option in the **Get Started** section is used to download additional template files.

Explore Sample Drawings
The **Explore Sample Drawings** option is used to open sample drawing files of AutoCAD.

AutoCAD 2019: A Power Guide > 23

Recent Documents
The **Recent Documents** section of the initial screen displays the list of recently opened drawing files. You can click on any recently opened drawing file in the list to open it again.

Connect
The **Connect** section of the initial screen is used to login into **A360** account to access the online services. Also, you can access the online form to provide feedback.

Starting a New Drawing File
To start a new drawing file, click on the **Start Drawing** option/icon in the **Get Started** section of the initial screen, see Figure 1.9. Alternatively, click on the **+sign**, next to the **Start** tab in the initial screen of AutoCAD to start a new drawing file with the default template, see Figure 1.10. Besides, click on the **New** tool in the **Quick Access Toolbar**, see Figure 1.11. The **Select template** dialog box appears, see Figure 1.12. In this dialog box, select the *acad.dwt* drawing template. The *acad.dwt* drawing template is used to start the 2D drawing environment whereas the *acad3D.dwt* drawing template is used to start the 3D modeling environment. Next, click on the **Open** button in the dialog box. The new drawing gets started with the *acad.dwt* drawing template.

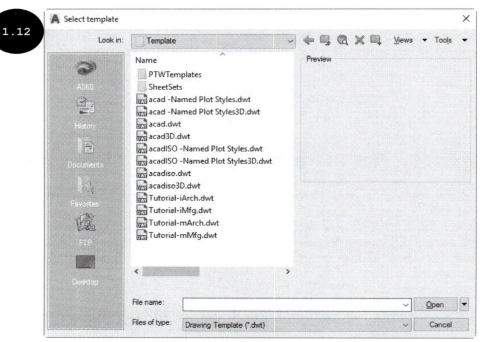

1.12

You can also start a new drawing file without a drawing template either in metric or imperial unit system by using the **Select template** dialog box. For doing so, click on the down arrow, next to the **Open** button in the **Select template** dialog box, see Figure 1.13. A drop-down list appears. In this drop-down list, the **Open with no Template - Imperial** and **Open with no Template - Metric** options are available. You can click on the required option to start a new drawing file.

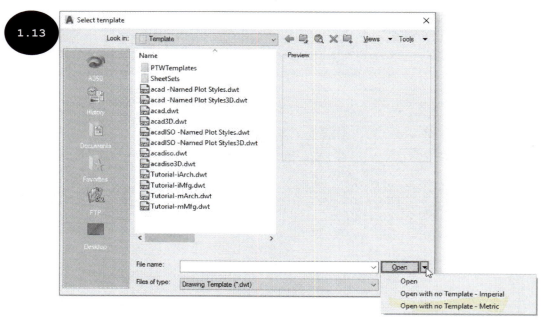

1.13

Note: As discussed, when you click on the **New** tool in the **Quick Access Toolbar**, the **Select template** dialog box appears for starting a new drawing file. It is because the system variable for STARTUP set to 3. If you set it to 1 then by clicking on the **New** tool, the **Create New Drawing** dialog box appears, see Figure 1.14. You can also start a new drawing by using this **Create New Drawing** dialog box. You will learn about setting system variable and start a new drawing file by using the **Create New Drawing** dialog box later in this chapter.

Figure 1.15 shows various components of a new drawing file such as **Application Menu**, **Quick Access Toolbar**, **Ribbon**, **ViewCube**, **Command Line** window, **Navigation Bar**, and **Status Bar**. Note that the background color of the drawing area has changed to white, and the display of grids is turned off for better clarity. You will learn about changing the background color of the drawing area and controlling the display of grids later in this chapter.

Note that the availability of tools in the **Ribbon** depends upon the activated workspace. By default, the **Drafting and Annotation** workspace is the active workspace of a new drawing. As a result, the tools related to drafting and annotation are available in the **Ribbon**. You can switch among the **Drafting and Annotation**, **3D Basics**, and **3D Modeling** workspaces by using the **Workspace Switching** flyout, see Figure 1.16. You will learn more about workspaces later in this chapter.

Working with Various Components of a Drawing

The various components of a new drawing such as **Application Menu**, **Quick Access Toolbar**, **Ribbon**, **ViewCube**, **Command Line window**, **Navigation Bar**, and **Status Bar** are discussed next.

Application Menu

The **Application Menu** is used to access the commonly used tools to start, open, save, export, print/publish, and so on a drawing file. To invoke the **Application Menu**, click on the **Application** button (red AutoCAD icon) at the upper left corner of the screen, see Figure 1.17.

Quick Access Toolbar

The Quick Access Toolbar provided with frequently used tools such as **New**, **Open**, **Save**, **Save As**, **Plot**, and **Undo**, see Figure 1.18. It is available at the upper left corner of the screen. In addition to the default tools, you can customize to add or remove tools in the Quick Access Toolbar.

To add more tools in the **Quick Access Toolbar**, right-click on a tool in the **Quick Access Toolbar**. A flyout appears, see Figure 1.19. In this flyout, click on the **Customize Quick Access Toolbar** option. The **Customize User Interface** window appears. This window displays the list of all the available tools/command in AutoCAD. Move the cursor over the tool/command to be added to the **Quick Access Toolbar** and then press and hold the left mouse button on it. Next, drag the cursor where you want to add this tool in the **Quick Access Toolbar** and then release the left mouse button. The selected tool gets added to the specified location in the **Quick Access Toolbar**. Similarly, you can add multiple tools by dragging them one by one from the **Customize User Interface** window to the **Quick Access Toolbar**. You can also drag and drop multiple tools at a time in the **Quick Access Toolbar** from the **Customize User Interface** window by pressing and holding the CTRL key. After adding the required tools to the **Quick Access Toolbar**, click on the **OK** button to exit the **Customize User Interface** window.

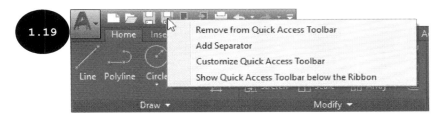

To remove a tool from the **Quick Access Toolbar**, move the cursor over the tool to be removed and then right-click. A flyout appears, see Figure 1.19. In this flyout, click on the **Remove from Quick Access Toolbar** option. The selected tool gets removed from the **Quick Access Toolbar**.

Ribbon

The **Ribbon** is composed of a series of tabs such as **Home**, **Insert**, and **Annotate** in which set of similar tools are grouped in different panels, see Figure 1.20. For example, the tools used to create drawing objects are arranged in the **Draw** panel and the tools used to modify or edit objects are grouped in the **Modify** panel, see Figure 1.20. Note that the availability of tools, panels, and tabs in the **Ribbon** depends upon the activated workspace.

By default, the **Ribbon** is docked horizontally at the top of the drawing area. You can dock the **Ribbon** vertically to the right or left of the drawing area. You can also undock the **Ribbon** such that it can float within the drawing area. To dock the **Ribbon** vertically to the right or left of the drawing area, right-click on a tab in the **Ribbon**. A shortcut menu appears, see Figure 1.21. In this shortcut menu, click on the **Undock** option. The **Ribbon** gets undocked and appears in floating state in the drawing area. Next, right-click on the title bar of the undocked **Ribbon**. A shortcut menu appears. In this shortcut menu, click on either the **Anchor Left <** or the **Anchor Right >** option. To dock the **Ribbon** back to the default position (horizontally at the top of the drawing area), press and hold the left mouse button on the title bar of the **Ribbon** and then drag the **Ribbon** toward the top of the drawing area. Next, release the left mouse button when the outline of a window appears at the top of the drawing area.

You can also change the default display state of the **Ribbon** (**Full Ribbon**) to three minimized states: **Minimize to Tabs**, **Minimize to Panel Titles**, and **Minimize to Panel Buttons**. For doing so, click on the down arrow available at the end of the last tab in the title bar of the **Ribbon**, see Figure 1.22. A flyout appears. In this flyout, click on the required display state. In the **Minimize to Tabs** display state, the **Ribbon** gets minimized such that only the tab titles appear in the **Ribbon**. In the **Minimize to Panel Titles** display state, only the tab and panel titles appear in the **Ribbon**. In the **Minimize to Panel Buttons** display state, only the tab titles and panel buttons appear in the **Ribbon**.

You can also cycle through the different states of the **Ribbon** by clicking on the small rectangular button with a black arrow in it, located at the end of the last tab in the **Ribbon**, see Figure 1.23. On clicking this rectangular button, you can cycle through all four display states of the **Ribbon** in a sequence, **Full Ribbon, Minimize to Panel Buttons, Minimize to Panel Titles, Minimize to Tabs**.

AutoCAD 2019: A Power Guide > 29

InfoCenter

The **InfoCenter** is available at the upper right corner of the AutoCAD window, see Figure 1.24. It is used to access help document for finding the information related to a topic. Also, it provides tools to access the Autodesk App Store, Sign In to Autodesk account, Autodesk YouTube/Facebook/Twitter channels, and so on. The various components of the **InfoCenter** are discussed next.

Search

The **Search** field is used to enter a keyword of a topic or command/tool to find the information related to it in the help document.

Sign In

The **Sign In** area is used to login to the Autodesk account. When you click on the **Sign In** area in the **InfoCenter**, a flyout appears, see Figure 1.25. In this flyout, click on the **Sign In to Autodesk account** tool to login into the Autodesk account. Note that if you are already logged in, then your name appears in this area.

Autodesk App Store

The **Autodesk App Store** tool is used to access the Autodesk App Store web page for downloading the plug-ins and Autodesk applications.

Stay Connected

The **Stay Connected** tool is used to stay connected with the Autodesk online community. When you click on **Stay Connected** in the **InfoCenter**, a flyout appears, see Figure 1.26. This flyout provides various options to stay connected with Autodesk.

Figure 1.26

Help

The **Help** tool is used to access online help document. When you click on the **Help** tool in the **InfoCenter**, the online help document gets opened. If you click on the down arrow next to the **Help** tool in the **InfoCenter**, a flyout appears, see Figure 1.27. By using the tools in this flyout, you can access the online help document, download offline help document, send feedback, get product information, and so on.

Figure 1.27

Command Line Window

A small horizontal window appears at the bottom of the drawing area is known as the Command Line window, see Figure 1.28.

Figure 1.28

The Command Line window is used to enter commands and displays subsequent command prompt sequence. By default, the Command Line window displays one line of text (command prompt), which provides the information about the action to be taken and various options based on the currently active command/tool. Notice that as you continue working through a command/tool, the previous command prompts get scrolled up and appear in the faded background just above the Command Line window, see Figure 1.29. Note that, by default, only last three command prompt lines appear above the Command Line window. To display all the previous command prompt lines, press the F2 key. You can also increase or decrease the display area of the Command Line window to show the previous command prompts. For doing so, move the cursor over the top edge of the Command Line window and then drag it by pressing and holding the left mouse button.

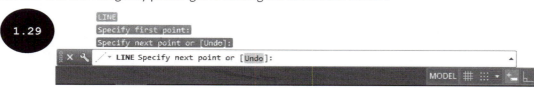

Figure 1.29

AutoCAD 2019: A Power Guide > 31

Tip: It is recommended for new users to pay attention to the command prompt as through it AutoCAD communicates with you and inform you about the action to be taken.

Note: If the display of the Command Line window is turned off or it does not appears in the drawing area, then press the CTRL + 9 key to display it again in the drawing area.

ViewCube

The **ViewCube** is available at the upper right corner of the drawing area, see Figures 1.30 and 1.31.

The **ViewCube** is used to change the view/orientation of a drawing/model. You can switch between standard and isometric views of a model by using the **ViewCube**. It primarily used for 3D modeling environment where you can view the 3D model in different standard and isometric views. By default, it is in an inactive state. When you move the cursor over the **ViewCube**, it becomes active and works as a navigation tool. You can navigate the drawing by using the **ViewCube** components, see Figure 1.31. The various **ViewCube** components are discussed next.

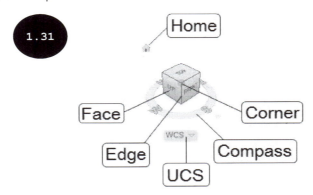

Home
The **Home** icon of the **ViewCube** is used to bring the current view of the drawing to the default home position.

Corner
A corner of the **ViewCube** is used to get an isometric view or to rotate the view freely in all directions. To get an isometric view, click on a corner of the **ViewCube** and to rotate the view freely in all directions, drag a corner of the **ViewCube** by pressing and holding the left mouse button.

32 Chapter 1 > Introduction to AutoCAD

Compass
The **Compass** is used to rotate the view. For doing so, press and hold the left mouse button on the **Compass** ring and then drag the cursor.

Edge
An edge of the **ViewCube** is used to get an edge-on view or to rotate the view freely in all directions. To get an edge-on view, click on the edge of the **ViewCube** and to rotate the view freely in all directions, drag an edge of the **ViewCube** by pressing and holding the left mouse button.

Face
A face of the **ViewCube** is used to get an orthogonal view such as a top, front, or right. For example, to get a top view of the drawing/model, click on the top face of the **ViewCube**.

UCS
When you click on the down arrow available in the **UCS** option of the **ViewCube**, the **UCS** drop-down list appears, see Figure 1.32. By using the options in this drop-down list, you can select an existing UCS or create a new UCS, see Figure 1.32. The term UCS stands for User Coordinate System, which is used to define points in 2D and 3D environments. By default, AutoCAD is provided with World Coordinate System (WCS), which is a global system. You will learn more about coordinate systems in later chapters.

1.32

Note: If the **ViewCube** does not display on the right corner of the drawing area, then click on the **View Cube** tool in the **Viewport Tools** panel of the **View** tab in the **Ribbon**, see Figure 1.33.

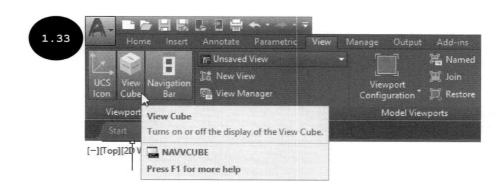

1.33

Navigation Bar

The **Navigation Bar** is used to access navigation tools such as **Zoom** and **Pan**, see Figure 1.34. It is available to the right of the drawing area. You can turn on or off the display of the **Navigation Bar** by clicking on the **Navigation Bar** tool in the **Viewport Tools** panel of the **View** tab in the **Ribbon**, see Figure 1.35. The various navigation tools of the **Navigation Bar** are discussed in Chapter 2.

Status Bar

The Status Bar provides quick access to some of the commonly used drawing tools, which allow you to toggle settings such as grid, snap, dynamic input mode, ortho mode, polar tracking, and object snap, see Figure 1.36. In addition to the default tools in the Status Bar, you can customize to add or remove tools in it, as per the requirement. To customize the Status Bar, click on the **Customization** tool in the Status Bar, see Figure 1.36. The **Customization** menu appears, see Figure 1.37.

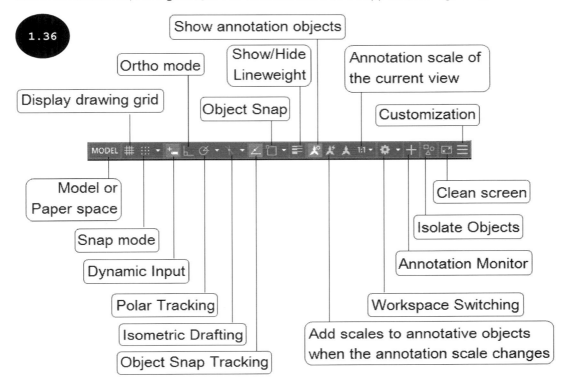

34   Chapter 1 > Introduction to AutoCAD

1.37

In the **Customization** menu, a tick mark in front of the tools indicates that they are currently available in the Status Bar. Click on the tools in the **Customization** menu to add or remove them in the Status Bar. Some of the tools in the Status Bar are discussed next.

Model or Paper space

The **Model or Paper space** tool of the Status Bar is used to toggle between the Model space and Paper space environments. When you start AutoCAD, the Model space is the default activated environment for creating drawings. You can create drawings in the Model space, whereas the Paper space used for plotting drawings and generating different drawing views. You will learn more about the Model space and Paper space in Chapter 11.

Display drawing grid

The **Display drawing grid** tool of the Status Bar is used to turn on or off the display of grids in the drawing area. To turn on or off the display of grids, click on the **Display drawing grid** tool in the Status Bar or press the F7 key. Moreover, you can change the grid settings by using this tool. For doing so, right-click on the **Display drawing grid** tool in the Status Bar. The **Grid Settings** option appears. Click on the **Grid Settings** option. The **Drafting Settings** dialog box appears. By using the options in the **Snap and Grid** tab of this dialog box, you can change the grid settings as required. You will learn more about specifying the grid settings in Chapter 2.

Snap Mode

The **Snap mode** tool of the Status Bar is used to turn on or off the snap mode. You can also press the F9 key to turn it on or off. The snap mode allows the cursor to move in a fixed incremental distance in the drawing area. For example, if the snap mode setting specified to 1 unit in both the X and Y directions, then the cursor will move 1 unit incremental distance in the X-direction as well as in the Y-direction. To specify the snap mode settings, right-click on the **Snap mode** tool in the Status Bar and then click on the **Snap Settings** option in the shortcut menu appeared. The **Drafting Settings** dialog box appears. By using the options in the **Snap and Grid** tab of this dialog box, you can specify the snap settings as required. You will learn more about specifying the snap settings in Chapter 2.

Dynamic Input

The **Dynamic Input** tool of the Status Bar is used to turn on or off the Dynamic Input mode. If the Dynamic Input mode is turned on, you can enter inputs such as commands and coordinates near the cursor tip in the drawing area instead of entering in the Command Line window. It acts as an alternative method of entering commands in AutoCAD. For example, when a command is in progress, the Dynamic Input boxes appear near the cursor tip which allows you to enter coordinates and specify options, see Figure 1.38. You will learn more about entering coordinates and commands by using the Dynamic Input boxes and Command Line window in later chapters.

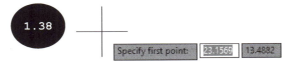

Ortho Mode

The **Ortho Mode** tool of the Status Bar is used to turn on or off the Ortho mode. You can also press the F8 key to turn on or off the Ortho mode. When the Ortho mode is turned on, the movement of the cursor gets restricted to horizontal and vertical only. As a result, you can only draw the straight lines at right angles.

Polar Tracking

The **Polar Tracking** tool of the Status Bar is used to turn on or off the Polar tracking mode. When the Polar tracking mode is activated, the movement of the cursor gets snapped to the specified increment angle in the drawing area. To specify the incremental angle value, right-click on the **Polar Tracking** button in the Status Bar. A flyout appears, see Figure 1.39. This flyout displays a list of pre-defined incremental angles. You can select the required increment angle in this flyout. You can also specify a new increment angle other than the increment angles listed in the flyout. To specify a new increment angle, click on the **Tracking Settings** option in the flyout. The **Drafting Settings** dialog box appears. In this dialog box, specify the increment angle in the **Increment angle** field of the **Polar Tracking** tab and then click on the **OK** button. The new increment angle for polar tracking has specified.

Isometric Drafting

The **Isometric Drafting** tool of the Status Bar is used to turn on or off the Isometric Drafting mode. When the Isometric Drafting mode is turned on, you can easily create the 2D isometric representation of a 3D model. You can select the **isoplane Left**, **isoplane Top**, or **isoplane Right** as the current 2D isometric drafting plane for creating the 2D isometric drawing. By default, the **isoplane Left** drafting plane selected as the current 2D isometric drafting plane. To select the required 2D isometric drafting plane, click on the down arrow next to the **Isometric Drafting** tool in the Status Bar. A flyout appears, see Figure 1.40. In this flyout, click on the required 2D isometric drafting plane for creating an isometric drawing.

Object Snap Tracking

The **Object Snap Tracking** tool of the Status Bar is used to turn on or off the Object Snap Tracking mode. The Object Snap Tracking mode works in conjunction with the Object Snap mode and is used to specify new points aligned to the existing points or locations in a drawing. For example, to draw a circle at the center of a rectangle, move the cursor over the midpoint the horizontal line 'A' (see Figure 1.41) and then move the cursor vertically downward when the cursor snaps to the midpoint of the horizontal line. A vertical tracking line appears, see Figure 1.41. Next, move the cursor over the midpoint of the vertical line 'B' and then move the cursor horizontally toward the right. A horizontal tracking line appears, see Figure 1.42. Next, move the cursor at the intersection of both the tracking lines and then click to specify the midpoint of the circle, see Figure 1.43.

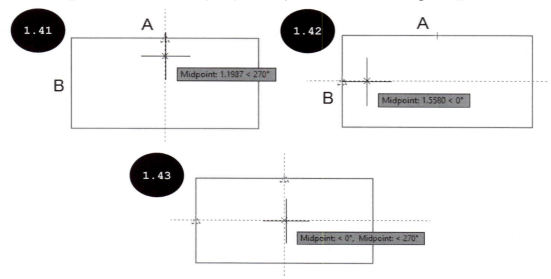

Object Snap

The **Object Snap** tool of the Status Bar is used to turn on or off the Object Snap mode. The Object Snap mode is used to snap the cursor over the existing objects of the drawing such as midpoint, endpoint, and intersection. It is a very useful method of specifying exact points in the drawing area. When the Object Snap mode is turned on, the cursor snaps to the existing objects of the drawing as per the specified object snap settings. To specify or control the object snap settings, right-click on the **Object Snap** tool in the Status Bar. A flyout appears, see Figure 1.44. This flyout displays a list of all the object snaps. Note that a tick mark in the front of the object snaps in the flyout indicates that they are activated. You can click on the required object snaps to activate or deactivate them in the flyout. Note that the cursor snaps to the objects in the drawing area depending upon the activated object snaps. For example, if only the **Endpoint** object snap is activated then the cursor only snaps to the end points of the existing objects in the drawing area, see Figure 1.45.

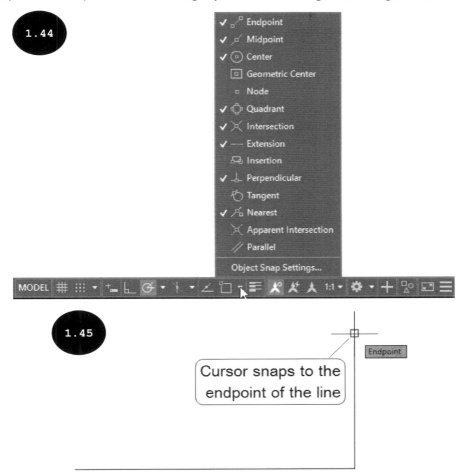

1.44

1.45

Cursor snaps to the endpoint of the line

You can also invoke the **Drafting Settings** dialog box by clicking on the **Object Snap Settings** option in the flyout to control the object snap setting, see Figure 1.46. In the **Object Snap** tab of the dialog box, select the required object snap check boxes to activate them. For example, on selecting the **Endpoint** check box, the Endpoint object snap is activated, and the cursor snaps to the endpoints of the existing drawing objects in the drawing area. Similarly, on selecting the **Midpoint** check box, the Midpoint object snap is activated, and the cursor snaps to the midpoints of the drawing objects in the drawing area. To select all the object snap check boxes, click on the **Select All** button in the dialog box. Similarly, to uncheck all the object snap check boxes, click on the **Clear All** button in the dialog box. After selecting the required object snap check boxes in the dialog box, click on the **OK** button.

38 Chapter 1 > Introduction to AutoCAD

Show/Hide Lineweight
The **Show/Hide Lineweight** tool is used to turn on or off the display of the object lineweight in the drawing area. You will learn more about specifying lineweight to drawing objects in later chapters.

Show annotation objects
The **Show annotation objects** tool is used to turn on or off the display of annotative objects in the drawing area.

Annotation scale of the current view
The **Annotation scale of the current view** flyout is used to select the annotation scale for the annotative objects in the Model space. To invoke this flyout, click on the down arrow next to the **Annotation scale of the current view** button in the Status Bar.

Workspace Switching
The **Workspace Switching** flyout is used to switch among the AutoCAD workspaces: **Drafting & Annotation, 3D Basics,** and **3D Modeling**. To invoke the **Workspace Switching** flyout, click on the down arrow next to the **Workspace Switching** button in the Status Bar, see Figure 1.47. Note that the availability of tools in the **Ribbon** depends upon the currently active workspace.

AutoCAD 2019: A Power Guide > 39

Isolate Objects

The **Isolate Objects** tool is used to isolate objects in the drawing area. You can isolate an object or a set of objects in the drawing area. To isolate objects, click on the **Isolate Objects** tool in the Status Bar. A flyout appears, see Figure 1.48. In this flyout, click on the **Isolate Objects** tool. You are prompted to select objects to be isolated in the drawing area. Select the objects to be isolated and then right-click or press ENTER. The selected objects get isolated such that the remaining drawing objects become invisible. You can also hide an object or a set of objects in the drawing area by using the **Hide Objects** tool of the flyout. To hide objects in the drawing area, click on the **Hide Objects** tool in the flyout, see Figure 1.48. You are prompted to select objects to be hidden. Select the objects to be hidden and then right-click or press ENTER. The selected objects get hidden in the drawing area. To display all the drawing objects back in the drawing area or end the object isolation, click on the **End Object Isolation** tool in the flyout, see Figure 1.49.

Clean Screen

The **Clean screen** tool of the Status Bar is used to expand the drawing display area by hiding the **Ribbon** and all the available toolbars except the Command Line window, Status Bar, and Quick Access Toolbar.

Customization

The **Customization** tool is used to customize the Status Bar such that you can add or remove tools in it. To customize the Status Bar, click on the **Customization** tool in the Status Bar. The **Customization** menu appears, which displays a list of all the tools that can add to the Status Bar. Note that a tick mark in front of the tools in the **Customization** menu indicates that they are currently available in the Status Bar. You can click on the tools in the **Customization** menu to add or remove them in the Status Bar.

Starting a New Drawing File by using the Create New Drawing dialog box

As discussed, when you click on the **New** tool in the **Quick Access Toolbar** for starting a new drawing file, the **Select template** dialog box appears, by default. It is because the system variable for STARTUP set to 3. If you set up the system variable for STARTUP to 1, then on clicking the **New** tool in the **Quick Access Toolbar**, the **Create New Drawing** dialog box appears for starting a new drawing file. For doing so, enter **STARTUP** in the Command Line window and then press ENTER. You are prompted to enter a new value for STARTUP.

```
Enter new value for STARTUP <3>:
```

Next, enter **1** in the Command Line window and then press ENTER. The new system variable for the STARTUP is set to 1. Now, when you click on the **New** tool in the **Quick Access Toolbar** for starting a new drawing file, **the Create New Drawing** dialog box appears, see Figure 1.50. By using the **Create New Drawing** dialog box, you can start a new drawing file from scratch, using a template, or a wizard. The methods of starting a new drawing file by using the **Create New Drawing** dialog box are discussed next.

Starting a New Drawing file from Scratch

To start a new drawing file from scratch by using the **Create New Drawing** dialog box, make sure that the **Start from Scratch** button is activated in the dialog box, see Figure 1.50. You can start a new drawing file from scratch either with the default imperial (*acad.dwt*) or metric (*acadiso.dwt*) settings. By default, the **Metric** radio button selected in the dialog box. As a result, on clicking the **OK** button, a new drawing file with default metric settings is invoked. To start a new drawing file with default imperial settings, select the **Imperial (feet and inches)** radio button in the dialog box and then click on the **OK** button.

Starting a New Drawing file by using a Template

To start a new drawing file by using a standard drawing template, click on the **Use a Template** button in the **Create New Drawing** dialog box. A list of drawing templates appears in the dialog box, see Figure 1.51. By default, the *Acad.dwt* drawing template is selected in the dialog box. Note that the selection of default template depends on the settings specified while installing AutoCAD. Select a required template in this dialog box to start a new drawing file. Note that a drawing template contains drawing settings such as units, limits, text height, and scale factor. After selecting a required drawing template, click on the **OK** button. The new drawing file gets started.

Starting a New Drawing file by using a Wizard

In AutoCAD, you can also start a new drawing with the **Advanced Setup** and **Quick Setup** wizards which allow you to specify settings such as unit, angle, angle measurement, angle direction, and area for the new drawing. To start a new drawing file by using a wizard, click on the **Use a Wizard** button in the **Create New Drawing** dialog box, see Figure 1.52. The **Advanced Setup** and **Quick Setup** options appear in the **Select a Wizard** area of the dialog box, see Figure 1.52.

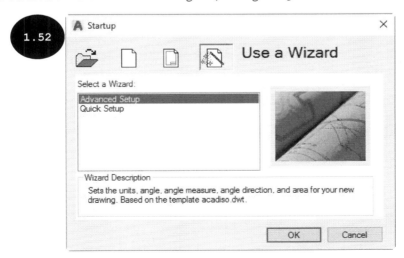

42 Chapter 1 > Introduction to AutoCAD

The **Advanced Setup** option allows you to specify a unit, angle, angle measurement, angle direction, and so on for the new drawing file, whereas the **Quick Setup** option only allows you to specify unit and area settings for the drawing file.

To start a new drawing with the **Advanced Setup** wizard, select the **Advanced Setup** option in the **Select a Wizard** area of the dialog box and then click on the **OK** button. The **Advanced Setup** dialog box appears with the **Units** page, see Figure 1.53. The options in the **Units** page of the **Advanced Setup** dialog box are used to set the unit format of measurement in the drawing. Select the required unit format: Decimal, Engineering, Architectural, Fractional, or Scientific by choosing the respective radio button. You can also specify the precision for the measurement by using the **Precision** drop-down list of the **Units** page. After selecting the unit and precision, click on the **Next** button. The **Angle** page of the **Advanced Setup** dialog box appears, see Figure 1.54.

1.53

1.54

The options in the **Angle** page of the **Advanced Setup** dialog box are used to set the angle of measurement and the precision of angle measurement for the drawing. Select the required angle of measurement: Decimal Degrees, Deg/Min/Sec, Grads, Radians, or Surveyor by choosing the respective radio button. Also, select the precision of angle measurement by using the **Precision** drop-down list of the **Angle** page. After selecting the required angle and precision, click on the **Next** button. The **Angle Measure** page of the **Advanced Setup** dialog box appears, see Figure 1.55.

The options in the **Angle Measure** page are used to select the direction of angle measurement: East, North, West, or South by choosing the respective radio button. You can also set the direction of angle measurement as per your requirement by using the **Other** radio button on this page. On selecting the **Other** radio button, the field below it gets enabled. In this field, you can specify the direction of angle measurement, as required. Note that by default, the **East** radio button is selected on this page. As a result, the angle measures from the east (0-degree) in the counter-clockwise orientation. You can set the orientation (clockwise or counter-clockwise) for angle measurement in the **Angle Direction** page which appears on clicking the **Next** button in the **Angle Measure** page after specifying the direction of angle measurement, see Figure 1.56.

The **Angle Direction** page of the **Advanced Setup** dialog box is used to specify the orientation for the angle measurement. You can select either the counter-clockwise or clockwise orientation for the angle measurement by selecting the respective radio button on this page. After selecting the orientation for angle measurement, click on the **Next** button. The **Area** page of the **Advanced Setup** dialog box appears, see Figure 1.57.

The **Area** page of the **Advanced Setup** dialog box is used to specify the drawing area for creating the drawing. You can specify the drawing area by entering the width and length in the **Width** and **Length** fields of the page, respectively. After specifying all the drawing settings, click on the **Finish** button. A new drawing with the specified settings gets started.

Similar to the **Advanced Setup** wizard, you can also start a new drawing with the **Quick Setup** wizard of the **Create New Drawing** dialog box. The only difference is that the **Quick Setup** wizard allows you to specify only unit and area settings of the dialog box, see Figure 1.58.

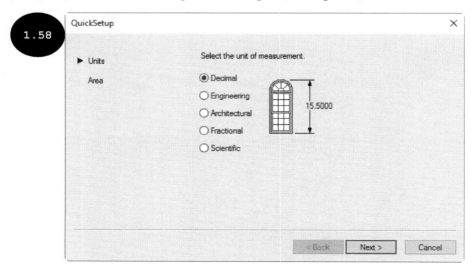

Changing the Color Scheme

AutoCAD provided with two color schemes: dark color scheme and light color scheme. The dark color scheme is the default color scheme of AutoCAD. As a result, the **Ribbon**, **Palettes**, and several other interface components of AutoCAD appear in the dark color scheme, see Figure 1.59. You can change the color scheme by using the **Options** dialog box. To invoke the **Options** dialog box, enter OP in the Command Line window and then press ENTER. Figure 1.60 shows the **Options** dialog box.

In the **Options** dialog box, click on the **Display** tab. The options related to display settings of AutoCAD appear in the dialog box, see Figure 1.60. Next, select either the **Light** or **Dark** option in the **Color scheme** drop-down list of the **Window Elements** area in the dialog box to display the AutoCAD elements/components in the light color scheme or dark color scheme, respectively.

Changing the Background Color

In AutoCAD, you can change the background color of the drawing area/screen, sheet/layout, Command Line window, plot preview, and so on by using the **Options** dialog box. To change the background color of the drawing area/screen, enter **OP** in the Command Line window and then press ENTER. The **Options** dialog box appears. In the **Options** dialog box, click on the **Display** tab. The options related to display settings of AutoCAD appear in the dialog box. Next, click on the **Colors** button in the **Window Elements** area of the dialog box. The **Drawing Window Colors** dialog box appears, see Figure 1.61.

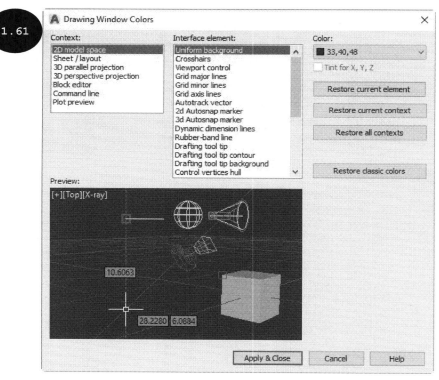

In this dialog box, make sure that the **2D model space** option selected in the **Context** area, and the **Uniform background** option is selected in the **Interface element** area of the dialog box, see Figure 1.61. Next, select the color to be assigned to the background of the drawing area/screen in the **Color** drop-down list. Similarly, you can specify the background color of other drawing contexts such as sheet/layout, Command Line window, and plot preview by using the **Drawing Window Colors** dialog box. After selecting the color to be assigned to the background, click on the **Apply & Close** button in the dialog box. The selected color assigned to the background of the drawing area, and the dialog box gets closed.

Working with Workspaces

A workspace defined as a task-oriented drawing environment in which you can control or organize the display of sets of user interface elements such as **Ribbon**, toolbars, menus, and palettes as per the requirement for accomplishing the tasks. By default, AutoCAD has three predefined workspaces: **Drafting & Annotation**, **3D Basics**, and **3D Modeling**. When you start a new drawing file in AutoCAD, the **Drafting & Annotation** workspace is the default active workspace for creating the drawing. The **Drafting & Annotation** workspace display the necessary tools, menus, and palettes that used for creating and annotating 2D drawings. The **3D Basics** and **3D Modeling** workspaces provide necessary tools, menus, and palettes which used for creating 3D drawings. You can switch between the predefined workspaces and create a new workspace as per the requirement. The methods of switching between workspaces and creating a new workspace are discussed next.

Switching between Workspaces

To switch between workspaces, click on the **Workspace Switching** button in the Status Bar. The **Workspace Switching** flyout appears, see Figure 1.62. It displays a list of all the available workspaces. You can click on the required workspace in this flyout to make it the currently active workspace for the drawing.

Creating a New Workspace

In addition to the predefined workspaces, you can create a new workspace in which you can customize the arrangement of sets of user interface elements such as **Ribbon**, toolbars, menus, and palettes as per the requirement. To create a new workspace, first of all, customize the arrangement of tools in the **Ribbon**, toolbars, menus, and palettes, as required. Next, click on the **Workspace Switching** button in the Status Bar. The **Workspace Switching** flyout appears, see Figure 1.62. In this flyout, click on the **Save Current As** option. The **Save Workspace** window appears, see Figure 1.63. In this window, enter the name of the workspace and then click on the **Save** button. The new workspace is created and added to the list of workspaces in the **Workspace Switching** flyout. Also, it becomes the currently active workspace of the drawing.

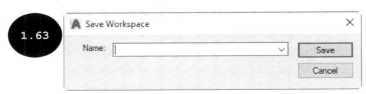

Working with Sheet Sets

Most of the real world projects require multiple drawing sheets, sometimes more than hundreds in number. The cross-referencing between multiple drawing sheets of a project is a very time-consuming process. Also, plotting, publishing, and opening multiple drawing sheets of a project require considerable time. To manage multiple drawing sheets of a project easily and efficiently, AutoCAD provides the sheet set feature. A sheet set is a very powerful feature of AutoCAD, which is used to manage or organize a set of multiple drawings (sheets) of a project in proper order. All drawings of a sheet set act as a single unit and displayed in a tree view. In AutoCAD, you can create two types of sheet sets: Example sheet set and Existing Drawings sheet set. An Example sheet set uses a sample sheet set with default settings to create a new sheet set in a well-organized structure, whereas the Existing Drawings sheet set is used to create a new sheet set to organize existing drawings. You can create both these types of sheet sets by using the **SHEET SET MANAGER** palette. The methods of creating different types of sheet sets are discussed next.

Creating an Example Sheet Set

To create an Example sheet set, click on the **Sheet Set Manager** tool in the **Palettes** panel of the **View** tab in the **Ribbon**. The SHEET SET MANAGER palette appears, see Figure 1.64. Alternatively, enter **SHEETSET** in the Command Line window and then press ENTER to invoke the **SHEET SET MANAGER** palette. In the **SHEET SET MANAGER** palette, make sure that the **Sheet List** tab is activated, see Figure 1.64. Next, click on the down arrow next to the **Open** button in the **SHEET SET MANAGER** palette. A drop-down list appears, see Figure 1.65. In this drop-down list, click on the **New Sheet Set** option. The **Create Sheet Set** dialog box appears with the **Begin** page, see Figure 1.66.

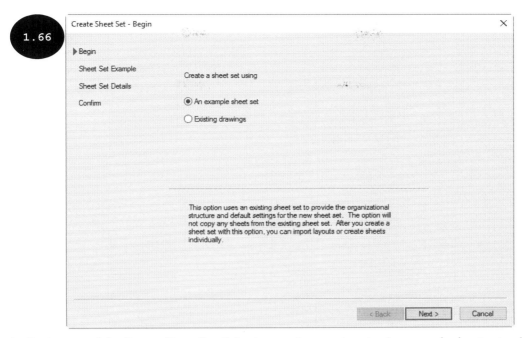

1.66

In the **Begin** page of the **Create Sheet Set** dialog box, make sure that the **An example sheet set** radio button is selected. Next, click on the **Next** button in the dialog box. The **Sheet Set Example** page of the **Create Sheet Set** dialog box appears, see Figure 1.67. In this page, the **Select a sheet set to use as an example** radio button is selected, by default. As a result, a list of all the available sample sheet sets is displayed below this radio button, see Figure 1.67. Select a required example sheet set in this field for creating new sheet set.

1.67

You can also select a sheet set which is in a different location and not available in the list of example sheet set. For doing so, select the **Browse to another sheet set to use as an example** radio button in the **Sheet Set Example** page of the dialog box and then click on the **Browse** button [...]. The **Browse for Sheet Set** dialog box appears. In this dialog box, browse to the location where the required sheet set is saved and then select it. Next, click on the **Open** button. After selecting the required example sheet set for creating a new sheet set in this page, click on the **Next** button. The **Sheet Set Details** page of the dialog box appears. In this page, enter the name of the new sheet set, description, and location to save the file by using the **Name of new sheet set**, **Description**, and **Store sheet set data file (.dst) here** fields, respectively. Next, click on the **Next** button. The **Confirm** page of the dialog box appears, see Figure 1.68. This page displays the structure of the sheet set and details of the sheet set properties. Review all the sheet set properties and then click on the **Finish** button. A new sheet set created with the specified properties and displayed in the **SHEET SET MANAGER** palette, see Figure 1.69.

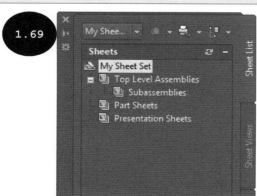

Now, you can add multiple drawing sheets in different subsets of the newly created sheet set and then create drawings in it. To add a new drawing sheet in a subset, right-click on a subset and then click on the **New Sheet** option in the shortcut menu appeared, see Figure 1.70. The **New Sheet** window appears. In this window, specify the sheet number, title, and file name and then click on the OK button. A new drawing sheet added and displayed under the selected subset, see Figure 1.71. Similarly, you can add multiple drawing sheets under different subsets. You can also add a new subset to the main sheet set. For doing so, right-click on the name of the sheet set in the **SHEET SET MANAGER** palette and then click on the **New Subset** option in the shortcut menu appeared. The **Subset Properties** window appears. In this window, specify the subset name and other properties. Next, click on the OK button. A new subset with the specified name and the properties gets added in the sheet set. After adding the required drawing sheets and subsets, you can open a drawing sheet and then create the drawing in it. To open a drawing sheet for creating the drawing, right-click on the drawing sheet in the **SHEET SET MANAGER** palette and then click on the **Open** option in the shortcut menu appeared. The drawing sheet gets opened in a separate window with default drawing template. Now, you can create the drawing in this sheet by using the drawing tools. You will learn about creating drawings by using the drawing tools in later chapters.

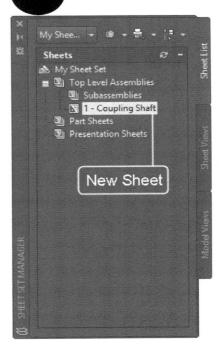

Creating an Existing Drawing Sheet Set

An Existing Drawing sheet set created by using the existing drawings of a project. To create a sheet set by using the existing drawings, invoke the **SHEET SET MANAGER** palette and then click on the down arrow next to the **Open** button. A drop-down list appears. In this drop-down list, click on the **New Sheet Set** option. The **Create Sheet Set** dialog box appears with the **Begin** page, see Figure 1.72.

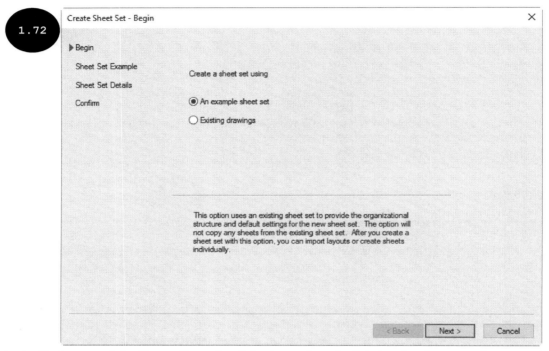

In the **Begin** page of the **Create Sheet Set** dialog box, select the **Existing drawings** radio button and then click on the **Next** button. The **Sheet Set Details** page of the dialog box appears. In this page, enter the sheet set details such as name, description, and location to save the file. Next, click on the **Next** button. The **Choose Layouts** page of the dialog box appears, see Figure 1.73. Click on the **Browse** button in this page. The **Browse for Folder** window appears. In this window, browse to the folder in which drawing files to add in the sheet set are saved and then select it. Next, click on the **OK** button. All the drawing files of the selected folder with their initial layouts get listed in the box available in the **Choose Layouts** page. You can browse to multiple folders one by one to add the drawing files.

Note that the drawing files and their first layouts listed in the box of the **Choose Layout** page have a tick mark in the front. You can uncheck the drawing files and layouts which you do not want to include in the sheet set. After selecting the drawing files and layouts to be included in the sheet set, click on the **Next** button. The **Confirm** page of the dialog box appears. This page displays the information about the layouts included in the sheet set. Next, click on the **Finish** button. A sheet set created by using the existing drawing files and displayed in the **SHEET SET MANAGER** palette.

Opening a Drawing File

To open an existing drawing, click on the **Open** tool in the **Quick Access Toolbar**, see Figure 1.74. The **Select File** dialog box appears. You can also enter **OPEN** in the Command Line window and then press ENTER to invoke the **Select File** dialog box. In this dialog box, browse to the location where the file is saved. Note that by default, the **Drawing (*.dwg)** file extension selected in the **Files of type** drop-down list in the dialog box. As a result, the drawing files having *.dwg* file extension appear in the dialog box. Select the drawing file to be opened and then click on the **Open** button. The selected drawing gets opened in AutoCAD. You can also open the *.dxf* files or *.dwt* (template) files by selecting the **DXF (*.dxf)** or **Drawing Template (*.dwt)** file extension in the **Files of type** drop-down list, respectively.

54 Chapter 1 > Introduction to AutoCAD

You can also open a drawing file as a read only which protects the drawing from any change, and it is used for review only. Note that AutoCAD does not restrict you to make a change in the read only file, but at the same time, it does not allow you to save the changes made in the read only file. To open a drawing as a read-only file, click on the **Open** tool in the **Quick Access Toolbar** to invoke the **Select File** dialog box. Next, select the drawing to be opened and then click on the down arrow next to the **Open** button in the **Select File** dialog box. The **Open** drop-down list appears, see Figure 1.75. In this drop-down list, select the **Open Read-Only** option. The selected drawing gets opened as a read-only file.

1.75

Note: When you save the read-only file after making some modifications or changes, the **AutoCAD Message** window appears, which inform you that the current drawing file is write protected. However, you can save the modified read-only file with a different name by using the **Save As** tool.

In AutoCAD, you can also open a partial view or a small portion of a drawing instead of opening the entire drawing by using the **Partial Open** option of the **Open** drop-down list, see Figure 1.75. This option is very useful if you want to modify a small portion of a big complex drawing. To open a partial view of a drawing, select the drawing in the **Select File** dialog box and then invoke the **Open** drop-down list, see Figure 1.75. Next, click on the **Partial Open** option. The **Partial Open** dialog box appears, which displays different views and layers of the selected drawing. Select the check boxes corresponding to the layers whose geometries are to be opened. Next, click on the **Open** button in the dialog box. The geometries/objects associated with the selected layers get displayed in the drawing area.

Saving a Drawing File

While creating a drawing or editing an existing drawing, it is imperative to save your work periodically to avoid any data loss. To save a drawing file, click on the **Save** tool in the **Quick Access Toolbar**, see Figure 1.76. Alternatively, press CTRL + S or enter **SAVE** in the Command Line window. Note that if you are saving a drawing first time then on clicking the **Save** tool, the **Save Drawing As** dialog box appears. In this dialog box, browse to the location where you want to save the drawing file and then enter the name of the drawing file in the **File name** field of the dialog box. Next, click on the **Save** button.

The drawing file gets saved in the specified location of your computer with the specified name in the *.dwg* file extension. The *.dwg* is the file extension of AutoCAD. Note that if the drawing have already saved with a particular name on your computer and you have made modifications to it then by clicking the **Save** tool, the drawing gets saved directly without the display of **Save Drawing As** dialog box.

You can also save an already saved drawing file with a different name. To save an already saved drawing file with different name, click on the **Save As** tool in the **Quick Assess Toolbar**, see Figure 1.77. Alternatively, enter SAVEAS in the Command Line window and then press ENTER. The **Save Drawing As** dialog box appears. In this dialog box, enter a new name for the drawing file in the **File name** field and then click on the **Save** button. The drawing file gets saved with the newly specified name without affecting the original drawing file.

Note: AutoCAD allows you to save your drawing file in previous versions of AutoCAD. For doing so, select the required version of AutoCAD in the **Files of type** drop-down list of the **Save Drawing As** dialog box, see Figure 1.78 and then click on the **Save** button.

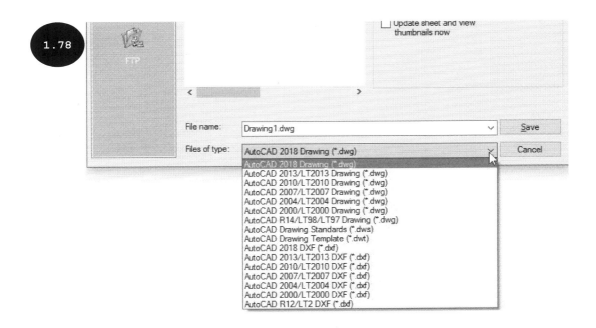

Chapter 1 > Introduction to AutoCAD

In addition to saving a drawing file by using the **Save** or **Save As** tools, AutoCAD automatically saves your drawing file after every 10 minutes. You can change the default time interval for automatically saving drawing files by using the **Options** dialog box. For doing so, enter **OP** in the Command Line window and the press ENTER. The **Options** dialog box appears. In this dialog box, click on the **Open and Save** tab and then enter the time interval in the **Minutes between saves** field of the **File Safety Precautions** area in the dialog box. Next, click **OK** to accept the change and exit the dialog box.

Summary

In this chapter, you have learned about system requirements for installing AutoCAD and how to start a new drawing file. You have also learned about various screen components of AutoCAD, how to change the color scheme and background color. Also, you have learned about different workspaces of AutoCAD and how to create a sheet set. Besides, you have learned how to open and save drawing files in AutoCAD.

Questions

- The _____ is used to enter commands and displays command prompt sequence.

- The _____ tool is used to turn on or off the display of grids in the drawing area.

- If the _____ mode is turned on, the cursor snaps to the existing objects of the drawing.

- AutoCAD is provided with two color schemes: _____ and _____ .

- By default, AutoCAD has three predefined workspaces: _____ , _____ , and _____ .

CHAPTER 2

Creating Drawings - I

In this chapter, you will learn the following:

- Setting up Drawing Units
- Setting Drawing Limits
- Specifying Grid and Snap Settings
- Understanding Coordinate Systems
- Creating a Drawing
- Drawing a Line
- Drawing a Circle
- Drawing an Arc
- Canceling, Erasing and Restoring Objects
- Navigating 2D Drawing

Before you start creating drawings in AutoCAD, it is important first to specify drawing units, limits, and grid and snap settings. Also, you should be familiar with the coordinate systems used in AutoCAD.

Setting up Drawing Units

The first and foremost step to create a drawing is to set up the units of measurement for the drawing. As discussed in Chapter 1, while starting a new drawing in AutoCAD, you can define a unit system for the measurement: Architectural, Decimal, Engineering, Fractional, or Scientific. Besides, you can also change or modify the unit settings at any point in time during the process of creating a drawing by using the UNITS command.

To set up a unit for the current drawing, type **UNITS** in the Command Line window and then press ENTER, see Figure 2.1. The **Drawing Units** dialog box appears, see Figure 2.2.

2.1 Command Line Window

2.2

Tip: You can also type **UN** instead of **UNITS** in the Command Line window for invoking the **Drawing Units** dialog box. The **UN** is the shortcut for the **UNITS** command.

After invoking the **Drawing Units** dialog box, you can set the required unit format for the measurement of length and angle. The options in the **Drawing Units** dialog box are discussed next.

Length
The options in the **Length** area of the **Drawing Units** dialog box are used to set the required unit format and precision for the measurement of length. The options of the **Length** area are discussed next.

Type
The **Type** drop-down list of the **Length** area is used to select the required unit format. You can select the architectural, decimal, engineering, fractional, or scientific unit format for the measurement of length from this drop-down list. Different unit formats are discussed next.

Architecture
The **Architectural** unit format is used to specify units in feet and inches. As the name suggests, this unit format is mostly used by the architects to specify units in feet and inches. In this unit format, the inches represented in the fraction form.

Note: The **Sample Output** area of the dialog box displays example of the current unit format selected in the **Type** drop-down list of the dialog box.

Decimal
The **Decimal** unit format is used to specify units in the metric unit system. This format is mostly used by users those work with the metric unit system for measurement.

Engineering
Similar to the **Architectural** unit format, the **Engineering** unit format is used to specify units in feet and inches. The only difference between these two unit formats is that the inches in the **Engineering** unit format represented in the decimal form.

Fractional
The **Fractional** unit format is used to specify units in the fractional unit system. For example, 5 feet, 6½ inches means 66-1/2 inches in the fractional unit system.

Scientific
The **Scientific** unit format is used to specify units in the scientific units system. For example, 10 million parsecs means 10E+06 in the scientific units system, where 10 represents ten accurate and E+06 represents the exponential function to the sixth power.

Precision
The **Precision** drop-down list of the **Length** area is used to set precision of units. The availability of options in the **Precision** drop-down list depends on the type of unit format selected in the **Type** drop-down list.

Angle
The options of the **Angle** area are used to specify a unit format and precision for the measurement of angle. You can select the **Decimal Degrees**, **Deg/Min/Sec**, **Grads**, **Radians**, or **Surveyor's Units** format for the measurement of an angle by using the **Type** drop-down list of the **Angle** area. The **Precision** drop-down list of the **Angle** area is used to specify precision for the angle measurements.

If you have selected the **Decimal Degrees**, **Deg/Min/Sec**, **Grads**, or **Radians** unit format for the measurement of angle, you can specify the angle in decimal, degrees/minutes/seconds, grads, or radians, respectively. Whereas, if you have selected the **Surveyor's Units** format, you can specify angle on the deviation of north and south, see Figure 2.3. Note that the angle value used in the surveyor unit is not greater than 90-degree. For example, to set an angle which measured 40-degree from north and 30 minutes toward the east, you need to specify **N40d30'E**.

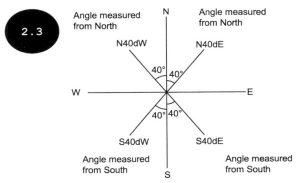

Clockwise

By default, the **Clockwise** check box is unchecked in the **Angle** area of the dialog box. As a result, the direction of a positive angle is measured in the counterclockwise direction, see Figure 2.4. To measure a positive angle in the clockwise direction, select the **Clockwise** check box, see Figure 2.5.

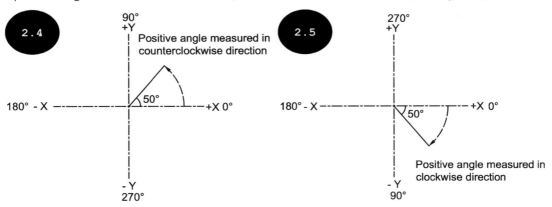

> **Note:** It is evident from Figures 2.4 and 2.5 that the position of 0-degree set at East position, by default. You can change the position of zero degrees from East to other position, such as north, south, or west by using the **Direction** button in the **Drawing Units** dialog box. To set the position of zero degrees, click on the **Direction** button in the **Drawing Units** dialog box. The **Direction Control** dialog box appears, see Figure 2.6. Using this dialog box, you can set base angle (zero degrees) at any position by selecting the appropriate radio button. You can also specify an angle value other than 0 (zero) by selecting the **Other** radio button and then entering the required angle value in the **Angle** field.

Insertion scale

The **Units to scale inserted content** drop-down list of the **Insertion Scale** area is used to set unit for the blocks and drawings that are inserted in the current drawing. Note that the unit selected in this drop-down list is applied automatically to the blocks or drawings inserted in the current drawing. If the blocks and drawings inserted in the current drawing have different unit, then AutoCAD may scale them to correct the mismatch and set the unit specified in the **Units to scale inserted content** drop-down list.

Sample Output

The **Sample Output** area of the **Drawing Units** dialog box is used to display the sample output or example of the current length and angle units settings specified in the dialog box.

Lighting

The **Units for specifying the intensity of lighting** drop-down list of the **Lighting** area is used to set the unit of measurement for the intensity of photometric light in the current drawing.

After specifying the desired settings for measurement of units in the **Drawing Units** dialog box, click OK to accept the settings and close the dialog box.

Setting Drawing Limits

After defining drawing units, it is important to set drawing limits (work area) in the drawing area. Drawing limit is an invisible and imaginary rectangular boundary in the drawing area, which defines the size of the workspace. Setting drawing limit helps in defining the grid display within the drawing limit, zooming drawing within the drawing limit, and plotting the drawing. You can set drawing limit for a drawing depending on the overall size of the drawing. For example, if you are drawing a plan view of a building that is roughly around 28 x 36 feet then you can set the drawing limit around 56 x 72 feet. Note that drawing limit is the size of your work area that accommodates the entire drawing and dimensions with some extra space, see Figure 2.7.

To define drawing limit for a drawing, enter **LIMITS** in the Command Line window and then press ENTER. The command prompt for setting drawing limit is as discussed next.

Command: **LIMITS**
Reset Model space limits:
Specify lower left corner or [ON/OFF] <0.0000,0.0000>: **0,0**
Specify upper right corner <12.0000,9.0000>: **56,72**

> **Note:** If the display of grids is turned on, the grids appear in the entire drawing area, by default. To display grids within the drawing limit, enter **GRIDDISPLAY** in the Command Line window and then enter **0** in the command prompt. Next, press ENTER. You will learn more about grid settings later in this chapter.

Specifying Grid and Snap Settings

The grid is a rectangular pattern of lines or dots, which is intended to speed up the creation of drawing by aligning objects and visualizing the distance between drawing entities. Grid lines can use as reference lines for creating drawings. Also, grid lines appear similar to the sheet of graph paper for creating a drawing, see Figure 2.8.

Note: The background color of the drawing area shown in Figure 2.8 has changed to white for clear visualization. The method of changing background color has discussed in Chapter 1.

You can control the spacing, angle, and alignment of grid lines. Also, you can restrict the movement of the cursor over grid lines by specifying the grid and snap settings.

To define the grid and snap settings in AutoCAD, right-click on the **Display drawing grid** button in the Status Bar, see Figure 2.9. The **Grid Settings** option appears. Next, click on the **Grid Settings** option. The **Drafting Settings** dialog box appears, see Figure 2.10.

Figure 2.10

Make sure that the **Snap and Grid** tab activated in the **Drafting Settings** dialog box, see Figure 2.10. The options in the **Snap and Grid** tab of the dialog box are used to specify snap and grid settings. Some of these options are discussed next.

Grid On (F7)
The **Grid On** check box of this dialog box is used to toggle the display of grid lines in the drawing area. Alternatively, you can click on the **Display drawing grid** button in the Status Bar or press the **F7** key to toggle the display of grid lines.

Grid style
The options in the **Grid style** area of the dialog box are used to specify grid styles in 2D context. These options are discussed next.

2D model space
The **2D model space** check box of the **Grid style** area is used to set grid style to dotted grid lines in the 2D model space (drawing area).

Block editor
The **Block editor** check box is used to set grid style to dotted grid lines in the Block editor. You will learn more about the Block editor in later chapters.

Sheet/layout
The **Sheet/layout** check box is used to set grid style to dotted grid lines in sheet and layout. You will learn more about sheet and layout in later chapters.

Grid spacing
The options in the **Grid spacing** area of the dialog box are used to specify spacing between grid lines. These options are discussed next.

Grid X spacing
The **Grid X spacing** field of the **Grid spacing** area is used to specify the spacing between grid lines along the X direction.

Grid Y spacing
The **Grid Y spacing** field of this area is used to specify the spacing between grid lines along the Y direction.

Major line every
The **Major line every** field is used to specify the display of the major grid lines concerning minor grid lines. For example, if you enter 5 in this field, the major grid lines will appear on every 5 counts of minor grid lines. Grid lines are of two types: major grid lines and minor grid lines. The major grid lines appear darker than the minor grid lines.

Snap On (F9)
The **Snap On** check box of the dialog box is used to toggle the snap mode on or off. Alternatively, you can click on the **Snap mode** button in the Status Bar or press the **F9** key to turn the snap mode on or off. Note that by turning the snap mode on, the movement of the cursor gets restricted in the specified X and Y intervals. You can specify the X and Y intervals in the **Snap spacing** area of this dialog box, which is discussed next.

Snap spacing
The options of the **Snap spacing** area are used to snap the movement of the cursor in the specified X and Y intervals along the X and Y directions, respectively. These options are discussed next.

Snap X spacing
The **Snap X spacing** field is used to specify the snap spacing along the X direction. For example, if you enter 5 in this field then the cursor will snap after every 5 units along the X direction.

Snap Y spacing
The **Snap Y spacing** field is used to specify the snap spacing along the Y direction. For example, if you enter 5 in this field then the cursor will snap after every 5 units along the Y direction.

Equal X and Y spacing
The **Equal X and Y spacing** check box is used to make the snap spacing same along the X and Y directions.

Once you have specified the grid and snap settings in the **Drafting Settings** dialog box, click on the **OK** button to accept changes and exit from the dialog box.

Tip: In AutoCAD, you are provided with shortcuts to toggle the display of grids and snap settings. To toggle the display of grids in the drawing area, you can click on the **Display drawing grid** button ▦ in the Status Bar or press the **F7** key. Similarly, to toggle the snap settings on and off, you can click on the **Snap mode** button ▦ in the Status Bar or press the **F9** key.

Understanding Coordinate Systems

In AutoCAD, the Cartesian and Polar coordinate systems used for specifying points in the drawing area. The Cartesian coordinate system is also known as the rectangular coordinate system, and it consists of two perpendicular lines (x-axis and y-axis) that intersect at a point called origin, see Figure 2.11. The origin has coordinate values of X = 0, Y = 0. In the Cartesian coordinate system, the location of every point specified by entering the X and Y coordinates values that measured from perpendicular lines (x-axis and y-axis), see Figure 2.11. Note that in two-dimensional space (2D plane), the Cartesian coordinate system has two perpendicular axes. Whereas, in three-dimensional space (3D), the system has three mutually perpendicular axes (x-axis, y-axis, and z-axis).

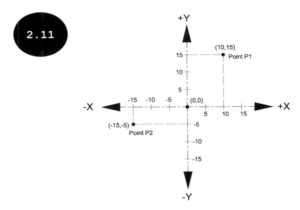

It is evident from Figure 2.11 that in the Cartesian coordinate system, you need to specify the X and Y coordinates concerning the X and Y axes for defining a point.

In the Polar coordinate system, to define the position of a point, you need to specify the distance and angle values rather than the X and Y coordinates, see Figure 2.12. Note that in the Polar coordinate system, the distance measured from the origin and the angle measured from an axis representing zero degrees, see Figure 2.12. In AutoCAD, the +X axis (East) represents zero degrees for measuring the angle, by default. You can change the position of zero degrees other than the +X axis (East) as discussed earlier in this Chapter.

66 Chapter 2 > Creating Drawings - I

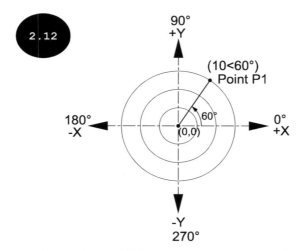

2.12

The different types of Cartesian and Polar coordinate system are discussed next.

Cartesian Coordinate System
The Cartesian coordinate system are of two types and are discussed next.

1. Absolute Cartesian coordinate system
2. Relative Cartesian coordinate system

Absolute Cartesian Coordinate System
In the Absolute Cartesian coordinate system, every point you specify in the drawing area measures from the origin (0,0) and the location of a point is defined by the X and Y coordinates, see Figure 2.13. Note that a comma should separate the X and Y coordinates you specify for locating a point. In Figure 2.13, the Point P1 has coordinates (X=10, Y=15) which measure 10 units along the X axis and 15 units along the Y axis from the origin. Similarly, the Point P2 coordinates (X=25, Y=20) measure 25 units along the X axis and 20 units along the Y axis from the origin.

2.13

> **Note:** In AutoCAD, you can specify coordinates either by using the Command Line window or by using the Dynamic Input boxes. As discussed, the Command Line window is available at the bottom of the drawing area, see Figure 2.14. The Dynamic Input boxes appear near the cursor in the drawing area, when the Dynamic Input mode is turned on, see Figure 2.15. To turn on or off the Dynamic Input mode, click on the **Dynamic Input** button in the Status Bar. If the **Dynamic Input** button is not available in the Status Bar by default, click on the **Customization** button in the Status Bar. A flyout appears. In this flyout, click on the **Dynamic Input** option. The **Dynamic Input** button becomes available in the Status Bar.

In the Absolute Cartesian coordinate system, the method of specifying the X and Y coordinates of a point in the Command Line window as well as in the Dynamic Input boxes are discussed next.

Specifying a Point in the Command Line Window

To specify a point, according to the Absolute Cartesian coordinate system in the Command Line window, enter the X and Y coordinates, separated by a comma, see Figure 2.14. In this figure, the coordinates (**25, 20**) specified in the Command Line window measure 25 units along the X axis and 20 units along the Y axis for defining the start point of a line.

Specifying a Point in the Dynamic Input Boxes

To specify a point, according to the Absolute Cartesian coordinate system in the Dynamic Input boxes, enter # as a prefix to the X coordinate and then followed by the Y coordinate, see Figure 2.15. In this figure, the coordinates (**#25, 20**) specified in the Dynamic Input boxes measure 25 units along the X axis and 20 units along the Y axis for defining the start point of a line.

Tip: To switch between the Dynamic Input boxes for specifying the coordinates (X and Y), you need to press the TAB key. Alternatively, press the COMMA (,) key after specifying the X coordinate to switch to the next Dynamic Input box for specifying the Y coordinate.

Note: In the Absolute coordinate system, whether you specify coordinates in the Command Line window or the Dynamic Input boxes, the coordinates are measured from the origin.

Relative Cartesian Coordinate System

In the Relative Cartesian coordinate system, every point you specify in the drawing area measures from the last specified point in the drawing area and the location of a point is defined by the X and Y coordinates, see Figure 2.16. In Figure 2.16, the coordinates (X=10, Y=15) of the point 'P2' measure 10 units along the X axis and 15 units along the Y axis from the last specified point (point P1).

In the Relative coordinate system, the method of specifying the X and Y coordinates of a point in the Command Line window as well as in the Dynamic Input boxes are discussed next.

Specifying a Point in the Command Line Window

To specify a point, according to the Relative coordinate system in the Command Line window, enter @ as a prefix to the X coordinate and then followed by the Y coordinate separated by a comma, see Figure 2.17. Note that the coordinates (@10, 15) of a point (Point 2) specified in the Command Line window are measured from the last specified point, refer to Figure 2.16.

Specifying a Point in the Dynamic Input Boxes

To specify a point, according to the Relative coordinate system in the Dynamic Input boxes, enter the coordinates (X and Y) of the point in the Dynamic Input boxes, without any prefix.

Note: As discussed, in the Relative coordinate system, whether you specify coordinates in the Command Line window or the Dynamic Input boxes, coordinates are measured from the last specified point in the drawing area.

Polar Coordinate System

The Polar coordinate system are of two types and are discussed next.

1. Absolute Polar coordinate system
2. Relative Polar coordinate system

Absolute Polar Coordinate System

In the Absolute Polar coordinate system, to define a point, you need to specify the distance and angle values separated by an angle bracket (<). Note that in the Absolute Polar coordinate system, the distance value measures from the origin and the angle value measures from an axis which represents zero degrees, see Figure 2.18.

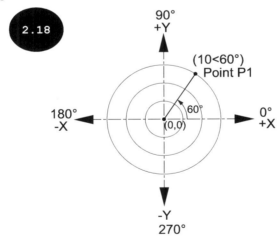

In the Absolute Polar coordinate system, the method of specifying a point in the Command Line window as well as in the Dynamic Input boxes are discussed next.

Specifying a Point in the Command Line Window

To specify a point, according to the Absolute Polar coordinate system in the Command Line window, enter the distance and angle values separated by an angle bracket (<), see Figure 2.19. In this figure, the distance and angle values (10<60) specified in the Command Line window measure 10 units distance from the origin and 60-degree angle from the X axis, refer to Figure 2.18.

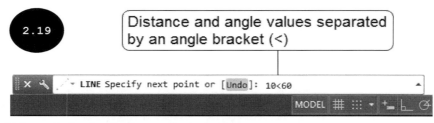

Figure 2.19

Specifying a Point in the Dynamic Input Boxes

To specify a point, according to the Absolute Polar coordinate system in the Dynamic Input boxes, enter # as a prefix to the distance value and then followed by the angle value, see Figure 2.20. In this figure, the coordinates (#10<60) specified in the Dynamic Input boxes measure 10 units distance from the origin and 60-degree angle from the X axis, which represents zero degrees.

Figure 2.20

Relative Polar Coordinate System

In the Relative Polar coordinate system, every point you specify in the drawing area measures from the last specified point in the drawing area and the location of a point is defined by entering the distance and angle values, see Figure 2.21. In Figure 2.21, the distance and angle values (10<25°) of the point 'P2" measure from the last specified point (P1).

Figure 2.21

In the Relative Polar coordinate system, the method of specifying a point in the Command Line window as well as in the Dynamic Input boxes are discussed next.

Specifying a Point in the Command Line Window

To specify a point, according to the Relative Polar coordinate system in the Command Line window, enter @ as a prefix to the distance value and then followed by the angle value separated by an angle bracket (<), see Figure 2.22. In this figure, the distance and angle values (@25<60) are specified for a point which measure 25 units distance form the last specified point and 60-degree angle from the X axis originating from the last specified point.

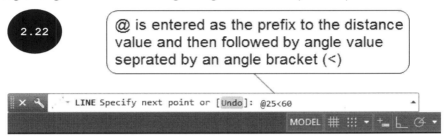

Specifying a Point in the Dynamic Input Boxes

To specify a point, according to the Relative Polar coordinate system in the Dynamic Input boxes, enter distance and angle values in the Dynamic Input boxes, without any prefix, see Figure 2.23.

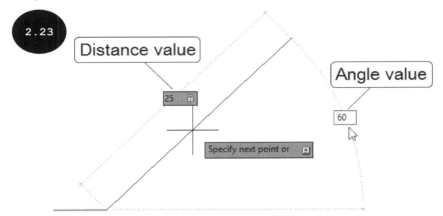

The following table summarizes about the different coordinate systems discussed earlier:

Coordinate System		Command Line	Dynamic Input
Cartesian Coordinate System	Absolute cartesian coordinate system	X,Y For example: 10,25	# X,Y For example: #10,25
	Relative cartesian coordinate system	@X,Y For example: @10,25	X,Y For example: 10,25
Polar Coordinate System	Absolute polar coordinate system	distance<angle For example: 25<60	#distance<angle For example: #25<60
	Relative polar coordinate system	@distance<angle For example: @25<60	distance<angle For example: 25<60

Creating a Drawing

Once you have setup drawing units, limits, grid and snap settings, and understand about different coordinate systems, you can start creating a drawing in AutoCAD. In AutoCAD, the tools used for creating drawings are grouped together in the **Draw** panel of the **Home** tab, see Figure 2.24. To activate a tool, click on it in the **Draw** panel or enter its shortcut key/command into the Command Line window. For example, to activate the **Line** tool, click on the **Line** tool in the **Draw** panel or enter L in the Command Line window and then press ENTER.

Drawing a Line

A line defines the shortest distance between two points. You can draw a line by specifying its start point and endpoint. To draw a line, click on the **Line** tool in the **Draw** panel of the **Home** tab or enter L in the Command Line window and then press ENTER. The **Line** tool gets activated, and you are prompted to specify the first point of the line. You can specify the coordinates (X and Y) of the first point of the line in the Command Line window or the Dynamic Input boxes. You can also click in the drawing area to specify points.

> **Note:** As discussed, you can specify points by entering their coordinates according to the Absolute coordinate system, Relative coordinate system, or Polar coordinate system in the Command Line window or the Dynamic Input boxes. You can also pick points directly in the drawing area by clicking the left mouse button.

Procedure for Drawing a Line

1. Click on the **Line** tool in the **Draw** panel or enter L in the Command Line window and then press ENTER. You are prompted to specify the first point of the line.

   ```
   Specify first point:
   ```

2. Enter the coordinates (X and Y) of the first point in the Command Line window or the Dynamic Input boxes. As soon as you specify the coordinates of the first point, you are prompted to specify the next (second) point of the line.

   ```
   Specify next point or [Undo]:
   ```

> **Note:** To specify coordinates in the Command Line window, you may need to turn off the Dynamic Input mode. You can turn on or off the Dynamic Input mode by clicking on the **Dynamic Input** button in the Status Bar.

3. Enter the coordinates (X and Y) of the second point in the Command Line window or the Dynamic Input boxes. A line is drawn between the two specified points in the drawing area, see Figure 2.25. Also, a rubber band line attached to the cursor, and you are prompted to specify the next (third) point of the line.

   ```
   Specify next point or [Undo]:
   ```

   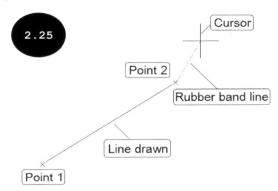

4. Similarly, you can continue specifying points in the drawing area for creating a chain of lines.

Note: After specifying the third point of the line, the command sequence appears as "`Specify next point or [Close Undo]:`" By using the options (Close and Undo) of the command sequence, you can create the closed loop of the line entities and undo the last specified point.

To undo or cancel the last specified point, click on the **Undo** option that appears in the command sequence. Alternatively, enter **U** in the Command Line window and then press ENTER. You can undo or cancel multiple points one after another by continuously using this option.

To create a close loop of the line entities where the last point joins to the first specified point, click on the **Close** option that appears in the command sequence or enter **C** in the Command Line window and then press ENTER, see Figure 2.26.

---

5. Once all the line entities have been drawn, exit from the **Line** tool by pressing the ENTER key. You can also press the **ESC** or **SPACEBAR** key to exit from the **Line** tool. Alternatively, right-click in the drawing area and then click on the **Enter** or **Cancel** option in the shortcut menu that appears to exit from the **Line** tool, see Figure 2.27.

74 Chapter 2 > Creating Drawings - I

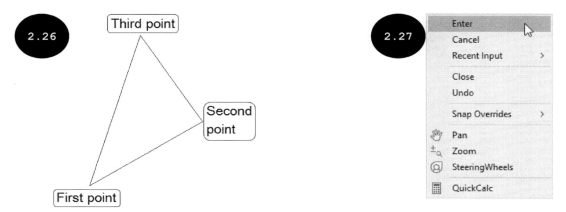

Command Sequence for Drawing a Line

```
Tool/Command: Line or L  (ENTER)
Specify first point: (Specify X, Y coordinates)
Specify next point or [Undo]: (Specify X, Y coordinates)
Specify next point or [Undo]: (Specify X, Y coordinates)
Specify next point or [Close Undo]: ENTER
```

Note: While creating a drawing, it does not matter which coordinate system to use for specifying points in the drawing area. You can use any of the coordinate systems or in the combination of coordinate systems to specify points in the drawing area as per your convenience.

Example 1

Create the drawing shown in Figure 2.28 by using the Absolute Cartesian coordinate system. Also, specify the coordinates of the points by using the Command Line window.

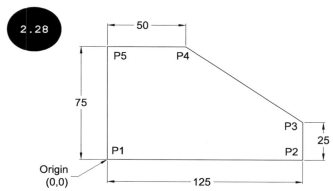

Section 1: Starting AutoCAD

1. Double-click on the AutoCAD icon on your desktop. The initial screen of AutoCAD appears with the **Start** tab, see Figure 2.29.

2.29

2. In the **Get Started** section of the **Start** tab, click on **Start Drawing**, see Figure 2.29. The new drawing file with the default drawing template gets invoked.

   Alternatively, to invoke a new drawing file, click on the **New** tool in the **Quick Access Toolbar**, which is at the top left corner of AutoCAD. The **Select template** dialog box appears. In this dialog box, choose the *acad.dwt* template and then click on the **Open** button. A new drawing file with *acad.dwt* template invoked. You can also right-click on the **Start** tab and then click on the **New** option in the shortcut menu appeared to invoke a new drawing file. Additionally, you can click on the + sign available next to the **Start** tab to invoke a new drawing file.

Section 2: Selecting Workspace for Creating Drawing

1. Click on the **Workspace Switching** button in the Status Bar. A flyout appears, see Figure 2.30.

2.30

2. In this flyout, make sure that the **Drafting & Annotation** option is tick-mark to create drawings in the Drafting & Annotation workspace.

   Note: A tick-mark next to a workspace indicates that it selected as the current workspace for creating drawings. By default, the Drafting & Annotation workspace selected as the current workspace for creating drawings.

Section 3: Defining Limits for Drawing

1. Follow the command sequence given below for defining the limits of the drawing.

   ```
   Command: LIMITS (ENTER)
   Specify lower left corner or [ON/OFF]<0.0000,0.0000>: 0,0 (ENTER)
   Specify upper right corner <12.0000,9.0000>: 250,150 (ENTER)
   ```

Section 4: Creating Drawing by using the Absolute Coordinate System

As stated in the description of the example, you need to enter coordinates in the Command Line window according to the Absolute coordinate system for specifying points. It is recommended to turn off the Dynamic Input mode to enter coordinates in the Command Line window.

1. Click on the **Dynamic Input** button in the Status Bar to turn off the Dynamic Input mode. Note that it is a toggle button.

2. Click on the **Line** tool in the **Draw** panel of the **Home** tab. The **Line** tool is activated, and you are prompted to specify the first point of the line. You can also enter **L** in the Command Line window and then press ENTER to activate the **Line** tool.

3. Follow the command sequence given below for creating the drawing.

   ```
   Specify first point: 0,0 (ENTER)
   Specify next point or [Undo]: 125,0 (ENTER)
   Specify next point or [Undo]: 125,25 (ENTER)
   Specify next point or [Undo]: 50,75 (ENTER)
   Specify next point or [Undo]: 0,75 (ENTER)
   Specify next point or [Close Undo]: C or Close
   ```

Tip: To specify points in the Dynamic Input boxes according to the Absolute coordinate system, you need to enter **#** as a prefix to the X coordinate and then followed by the Y coordinate in the Dynamic Input boxes.

Note: To fit the drawing complete in the drawing area, enter **ZOOM** in the Command Line window and then press ENTER. Next, enter **All** in the Command Line window and then press ENTER. The drawing is fit entirely inside the drawing area.

Hands-on Test Drive 1

Create the same drawing created in Example 1 by using the Relative Cartesian coordinate system, see Figure 2.31. Also, specify the coordinates of the points by using the Command Line window.

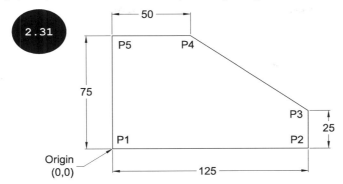

Hint: In the Relative Cartesian coordinate system, every point you specify in the drawing area measures from the last specified point in the drawing area.

Command sequence for creating drawing with some of the coordinates of the points are as follows:

```
Tool/Command:  Line or L  (ENTER)
Specify first point:  0,0  (ENTER)
Specify next point or [Undo]:  @125,0  (ENTER)
Specify next point or [Undo]:  @0,25   (ENTER)
Specify next point or [Undo]:  _____  (ENTER)
Specify next point or [Undo]:  _____  (ENTER)
Specify next point or [Close Undo]:  C or Close
```

Example 2

Create the drawing shown in Figure 2.32 by using the Relative Polar coordinate system. Also, specify the coordinates of the points by using the Command Line window.

78　Chapter 2 > Creating Drawings - I

Section 1: Starting AutoCAD

1. Start AutoCAD by double-clicking on the AutoCAD icon on your desktop, if not already started.

2. In the **Get Started** section of the initial screen, click on **Start Drawing**. The new drawing file with the default drawing template gets invoked.

Section 2: Selecting Workspace for Creating Drawing

1. Click on the **Workspace Switching** button in the Status Bar. A flyout appears, see Figure 2.33.

2. Make sure that the **Drafting & Annotation** option is tick-mark in this flyout.

Section 3: Defining Limits for Drawing

1. Follow the command sequence given below for defining the limits of the drawing.

   ```
   Command: LIMITS (ENTER)
   Specify lower left corner or [ON/OFF]<0.0000,0.0000>: 0,0 (ENTER)
   Specify upper right corner <12.0000,9.0000>: 120,200 (ENTER)
   ```

Section 4: Creating Drawing by using the Relative Polar Coordinate System

As stated in the description of the example, you need to enter coordinates in the Command Line window according to the Relative Polar coordinate system for specifying points. It is recommended to turn off the Dynamic Input mode to enter coordinates in the Command Line window.

1. Click on the **Dynamic Input** button in the Status Bar to turn off the Dynamic Input mode. Note that it is a toggle button.

2. Click on the **Line** tool in the **Draw** panel of the **Home** tab. The **Line** tool is activated, and you are prompted to specify the first point of the line. Alternatively, you can enter L into the Command Line window and then press ENTER to activate the **Line** tool.

Note: In the Relative Polar coordinate system, you need to enter @ as a prefix to the distance value and then followed by the angle value separated by an angle bracket (<) in the Command Line window. Note that in the Relative Polar coordinate system, every point you specify in the drawing area by defining its distance and angle values measures from the last specified point in the drawing area.

3. Follow the command sequence given below for creating the drawing.

```
Specify first point: 0,0 (ENTER)
Specify next point or [Undo]: @60<0 (ENTER)
Specify next point or [Undo]: @10<90 (ENTER)
Specify next point or [Undo]: @52<120 (ENTER)
Specify next point or [Undo]: @24<180 (ENTER)
Specify next point or [Undo]: @34<90 (ENTER)
Specify next point or [Undo]: @35<0 (ENTER)
Specify next point or [Undo]: @10<90 (ENTER)
Specify next point or [Undo]: @45<180 (ENTER)
Specify next point or [Close Undo]: C or Close
```

Hands-on Test Drive 2

Create the same drawing created in Example 2, by using the Relative Polar coordinate system, see Figure 2.34. You need to specify the coordinates of the points by using the Dynamic Input boxes.

Hint: For specifying points by using the Relative Polar coordinate system in the Dynamic Input boxes, you first need to turn on the Dynamic Input mode by clicking on the **Dynamic Input** button in the Status Bar. Next, you can directly enter the distance and angle values without any prefix in the respective Dynamic Input boxes, which appear near the cursor tip.

Drawing a Circle

In AutoCAD, you can draw a circle by using the following methods:

- Drawing a circle by defining center point and radius
- Drawing a circle by defining center point and diameter
- Drawing a circle by defining two points on the circumference of a circle
- Drawing a circle by defining three points on the circumference of a circle
- Drawing a circle by defining two tangent points and radius
- Drawing a circle by defining three tangent points

2.35

In AutoCAD, the tools for drawing a circle are available in the **Circle** flyout of the **Draw** panel in the **Home** tab, see Figure 2.35. Alternatively, you can invoke the **Circle** command for drawing a circle by entering **CIRCLE** or **C** in the Command Line window and then pressing ENTER. Different methods of drawing a circle are discussed next.

Drawing a Circle by Defining Center Point and Radius

You can draw a circle by defining its center point and radius by using the **Center, Radius** tool of the **Circle** flyout. For doing so, click on the down arrow in the circle tool of the **Draw** panel. The **Circle** flyout appears, see Figure 2.35. In this flyout, click on the **Center, Radius** tool. The **Center, Radius** tool gets activated, and you are prompted to specify the center point of the circle. Alternatively, you can enter **C** or **CIRCLE** in the Command Line window and then press ENTER to activate this tool. Once the **Center, Radius** tool has been activated, you can specify the coordinates (X, Y) of the center point of the circle either in the Command Line window or the Dynamic Input boxes. Additionally, you can click in the drawing area to specify the center point of the circle. The procedure for drawing a circle by defining center point and radius is discussed next.

Procedure for Drawing a Circle by Defining Center Point and Radius

1. Invoke the **Circle** flyout and then click on the **Center, Radius** tool. You are prompted to specify the center point of the circle. Alternatively, you can enter **C** in the Command Line window and then press ENTER to activate the tool.

    ```
    Specify center point for circle or [3P 2P Ttr (tan tan radius)]:
    ```

2. Specify the coordinates (X, Y) of the center point either in the Command Line or the Dynamic Input boxes. You are prompted to specify the radius of the circle.

    ```
    Specify radius of circle or [Diameter]:
    ```

Tip: To create a circle by defining its diameter, click on the **Diameter** option in the command prompt or enter **D** in the Command Line window and then press ENTER. Next, specify the diameter of the circle in the Command Line window.

3. Enter the radius value of the circle and then press ENTER. The circle of the specified radius is created in the drawing area, see Figure 2.36.

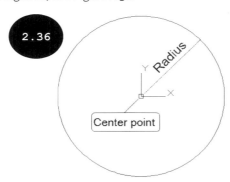

Drawing a Circle by Defining Center Point and Diameter
You can draw a circle by defining its center point and diameter by using the **Center, Diameter** tool of the **Circle** flyout, see Figure 2.37.

Procedure for Drawing a Circle by Defining Center Point and Diameter
1. Invoke the **Circle** flyout and then click on the **Center, Diameter** tool. You are prompted to specify the center point of the circle. Alternatively, enter **C** in the Command Line window and then press ENTER.

   `Specify center point for circle or [3P 2P Ttr (tan tan radius)]:`

2. Specify the coordinates (X, Y) of the center point either in the Command Line window or the Dynamic input boxes. You are prompted to specify the diameter of the circle.

   `Specify radius of circle or [Diameter]:_d Specify diameter of circle:`

Note: If you invoke the tool for creating a circle by entering the **C** or **CIRCLE** in the Command Line window, then after specifying the center point of the circle, you need to click on the **Diameter** option in the command prompt for specifying the diameter of the circle.

3. Enter diameter of the circle and then press ENTER. The circle of specified diameter is created, see Figure 2.38.

Drawing a Circle by Defining 2 Points

You can draw a circle by defining two points on the circumference of the circle by using the **2 Point** tool, see Figure 2.39. You can also enter **C** or **CIRCLE** into the Command Line window and then click on the **2P** option in the command prompt appeared for creating the circle by defining two points on the circumference of the circle.

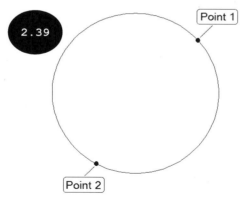

Procedure for Drawing a Circle by Defining 2 Points

1. Invoke the **Circle** flyout and then click on the **2 Point** tool. You are prompted to specify the first point on the circumference of the circle. Alternatively, enter **C** in the Command Line window and then press ENTER. Next, click on the **2P** option in the command prompt appeared.

   ```
   Specify center point for circle or [3P 2P Ttr (tan tan radius)]: _2p
   Specify first end point of circle's diameter:
   ```

2. Enter the coordinate (X, Y) of the first point either in the Command Line window or the Dynamic Input boxes and then press ENTER. Alternatively, click in the drawing area to define the first point on the circumference of the circle. As soon as you specify the first point, you are prompted to specify the second point of the circle.

   ```
   Specify second end point of circle's diameter:
   ```

3. Enter the coordinate (X, Y) of the second point on the circumference of the circle either in the Command Line window or the Dynamic Input boxes and then press ENTER. The circle drawn, see Figure 2.39. You can also click directly in the drawing area to define the second point on the circumference of the circle.

Drawing a Circle by Defining 3 Points

In AutoCAD, you can draw a circle by defining three points on the circumference of the circle, see Figure 2.40. To draw a circle by defining 3 points on its circumference, invoke the **Circle** flyout of the **Draw** panel and then click on the **3 Point** tool. Alternatively, enter C or CIRCLE in the Command Line window and then press ENTER. Next, click on the 3P option in the command prompt or enter 3P in the Command Line window.

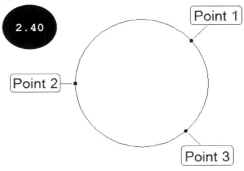

Procedure for Drawing a Circle by Defining 3 Points

1. Invoke the **Circle** flyout and then click on the **3 Point** tool. You are prompted to specify the center point of the circle.

   ```
   Specify center point for circle or [3P 2P Ttr (tan tan radius)]: _3p
   Specify first point on circle:
   ```

2. Enter the coordinate (X, Y) of the first point either in the Command Line window or the Dynamic Input boxes. Alternatively, you can click directly in the drawing area to define the first point. As soon as you specify the first point, you are prompted to specify the second point of the circle.

   ```
   Specify second point on circle:
   ```

84   Chapter 2 > Creating Drawings - I

3. Enter the coordinate (X, Y) of the second point. You are prompted to specify the third point. Also, the preview of the circle appears such that it has passed through the two specified points.

    ```
    Specify third point on circle:
    ```

4. Enter the coordinate (X, Y) of the third point. The circle drawn, see Figure 2.40.

Drawing a Circle by Defining Tangent, Tangent, Radius

In AutoCAD, you can draw a circle that is tangent to two objects/entities. To draw a circle tangent to two objects/entities, you need to define two tangent objects and the radius of the circle by using the **Tan, Tan, Radius** tool, see Figure 2.41.

Procedure for Drawing a Circle by Defining Tangent, Tangent, Radius

1. Invoke the **Circle** flyout and then click on the **Tan, Tan, Radius** tool. You are prompted to specify the first tangent object. Alternatively, enter **C** in the Command Line window and then press ENTER. Next, click on the **Ttr (tan tan radius)** option in the command prompt or enter **ttr** in the Command Line window.

    ```
    Specify point on object for first tangent of circle:
    ```

2. Click on the first tangent object in the drawing area, see Figure 2.41. You are prompted to specify the second tangent object.

    ```
    Specify point on object for second tangent of circle:
    ```

3. Click on the second tangent object in the drawing area, see Figure 2.41. You are prompted to specify the radius of the circle.

    ```
    Specify radius of circle:
    ```

4. Enter the radius value of the circle either in the Command Line window or the Dynamic Input boxes and then press ENTER. The circle tangent to the two selected objects drawn, see Figure 2.41.

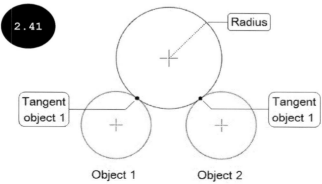

Drawing a Circle by Defining Tangent, Tangent, Tangent

In AutoCAD, you can draw a circle that is tangent to three objects/entities. To draw a circle tangent to three objects/entities, you need to define three tangent objects by using the **Tan, Tan, Tan** tool, see Figure 2.42.

Procedure for Drawing a Circle by Defining Tangent, Tangent, Tangent

1. Invoke the **Circle** flyout and then click on the **Tan, Tan, Tan** tool. You are prompted to specify the first tangent object.

   ```
   Specify center point for circle or [3P 2P Ttr (tan tan radius)]:_3p
   Specify first point on circle:_tan to
   ```

2. Click on the first tangent object in the drawing area, see Figure 2.42. You are prompted to specify the second tangent object.

   ```
   Specify second point on circle:_tan to
   ```

3. Click on the second tangent object in the drawing area, see Figure 2.42. You are prompted to specify the third tangent object.

   ```
   Specify third point on circle:_tan to
   ```

4. Click on the third tangent object, see Figure 2.42. The circle tangent to three selected objects drawn, see Figure 2.42.

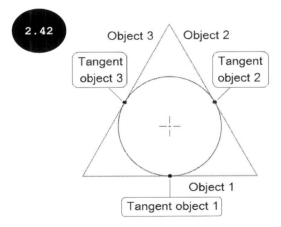

Drawing an Arc

In AutoCAD, you can draw an arc by using different methods. The tools for drawing an arc are available in the **Arc** flyout of the **Draw** panel in the **Home** tab, see Figure 2.43. Alternatively, you can enter **ARC** or **A** in the Command Line window and then press ENTER for drawing an arc. Different methods to create an arc are discussed next.

Drawing an Arc by Defining 3 Points

You can draw an arc by defining three points on the circumference of the arc by using the **3-Point** tool, see Figure 2.44. For doing so, click on the down arrow in the arc tool of the **Draw** panel. The **Arc** flyout appears, see Figure 2.43. Next, click on the **3-Point** tool in the flyout. The **3-Point** tool gets activated. Alternatively, you can enter **A** or **ARC** in the Command Line window and then press ENTER to invoke the **3-Point** tool. Once the **3-Point** tool gets activated, you are prompted to specify the start point of the arc. You can specify the coordinate (X, Y) of the start point of the arc either in the Command Line window or the Dynamic Input boxes. You can also click the left mouse button in the drawing area to specify the point.

Procedure for Drawing an Arc by Defining 3 Points

1. Click on the down arrow in the arc tool of the **Draw** panel to invoke the **Arc** flyout and then click on the **3-Point** tool. You are prompted to specify the start point of the arc. Alternatively, enter **A** in the Command Line window and then press ENTER.

    ```
    Specify start point of arc or [Center]:
    ```

2. Enter the coordinate (X, Y) of the start point and then press ENTER. You are prompted to specify the second point of the arc. You can also click in the drawing area to specify the start point of the arc.

   ```
   Specify second point of arc or [Center End]:
   ```

3. Move the cursor counter-clockwise or clockwise in the drawing area and then click the left mouse button to specify the second point of the arc on the circumference of the arc. You can also specify the second point of the arc by entering its coordinate (X, Y). As soon as you specify the second point, you are prompted to specify the end point of the arc. Also, the preview of the arc appears such that it has passed through the first and second points specified in the drawing area.

   ```
   Specify end point of arc:
   ```

4. Specify the end point of the arc on the circumference of the arc by clicking the left mouse button in the drawing area. The arc drawn such that it has passed through the three specified points, see Figure 2.45.

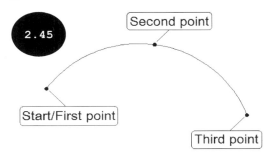

Drawing an Arc by Defining Start, Center, and End Points
You can draw an arc by defining the start, center, and end points using the **Start, Center, End** tool of the **Arc** flyout, see Figure 2.46.

Procedure for Drawing an Arc by Defining Start, Center, and End Points
1. Invoke the **Arc** flyout and then click on the **Start, Center, End** tool. You are prompted to specify the start point of the arc. Alternatively, enter **A** in the Command Line window and then press ENTER.

   ```
   Specify start point of arc or [Center]:
   ```

2. Enter the coordinate (X, Y) of the start point and then press ENTER. You are prompted to specify the center point of the arc. You can also click the left mouse button in the drawing area to specify the start point of the arc.

   ```
   Specify second point of arc or [Center End]:_c Specify center point of arc:
   ```

88 Chapter 2 > Creating Drawings - I

Note: If you invoke the tool for creating an arc by entering **A** or **ARC** in the Command Line window then after specifying the start point of the arc, you need to click on the **Center** option in the command prompt for specifying the center point of the arc.

3. Move the cursor to the required location in the drawing area and then click to specify the center point of the arc. You can also enter the coordinate (X, Y) for specifying the center point of the arc. As soon as you specify the center point, you are prompted to specify the end point of the arc. Also, the preview of the arc appears in the counter-clockwise direction in the drawing area.

   ```
   Specify end point of arc or [Angle chord Length]:
   ```

Note: By default, an arc created in the counter-clockwise direction. To change the direction of the arc from counter-clockwise direction to clockwise direction, press and hold the CTRL key and then specify the end point of the arc.

4. Specify the end point of the arc by clicking the left mouse button in the drawing area. The arc is drawn, see Figure 2.46.

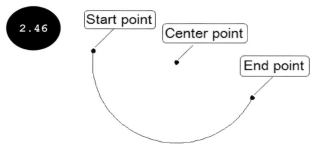

Drawing an Arc by Defining Start Point, Center Point, and Angle

You can draw an arc by defining start point, center point, and angle using the **Start, Center, Angle** tool of the **Arc** flyout, see Figure 2.47. Below is the command sequence for drawing an arc by specifying the start point, center point, and angle.

```
Tool/Command:  Click on the Start, Center, Angle tool in the Arc flyout
Specify start point of arc or [Center]: Specify the start point of the arc
Specify center point of arc: Specify the center point of the arc
Specify included angle (hold Ctrl to switch direction): Specify the
```
angle of the arc (see Figure 2.47)

Tip: As discussed, you can specify coordinates (X, Y) either in the Command Line window or in the Dynamic Input boxes. Alternatively, you can also click the left mouse button in the drawing area for specifying points.

2.47 Arc being drawn by defining start point (1), center point (2), and angle

Drawing an Arc by Defining Start Point, Center Point, and Length

You can draw an arc by defining start point, center point, and length using the **Start, Center, Length** tool of the **Arc** flyout, see Figure 2.48. Below is the command sequence for drawing an arc by specifying the start point, center point, and length.

```
Tool/Command:    Click on the Start, Center, Length tool in the Arc flyout
Specify start point of arc or [Center]:  Specify the start point of the arc
Specify center point of arc:  Specify the center point of the arc
Specify length of chord (hold Ctrl to switch direction):  Specify the
```
length of the arc (see Figure 2.48)

2.48 Arc being drawn by defining start point (1), center point (2), and length (3)

Drawing an Arc by Defining Start Point, End Point, and Angle

You can draw an arc by defining start point, end point, and angle using the **Start, End, Angle** tool of the **Arc** flyout, see Figure 2.49. Below is the command sequence for drawing an arc by specifying the start point, end point, and angle.

```
Command/Tool:    Click on the Start, End, Angle tool in the Arc flyout
Specify start point of arc or [Center]:  Specify the start point of the arc
Specify end point of arc:  Specify the end point of the arc
Specify center point of arc or [Angle Direction Radius]:_a Specify
included angle:  Specify the angle of the arc (see Figure 2.49)
```

Drawing an Arc by Defining Start Point, End Point, and Direction

You can draw an arc by defining start point, end point, and direction using the **Start, End, Direction** tool of the **Arc** flyout, see Figure 2.50. Below is the command sequence for drawing an arc by specifying the start point, end point, and direction.

```
Tool/Command:   Click on the Start, End, Direction tool in the Arc flyout
Specify start point of arc or [Center]:  Specify the start point of the arc
Specify end point of arc:  Specify the end point of the arc
Specify center point of arc or [Angle Direction Radius]:_d Specify
tangent direction for the start point of arc:  Specify the direction of the arc
(see Figure 2.50)
```

Drawing an Arc by Defining Start Point, End Point, and Radius

You can draw an arc by defining start point, end point, and radius using the **Start, End, Radius** tool of the **Arc** flyout, see Figure 2.51. Below is the command sequence for drawing an arc by specifying the start point, end point, and radius.

```
Tool/Command:   Click on the Start, End, Radius tool in the Arc flyout
Specify start point of arc or [Center]:  Specify the start point of the arc
Specify end point of arc:  Specify the end point of the arc
Specify radius of arc:  Specify the radius of the arc (see Figure 2.51)
```

Figure 2.51 Arc being drawn by defining start point (1), end point (2), and radius

Drawing an Arc by Defining Center Point, Start Point, and End Point

You can draw an arc by defining the center point, start point, and end point using the **Center, Start, End** tool of the **Arc** flyout, see Figure 2.52. Below is the command sequence for drawing an arc by specifying the center point, start point, and end point.

```
Tool/Command:   Click on the Center, Start, End tool in the Arc flyout
Specify start point of arc or [Center]: _c Specify center point of
arc: Specify the center point of the arc (see Figure 2.52)
Specify start point of arc: Specify the start point of the arc (see Figure 2.52)
Specify end point of arc or [Angle chord Length]: Specify the end point of
the arc (see Figure 2.52)
```

Figure 2.52 Arc drawn by defining center point, start point, and end point

Drawing an Arc by Defining Center Point, Start Point, and Angle

You can draw an arc by defining the center point, start point, and angle using the **Center, Start, Angle** tool of the **Arc** flyout, see Figure 2.53. Below is the command sequence for drawing an arc by specifying the center point, start point, and angle.

```
Tool/Command:   Click on the Center, Start, Angle tool in the Arc flyout
Specify start point of arc or [Center]: _c Specify center point of
arc: Specify the center point of the arc (see Figure 2.53)
Specify start point of arc: Specify the start point of the arc (see Figure 2.53)
Specify included angle: Specify the angle of the arc (see Figure 2.53)
```

Drawing an Arc by Defining Center Point, Start Point, and Length

You can draw an arc by defining the center point, start point, and length using the **Center, Start, Length** tool of the **Arc** flyout, see Figure 2.54. Below is the command sequence for drawing an arc by specifying the center point, start point, and length.

Command/Tool: *Click on the Center, Start, Length tool of the Arc flyout*
Specify start point of arc or [Center]: _c Specify center point of arc: *Specify the center point of the arc*
Specify start point of arc: *Specify the start point of the arc*
Specify end point of arc or [Angle chord Length]: _l Specify length of chord: *Specify length to draw an arc (see Figure 2.54)*

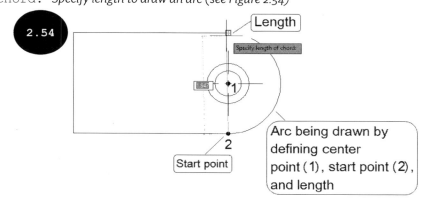

Drawing an Arc by using the Continue Tool

You can draw an arc tangent to the last drawn line or arc entity by using the **Continue** tool of the **Arc** flyout. Below is the command sequence for drawing an arc tangent to the last drawn line or arc entity.

Tool/Command: *Click on the Continue tool in the Arc flyout. The preview of an tangent arc appears such that its start point is fixed with the end point of the last drawn entity*
Specify end point of arc: *Click to specify the end point of the arc*

Canceling, Erasing and Restoring Objects

In AutoCAD, you can cancel or exit the currently active command/tool, erase or delete unwanted entities, and restore the erased or deleted entities in the drawing area. To cancel or exit the currently active command/tool, press the ESC or ENTER key. Alternatively, right-click in the drawing area and then click on the **Cancel** or **Enter** option in the shortcut menu displayed. For example, if you are creating line entities by using the **Line** tool then press the ESC or ENTER key to terminate the creation of lines and exit from the **Line** tool. Refer to the command sequence given below:

```
Tool/Command:   Line or L  (ENTER)
Specify first point:  Specify X, Y coordinates
Specify next point or [Undo]:  Specify X, Y coordinates
Specify next point or [Undo]:  ESC or ENTER
```

To erase the drawing entities which are drawn by mistake, enter **E** or **ERASE** in the Command Line window and then press ENTER. The erase command gets activated, and you are prompted to select the objects to be erased. Click on the objects to be erased from the drawing. You can click on multiple objects one by one for erasing them. Next, press the ENTER key or right-click in the drawing area. The selected objects deleted from the drawing. Refer to the command sequence given below:

```
Command:   ERASE or E  (ENTER)
Select objects:  Click on the first object to be erased
Select objects:  Click on the second object to be erased
Select objects:  ENTER
```

Tip: You can also click on the **ERASE** tool in the **Modify** panel of the **Home** tab to erase the drawing entities.

To erase all objects/entities of a drawing at a time, invoke the **ERASE** tool/command and then enter **All** in the Command Line window.

You can restore an object which is deleted by mistake or accidentally in a drawing. For doing so, enter **Undo** or **U** in the Command Line window and then press ENTER. The undo command gets activated, and the previously deleted object gets restored in the drawing area. You can use the undo command multiple times to restore the previously deleted objects one by one. Alternatively, press the CTRL + Z to restore the previously deleted objects.

94   Chapter 2 > Creating Drawings - I

Navigating 2D Drawing

In AutoCAD, you can navigate drawing by using the navigating tools. The navigating tools such as **Zoom** and **Pan** can be accessed from the **Navigation Bar**, which is on the right of the drawing area, see Figure 2.55. Different navigating tools are discussed next.

2.55

Zoom

AutoCAD has many powerful tools to zoom in or zoom out drawing for better control over it. The tools to zoom in or zoom out a drawing are available in the **Zoom** flyout of the **Navigation Bar**. To invoke the **Zoom** flyout, click on the down arrow in the zoom tool of the **Navigation Bar**, see Figure 2.56. Some of the zoom tools are discssed next.

Zoom Realtime

The **Zoom Realtime** tool is used to zoom in or zoom out the drawing area, dynamically. In other words, you can dynamically enlarge or reduce the view of the drawing area by using the **Zoom Realtime** tool. To invoke the **Zoom Realtime** tool, click on the down arrow in the zoom tool of the Navigation Bar. The **Zoom** flyout appears, see Figure 2.56. In this flyout, click on the **Zoom Realtime** tool, see Figure 2.57. Alternatively, to invoke the **Zoom Realtime** tool, enter **Z** or **ZOOM** in the Command Line window and then press ENTER twice. Refer to the command sequence given below:

2.56

2.57

```
Tool/Command: Zoom or Z (ENTER)
Specify corner of window, enter a scale factor (nX or nXP), or
[All/Center/Dynamic/Extents/Previous/Scale/Window/Object]<real
time>: ENTER
```

After invoking the **Zoom Realtime** tool, press and hold the left mouse button in the drawing area and then drag the cursor upward or downward in the drawing area. On dragging the cursor upward, the drawing view starts enlarging, and on dragging the cursor downward, the drawing view starts reducing. Note that in the process of enlarging or reducing the drawing view, the scale of the drawing remains the same; only the viewing distance changes to enlarge or reduce the view.

Zoom All

The **Zoom All** tool is used to zoom the entire drawing or drawing limit to fit inside the drawing area. If the drawing is large and goes outside the drawing limit, then the entire drawing fits inside the drawing area on using the **Zoom All** tool, see Figure 2.58. However, if the drawing is smaller than the drawing limit, then the drawing limit fits inside the drawing area on using the **Zoom All** tool, see Figure 2.59. To invoke the **Zoom All** tool, click on the down arrow in the zoom tool of the **Navigation Bar**. The **Zoom** flyout appears. In this flyout, click on the **Zoom All** tool. Alternatively, enter Z or ZOOM in the Command Line window and then press ENTER. Next, enter **A** or **ALL** to invoke the **Zoom All** tool. Refer to the command sequence given below:

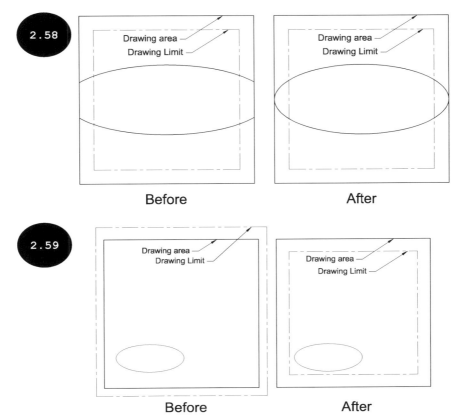

```
Command: Z or Zoom (ENTER)
Specify corner of window, enter a scale factor (nX or nXP), or
[All/Center/Dynamic/Extents/Previous/Scale/Window/Object]<real
time>: A or ALL (ENTER)
```

As soon as you invoke the **Zoom All** tool/command, the entire drawing or drawing limit fits inside the drawing area.

Zoom Window

The **Zoom Window** tool is used to zoom in an area of a drawing. You can specify an area of a drawing to be zoomed in by drawing a rectangular window around it. To invoke the **Zoom Window** tool, invoke the **Zoom** flyout of the Navigation Bar and then click on the **Zoom Window** tool. Alternatively, enter **Z** or **ZOOM** in the Command Line window and then press ENTER. Next, enter **W** in the Command Line window to invoke the **Zoom Window** tool. Refer to the command sequence given below:

```
Command: Z or Zoom (ENTER)
Specify corner of window, enter a scale factor (nX or nXP), or
[All/Center/Dynamic/Extents/Previous/Scale/Window/Object]<real
time>: W (ENTER)
Specify first corner:  Click to specify the first corner of the rectangular window in the drawing area
Specify first corner: Specify opposite corner:  Click to specify the opposite corner of the rectangular window
```

After drawing a rectangular window, the area lies inside it gets magnified and fits inside the drawing area.

Zoom Previous

The **Zoom Previous** tool is used to display the previously zoomed view of a drawing. To invoke the **Zoom Previous** tool, invoke the **Zoom** flyout of the Navigation Bar and then click on the **Zoom Preview** tool. Alternatively, enter **Z** or **Zoom** in the Command Line window and then press ENTER. Next, enter **P** in the Command Line window to invoke the **Zoom Previous** tool. Refer to the command sequence given below:

```
Command: Z or Zoom (ENTER)
Specify corner of window, enter a scale factor (nX or nXP), or
[All/Center/Dynamic/Extents/Previous/Scale/Window/Object]<real
time>: P (ENTER)
```

Zoom Extents

The **Zoom Extents** tool is used to fit a drawing completely inside the drawing area by expanding or shrinking the drawing view. By using this tool, all the entities in the drawing get magnified to their largest possibilities in the drawing area. To invoke the **Zoom Extents** tool, invoke the **Zoom** flyout of the Navigation Bar and then click on the **Zoom Extents** tool. Alternatively, enter **Z** or **ZOOM** in the Command Line window and then press ENTER. Next, enter E to invoke this tool. Refer to the command sequence given below:

```
Command: Z or Zoom (ENTER)
Specify corner of window, enter a scale factor (nX or nXP), or
[All/Center/Dynamic/Extents/Previous/Scale/Window/Object]<real
time>: E (ENTER)
```

Zoom In

The **Zoom In** tool is used to zoom in a drawing by doubling its size in the drawing area. To invoke the **Zoom In** tool, invoke the **Zoom** flyout of the **Navigation Bar** and then click on the **Zoom In** tool. Alternatively, enter Z or ZOOM in the Command Line window and then press ENTER. Next, enter 2X to invoke this tool. Refer to the command sequence given below:

```
Command: Z or Zoom (ENTER)
Specify corner of window, enter a scale factor (nX or nXP), or
[All/Center/Dynamic/Extents/Previous/Scale/Window/Object]<real
time>: 2X (ENTER)
```

Zoom Out

The **Zoom Out** tool is used to zoom out the drawing by decreasing its size to half of the original size of the drawing. To invoke the **Zoom Out** tool, invoke the **Zoom** flyout of the Navigation Bar and then click on the **Zoom Out** tool. Alternatively, enter Z or ZOOM in the Command Line window and then press ENTER. Next, enter .5X in the Command Line window to invoke this tool. Refer to the command sequence given below:

```
Command: Z or Zoom (ENTER)
Specify corner of window, enter a scale factor (nX or nXP), or
[All/Center/Dynamic/Extents/Previous/Scale/Window/Object]<real
time>: .5X (ENTER)
```

Note: You can turn on or off the display of the Navigation Bar in the drawing area by using the **Navigation Bar** tool in the **Viewport Tools** panel of the **View** tab in the **Ribbon**, see Figure 2.60. By default, this tool activated in the **Viewport Tools** panel of the **View** tab. As a result, the display of **Navigation Bar** is turned on in the drawing area.

Pan

The **Pan** tool is used to pan/move a drawing in the drawing area. To invoke the **Pan** tool, click on the **Pan** tool in the **Navigation Bar**, see Figure 2.61. After invoking the **Pan** tool, you can pan the drawing by pressing and holding the left mouse button and then dragging the cursor.

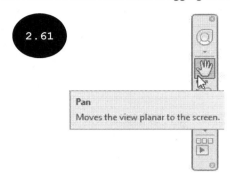

Tutorial 1

Draw the drawing shown in Figure 2.62 by specifying points using the Absolute Cartesian coordinate system. Also, use the Dynamic Input boxes for specifying coordinates. The dimensions shown in this figure are for your reference only. You will learn about applying dimensions in the later chapters.

Section 1: Starting AutoCAD

1. Double-click on the AutoCAD icon on your desktop. The initial screen of AutoCAD appears with the **Start** tab, see Figure 2.63.

AutoCAD 2019: A Power Guide > 99

2. In the **Get Started** section of the **Start** tab, click on **Start Drawing**, see Figure 2.63. The new drawing file with the default drawing template gets invoked.

 Alternatively, to invoke a new drawing file, click on the **New** tool in the **Quick Access Toolbar**, which is at the top left corner of AutoCAD. The **Select template** dialog box appears. In this dialog box, choose the *acad.dwt* template and then click on the **Open** button. A new drawing file with the *acad.dwt* template invoked. You can also right-click on the **Start** tab and then click on the **New** option in the shortcut menu appeared. Additionally, you can click on the + sign available next to the **Start** tab to invoke a new drawing file.

Section 2: Selecting Workspace for Creating Drawing

1. Click on the **Workspace Switching** button in the Status Bar. A flyout appears, see Figure 2.64.

2. In this flyout, make sure that the **Drafting & Annotation** option is tick-mark to create drawings in the Drafting & Annotation workspace.

Note: A tick-mark next to a workspace indicates that it selected as the current workspace for creating drawings. By default, the Drafting & Annotation workspace selected as the current workspace for creating drawings. You can click on any workspace to make it current for creating drawings.

Section 3: Defining Limits for the Drawing

1. Follow the command sequence given below for defining limits for the drawing.

   ```
   Command: LIMITS (ENTER)
   Specify lower left corner or [ON/OFF]<0.0000,0.0000>: 0,0 (ENTER)
   Specify upper right corner <12.0000,9.0000>: 160,130 (ENTER)
   ```

Section 4: Creating Drawing by Using the Absolute Coordinate System

As stated in the tutorial description, you need to enter coordinates in the Dynamic Input boxes according to the Absolute Cartesian coordinate system for specifying points. To enter coordinates in the Dynamic Input boxes, you need to make sure that the Dynamic Input mode is turned on.

1. Make sure that the Dynamic Input mode is turned on. You can turn on or off the Dynamic Input mode by clicking on the **Dynamic Input** button in the Status Bar. It is a toggle button.

2. Click on the **Line** tool in the **Draw** panel of the **Home** tab. The **Line** tool gets activated, and you are prompted to specify the first point of the line. Alternatively, you can enter L in the Command Line window and then press ENTER to activate the **Line** tool.

Note: In the Absolute coordinate system, the coordinate values measure from the origin. To specify coordinates in the Dynamic Input boxes according to the Absolute coordinate system, you need to enter # as a prefix to the X coordinate and then followed by the Y coordinate.

3. Follow the command sequence given below for creating the drawing.

   ```
   Specify first point: 0,0 (ENTER)
   Specify next point or [Undo]: #55,0 (ENTER)
   Specify next point or [Undo]: #55,25 (ENTER)
   Specify next point or [Undo]: #80,25 (ENTER)
   Specify next point or [Undo]: #80,55 (ENTER)
   Specify next point or [Close Undo]: #65,65 (ENTER)
   Specify next point or [Close Undo]: #0,65 (ENTER)
   Specify next point or [Close Undo]: C or Close (See Figure 2.65)

   Command: Z or Zoom (ENTER)
   Specify corner of window, enter a scale factor (nX or nXP), or
   [All/Center/Dynamic/Extents/Previous/Scale/Window/Object]<real
   time>: A or ALL (ENTER)
   ```

2.65

```
Command: C or Circle (ENTER)
Specify center point for circle or [3P 2P Ttr (tan tan radius)]: 25,30 (ENTER)
Specify radius of circle or [Diameter] <7.6802>: D (ENTER)
Specify diameter of circle <15.3603>: 25 (ENTER)  (See Figure 2.66)

Command: C or Circle (ENTER)
Specify center point for circle or [3P 2P Ttr (tan tan radius)]: 50,50 (ENTER)
Specify radius of circle or [Diameter] <7.6802>: D (ENTER)
Specify diameter of circle <15.3603>: 15 (ENTER)  (See Figure 2.67)
```

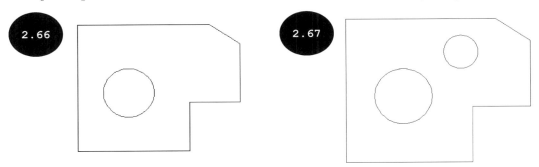

2.66   2.67

Section 5: Saving the Drawing

After creating the drawing, you need to save it.

1. Click on the **Save** tool in the **Quick Access Toolbar**. The **Save Drawing As** dialog box appears.

2. Browse to a local drive of your system and then create a folder with the name *AutoCAD*.

3. Create another folder with the name *Chapter 2* inside the *AutoCAD* folder. Next, enter **Tutorial 1** in the **File name** field of the dialog box.

4. Click on the **Save** button in the dialog box. The drawing saved with the name Tutorial 1.

Tutorial 2

Draw the drawing shown in Figure 2.68 by using the Relative Polar coordinate system. Also, use the Dynamic Input mode for specifying coordinate points. The dimensions shown in this figure are for your reference only. You will learn about applying dimensions in the later chapters.

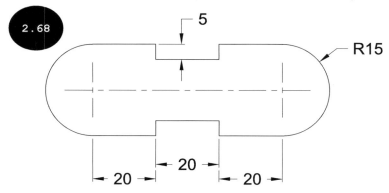

Section 1: Starting AutoCAD

1. Start AutoCAD and then click on the **New** tool in the **Quick Access Toolbar**, which is at the top left corner of the screen, see Figure 2.69. The **Select template** dialog box appears, see Figure 2.70.

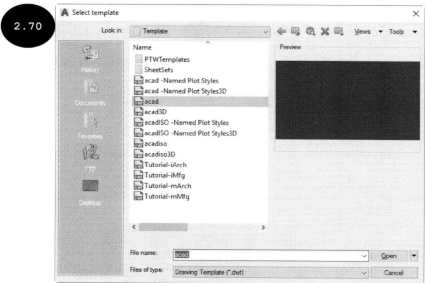

AutoCAD 2019: A Power Guide > 103

2. In the dialog box, click on the *acad.dwt* template and then click on the **Open** button. A new drawing file with the *acad.dwt* template invoked.

3. Make sure that the Drafting & Annotation workspace selected as the current workspace for creating the drawing.

Section 2: Drawing Line Entities

As stated in the tutorial description, you need to enter coordinates in the Dynamic Input boxes as per the Relative Polar coordinate system for specifying points.

1. Make sure that the Dynamic Input mode is turned on. You can turn on or off the Dynamic Input mode by clicking on the **Dynamic Input** button in the Status Bar. It is a toggle button.

2. Click on the **Ortho Mode** button in the Status Bar or press the **F8** key to turn on the Ortho mode. By activating the Ortho mode, you can create horizontal or vertical straight lines only.

3. Click on the **Line** tool in the **Draw** panel of the **Home** tab. The **Line** tool invoked, and you are prompted to specify the first point of the line.

> **Note:** In the Relative Polar coordinate system, the distance and angle values measure from the last specified point in the drawing area.

4. Follow the command sequence given below for creating the drawing.

    ```
    Specify first point:
    ```
    Click the left mouse button in the drawing area to specify the first point
    ```
    Specify next point or [Undo]:
    ```
    Move the cursor horizontally toward the right and then enter **20** *in the Dynamic Input box* (**ENTER**) *(See Figure 2.71)*
    ```
    Specify next point or [Undo]:
    ```
    Move the cursor vertically upward and then enter **5** (**ENTER**)
    ```
    Specify next point or [Undo]:
    ```
    Move the cursor horizontally toward the right and then enter **20** (**ENTER**)
    ```
    Specify next point or [Undo]:
    ```
    Move the cursor vertically downward and then enter **5** (**ENTER**)
    ```
    Specify next point or [Close Undo]:
    ```
    Move the cursor horizontally toward the right and then enter **20** (**ENTER**)
    ```
    Specify next point or [Close Undo]:
    ```
    Move the cursor vertically upward and then enter **30** (**ENTER**) *(See Figure 2.72)*

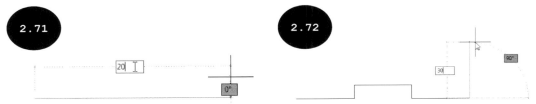

2.71

2.72

104 Chapter 2 > Creating Drawings - I

```
Specify next point or [Close Undo]:
```
Move the cursor horizontally toward the left and then enter 20 (**ENTER**)
```
Specify next point or [Close Undo]:
```
Move the cursor vertically downward and then enter 5 (**ENTER**)
```
Specify next point or [Close Undo]:
```
Move the cursor horizontally toward the left and then enter 20 (**ENTER**)
```
Specify next point or [Close Undo]:
```
Move the cursor vertically upward and then enter 5 (**ENTER**)
```
Specify next point or [Close Undo]:
```
Move the cursor horizontally toward the left and then enter 20 (**ENTER**)
```
Specify next point or [Close Undo]:
```
C or Close (See Figure 2.73)

```
Command: Z or Zoom (ENTER)
Specify corner of window, enter a scale factor (nX or nXP), or
[All/Center/Dynamic/Extents/Previous/Scale/Window/Object]<real
time>: A or ALL (ENTER)
```

Section 3: Erasing the Unwanted Entities of the Drawing

1. Click on the **Erase** tool of the **Modify** panel of the **Home** tab or enter **E** in the Command Line. The **Erase** tool is activated, and you are prompted to select the objects to be erased.

   ```
   Select objects:
   ```

2. Click on the right and left most vertical entities one after another as the entities to be erased, see Figure 2.74. Next, press ENTER. The selected entities are deleted, see Figure 2.75.

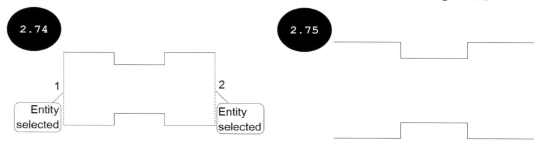

Section 4: Drawing Arcs

1. Click on the down arrow at the bottom of the arc tool. The **Arc** flyout appears, see Figure 2.76.

2. In this flyout, click on the **Start, End, Radius** tool, see Figure 2.76. The **Start, End, Radius** tool is activated, and you are prompted to specify the start point of the arc.

   ```
   Specify start point of arc or [Center]:
   ```

2.76

3. Click on the **Object Snap** button in the Status Bar to activate the Object Snap mode. You will learn more about Object Snap mode in later chapters.

4. Move the cursor over the end point of the lower rightmost horizontal line and then click to specify the start point of the arc when the cursor snaps to the end point of the line, see Figure 2.77.

```
Specify end point of arc:
```

2.77

5. Move the cursor over the end point of the upper rightmost horizontal line and then click to specify the end point of the arc when the cursor snaps to it, see Figure 2.78.

```
Specify center point of arc or [Angle Direction Radius]:_r Specify
radius of arc:
```

106 Chapter 2 > Creating Drawings - I

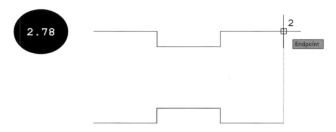

Figure 2.78

6. Move the cursor horizontally toward the right and then enter **15** as the radius of arc in the **Dynamic Input** box, which appears near the cursor in the drawing area. The arc is drawn, see Figure 2.79.

Figure 2.79

7. Similarly, draw an arc on the left side of the drawing by using the **Start, End, Radius** tool, see Figure 2.80.

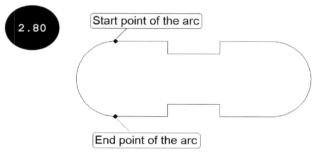

Figure 2.80

Section 5: Saving the Drawing

After creating the drawing, you need to save it.

1. Click on the **Save** tool in the **Quick Access Toolbar**. The **Save Drawing As** dialog box appears.

2. Browse to the *Chapter 2* folder, inside the *AutoCAD* folder. If the folders have not created in Tutorial 1 of this chapter, then you need to first create these folders on a local drive of your system.

3. Enter **Tutorial 2** in the **File name** field of the dialog box and then click on the **Save** button. The drawing saved with the name Tutorial 2.

Hands-on Test Drive 3

Draw the drawing shown in Figure 2.81 by using the Relative Cartesian coordinate system. Also, use the Dynamic Input boxes for specifying coordinate points. The dimensions shown in this figure are for your reference only. You will learn about applying dimensions in the later chapters.

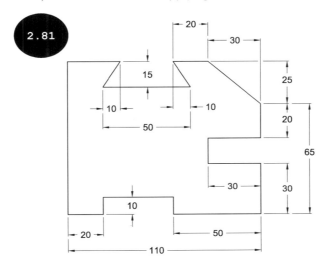

Hands-on Test Drive 4

Draw the drawing shown in Figure 2.82 by using the Relative Cartesian coordinate system. Also, use the Dynamic Input boxes for specifying coordinate points.

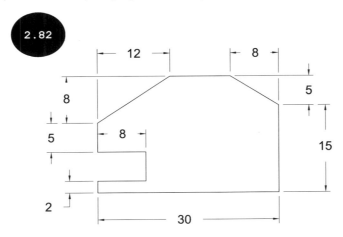

Summary

In this chapter, you have learned how to set drawing units, drawing limits, and grid and snap settings. You have also learned about various coordinate systems used in AutoCAD and how to create a line, circle, and arc entities in AutoCAD. Also, you have learned how to cancel, erase, undo, and to navigate 2D drawing.

Questions

- The _____ is the shortcut for the UNITS command.

- In the _____ coordinate system, every point you specify in the drawing area measures from the origin (0,0), and the location of a point is specified by the X and Y coordinates.

- In AutoCAD, you can specify coordinates either by using the _____ or _____ .

- In the _____ coordinate system, every point you specify in the drawing area measures from the last specified point in the drawing area and the location of a point is specified by the X and Y coordinates.

- In the _____ coordinate system, to define a point, you need to specify the distance and angle values separated by an angle bracket (<).

- The _____ tool is used to draw a circle by defining two points on the circumference of the circle.

- The _____ tool is used to draw an arc by defining the start, center and end points.

- The _____ tool is used to display the previously zoomed view of a drawing.

CHAPTER 3

Working with Drawing Aids and Layers

In this chapter, you will learn the following:

- Working with Ortho Mode
- Working with Polar Tracking
- Working with Object Snap
- Working with Object Snap Tracking
- Working with Layers
- Assigning Objects to a Layer

Drawing aids such as grid and snap, ortho, polar tracking, and object snap tracking are highly essential for creating drawings accurately and quickly, in AutoCAD. Of all these drawing aids, the grid and snap settings have already discussed in Chapter 2. The remaining drawing aids discussed next.

Working with Ortho Mode

The Ortho mode is used to create horizontal or vertical straight lines. You can turn on the Ortho mode to create horizontal or vertical lines (lines at an incremental angle of 90-degree). By doing so, you can quickly and accurately draw the horizontal or vertical line entities of a drawing. To activate the Ortho mode, click on the **Ortho Mode** button in the Status Bar, see Figure 3.1. Note that it is a toggle button. You can also press F8 key to turn on or off the Ortho mode to create horizontal or vertical lines.

110 Chapter 3 > Working with Drawing Aids and Layers

Example 1

Draw the drawing shown in Figure 3.2 by turning on the Ortho mode.

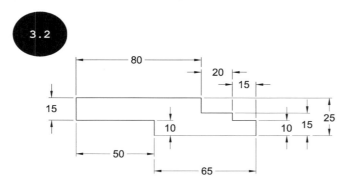

Section 1: Starting AutoCAD

1. Double-click on the AutoCAD icon on your desktop to start AutoCAD. The initial screen of AutoCAD appears with the **Start** tab, see Figure 3.3.

2. In the **Get Started** section of the **Start** tab, click on **Start Drawing**, see Figure 3.3. The new drawing file with the default drawing template gets invoked. Alternatively, click on the **New** tool in the **Quick Access Toolbar**, which is at the top left corner of AutoCAD screen. The **Select template** dialog box appears. In this dialog box, choose the **acad.dwt** template and then click on the **Open** button. A new drawing file with the acad.dwt template invoked.

Section 2: Creating Drawing by Using the Ortho Mode

As stated in the description of the example, you need to create the drawing by turning on the Ortho mode.

1. Click on the **Ortho Mode** button in the Status Bar to turn on the Ortho mode, see Figure 3.4. Alternatively, press the F8 key to activate the Ortho mode.

2. Make sure that the Dynamic Input mode is activated. You can turn on the Dynamic Input mode by clicking on the **Dynamic Input** button in the Status Bar.

> **Note:** If the Dynamic Input button is not available in the Status Bar by default, then click on the **Customization** button in the Status Bar. A flyout appears. In this flyout, click on the **Dynamic Input** option. The **Dynamic Input** button becomes available in the Status Bar.

3. Click on the **Line** tool in the **Draw** panel of the **Home** tab. The **Line** tool is activated, and you are prompted to specify the first point of the line. Alternatively, enter **L** in the Command Line window and then press ENTER to activate the **Line** tool.

        Specify first point:

4. Follow the command sequence given below for creating the drawing:

        Specify first point: *Click in the drawing area to specify the first point of the line*
        Specify next point or [Undo]: *Move the cursor horizontally toward the right and then enter* **65** *in the Dynamic Input box* (***ENTER***) *(See Figure 3.5)*
        Specify next point or [Undo]: *Move the cursor vertically upward and then enter* **10** (***ENTER***)
        Specify next point or [Undo]: *Move the cursor horizontally toward the left and then enter* **15** (***ENTER***)
        Specify next point or [Undo]: *Move the cursor vertically upward and then enter* **5** (***ENTER***)
        Specify next point or [Close Undo]: *Move the cursor horizontally toward the left and then enter* **20** (***ENTER***)
        Specify next point or [Undo]: *Move the cursor vertically upward and then enter* **10** (***ENTER***)
        Specify next point or [Close Undo]: *Move the cursor horizontally toward the left and then enter* **80** (***ENTER***)
        Specify next point or [Undo]: *Move the cursor vertically downward and then enter* **15** (***ENTER***)

```
Specify next point or [Close Undo]:  Move the cursor horizontally toward the right
and then enter 50  (ENTER)
Specify next point or [Close Undo]:  C or Close (ENTER)   (See Figure 3.6)
```

3.5

3.6

Tip: If the drawing has horizontal/vertical lines as well as inclined line entities, then you can create horizontal/vertical lines by turning on the Ortho mode. For creating inclined lines, you need to deactivate the Ortho mode. You can turn on or off the Ortho mode at any point while creating a drawing.

Working with Polar Tracking

The Polar Tracking mode is used to create line entities at an increment of predefined incremental angle. For doing so, turn on the Polar Tracking mode by clicking on the **Polar Tracking** button in the Status Bar, see Figure 3.7. Alternatively, press the F10 key. Once the Polar Tracking mode has been turned on, the cursor snaps at the predefined incremental angle for creating a line, see Figure 3.8. For example, if the incremental angle is defined to 45-degree then the cursor snaps at 0-degree, 45-degree, 90-degree, 135-degree, 180-degree, and so on for creating line entities. Figure 3.8 shows the preview of a line at 45-degree angle, which is defined as the incremental angle.

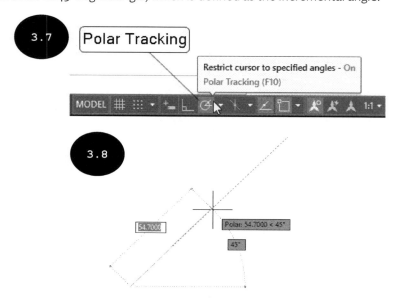

3.7

3.8

AutoCAD 2019: A Power Guide > 113

You can specify an incremental angle by using the **Drafting Settings** dialog box. To invoke the **Drafting Settings** dialog box, right-click on the **Polar Tracking** button in the Status Bar. A flyout appears, see Figure 3.9. In this flyout, click on the **Tracking Settings** option. The **Drafting Settings** dialog box appears with the **Polar Tracking** tab activated in it, see Figure 3.10. In the **Increment angle** field of the **Drafting Settings** dialog box, you can enter incremental angle value for polar tracking, as required.

Note: In addition to specifying an incremental angle for polar tracking in the **Drafting Settings** dialog box, you can also select the predefined incremental angle directly from the flyout, see Figure 3.9. The flyout shows a list of commonly used increment angles, such as **90, 180, 270, 360** and **45, 90, 135, 180**.

114 Chapter 3 > Working with Drawing Aids and Layers

Note: Among the Ortho and Polar Tracking modes, only one mode can activate at a time. If you turn on the Ortho mode, the Polar Tracking mode automatically deactivates, and vice-versa.

Example 2
Draw the drawing shown in Figure 3.11 by using the Polar Tracking mode.

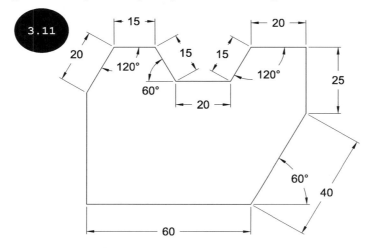

Section 1: Starting AutoCAD
1. Start a new AutoCAD drawing file.

Section 2: Creating Drawing by Using the Polar Tracking Mode
1. Click on the **Line** tool in the **Draw** panel of the **Home** tab. The **Line** tool is activated, and you are prompted to specify the first point of the line. Alternatively, enter **L** in the Command Line window and then press ENTER to activate the **Line** tool.

    ```
    Specify first point:
    ```

    It cleared from the drawing of this exercise that the inclined line entities have an increment angle of 60-degree. Therefore, you need to set the incremental angle for Polar Tracking to 60-degree for creating these entities quickly and easily.

2. Move the cursor over the **Polar Tracking** button in the Status Bar and then right-click to display a flyout, see Figure 3.12.

3. Click on the **30, 60, 90, 120** option in the flyout. The 30-degree is specified as the incremental angle for polar tracking.

3.12

4. Make sure that the Dynamic Input mode is activated. If not, click on the **Dynamic Input** button ![] in the Status Bar to activate it.

5. Follow the command sequence given below for creating the drawing:

   ```
   Specify first point:
   ```
   Click in the drawing area to specify the first point of the line
   ```
   Specify next point or [Undo]:
   ```
   *Move the cursor horizontally toward the right and then enter **60** in the Dynamic Input box* (**ENTER**) *(See Figure 3.13)*
   ```
   Specify next point or [Undo]:
   ```
   *Move the cursor at an angle and then enter **40** when the cursor snaps at the angle of 60-degree* (**ENTER**) *(See Figure 3.14)*

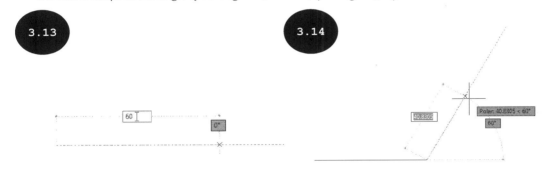

3.13

3.14

   ```
   Specify next point or [Undo]:
   ```
   *Move the cursor vertically upward and then enter **25*** (**ENTER**) *(See Figure 3.15)*
   ```
   Specify next point or [Undo]:
   ```
   *Move the cursor horizontally toward the left and then enter **20*** (**ENTER**)
   ```
   Specify next point or [Close Undo]:
   ```
   *Move the cursor clockwise and then enter **15** when the cursor snaps at the angle of 120-degree* (**ENTER**) *(See Figure 3.16)*

116   Chapter 3 > Working with Drawing Aids and Layers

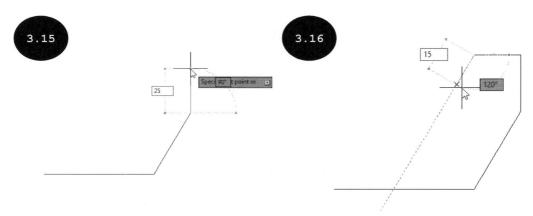

```
Specify next point or [Close Undo]:
```
Move the cursor horizontally toward the left and then enter 20 (**ENTER**)
```
Specify next point or [Close Undo]:
```
Move the cursor counter-clockwise and then enter 15 when the cursor snaps at the angle of 120-degree (**ENTER**) *(See Figure 3.17)*
```
Specify next point or [Close Undo]:
```
Move the cursor horizontally toward the left and then enter 15 (**ENTER**)
```
Specify next point or [Close Undo]:
```
Move the cursor clockwise and then enter 20 when the cursor snaps at the angle of 120-degree (**ENTER**) *(See Figure 3.18)*
```
Specify next point or [Close Undo]:
```
C or Close (**ENTER**) *(See Figure 3.19)*

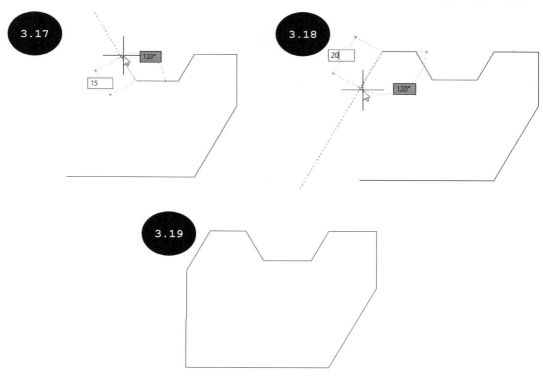

Working with Object Snap

The Object Snap mode is used to specify points on the existing geometry of a drawing. For doing so, you need to turn on the Object Snap mode, so that points can be defined quickly and accurately on the existing geometry of the drawing. The Object Snap mode is one of the important features of AutoCAD. On turning on the Object Snap mode, the cursor snaps to the existing geometries, such as midpoint, center, node, insertion, and end point, which helps in specifying exact points in the drawing area. For example, if you want to create a line starting from the end point of an arc then first invoke the **Line** tool and then turn on the Object Snap mode. Next, move the cursor over the end point of the arc and then click the left mouse button when the cursor snaps to the end point of the arc, see Figure 3.20.

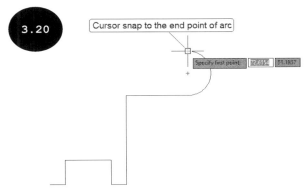

To turn on or off the Object Snap mode, click on the **Object Snap** button in the Status Bar or press the **F3** key, see Figure 3.21.

In the Object Snap mode, the cursor snaps to the geometries depending upon the Object snap settings specified in the **Drafting Settings** dialog box. To define the Object snap settings, move the cursor over the **Object Snap** button in the Status Bar and then right-click. A flyout appears, see Figure 3.22. You can also click on the down arrow next to the **Object Snap** button in the Status Bar to display this flyout. In this flyout, click on the **Object Snap Settings** option. The **Drafting Settings** dialog box appears with the **Object Snap** tab activated in it, see Figure 3.23.

118   Chapter 3 > Working with Drawing Aids and Layers

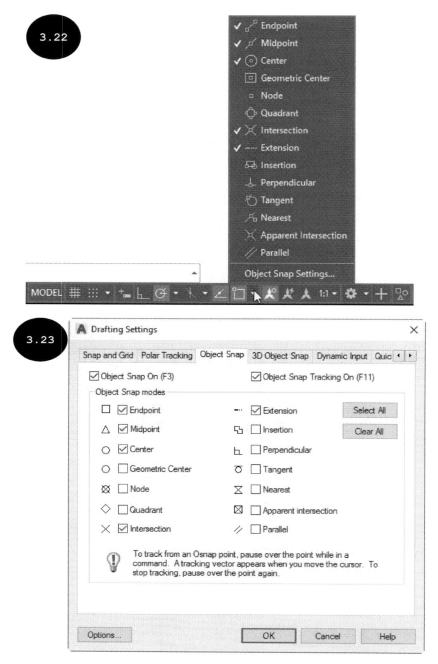

3.22

3.23

In the **Drafting Settings** dialog box, you can select the respective object snap check boxes for snapping the cursor while specifying points in the drawing area. For example, if you want to define points on the midpoint, endpoint, and center point of a geometry then you can select their respective check boxes in this dialog box. Note that the cursor snaps only to the geometries/points that are selected in the **Drafting Settings** dialog box. Figures 3.24 through 3.27 shows geometries with different object snaps.

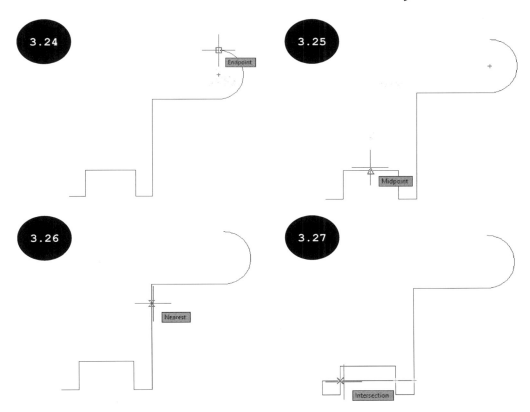

You can also select the **Select All** button in the dialog box to select all the object snap check boxes. To remove all the existing selected check boxes, click on the **Clear All** button in the **Drafting Settings** dialog box. After selecting the required object snap check boxes, click on the **OK** button in the dialog box to accept the change made as well as to exit the dialog box.

Note: In addition to specifying Object snap settings in the **Drafting Settings** dialog box, you can also select the required object snap, such as **Endpoint**, **Midpoint**, and **Center** directly from the flyout, which appears on right-clicking on the **Object Snap** button in the Status Bar, refer to Figure 3.22.

Working with Object Snap Tracking

The Object Snap Tracking mode is used to specify new points aligned to the existing points of a drawing, see Figure 3.28. In this figure, the center point of the circle being defined by aligning it to the end points of the inclined line entity of the drawing. Note that the Object Snap Tracking mode works in conjunction with the Object Snap. When the Object Snap Tracking is turned on, reference/tracking lines appear originating from the existing points of the drawing which guide the pointer of the cursor to specify a new point in the drawing area, see Figure 3.28.

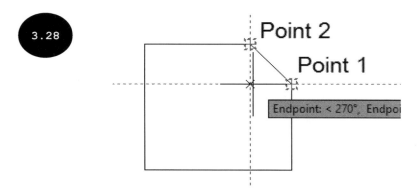

3.28

To specify points in the drawing by using the Object Snap Tracking mode, click on the **Object Snap Tracking** button in the Status Bar to turn it on. Alternatively, press the F11 key to turn on the Object Snap Tracking mode, see Figure 3.29. It is a toggle button.

3.29

Once the Object Snap Tracking has been turned on, move the cursor to a reference point in the drawing area. When the cursor snaps to the reference point, move the cursor to a distance in the drawing area. A reference/tracking line appears, which originated from the reference point. You can use this reference/tracking line for specifying new points in the drawing area. For example, to draw a circle as shown in Figure 3.30 whose center point is at the intersection of end points (Point 1 and Point 2), you need to first move the cursor to Point 1 and then move it horizontally toward the left. A reference/tracking line appears. Next, move the cursor to Point 2 and when the cursor snaps to it, move the cursor vertically downward. A reference/tracking line appears. Continue moving the cursor vertically downward until the cursor snaps to the intersection of both the end points with the help of reference/tracking lines, see Figure 3.31. Next, click the left mouse button to specify the center point of the circle at the intersection of the endpoints, see Figure 3.31.

3.30 3.31

Working with Layers

In AutoCAD, you need to understand the concept of layers to create drawings easily and faster. With layers, you can have better control over a drawing and create complex drawings faster and accurate. Layers work similar to tracing overlays on a drawing board, see Figure 3.32. You can have multiple layers in a drawing and organize your drawing by assigning the different set of drawing objects to different layers. For example, all dimensions are in one layer, and all hidden entities are in another layer. You can also assign different properties such as color, linetype, and lineweight to different layers of a drawing. For example, you can assign hidden linetype to hidden layer with different lineweight. Note that in AutoCAD, all layers of a drawing give you combined look as you view the layers from the top and appear as you are working on a single sheet, see Figure 3.33. In this figure, object entities are in one layer with different lineweight, dimensions are in another layer with different color and lineweight, and center marks are in the different layer with different color and lineweight.

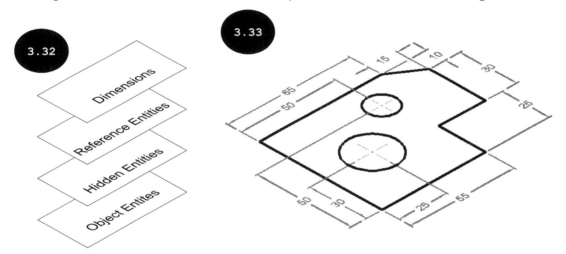

In AutoCAD, you can control the visibility, color, linetype, lineweight, and so on of layers, independently. As a result, you can work with intricate drawings very efficiently. For example, while working on a complicated drawing, you may have to create many reference/construction lines, which you do not want to be the part of the final drawing. In such case, you can create a layer with the name "Reference layer" and assign all the reference lines to this layer. When the drawing completed, you can just turn off the "Reference layer" to hide all reference entities of the drawing. Note that you can turn on or off layers at any point of your drawing as per your requirement. It is always recommended to use layers functionally when working with AutoCAD. The proper use of layers is the most famous for creating drawings with good practice.

In AutoCAD, whenever you start a new drawing, only one layer is provided by default with default parameters. This default layer named as "**0**" (zero) layer. The default "0" layer acts as the current layer, by default. It means anything you draw in the drawing area is assigned automatically to this "0" layer.

All the operations of a layer such as creating a new layer, specifying layer properties, and so on can perform by using the **LAYER PROPERTIES MANAGER**. To invoke the **LAYER PROPERTIES MANAGER,** click on the **Layer Properties** tool in the **Layers** panel of the **Home** tab, see Figure 3.34.

122 Chapter 3 > Working with Drawing Aids and Layers

Alternatively, you can invoke the **LAYER PROPERTIES MANAGER** by entering **LAYER** or **LA** in the Command Line window. Figure 3.35 shows the **LAYER PROPERTIES MANAGER** invoked with default "0" layer. Different operations that can perform by using the **LAYER PROPERTIES MANAGER** are discussed next.

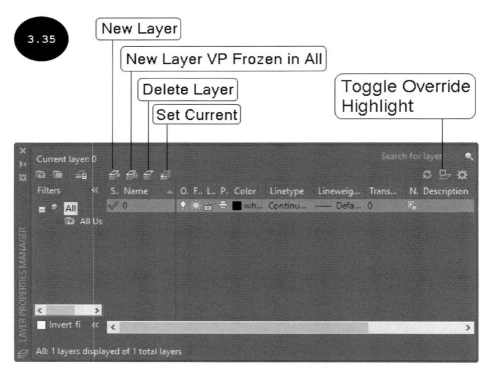

Creating a New Layer

You can create a new layer by clicking on the **New Layer** button in the **LAYER PROPERTIES MANAGER**, see Figure 3.35. Alternatively, you can press the ALT + N key after invoking the **LAYER PROPERTIES MANAGER** for creating a new layer. As soon as you click on the **New Layer** button, a new layer with the default name "**Layer 1**" is created with the default properties, see Figure 3.36. Note that the name of the newly created layer appears in an edit field, which indicates that the default name of the layer can change as per the requirement.

Note: The default properties of the newly created layer are the same as those of the existing selected layer.

Similarly, you can create multiple layers in a drawing one by one by using the **New Layer** button of the LAYER PROPERTIES MANAGER. Figure 3.37 shows the LAYER PROPERTIES MANAGER with multiple layers.

Setting the Current Layer

In AutoCAD, by default, the "0" layer is set as the current layer for a drawing. As a result, anything drawn in AutoCAD is assigned automatically to the "0" layer. Also, the properties such as color, linetype, and lineweight of the "0" layer get assigned to the objects drawn. Note that a green tick mark in the **Status** field of the layer, under the **Status** column indicates that the layer is specified as the current layer of the drawing, see Figure 3.38.

124 Chapter 3 > Working with Drawing Aids and Layers

You can set a layer as the current layer for a drawing by double-clicking either on the **Status** or **Name** field of the layer to be made current. Alternatively, you can select a layer to be made current and then click on the **Set Current** button available at the top of the LAYER PROPERTIES MANAGER, see Figure 3.39. You can also right-click on the layer and then click on the **Set current** option in the shortcut menu appeared. Note that as discussed, the objects/entities drawn in the drawing area automatically assigned to the currently active layer of the drawing. However, you can further transfer the objects of one layer to another layer. The method of transferring objects from one layer to another is discussed later in this chapter.

Note: You can also set a layer as the current layer without invoking the LAYER PROPERTIES MANAGER. For doing so, move the cursor over the **Layer** drop-down list in the **Layers** panel of the **Home** tab and then click the left mouse button. The **Layer** drop-down list appears, see Figure 3.40. The **Layer** drop-down list displays a list of all the layers created in the current drawing. Next, move the cursor over the layer to be made current in the drop-down list and then click the left mouse button on it. The selected layer becomes the current layer of the drawing.

Assigning Color to a Layer

You can assign unique colors to different layers of a drawing. To assign a color for a layer, click on the **Color** field of the layer in the **LAYER PROPERTIES MANAGER**, see Figure 3.41. The **Select Color** dialog box appears, see Figure 3.42.

In the **Select Color** dialog box, click on the required color swatch to be assigned to the layer. Next, click on the **OK** button. The chosen color assigned to the layer. Similarly, you can assign different colors to other layers of a drawing.

Note: All entities/objects in the drawing area appear in color, which assigned to their respective layers.

Assigning Linetype to a Layer

You can assign different linetypes to different layers of a drawing according to your requirement. For example, you can assign **Center** linetype to a layer that associated with the centerlines of a drawing and **Hidden** linetype to a layer that associated with hidden lines. To assign a linetype to a layer, click on the **Linetype** field of the layer in the **LAYER PROPERTIES MANAGER**, see Figure 3.43. The **Select Linetype** dialog box appears, see Figure 3.44.

In case the **Select Linetype** dialog box appears similar to the one shown in Figure 3.44, in which only the Continuous linetype is listed, then you need to load the required linetypes into this dialog box. To load linetypes, click on the **Load** button in the **Select Linetype** dialog box. The **Load or Reload Linetypes** dialog box appears with the list of all available linetypes, see Figure 3.45. Next, click on the linetype to be loaded. You can select multiple linetypes by pressing the CTRL key. Once you have selected the linetypes to be loaded, click on the **OK** button. All the selected linetypes are listed or loaded into the **Select Linetype** dialog box. Figure 3.46 shows the **Select Linetype** dialog box with the **Center** and **Hidden** linetypes loaded.

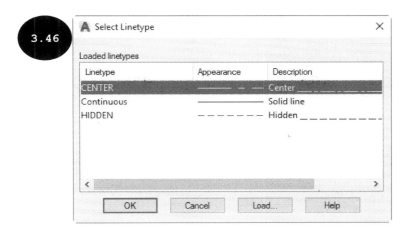

3.46

Once the required linetypes are loaded in the **Select Linetype** dialog box, click on the linetype to be assigned to the layer. Next, click the **OK** button in the **Select Linetype** dialog box. The selected linetype assigned to the layer. Similarly, you can assign the required linetype of other layers of the drawing.

Assigning Lineweight to a Layer

Similar to assigning color and linetype to a layer, you can assign the lineweight/thickness to a layer. For doing so, click on the **Lineweight** field of the layer in the **LAYER PROPERTIES MANAGER**, see Figure 3.47. The **Lineweight** dialog box appears, see Figure 3.48.

3.47

3.48

In this **Lineweight** dialog box, click on the lineweight to be assigned and then click on the **OK** button. The selected lineweight/thickness assigned to the layer. Similarly, you can assign the required lineweight to other layers of the drawing.

Note: You can turn on or off the display of the lineweight/thickness of objects in the drawing area by using the **Show/Hide Lineweight** button. It is a toggle button available in the Status Bar.

Turning a Layer On or Off

You can turn on or off a layer by clicking on the **On** field of a layer, see Figure 3.49. Note that when you turn off a layer, the objects assigned to the layer become hidden or invisible in the drawing area. Also, if you plot the drawing, the objects of the hidden layer will not be plotted.

Note: If you turn off the current layer by clicking on its **On** field, then the **Layer - Current Layer Off** window appears, see Figure 3.50. This window confirms whether you want to turn off the current layer or keep it on. Also, it informs that if you turn off the current layer, then the objects drawn now onwards will not be visible in the drawing area until you have turned on the layer.

Freezing a Layer

Similar to turning a layer on or off, you can also freeze or thaw a layer by clicking on the **Freeze** field of the layer, see Figure 3.51. When you freeze a layer, the respective objects assigned to the layer get hidden in the drawing area and cannot be ploted. Note that the freezing/thawing a layer is same as turning off/on a layer with the only difference that on freezing a layer, the frozen layer does not consider while regenerating drawing. As a result, regeneration time of the drawing gets reduced. Also, it improves the overall performance of the system and speeds up the zoom, pan, and other drawing operations.

Note: You cannot freeze the current layer. If you click on the **Freeze** field of a current layer, the **Layer - Cannot Freeze** window appears, see Figure 3.52, which informs you that this layer cannot be frozen.

Locking or Unlocking a Layer

You can lock or unlock a layer by clicking on the **Lock** field of a layer, see Figure 3.53. The objects assigned to the locked layer cannot edit or modify. Also, the objects of the locked layer appear faded in the drawing area. Locking a layer is very useful if you do not want any editing or modification to be done by mistake in the objects of a layer

Deleting a Layer

You can delete an unwanted layer of a drawing. For doing so, select the layer to be deleted in the **LAYER PROPERTIES MANAGER** and then click on the **Delete Layer** button, see Figure 3.54. Alternatively, press ALT + D to delete the selected layer. Note that you cannot delete the default '0' layer, Defpoints layer (the Defpoints layer is created automatically as soon as you apply dimensions to objects in the drawing area), current layer, layers containing objects, and Xref-dependent layers.

Setting Transparency of a Layer

You can define transparency for the objects of a layer by using the **Transparency** field in the **LAYER PROPERTIES MANAGER**. On clicking the **Transparency** field of the layer, the **Layer Transparency** dialog box appears, see Figure 3.55. By using the drop-down list of this dialog box, you can select transparency for the layer from "0" to "90". The objects assigned to the layer become faded in the drawing area when the transparency of the layer is defined to 10 or higher. Higher the transparency, more faded the appearance of the objects in the drawing area.

Restricting a Layer for Plotting

You can restrict a layer for plotting by using the **LAYER PROPERTIES MANAGER**. If you do not want the objects of a layer to be plotted, then you can restrict the layer for plotting. For doing so, click on the **Plot** field of the layer, see Figure 3.56. A red color symbol ⊘ appears in the **Plot** field, which indicates that the layer has restricted for plotting. You can click again on the **Plot** field of the layer to remove the restriction.

Freezing a Layer in New Viewports

You can freeze a layer in the newly created viewports by using the **New VP Freeze** field of a layer, see Figure 3.57. After freezing a layer by clicking on the **New VP Freeze** field, when you create a new viewport, all the objects of the layer become hidden/invisible in the newly created viewport. You can create multiple viewports of a drawing in the **Layout** tab. You will learn about the **Layout** tab and creating create viewports in later chapters.

Freezing the New Layer in All Viewports

You can also freeze the newly created layer in all viewports by using the **New Layer VP Frozen in All Viewports** button of the LAYER PROPERTIES MANAGER, Figure 3.58. When you click on the **New Layer VP Frozen in All Viewports** button, a new layer gets created such that it becomes frozen in all viewports.

Toggle Override Highlight

In AutoCAD 2019, you can highlight the overrides of the Xrefs (external references) layers in the drawing by using the **Toogle Override Highlight** button of the LAYER PROPERTIES MANAGER, see Figure 3.59. This functionality is added in AutoCAD 2019 and is used to easily identify the Xrefs layers of the drawing that are modified in the current drawing, see Figure 3.59. In this figure, the **External|Center** and **External|Object** layers are modified.

132   Chapter 3 > Working with Drawing Aids and Layers

Note that when you move the cursor over the Status icon of an override Xref layer, all the applied overrides of the Xref layer appears near the cursor, see Figure 3.60.

You can also reset the Xref layer properties. For doing so, right-click on the layer and then click on **Reset Xref Layer Properties > Selected layer > All Properties** in the shortcut menu that appears, see Figure 3.61. All the overrides of the selected layer gets reset to its orginal state.

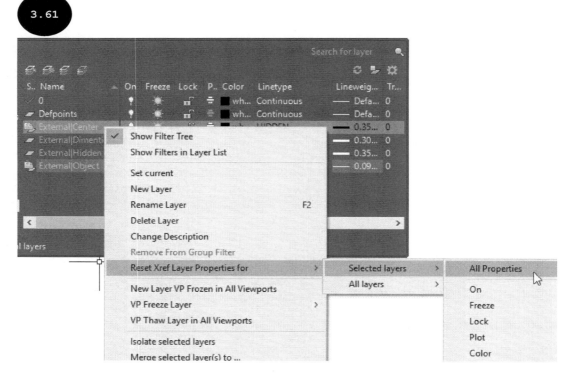

Once you have created layers and assigned layer properties, you can close the **LAYER PROPERTIES MANAGER** by clicking on the cross mark ☒ on the title bar of the **LAYER PROPERTIES MANAGER**.

Assigning Objects to a Layer

As discussed earlier, when you draw objects in the drawing area, by default, all the objects drawn get assigned automatically to the currently active layer. However, you can assign objects to other layers as well. For doing so, select the objects in the drawing area, see Figure 3.62. Next, move the cursor over the **Layer** drop-down list in the **Layers** panel of the **Home** tab and then click on it. The **Layer** drop-down list appears, see Figure 3.63. The **Layer** drop-down list displays all the layers created in the drawing. Next, click on the layer in the **Layer** drop-down list to assign the selected objects. The selected objects are assigned to the layer selected, see Figure 3.64. In this figure, the selected entities of the drawing are assigned to the Hidden layer. As a result, the entities are appeared in hidden lines. Next, press the ESC key to exit from the current selection set. Similarly, you can assign the different set of objects to different layers. In Figure 3.65, the hidden lines of the drawing assigned to the Hidden layer and the centerlines assigned to the Centerline layer.

134 Chapter 3 > Working with Drawing Aids and Layers

Tutorial 1

Create the drawing shown in Figure 3.66. The dimensions shown in this figure are for your reference only. You will learn about applying dimensions in the later chapters. Also, create three layers: Object, Hidden, and Centerline with the layer properties given below.

Layer Name	Color	Linetype	Lineweight
Object	Black	Continuous	0.40 mm
Hidden	Blue	Hidden	0.30 mm
Centerline	Red	Center	0.25 mm

Section 1: Starting AutoCAD

1. Double-click on the AutoCAD icon on your desktop to start AutoCAD. The initial screen of AutoCAD with the **Start** tab appears, see Figure 3.67.

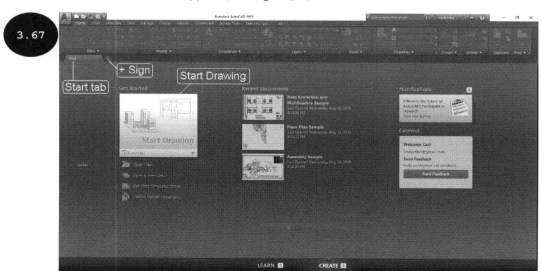

2. Click on the + sign next to the **Start** tab, see Figure 3.67. The new drawing file with the default drawing template gets invoked. Alternatively, click on **Start Drawing** in the **Get Started** section of the **Start** tab to start a new drawing file with the default template. You can also start a new drawing file by using the **New** tool of the **Quick Access Toolbar**, which is at the top left corner of AutoCAD.

Section 2: Selecting Workspace for Creating Drawing

1. Click on the **Workspace Switching** button in the Status Bar. A flyout appears, see Figure 3.68.

2. In this flyout, make sure that the **Drafting & Annotation** option is tick-mark to create drawings in the Drafting & Annotation workspace.

Note: A tick-mark next to the workspace indicates that it selected as the current workspace for creating drawings. By default, the Drafting & Annotation workspace chosen as the current workspace for creating drawings. You can click on any workspace to make it current for creating drawings.

Section 3: Creating Layer and Assigning Layer Properties

1. Click on the **Layer Properties** tool in the **Layers** panel, see Figure 3.69. The LAYER PROPERTIES MANAGER appears, see Figure 3.70. Alternatively, enter **LAYER** or **LA** in the Command Line window and then press ENTER to invoke the LAYER PROPERTIES MANAGER.

136   Chapter 3 > Working with Drawing Aids and Layers

2. Click on the **New Layer** button in the **LAYER PROPERTIES MANAGER**. A new layer with default name "**Layer 1**" is created.

3. Enter **Object** as the name of the newly created layer in the **LAYER PROPERTIES MANAGER**.

   After creating the **Object** layer, you need to define its properties such as color and lineweight. Note that the default color and linetype of the **Object** layer are the same as those mentioned in the tutorial description. Therefore, you need to only assign lineweight for the **Object** layer.

4. Click on the **Lineweight** field in the **Object** layer, see Figure 3.71. The **Lineweight** dialog box appears, see Figure 3.72.

5. Click on the **0.40 mm** lineweight in the **Lineweight** dialog box, see Figure 3.72.

AutoCAD 2019: A Power Guide > 137

6. Click on the **OK** button in the dialog box to accept the selection as well as to exit the dialog box.

   Now, you need to create the Hidden layer.

7. Click on the **New Layer** button in the LAYER PROPERTIES MANAGER. A new layer with default name "**Layer 1**" is created.

8. Enter **Hidden** as the name of the newly created layer in the LAYER PROPERTIES MANAGER.

   After creating the Hidden layer, you need to assign color, linetype, and lineweight to it.

9. Click on the **Color** field of the Hidden layer, see Figure 3.73. The **Select Color** dialog box appears, see Figure 3.74.

3.73

10. Click on the **Blue** color swatch in the **Select Color** dialog box, see Figure 3.74 and then click on the **OK** button in the **Select Color** dialog box. The blue color is assigned to the layer.

3.74

After assigning the color to the Hidden layer, you need to define Linetype and Lineweight.

11. Click on the **Linetype** field of the Hidden layer. The **Select Linetype** dialog box appears.

    If the Hidden linetype is not available in the **Select Linetype** dialog box, then you need first to load it in the dialog box.

12. Click on the **Load** button in the **Select Linetype** dialog box. The **Load or Reload Linetypes** dialog box appears, see Figure 3.75.

13. Click on the **HIDDEN** linetype in the **Load or Reload Linetypes** dialog box, see Figure 3.75.

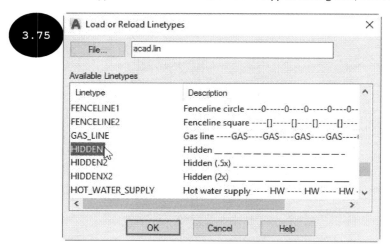

14. Click on the **OK** button in the **Load or Reload Linetypes** dialog box. The Hidden linetype is loaded in the **Select Linetype** dialog box.

15. Select the **HIDDEN** linetype in the **Select Linetype** dialog box.

16. Click on the **OK** button in the dialog box. The Hidden linetype assigned to the layer.

    Now, you need to assign Lineweight to the Hidden layer.

17. Click on the **Lineweight** field of the **Hidden** layer. The **Lineweight** dialog box appears, see Figure 3.76.

18. Click on the **0.30 mm** lineweight in the **Lineweight** dialog box, see Figure 3.76.

19. Click on the **OK** button in the dialog box to accept the selection as well as to exit the dialog box.

AutoCAD 2019: A Power Guide > 139

3.76

20. Similarly, create the Centerline layer and then assign the layer properties: Color = Red, Linetype = Center, and Lineweight = 0.25 mm. Figure 3.77 shows the **LAYER PROPERTIES MANAGER** after creating the layers: Object, Hidden, and Centerline.

21. After creating the layers and assigning the layer properties, close the **LAYER PROPERTIES MANAGER** by clicking on the cross mark ⊠ in the title bar of the **LAYER PROPERTIES MANAGER**.

3.77

Section 4: Defining Limits for Drawing

1. Follow the command sequence given below for defining limits for the drawing.

```
Command: LIMITS (ENTER)
Specify lower left corner or [ON/OFF]<0.0000,0.0000>: 0,0 (ENTER)
Specify upper right corner <12.0000,9.0000>: 820,540 (ENTER)
```

140   Chapter 3 > Working with Drawing Aids and Layers

Section 5: Creating Object Entities in the Object Layer

Before creating the entities of the Object layer, you need to make the Object layer as the current layer so that the entities you create in the drawing area assigned automatically to the Object layer.

1. Move the cursor over the **Layer** drop-down list in the **Layers** panel of the **Home** tab and then click the left mouse button to display the **Layer** drop-down list, see Figure 3.78.

2. Click on the **Object** layer in the **Layer** drop-down list to make it current layer.

    Now, you can create the entities of the Object layer.

3. Click on the **Line** tool in the **Draw** panel of the **Home** tab. You are prompted to specify the first point of the line.

    ```
    Specify first point:
    ```

4. Click on the **Ortho Mode** button in the Status Bar or press the F8 key to turn on the Ortho mode. Note that this is a toggle button.

5. Make sure that the Dynamic Input mode is activated. You can turn on the Dynamic Input mode by clicking on the **Dynamic Input** button in the Status Bar.

6. Follow the command sequence given below for creating the drawing entities.

    ```
    Specify first point:
    ```
    0,0 (***ENTER***)
    ```
    Specify next point or [Undo]:
    ``` *Move the cursor horizontally toward the right and then enter* **60** *in the Dynamic Input box*   (***ENTER***)
    ```
    Specify next point or [Undo]:
    ``` *Move the cursor vertically upward and then enter* **24** (***ENTER***)
    ```
    Specify next point or [Undo]:
    ``` *Move the cursor horizontally toward the right and then enter* **400** (***ENTER***)
    ```
    Specify next point or [Undo]:
    ``` *Move the cursor vertically downward and then enter* **24** (***ENTER***)
    ```
    Specify next point or [Close Undo]:
    ``` *Move the cursor horizontally toward the right and then enter* **60** (***ENTER***)
    ```
    Specify next point or [Undo]:
    ``` *Move the cursor vertically upward and then enter* **80** (***ENTER***)
    ```
    Specify next point or [Close Undo]:
    ``` *Move the cursor horizontally toward the left and then enter* **220** (***ENTER***)

AutoCAD 2019: A Power Guide > 141

```
Specify next point or [Undo]: Move the cursor vertically upward and then enter 160
(ENTER)
Specify next point or [Close Undo]: Move the cursor horizontally toward the left
and then enter 80 (ENTER)
Specify next point or [Close Undo]: Move the cursor vertically downward and
then enter 160 (ENTER)
Specify next point or [Close Undo]: Move the cursor horizontally toward the left
and then enter 220 (ENTER)
Specify next point or [Close Undo]: C or Close (ENTER)    (See Figure 3.79)
```

Tip: You may need to fit the drawing within the drawing area. To fit the drawing into the drawing area, follow the command sequence given below.

```
Command: Z or ZOOM (ENTER)
Specify corner of window, enter a scale factor (nX or
nXP), or [All/Center/Dynamic/Extents/Previous/Scale/
Window/Object]<real time>: A or ALL (ENTER)
```

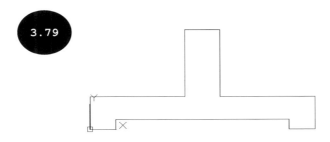

3.79

Note: To display entities in the drawing area with the lineweight/thickness assigned to the **Object** layer, click on the **Show/Hide Lineweight** button in the Status Bar to activate it.

Section 6: Creating Hidden Entities in the Hidden Layer

1. Invoke the **Layer** drop-down list in the **Layers** panel of the **Home** tab and then click on the **Hidden** layer. The Hidden layer becomes the current layer.

   Now, you can create the entities of the Hidden layer.

2. Click on the **Line** tool in the **Draw** panel of the **Home** tab. You are prompted to specify the first point of the line.

   ```
   Specify first point:
   ```

142   Chapter 3 > Working with Drawing Aids and Layers

3. Make sure that the Ortho mode is activated. You can activate/deactivate the Ortho mode by clicking on the **Ortho Mode** button in the Status Bar or by pressing the F8 key.

4. Make sure that the Object Snap mode is activated. You can activate/deactivate the Object Snap mode by clicking on the **Object Snap** button in the Status Bar or by pressing the F3 key.

5. Make sure that the Dynamic Input mode is activated. You can activate/deactivate the Dynamic Input mode by clicking on the **Dynamic Input** button in the Status Bar or by pressing the F12 key.

6. Follow the command sequence given below for creating the entities of the Hidden layer.

   ```
   Specify first point: 108,24 (ENTER)
   Specify next point or [Undo]:
   ```
   Move the cursor vertically upward and then click to specify the end point of the line when the cursor snaps to the upper horizontal object entity (**ENTER**) (see Figure 3.80)

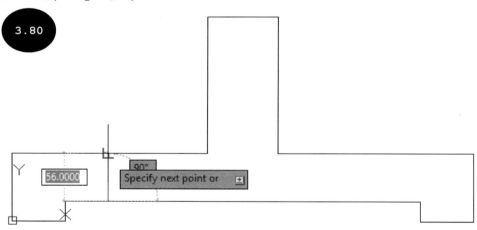

3.80

Note: If the cursor did not snap to the upper horizontal entity as shown in Figure 3.80, then you need to change the Object Snap settings. To change the Object Snap settings, right-click on the **Object Snap** button in the Status Bar. A flyout appears. In this flyout, click on the **Object Snap Settings** option. The **Drafting Settings** dialog box appears. In this dialog box, make sure that the **Perpendicular** check box is selected.

```
Tool/Command: Line or L (ENTER)
Specify first point: 172,24 (ENTER)
Specify next point or [Undo]:
```
Move the cursor vertically upward and then click to specify the end point of the line when the cursor snaps to the upper object line   (**ENTER**) (see Figure 3.81)

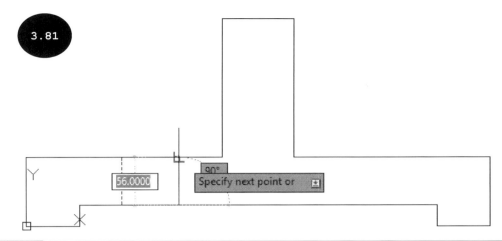

Note: If the entities of the Hidden layer appear as continuous linetype in the drawing area, then you need to increase or decrease its linetype scale by using the **Properties** panel. To increase or decrease the linetype scale, enter **PR** in the Command Line window and then press ENTER. The **Properties** panel appears on the left of the drawing area. Next, select the entity of the Hidden layer whose linetype scale to be changed in the drawing area. The **Properties** panel displays the properties of the selected entity. Next, enter **15** in the **Linetype scale** field of the **Properties** panel. If linetype scale 15 does not work, you can try any value as the linetype scale to match the display of the hidden line, as required.

```
Tool/Command:  Line or L  (ENTER)
Specify first point:  412,24 (ENTER)
Specify next point or [Undo]:  
```
Move the cursor vertically upward and then click to specify the end point of the line when the cursor snaps to the upper object line (**ENTER**) *(see Figure 3.82)*

```
Tool/Command:  Line or L  (ENTER)
Specify first point:  348,24 (ENTER)
Specify next point or [Undo]:  
```
Move the cursor vertically upward and then click to specify the end point of the line when the cursor snaps to the upper object line (**ENTER**) *(see Figure 3.83)*

144   Chapter 3 > Working with Drawing Aids and Layers

3.83

```
Command: Line or L (ENTER)
Specify first point: 220,200 (ENTER)
Specify next point or [Undo]:
```
 Move the cursor horizontally toward the right and then click to specify the end point of the line when the cursor snaps to the next object line (**ENTER**)

```
Command: Line or L (ENTER)
Specify first point: 220,120 (ENTER)
Specify next point or [Undo]:
```
 Move the cursor horizontally toward the right and then click to specify the end point of the line when the cursor snaps to the next object line (**ENTER**) *(see Figure 3.84)*

Figure 3.84 shows the drawing after creating the object and hidden line entities.

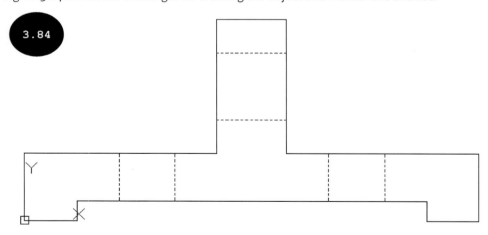

3.84

Section 7: Creating Centerlines in the Centerline Layer

1. Invoke the **Layer** drop-down list in the **Layers** panel and then click on the **Centerline** layer. The Centerline layer becomes the current layer.

After making the Centerline layer as the current layer, you can create the centerline entities of the drawing.

2. Click on the **Line** tool in the **Draw** panel of the **Home** tab. You are prompted to specify the first point of the line.

   ```
   Specify first point:
   ```

3. Move the cursor toward the midpoint of the first drawn hidden line and then click to specify the first point of the line when the cursor snaps to it, see Figure 3.85.

   Note: If the cursor did not snap to the midpoint as shown in Figure 3.85, then you need to change the Object Snap settings. For doing so, right-click on the **Object Snap** button in the Status Bar. A flyout appears. In this flyout, click on the **Midpoint** option. Next, click anywhere in the drawing area to exit the flyout.

4. Move the cursor horizontally toward the right and then click to specify the end point of the line when the cursor snaps to the midpoint of the next hidden line, see Figure 3.86. Next, press ENTER.

Note that the line entity drawn in the above three steps will use as the reference line for creating the centerline.

5. Click on the **Line** tool in the **Draw** panel of the **Home** tab.

   ```
   Specify first point:
   ```

6. Move the cursor toward the midpoint of the previously drawn reference line and when the cursor snaps to it (see Figure 3.87), move the cursor vertically upward to a little distance outside the drawing. A reference/tracking line appears, see Figure 3.88.

7. Click to specify the first point of the centerline somewhere near the upper horizontal line entity of the drawing, see Figure 3.88. Next, move the cursor vertically downward and click to specify the end point of the centerline somewhere outside the lower horizontal line entity of the drawing, see Figure 3.89.

Note: If the centerline appear as continuous linetype in the drawing area, then you need to increase or decrease its linetype scale by using the **Properties** panel. For doing so, enter **PR** in the Command Line window and then press ENTER. The **Properties** panel appears on the left of the drawing area. Next, select the centerline in the drawing area. The **Properties** panel displays the properties of the selected centerline. Next, in the **Linetype scale** field of the **Properties** panel, enter the linetype scale for the centerline. You can try any value as the linetype scale to match the display of the centerline, as required.

After creating the centerline, you need to delete the reference line drawn for creating the centerline.

8. Click on the reference line in the drawing area. The reference line gets selected, see Figure 3.90. Next, press the DELETE key. The reference line gets deleted. Figure 3.91 shows the drawing after deleting the reference line.

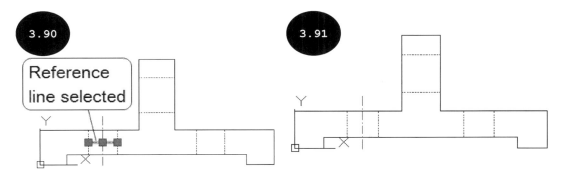

9. Similarly, draw the other centerlines of the drawing, see Figure 3.92. Figure 3.92 shows the final drawing after creating all the drawing entities.

Section 8: Saving the Drawing

After creating the drawing, you need to save it.

1. Click on the **Save** tool in the **Quick Access Toolbar**. The **Save Drawing As** dialog box appears.

2. Browse to the *AutoCAD* folder and then create another folder with the name *Chapter 3* inside the *AutoCAD* folder. If the *AutoCAD* folder not created in Chapter 2, then you need to first create this folder on a local drive of your system.

3. Enter **Tutorial 1** in the **File name** field of the dialog box and then click on the **Save** button. The drawing saved with the name Tutorial 1 in the *Chapter 3* folder.

148 Chapter 3 > Working with Drawing Aids and Layers

Tutorial 2

Create the drawing shown in Figure 3.93. The dimensions shown in this figure are for your reference only. You will learn about applying dimensions in the later chapters. Also, create three layers: Object, Hidden, and Centerline with the layer properties given below.

Layer Name	Color	Linetype	Lineweight
Object	Black	Continuous	0.50 mm
Hidden	Blue	Hidden2	0.40 mm
Centerline	Red	Center2	0.30 mm

3.93

Section 1: Starting AutoCAD
1. Start AutoCAD by double-clicking on the AutoCAD icon on your desktop, if not started already.

2. Click on the **New** tool in the **Quick Access Toolbar**, which is at the top left corner of AutoCAD. The **Select template** dialog box appears. In this dialog box, choose the *acad.dwt* template and then click on the **Open** button. A new drawing file with the *acad.dwt* template invoked.

Section 2: Creating Layers and Assigning Properties to Layers
1. Click on the **Layer Properties** tool in the **Layers** panel of the **Home** tab, see Figure 3.94. The LAYER PROPERTIES MANAGER appears, see Figure 3.95.

3.94

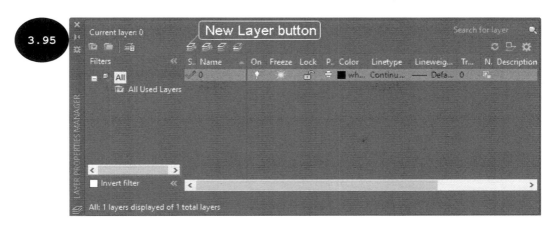

3.95

> **Tip:** You can also enter **LAYER** or **LA** in the Command Line window to invoke the **LAYER PROPERTIES MANAGER**.

2. Click on the **New Layer** button in the **LAYER PROPERTIES MANAGER**. A new layer with the default name "**Layer 1**" is created.

3. Enter **Object** as the name of the newly created layer in the **LAYER PROPERTIES MANAGER**.

   After creating the Object layer, you need to define its properties such as color and lineweight. Note that the default color and linetype assigned to the Object layer are the same as those mentioned in the tutorial description. Therefore, you need to assign only the lineweight to the Object layer.

4. Click on the **Lineweight** field in the Object layer, see Figure 3.96. The **Lineweight** dialog box appears, see Figure 3.97.

3.96

150   Chapter 3 > Working with Drawing Aids and Layers

5. Click on the **0.50 mm** lineweight in the **Lineweight** dialog box, see Figure 3.97.

6. Click on the **OK** button in the dialog box to accept the selection as well as to exit the dialog box.

Now, you need to create the Hidden layer.

7. Click on the **New Layer** button in the **LAYER PROPERTIES MANAGER**. A new layer with the default name "**Layer 1**" is created.

8. Enter **Hidden** as the name of the newly created layer in the **LAYER PROPERTIES MANAGER**.

    After creating the Hidden layer, you need to assign color, linetype, and lineweight to it.

9. Click on the **Color** field of the Hidden layer, see Figure 3.98. The **Select Color** dialog box appears.

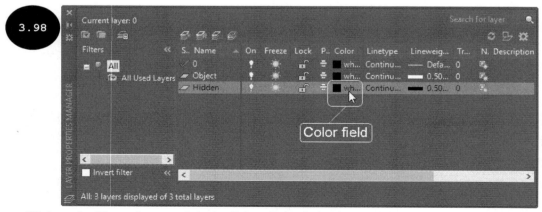

10. Click on the **Blue** color swatch in the **Select Color** dialog box and then click on the **OK** button. The chosen color assigned to the Hidden layer.

After assigning the color to the Hidden layer, you need to define linetype and lineweight.

11. Click on the **Linetype** field of the Hidden layer. The **Select Linetype** dialog box appears. In this dialog box, if the Hidden2 linetype is not available then you need to first add/load it in the dialog box.

12. Click on the **Load** button in the **Select Linetype** dialog box. The **Load or Reload Linetypes** dialog box appears, see Figure 3.99.

13. Click on the **HIDDEN2** linetype in the dialog box, see Figure 3.99. Next, click on the **OK** button. The Hidden2 linetype is loaded in the **Select Linetype** dialog box.

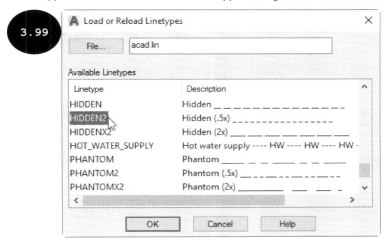

14. Click on the **HIDDEN2** linetype in the **Select Linetype** dialog box and then click on the **OK** button. The Hidden2 linetype is assigned to the Hidden layer.

15. Assign 0.40 mm lineweight to the Hidden layer.

16. Similarly, create the Centerline layer and then assign the layer properties: Color = Red, Linetype = Center2, and Lineweight = 0.3 mm, see Figure 3.100.

152 Chapter 3 > Working with Drawing Aids and Layers

17. After creating layers and assigning properties, close the **LAYER PROPERTIES MANAGER** by clicking on the cross mark ⊠ in the title bar of the **LAYER PROPERTIES MANAGER**.

Section 3: Creating Object Entities in the Object Layer

Before creating the entities of the Object layer, you need to make the Object layer as the current layer so that the entities you create in the drawing area assigned automatically to the Object layer.

1. Move the cursor over the **Layer** drop-down list in the **Layers** panel of the **Home** tab and then click the left mouse button on it to display the **Layer** drop-down list, see Figure 3.101.

2. Click on the **Object** layer in the **Layer** drop-down list to make it the current layer.

   Now, you can create the entities of the Object layer.

3. Invoke the **Arc** flyout and then click on the **Center, Start, End** tool. You are prompted to specify the center point of the arc.

   ```
   Specify start point of arc or [Center]:_c Specify center point of
   arc:
   ```

4. Click anywhere in the drawing area to specify the center point of the arc. You are prompted to specify the start point of the arc.

   ```
   Specify start point of arc:
   ```

5. Make sure that the Ortho mode and the Dynamic Input mode are activated.

6. Move the cursor horizontally toward the left and then enter **105** in the Dynamic Input box as the radius of the arc. Next, press ENTER. You are prompted to specify the end point of the arc.

   ```
   Specify end point of arc or [Angle chord Length]:
   ```

7. Press and hold the CTRL key and then move the cursor in the clockwise direction. Next, click to specify the end point of the arc when the angle value appears 90-degree near the cursor, see Figure 3.102.

AutoCAD 2019: A Power Guide > 153

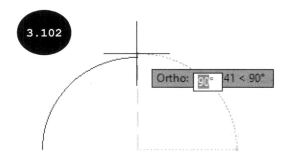

3.102

> **Note:** By default, an arc is created in the counter-clockwise direction. To change the direction of the arc from counter-clockwise to clockwise direction, press and hold the CTRL key and then specify the end point of the arc.

8. Invoke the **Center, Start, End** tool again. You are prompted to specify the center point of the arc.

   ```
   Specify start point of arc or [Center]:_c Specify center point of
   arc:
   ```

9. Move the cursor over the arc drawn earlier in the drawing area, see Figure 3.103. The center point of the arc highlighted in the drawing area, see Figure 3.103.

3.103

Center point of the arc

10. Move the cursor over the highlighted center point and then click the left mouse button when the cursor snaps to the center point of the arc. The center point of the arc is specified.

> **Note:** If the cursor did not snap to the existing entities, you need to specify the Object Snap settings by using the **Drafting Settings** dialog box. For doing so, right-click on the **Object Snap** button in the Status Bar. A flyout appears. Next, click on the **Object Snap Settings** option in the flyout. The **Drafting Settings** dialog box appears. In this dialog box, click on the **Select All** button to select all the check boxes.

11. Move the cursor horizontally toward the left and then enter **55** in the Dynamic Input box as the radius of the arc. You are prompted to specify the end point of the arc.

   ```
   Specify end point of arc or [Angle chord Length]:
   ```

12. Press and hold the CTRL key and then move the cursor in the clockwise direction. Next, click to specify the end point of the arc when the angle value appears 90-degree near the cursor, see Figure 3.104.

13. Click on the **Line** tool in the **Draw** panel. You are prompted to specify the first point of the line.

   ```
   Specify first point:
   ```

14. Move the cursor toward the start point of the first created arc and then click to specify the first point of the line when the cursor snaps to it, see Figure 3.105.

   ```
   Specify next point or [Undo]:
   ```

15. Move the cursor horizontally toward the left and then enter **5** in the Dynamic Input box as the length of the line, see Figure 3.106. Next, press ENTER.

16. Follow the command sequence given below for creating the remaining line entities.

   ```
   Specify next point or [Undo]:
   ```
   Move the cursor vertically downward and then enter 10 in the Dynamic Input box (**ENTER**)
   ```
   Specify next point or [Undo]:
   ```
   Move the cursor horizontally toward the right and then enter 60 (**ENTER**)
   ```
   Specify next point or [Undo]:
   ```
   Move the cursor vertically upward and then enter 10 (**ENTER**)

```
Specify next point or [Close Undo]:
```
Move the cursor horizontally toward the left and then click to specify the end point of the line when the cursor snaps to the start point of the first drawn arc (**ENTER**) *(See Figure 3.107)*

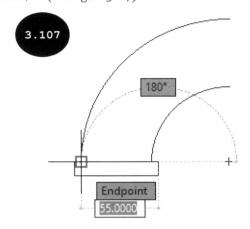

```
Tool/Command:
```
Line or L (**ENTER**)
```
Specify first point:
```
Move the cursor toward the end point of the first drawn arc and then click to specify the first point of the line when the cursor snaps to it *(See Figure 3.108)*
```
Specify next point or [Undo]:
```
Move the cursor vertically upward and then enter 5 in the Dynamic Input box (**ENTER**)
```
Specify next point or [Undo]:
```
Move the cursor horizontally toward the right and then enter 10 (**ENTER**)
```
Specify next point or [Close Undo]:
```
Move the cursor vertically downward and then enter 60 (**ENTER**)
```
Specify next point or [Close Undo]:
```
Move the cursor horizontally toward the left and then enter 10 (**ENTER**)
```
Specify next point or [Close Undo]:
```
C or Close (**ENTER**) *(See Figure 3.109)*

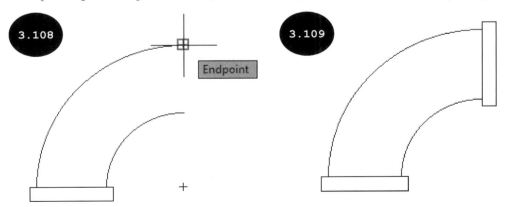

156　Chapter 3 > Working with Drawing Aids and Layers

Tip: You may need to fit the drawing within the drawing area. To fit the drawing, follow the command sequence given below.

```
Command: Z or Zoom (ENTER)
Specify corner of window, enter a scale factor (nX or
nXP), or [All/Center/Dynamic/Extents/Previous/Scale/
Window/Object]<real time>: A or ALL (ENTER)
```

Section 4: Creating Hidden Entities in the Hidden Layer

1. Invoke the **Layer** drop-down list in the **Layers** panel of the **Home** tab and then click on the **Hidden** layer. The Hidden layer becomes the current layer of the drawing.

2. Click on the **Line** tool in the **Draw** panel. You are prompted to specify the first point of the line.

   ```
   Specify first point:
   ```

3. Make sure that the Ortho mode, Dynamic Input mode, and Object Snap mode are activated.

4. Move the cursor toward the lower left vertex of the drawing and then click to specify the first point of the line when the cursor snaps to it, see Figure 3.110.

   ```
   Specify next point or [Undo]:
   ```

5. Move the cursor horizontally toward the right and then enter **10** in the Dynamic Input box as the length of the line. Next, press ENTER.

6. Move the cursor vertically upward and then click to specify the end point of the line when the cursor snaps to the next object line entity, see Figure 3.111. Next, press ENTER.

3.110

3.111

Note: If hidden line entity appears as continuous linetype in the drawing area, then you need to increase or decrease its linetype scale by using the **Properties** panel. To increase or decrease the linetype scale, enter **PR** in the Command Line window and then press ENTER. The **Properties** panel appears on the left of the drawing area. Next, select the hidden entity in the drawing area. The **Properties** panel displays the properties of the selected entity. Next, enter **10** in the **Linetype scale** field of the **Properties** panel. If linetype 10 does not work, you can try any value as the linetype scale to match the display of the hidden line, as required.

7. Click on the first drawn hidden line in the drawing area to select it, see Figure 3.112. Next, press the DELETE key. The line gets deleted. This line entity was drawn as a reference line for measuring 10 unit from the lower left vertex of the drawing to create the hidden line of the drawing.

8. Similarly, draw other hidden line entities by using the **Line** tool. Figure 3.113 shows the drawing after creating the hidden line entities of the drawing.

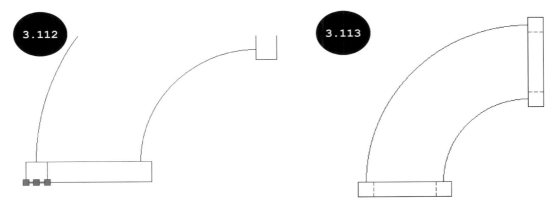

Now, you need to draw the hidden arcs of the drawing by using the **Center, Start, End** arc tool.

9. Invoke the **Arc** flyout in the **Draw** panel of the **Home** tab and then click on the **Center, Start, End** tool. You are prompted to specify the center point of the arc.

   ```
   Specify start point of arc or [Center]: _c Specify center point of arc:
   ```

10. Move the cursor over the first drawn arc in the drawing area. The center point of the first drawn arc gets highlighted in the drawing area, see Figure 3.114.

11. Move the cursor over the highlighted center point and then click the left mouse button when the cursor snaps to it. The center point of the hidden arc is specified.

    ```
    Specify start point of arc:
    ```

158 Chapter 3 > Working with Drawing Aids and Layers

12. Move the cursor over the end point of the first drawn hidden line entity and then click to specify the start point of the arc when the cursor snaps to it, see Figure 3.115.

    ```
    Specify end point of arc or [Angle chord Length]:
    ```

13. Press and hold the CTRL key and then move the cursor in the clockwise direction. Next, click to specify the end point of the arc when the cursor snaps to the end point of next hidden line entity, see Figure 3.116.

14. Similarly, draw the another hidden arc entity of the drawing by using the **Center, Start, End** arc tool. Figure 3.117 shows the drawing after drawing the hidden arc entities.

Section 5: Creating Centerlines in the Centerline Layer

1. Invoke the **Layer** drop-down list in the **Layers** panel of the **Home** tab and then click on the **Centerline** layer. The Centerline layer becomes the current layer of the drawing.

2. Invoke the **Arc** flyout in the **Draw** panel of the **Home** tab and then click on the **Center, Start, End** tool.

    ```
    Specify start point of arc or [Center]:_c Specify center point of
    arc:
    ```

3. Move the cursor over the first drawn arc in the drawing area, see Figure 3.118. The center point of the arc gets highlighted in the drawing area, see Figure 3.118.

4. Move the cursor over the highlighted center point and then click to specify the center point of the arc when the cursor snaps to it.

   ```
   Specify start point of arc:
   ```

5. Move the cursor horizontally toward the left and then enter **80** in the Dynamic Input box. Next, press ENTER.

   ```
   Specify end point of arc or [Angle chord Length]:
   ```

6. Press and hold the CTRL key and then move the cursor in the clockwise direction. Next, click to specify the end point of the arc when the cursor snaps to the next intersection, see Figure 3.119.

7. Click on the **Line** tool in the **Draw** panel of the **Home** tab. The **Line** tool is invoked.

   ```
   Specify first point:
   ```

8. Move the cursor toward the start point of the previously drawn arc and then click to specify the start point of the line when the cursor snaps to it, see Figure 3.120.

9. Move the cursor vertically downward a small distance and then click to specify the end point of the line below the horizontal line of the drawing, see Figure 3.121.

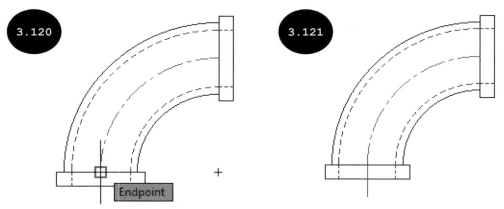

10. Similarly, draw a line on the other side of the arc. Figure 3.122 shows the final drawing.

> **Note:** To display entities in the drawing area with the lineweight/thickness assigned to the layers, click to activate the **Show/Hide Lineweight** button in the Status Bar. Figure 3.123 shows the drawing with the lineweight/thickness is turned on.

Section 6: Saving the Drawing

After creating the drawing, you need to save it.

1. Click on the **Save** tool in the **Quick Access Toolbar**. The **Save Drawing As** dialog box appears.

2. Browse to the *Chapter 3* folder, inside the *AutoCAD* folder. If these folders have not created in Tutorial 1 of this chapter, then you need to first create these folders in a local drive of your system.

3. Enter **Tutorial 2** in the **File name** field of the dialog box and then click on the **Save** button. The drawing saved with the name Tutorial 2 in the *Chapter 3* folder.

Hands-on Test Drive 1

Create the drawing shown in Figure 3.124. Also, create three layers: Object, Hidden, and Centerline with the layer properties given below.

Layer Name	Color	Linetype	Lineweight
Object	Blue	Continuous	0.50 mm
Hidden	Green	Hidden	0.35 mm
Centerline	Red	Center	0.30 mm

3.124

Summary

In this chapter, you have learned about Ortho mode, Polar Tracking, Object Snap, and Object Snap Tracking. You have also learned about how to specify grids and snaps settings. Besides, in this chapter, you have learned how to work with layers and to assign objects to layers.

Questions

- The _____ mode is used to create horizontal or vertical straight lines.

- The _____ mode is used to create line entities at an increment of set angle.

- When the _____ mode is turned on, the cursor snaps to the existing geometries of drawing such as midpoint, center, node, insertion, perpendicular, and tangent.

- The _____ is used to create new layers, specifying layer properties, and so on.

- The _____ tool is used to invoke the **LAYER PROPERTIES MANAGER**.

- You can set the transparency for the objects of a layer by using the _____ field in the **LAYER PROPERTIES MANAGER**.

- The objects drawn in the drawing get assigned automatically to the _____ layer.

CHAPTER 4

Creating Drawings - II

In this chapter, you will learn the following:

- Drawing a Rectangle
- Drawing a Polygon
- Drawing a Polyline
- Drawing an Ellipse
- Drawing an Elliptical Arc
- Drawing a Spline
- Drawing Donuts
- Drawing Construction and Ray lines
- Drawing Points and Defining Point Style/Size

In this chapter, you will learn about drawings rectangles, polygons, polylines, ellipses, elliptical arcs, splines, donuts, construction lines, ray lines, and points.

Drawing a Rectangle

A rectangle comprises of four line segments treated as a single object. In AutoCAD, you can draw a rectangle by different methods using the **Rectangle** tool in the **Draw** panel of the **Home** tab, see Figure 4.1. Various methods of creating a rectangle by using the **Rectangle** tool are discussed next.

1. Drawing a rectangle by specifying diagonally opposite corners
2. Drawing a rectangle by specifying its area and one side
3. Drawing a rectangle by specifying its dimensions
4. Drawing a rectangle at an angle by specifying rotation angle
5. Drawing a rectangle with chamfer
6. Drawing a rectangle with fillet
7. Drawing a rectangle with elevation
8. Drawing a rectangle with thickness
9. Drawing a rectangle with width

Drawing a Rectangle by Specifying Diagonally Opposite Corners

In AutoCAD, you can draw a rectangle by specifying it's two diagonally opposite corners. The first specified corner defines the position of the first corner of the rectangle and the second specified corner defines the length and width of the rectangle, see Figure 4.2.

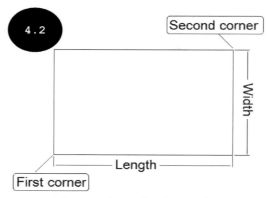

The procedure to draw a rectangle by specifying the diagonally opposite corner is discussed next.

Procedure for Drawing a Rectangle by Specifying Diagonally Opposite Corners

1. Click on the **Rectangle** tool in the **Draw** panel of the **Home** tab. Alternatively, enter **REC** in the Command Line window and then press ENTER. The **Rectangle** tool is activated and you are prompted to specify the first corner of the rectangle.

   ```
   Specify first corner point or [Chamfer Elevation Fillet Thickness Width]:
   ```

2. Click the left mouse button in the drawing area to specify the first corner of the rectangle. You are prompted to specify the second corner of the rectangle. Alternatively, you can enter coordinate (X, Y) in the Command Line window to specify the first corner of the rectangle.

   ```
   Specify other corner point or [Area Dimensions Rotation]:
   ```

3. Move the cursor diagonally to specify the second corner of the rectangle in the drawing area. The preview of the rectangle appears whose first corner fixed at the specified location and the other corner is attached to the cursor, see Figure 4.3.

4. Enter the length and width values of the rectangle in the Dynamic Input boxes that appear near the cursor for defining the second corner of the rectangle. You can press the TAB key to switch from the one Dynamic Input box to another for specifying the values. After entering the length and width values, press ENTER. The rectangle is created in the drawing area.

Note: If the Dynamic Input boxes do not appear near your cursor for specifying the length and width values of the rectangle, you need to turn on the Dynamic Input mode by clicking on the **Dynamic Input** button in the Status Bar.

Drawing a Rectangle by Specifying its Area and One Side

You can draw a rectangle by specifying its area and one side (length or width) by using the **Rectangle** tool. The procedure to draw a rectangle by specifying its area and one side is discussed next.

Note: On specifying the area and one side (length/width) of the rectangle, AutoCAD automatically calculates the other side of the rectangle by using the formula: *Area of rectangle = Length X Width*. For example, if you specify the Area of rectangle = 500 units and length = 50 units then the *Width* = *500/50*.

Procedure for Drawing a Rectangle by Specifying Area and One Side

1. Click on the **Rectangle** tool in the **Draw** panel of the **Home** tab. Alternatively, enter **REC** in the Command Line window and then press ENTER. The **Rectangle** tool is activated and you are prompted to specify the first corner of the rectangle.

   ```
   Specify first corner point or [Chamfer Elevation Fillet Thickness Width]:
   ```

2. Click the left mouse button in the drawing area or enter coordinate (X, Y) to specify the first corner of the rectangle. You are prompted to specify the second corner of the rectangle.

   ```
   Specify other corner point or [Area Dimensions Rotation]:
   ```

3. Enter **A** in the Dynamic Input box or the Command Line window and then press ENTER. You are prompted to specify the area of the rectangle. Alternatively, click on the **Area** option in the command prompt to specify the area of the rectangle.

   ```
   Enter area of rectangle in current units <10.0000>:
   ```

4. Enter the area of the rectangle and then press ENTER. You are prompted to specify either the length or width of the rectangle.

   ```
   Calculate rectangle dimensions based on [Length Width] <Length>:
   ```

5. Enter **L** and then press ENTER for defining the length of the rectangle. You are prompted to specify the length of the rectangle. Note that for defining the width of the rectangle, you need to enter **W** in the Command Line window.

   ```
   Enter rectangle length <5.0000>:
   ```

6. Enter the length value of the rectangle and then press ENTER. The rectangle of the defined area and length is drawn in the drawing area, see Figure 4.4.

> **Note:** The value entered inside the < > symbol in the command prompt is the last defined or default value of the command. For example, in the prompt "`Calculate rectangle dimensions based on [Length Width] <Length>:`", the length entered inside the <> is the default option of the command. If you want to go with the default selected option, you can directly press ENTER; else, specify the new option in the Command Line window and then press ENTER.

Drawing a Rectangle by Specifying Dimensions

You can draw a rectangle by specifying dimensions: length and width by using the **Rectangle** tool. The procedure to draw a rectangle by specifying dimensions is discussed next.

Procedure for Drawing a Rectangle by Specifying Dimensions

1. Click on the **Rectangle** tool or enter **REC** in the Command Line window. You are prompted to specify the first corner of the rectangle.

   ```
   Specify first corner point or [Chamfer Elevation Fillet Thickness Width]:
   ```

2. Click the left mouse button in the drawing area or specify coordinates (X, Y) to specify the first corner of the rectangle. You are prompted to specify the second corner of the rectangle.

   ```
   Specify other corner point or [Area Dimensions Rotation]:
   ```

3. Enter **D** and then press ENTER. You are prompted to specify the length of the rectangle. Alternatively, you can click on the **Dimensions** option in the command prompt.

   ```
   Specify length for rectangle <100.000>:
   ```

4. Enter the length value of the rectangle and then press ENTER. You are prompted to specify the width of the rectangle.

   ```
   Specify width for rectangle <2.0000>:
   ```

5. Enter the width value of the rectangle and then press ENTER. You are prompted to specify the other corner of the rectangle.

   ```
   Specify other corner point or [Area Dimensions Rotation]:
   ```

6. Click to specify the other corner point of the rectangle. The rectangle of the defined length and width is drawn in the drawing area, see Figure 4.5.

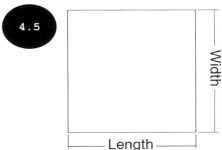

Drawing a Rectangle at an Angle

You can draw a rectangle at an angle by using the **Rectangle** tool. The procedure to draw a rectangle at an angle is discussed next.

Procedure for Drawing a Rectangle at an Angle

1. Click on the **Rectangle** tool. You are prompted to specify the first corner of the rectangle.

   ```
   Specify first corner point or [Chamfer Elevation Fillet Thickness Width]:
   ```

2. Click the left mouse button in the drawing area or enter coordinates (X, Y) to specify the first corner of the rectangle. You are prompted to specify the second corner of the rectangle.

   ```
   Specify other corner point or [Area Dimensions Rotation]:
   ```

168   Chapter 4 > Creating Drawings - II

3. Enter **R** and then press ENTER. You are prompted to specify the rotation angle of the rectangle. You can also click on the **Rotation** option in the command prompt to specify the rotation angle of the rectangle.

   ```
   Specify rotation angle or [Pick points] <0.0000>:
   ```

4. Enter the rotational angle and then press ENTER, see Figure 4.6. You are prompted to specify the other corner of the rectangle.

   ```
   Specify other corner point or [Area Dimensions Rotation]:
   ```

5. Move the cursor in the drawing area. The preview of the rectangle at the specified angle appears in the drawing area. Next, click the left mouse button in the drawing area to define the second corner of the rectangle, see Figure 4.6. You can also enter coordinates (X, Y) to define the second corner of the rectangle.

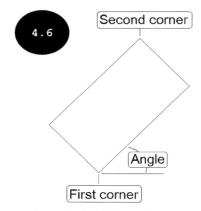

Drawing a Rectangle with Chamfer
In AutoCAD, you can draw a rectangle with chamfers on its corners by using the **Rectangle** tool, see Figure 4.7. The procedure to draw a rectangle with chamfer is discussed next.

Procedure for Drawing a Rectangle with Chamfer
1. Click on the **Rectangle** tool. You are prompted to specify the first corner of the rectangle.

   ```
   Specify first corner point or [Chamfer Elevation Fillet Thickness Width]:
   ```

2. Click on the **Chamfer** option in the command prompt or enter C and then press ENTER. You are prompted to specify the first chamfer distance.

   ```
   Specify first chamfer distance for rectangle <0.0000>:
   ```

3. Enter the first chamfer distance and then press ENTER. You are prompted to specify the second chamfer distance.

   ```
   Specify first chamfer distance for rectangle <0.0000>:
   ```

4. Enter the second chamfer distance and then press ENTER. You are prompted to specify the first corner of the rectangle.

   ```
   Specify first corner point or [Chamfer Elevation Fillet Thickness Width]:
   ```

5. Click the left mouse button in the drawing area or enter coordinates (X, Y) to specify the first corner of the rectangle. You are prompted to specify the second corner of the rectangle.

   ```
   Specify other corner point or [Area Dimensions Rotation]:
   ```

6. Click the left mouse button in the drawing area or enter coordinates (X, Y) to specify the second corner of the rectangle. The rectangle with chamfers on its each corner is drawn in the drawing area.

Drawing a Rectangle with Fillets

In AutoCAD, you can draw a rectangle with fillets on its corners by using the **Rectangle** tool, see Figure 4.8. The procedure to draw the rectangle with fillets is discussed next.

Procedure for Drawing a Rectangle with Fillets

1. Click on the **Rectangle** tool. You are prompted to specify the first corner of the rectangle.

   ```
   Specify first corner point or [Chamfer Elevation Fillet Thickness Width]:
   ```

2. Click on the **Fillet** option in the command prompt or enter **F** and then press ENTER. You are prompted to specify the fillet radius of the rectangle.

   ```
   Specify fillet radius for rectangle <0.0000>:
   ```

3. Enter the fillet radius of the rectangle and then press ENTER. You are prompted to specify the first corner of the rectangle.

   ```
   Specify first corner point or [Chamfer Elevation Fillet Thickness Width]:
   ```

4. Click the left mouse button in the drawing area or enter coordinates (X, Y) to specify the first corner of the rectangle. You are prompted to specify the second corner of the rectangle.

   ```
   Specify other corner point or [Area Dimensions Rotation]:
   ```

5. Click the left mouse button in the drawing area or enter coordinates (X, Y) to specify the second corner of the rectangle. The rectangle with fillets on its corners is drawn in the drawing area.

Drawing a Rectangle with Elevation

You can draw a rectangle at a specified elevation along the Z direction from the origin (0,0,0), see Figure 4.9 by using the **Rectangle** tool. The procedure to draw a rectangle with elevation is discussed next.

Procedure for Drawing a Rectangle with Elevation

1. Click on the **Rectangle** tool. You are prompted to specify the first corner of the rectangle.

   ```
   Specify first corner point or [Chamfer Elevation Fillet Thickness Width]:
   ```

2. Click on the **Elevation** option in the command prompt or enter **E** and then press ENTER. You are prompted to specify the elevation of the rectangle.

   ```
   Specify the elevation for rectangles <0.0000>:
   ```

3. Enter the elevation value along the z-axis from the origin (0,0,0) and then press ENTER. You are prompted to specify the first corner of the rectangle.

   ```
   Specify first corner point or [Chamfer Elevation Fillet Thickness Width]:
   ```

4. Specify the first corner of the rectangle. You are prompted to specify the second corner of the rectangle.

   ```
   Specify other corner point or [Area Dimensions Rotation]:
   ```

5. Specify the second corner of the rectangle. The rectangle with the specified elevation is drawn in the drawing area, see Figure 4.9.

   Note: You can change the orientation of the rectangle to isometric to view the elevation of the rectangle drawn by clicking on the **Home** button in the **ViewCube**, which is available at the upper right corner of the screen.

Drawing a Rectangle with Thickness

You can draw a rectangle with a specified thickness along the z-axis by using the **Rectangle** tool, see Figure 4.10. The procedure to draw a rectangle with a specified thickness is discussed next.

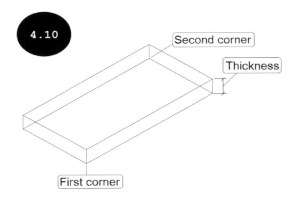

Procedure for Drawing a Rectangle with Thickness

1. Click on the **Rectangle** tool. You are prompted to specify the first corner of the rectangle.

   ```
   Specify first corner point or [Chamfer Elevation Fillet Thickness Width]:
   ```

2. Click on the **Thickness** option in the command prompt or enter **T** and then press ENTER. You are prompted to specify the thickness along the z-axis for the rectangle.

   ```
   Specify thickness for rectangles <0.0000>:
   ```

172 Chapter 4 > Creating Drawings - II

3. Enter thickness value along the z-axis from the origin (0,0,0) and then press ENTER. You are prompted to specify the first corner of the rectangle.

   ```
   Specify first corner point or [Chamfer Elevation Fillet Thickness Width]:
   ```

4. Specify the first corner of the rectangle. You are prompted to specify the second corner of the rectangle.

   ```
   Specify other corner point or [Area Dimensions Rotation]:
   ```

5. Specify the second corner of the rectangle. The rectangle with the specified thickness drawn in the drawing area.

6. Click on the **Home** button in the **ViewCube**, which is available at the upper right corner of the screen. The orientation of the drawing changed to isometric, see Figure 4.10.

Drawing a Rectangle with Width

You can draw a rectangle with the specified width by using the **Rectangle** tool, see Figure 4.11. The procedure to draw a rectangle with width is discussed next.

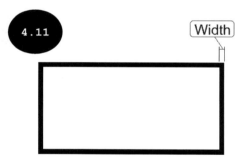

Procedure for Drawing a Rectangle with Width

1. Click on the **Rectangle** tool. You are prompted to specify the first corner of the rectangle.

   ```
   Specify first corner point or [Chamfer Elevation Fillet Thickness Width]:
   ```

2. Click on the **Width** option in the command prompt or enter **W** and then press ENTER. You are prompted to specify the width of the rectangle.

   ```
   Specify line width for rectangle <0.0000>:
   ```

3. Enter the width value of the rectangle and then press ENTER. You are prompted to specify the first corner of the rectangle.

   ```
   Specify first corner point or [Chamfer Elevation Fillet Thickness Width]:
   ```

4. Specify the first corner of the rectangle. You are prompted to specify the second corner of the rectangle.

   ```
   Specify other corner point or [Area Dimensions Rotation]:
   ```

5. Specify the second corner of the rectangle. The rectangle with the specified width is drawn in the drawing area, refer to Figure 4.11.

Drawing a Polygon

AutoCAD allows you to draw polygons of equal sides in the range from 3 to 1024. A polygon is a closed geometry having equal sides as well as the equal angle between sides. Figure 4.12 shows a polygon having five sides. You can draw a polygon by using the **Polygon** tool of the **Draw** panel, see Figure 4.13, or by entering **POL** in the Command Line window. POL is the shortcut of the POLYGON command.

In AutoCAD, you can draw two types of a polygon: Inscribed polygon and Circumscribed polygon by using the **Polygon** tool, see Figures 4.14 and 4.15. Both the types of the polygon discussed next.

Inscribed Polygon

An Inscribed polygon is created inside an imaginary circle such that its vertices touch the imaginary circle, see Figure 4.14.

Circumscribed Polygon

A Circumscribed polygon is created outside an imaginary circle such that the midpoints of the polygon sides touch the imaginary circle, see Figure 4.15.

The procedure to draw a polygon is discussed next.

Procedure for Drawing a Polygon (Inscribed and Circumscribed)

1. Click on the down arrow in the **Rectangle** tool of the **Draw** panel. A flyout appears, refer to Figure 4.13. In this flyout, click on the **Polygon** tool. The **Polygon** tool is activated, and you are prompted to specify the number of polygon sides. Alternatively, enter **POL** in the Command Line window and then press ENTER to activate the **Polygon** tool.

   ```
   Enter number of sides <4>:
   ```

2. Enter the number of polygon sides and then press ENTER. You are prompted to specify the center of the polygon.

   ```
   Specify center of polygon or [Edge]:
   ```

3. Click the left mouse button in the drawing area or enter coordinates (X, Y) to specify the center of the polygon. You are prompted to specify the type of polygon (Inscribed in circle or Circumscribed about circle).

   ```
   Enter an option [Inscribed in circle Circumscribed about circle]
   <I>:
   ```

4. Enter **I** or **C** in the Command Line window for drawing Inscribed or circumscribed polygon, respectively. Next, press ENTER. You are prompted to specify the radius of an imaginary circle.

   ```
   Specify radius of circle:
   ```

5. Enter the radius value of an imaginary circle and then press ENTER. The polygon is drawn depending upon the option: **Inscribed in circle** or **Circumscribed about circle** selected.

Drawing a Polyline

A Polyline consists of one or more than one line or arc segment and acts as a single object. In AutoCAD, drawing a polyline is similar to drawing a line with the only difference that the polyline consists of a series of line segments, arc segments, or the combination of line and arc segments and acts as a single object, see Figure 4.16. You can draw a polyline by using the **Polyline** tool of the **Draw** panel or by entering **PL** in the Command Line window. PL is the shortcut of the POLYLINE command. The procedures to draw a polyline are discussed next.

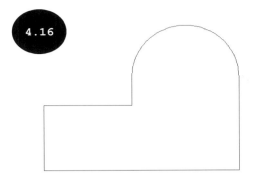

Procedure for Drawing a Polyline with Line Segments

1. Click on the **Polyline** tool in the **Draw** panel of the **Home** tab or enter **PL** in the Command Line window and then press ENTER. You are prompted to specify the start point of the polyline.

   ```
   Specify start point:
   ```

2. Click the left mouse button in the drawing area or specify coordinates (X, Y) to specify the start point of the polyline. You are prompted to specify the next point of the polyline.

   ```
   Specify next point or [Arc Halfwidth Length Undo Width]:
   ```

3. Specify the next point of the polyline. A line segment is created in the drawing area, and you are prompted to specify the next point of the polyline.

   ```
   Specify next point or [Arc Halfwidth Length Undo Width]:
   ```

4. Specify the next point of the polyline. The second line segment of polyline is drawn in the drawing area, see Figure 4.17. You are prompted to specify the next point of the polyline.

   ```
   Specify next point or [Arc Halfwidth Length Undo Width]:
   ```

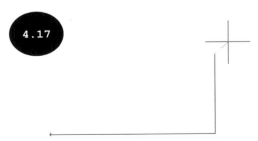

5. Similarly, you can draw a series of continuous line segments of a polyline, one after another by specifying points in the drawing area.

Procedure for Drawing a Polyline with Line and Arc Segments

1. Click on the **Polyline** tool in the **Draw** panel or enter **PL** in the Command Line window and then press ENTER. You are prompted to specify the start point of the polyline.

   ```
   Specify start point:
   ```

2. Specify the start point of the polyline. You are prompted to specify the next point of the polyline.

   ```
   Specify next point or [Arc Halfwidth Length Undo Width]:
   ```

3. Specify the next point of the polyline. A line segment is created, and you are prompted to specify the next point of the polyline.

   ```
   Specify next point or [Arc Halfwidth Length Undo Width]:
   ```

   You can also draw arc segments in a polyline.

4. Click on the **Arc** option in the command prompt. The Arc mode for drawing arc segment is activated, and you are prompted to specify the endpoint of the arc. Alternatively, enter **A** in the Command Line window and then press ENTER to activate the Arc mode.

   ```
   Specify endpoint of arc or [Angle CEnter CLose Direction Halfwidth Line Radius Second pt Undo Width]:
   ```

5. Click to specify the end point of the arc. An arc segment is created, see Figure 4.18. Note that the Arc mode still activated, and you are prompted to specify the endpoint of another arc.

   ```
   Specify endpoint of arc or [Angle CEnter CLose Direction Halfwidth Line Radius Second pt Undo Width]:
   ```

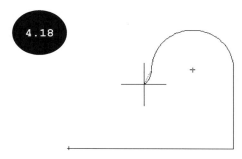

4.18

6. To draw the line segment again, enter **L** in the Command Line window and then press ENTER. Alternatively, click on the **Line** option in the command prompt. You are prompted to specify the endpoint of the line segment.

   ```
   Specify next point or [Arc Halfwidth Length Undo Width]:
   ```

7. Similarly, you can draw a polyline with a series of line and arc segments. Once you have drawn a polyline, press the ENTER key to exit from the **Polyline** tool.

> **Tip:** While drawing a polyline, when the Arc mode is activated, you are prompted to specify the endpoint of the arc segment as well as provided with additional options such as angle, center, direction, and radius in the command prompt for drawing the arc. These options discussed next.
>
> ```
> Specify endpoint of arc or [Angle CEnter CLose Direction
> Halfwidth Line Radius Second pt Undo Width]:
> ```
>
> **Angle:** By clicking on the **Angle** option in the command prompt, you can specify the angle of the arc segment from the start point, see Figure 4.19. The positive angle value creates counter-clockwise arc segment, and the negative angle value creates clockwise arc segment.
>
> **Center:** By clicking on the **Center** option in the command prompt, you can specify the center point of the arc segment to be drawn, see Figure 4.20.

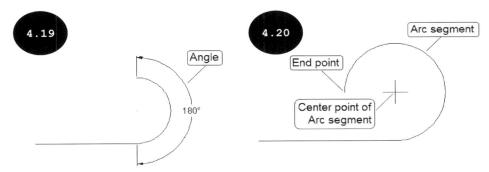

Direction: By clicking on the **Direction** option in the command prompt, you can specify the direction of the tangent for the arc segment, see Figure 4.21.

Radius: By clicking on the **Radius** option in the command prompt, you can specify the radius of the arc segment, see Figure 4.22.

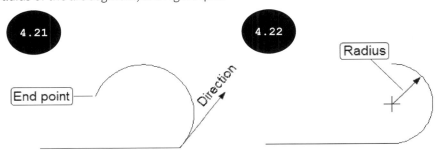

Procedure for Drawing a Polyline with Width

1. Click on the **Polyline** tool in the **Draw** panel of the **Home** tab or enter **PL** in the Command Line window and then press ENTER. You are prompted to specify the start point of the polyline.

   ```
   Specify start point:
   ```

2. Specify the start point of the polyline. You are prompted to specify the next point of the polyline.

   ```
   Specify next point or [Arc Halfwidth Length Undo Width]:
   ```

3. Click on the **Width** option in the command prompt. You are prompted to specify the starting width of the polyline. Alternatively, enter **W** and then press ENTER.

   ```
   Specify starting width <0.0000>:
   ```

4. Enter the starting width value (see Figure 4.23) and then press ENTER. You are prompted to specify the ending width of the polyline.

   ```
   Specify ending width <0.0000>:
   ```

5. Enter the ending width value (see Figure 4.23) and then press ENTER. You are prompted to specify the next point of the polyline.

   ```
   Specify next point or [Arc Halfwidth Length Undo Width]:
   ```

6. Specify the next point of the polyline. A line segment with specified width is created, and you are prompted to specify the next point of the polyline. Also, a rubber band line segment with the constant width (which defined as the ending width) appears in the drawing area whose one end fixed at the last specified point, and the other end attached to the cursor, see Figure 4.23.

   ```
   Specify next point or [Arc Halfwidth Length Undo Width]:
   ```

4.23

7. Similarly, you can draw a continuous series of line and arc segments in a polyline with specified width. Once you have drawn the polyline, press the ENTER key to exit the **Polyline** tool.

Note: By default, the fill mode for polyline set to 1. As a result, the polyline segments having width are drawn as solid, see Figure 4.23. However, if you change the fill mode to 0 (zero), the polyline segments having width are drawn as outlines only, see Figure 4.24. To change the fill mode, enter **FILLMODE** in the Command Line window and then press ENTER. Next, enter 1 or 0 in the Command Line window, as required.

The width specified for the endpoint of a polyline segment becomes uniform width for other polyline segments until have changed the width again.

Tip: Similar to defining the width of a line segment of a polyline, you can specify start width and end width for an arc segment of the polyline, see Figure 4.25.

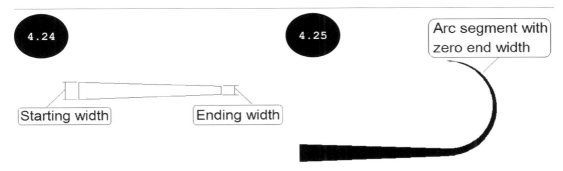

4.24

4.25

Arc segment with zero end width

Starting width

Ending width

Procedure for Drawing a Polyline with Halfwidth

1. Invoke the **Polyline** tool.

   ```
   Specify start point:
   ```

2. Specify the start point of the polyline.

   ```
   Specify next point or [Arc Halfwidth Length Undo Width]:
   ```

3. Click on the **Halfwidth** option in the command prompt or enter H and then press ENTER. You are prompted to specify the starting half width of polyline segment.

   ```
   Specify starting half-width <0.0000>:
   ```

   Note: The half width of a polyline segment measured from the center of the polyline segment to the one side edge of the polyline segment, see Figure 4.26.

4. Specify the starting half width of the polyline segment (see Figure 4.26) and then press ENTER. You are prompted to specify the ending half width of the polyline segment.

   ```
   Specify ending half-width <5.0000>:
   ```

180　Chapter 4 > Creating Drawings - II

5. Enter the ending half width value (see Figure 4.26) and then press ENTER. You are prompted to specify the next point of the polyline.

   ```
   Specify next point or [Arc Halfwidth Length Undo Width]:
   ```

6. Specify the next point of the polyline segment. A line segment with specified half width is drawn, and you are prompted to specify the next point of the polyline. Also, a rubber band line segment with the constant half width (which defined as the ending half width) appears in the drawing area whose one end fixed at the last specified point, and the other end attached to the cursor, see Figure 4.26.

   ```
   Specify next point or [Arc Halfwidth Length Undo Width]:
   ```

7. Similarly, you can draw a series of line and arc segments in a polyline. Once you have drawn the polyline, press the ENTER key to exit from the tool.

Drawing an Ellipse

An ellipse is created by defining its major axis and the minor axis, see Figure 4.27. In AutoCAD, you can draw an ellipse by using the **Center** and **Axis, End** tools. These tools are available in the **Ellipse** flyout of the **Draw** panel, see Figure 4.28. The procedures of creating an ellipse are discussed next.

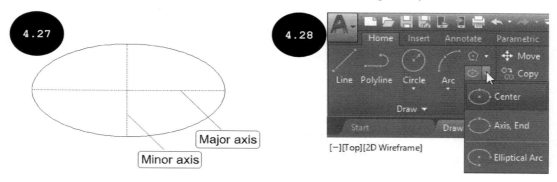

Procedure for Drawing an Ellipse by Using the Axis, End Tool

1. Invoke the **Ellipse** flyout by clicking on the down arrow next to an ellipse tool in the **Draw** panel, see Figure 4.28.

2. Click on the **Axis, End** tool in the **Ellipse** flyout. The **Axis, End** tool is activated, and you are prompted to specify the first endpoint of the ellipse axis. Alternatively, enter **EL** in the Command Line window and then press ENTER to activate the **Axis, End** tool.

   ```
   Specify axis endpoint of ellipse or [Arc Center]:
   ```

3. Click the left mouse button in the drawing area or enter coordinates (X, Y) to specify the first endpoint of the ellipse axis (P1), see Figure 4.29. You are prompted to specify the second endpoint of the ellipse axis.

   ```
   Specify other endpoint of axis:
   ```

4. Click the left mouse button in the drawing area or enter coordinates (X, Y)/length of the axis to specify the second endpoint (P2), see Figure 4.29. You are prompted to specify the distance of the other ellipse axis.

   ```
   Specify distance to other axis or [Rotation]:
   ```

5. Move the cursor, clockwise or anti-clockwise direction for a little distance. The preview of an ellipse appears in the drawing area, see Figure 4.30. Next, click the left mouse button or enter length to specify the distance of the other ellipse axis (P3), see Figure 4.29. The ellipse of specified major and minor axes is created.

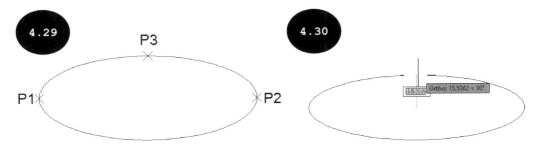

Procedure for Drawing an Ellipse by Using the Center Tool

1. Invoke the **Ellipse** flyout, see Figure 4.28.

2. Click on the **Center** tool in the **Ellipse** flyout. You are prompted to specify the center point of the ellipse axis. Alternatively, enter **EL** in the Command Line window and then press ENTER. Next, type **C** and then press ENTER to activate the **Center** tool.

   ```
   Specify center of ellipse:
   ```

3. Click the left mouse button in the drawing area or enter coordinates (X, Y) to specify the center point of the ellipse axis (P1), see Figure 4.31. You are prompted to specify the endpoint of the ellipse axis.

   ```
   Specify endpoint of axis:
   ```

4. Specify the endpoint of the ellipse axis (P2), see Figure 4.31. You are prompted to specify the distance to the other ellipse axis.

   ```
   Specify distance to other axis or [Rotation]:
   ```

5. Move the cursor, clockwise or anti-clockwise direction a distance. The preview of an ellipse appears in the drawing area. Next, enter the length of the ellipse axis and then press ENTER. The ellipse of specified major and minor axes is created in the drawing area.

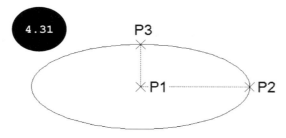

Drawing an Elliptical Arc

In addition to drawing an ellipse, you can also draw an elliptical arc, see Figure 4.32. You can draw an elliptical arc by using the **Elliptical Arc** tool of the **Ellipse** flyout, see Figure 4.33. You can also enter **EL** and then **A** in the Command Line window to activate this tool. The procedure to draw an elliptical arc is discussed next.

Procedure for Drawing an Elliptical Arc

1. Invoke the **Ellipse** flyout and then click on the **Elliptical Arc** tool, see Figure 4.33. Alternatively, enter **EL** in the Command Line window and then press ENTER. Next, enter **A** and then press ENTER to activate the **Elliptical Arc** tool.

   ```
   Specify axis endpoint of elliptical arc or [Center]:
   ```

2. Specify the start point of the elliptical arc axis (P1), see Figure 4.34. You are prompted to specify the endpoint of the elliptical arc axis.

   ```
   Specify other endpoint of axis:
   ```

3. Specify the endpoint of the elliptical arc axis (P2), see Figure 4.34. You are prompted to specify the distance to the other axis.

   ```
   Specify distance to other axis or [Rotation]:
   ```

4. Move the cursor clockwise or counter-clockwise to a small distance. The preview of an imaginary ellipse appears in the drawing area. Next, specify a point (P3) to define the length of the other axis, see Figure 4.34. You are prompted to specify start angle of the elliptical arc.

   ```
   Specify start angle or [Parameter]:
   ```

5. Move the cursor clockwise or counter-clockwise and then specify the start angle for the elliptical arc, see Figure 4.34. You are prompted to specify the end angle of the elliptical arc.

   ```
   Specify end angle or [Parameter Included angle]:
   ```

6. Move the cursor clockwise or counter-clockwise and then specify the end angle for the elliptical arc, see Figure 4.34. The elliptical arc is created in the drawing area.

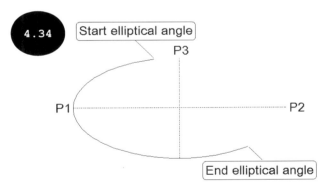

Drawing a Spline

A spline is defined as a smooth curve having a high degree of smoothness and passes through a set of fit points that influence the shape of the curve, see Figure 4.35. You can also create a spline that passes near the control vertices, see Figure 4.36. The smooth curves are technically known as NURBS (non-uniform rational B-splines). However, it referred as a spline. In AutoCAD, you can draw a spline by using the **Spline Fit** and **Spline CV** tools. Both these tools are discussed next.

184 Chapter 4 > Creating Drawings - II

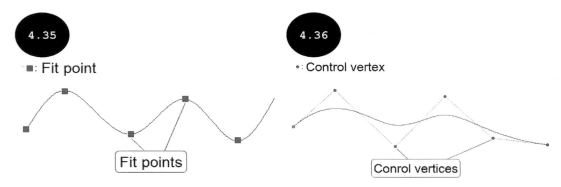

Drawing a Spline by Using the Spline Fit Tool

The **Spline Fit** tool is used to create a spline such that it passes through a set of fit points that influence the shape of the spline, see Figure 4.35. The procedure to draw a spline by using the **Spline Fit** tool is discussed next.

Procedure for Drawing a Spline by Using the Spline Fit Tool

1. Expand the **Draw** panel by clicking on the down arrow in the title bar of the **Draw** panel, see Figure 4.37. Figure 4.38 shows the expanded **Draw** panel.

2. Click on the **Spline Fit** tool in the expanded **Draw** panel, see Figure 4.38. The **Spline Fit** tool gets activated, and you are prompted to specify the first fit point of the spline. Alternatively, enter SPL in the Command Line window and then press ENTER to invoke the **Spline Fit** tool.

   ```
   Specify first point or [Method Knots Objects]:
   ```

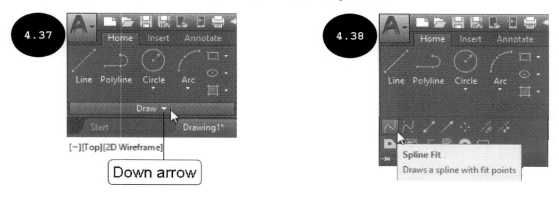

3. Click the left mouse button in the drawing area to specify the first fit point of the spline. You are prompted to specify the next fit point of the spline.

   ```
   Enter next point or [start Tangency toLerance]:
   ```

Note: Before you specify the second fit point of a spline, you can define its start tangency by entering T in the Command Line window or by clicking on the **start Tangency** option in the command prompt. Figure 4.39 shows a spline with start tangency point.

By default, the tolerance value for a spline set to 0 (zero). As a result, the resultant spline passes exactly through the specified fit points. On defining the positive tolerance value, the resultant spline deviates from the specified fit points and maintains uniform tolerance distance between the spline and fit points, see Figure 4.40. To define the tolerance for a spline, enter **L** in the Command Line window or click on the **toLerance** option in the command prompt, which appears after specifying the first fit point of a spline. The tolerance value gets applied to all fit points except the start and end fit points, see Figure 4.40.

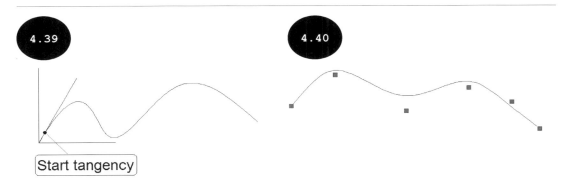

4. Click to specify the second fit point of the spline. You are prompted to specify the next fit point of the spline. Also, the preview of the spline appears such that it passes through the specified fit points.

   ```
   Enter next point or [end Tangency toLerance Undo]:
   ```

5. Click to specify the third fit point of the spline. You are prompted to specify the next fit point of the spline. Also, the preview of the spline appears such that it passes through the specified fit points.

   ```
   Enter next point or [end Tangency toLerance Undo Close]:
   ```

6. Similarly, you can continue specifying fit points for creating spline. Once you have defined all the fit points of the spline, press ENTER to exit the tool.

Note: Before you terminate the creation of spline, you can define its end tangency by entering the T in the Command Line window or by clicking on the **end Tangency** option in the command prompt. Figure 4.41 shows a spline with end tangency point.

You can also draw a close spline. To draw a close spline whose end fit point joins to the start point, enter **C** in the Command Line window and then press ENTER. Figure 4.42 shows a close spline. To draw a close spline, you need to define minimum three fit points.

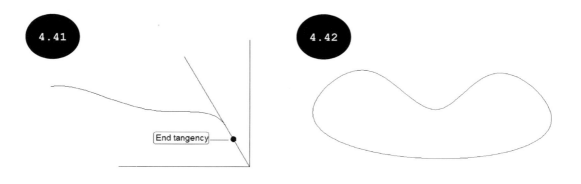

Tip: You can also undo/remove the last specified fit point by entering **U** in the Command Line window and then pressing the ENTER key. You can undo multiple specified last points one after the other by using this command.

Drawing a Spline by Using the Spline CV Tool

The **Spline CV** tool is used to create a spline such that it passes near a set of control vertices that influence the shape of the spline, see Figure 4.43. The procedure to draw a spline by using the **Spline CV** tool is discussed next.

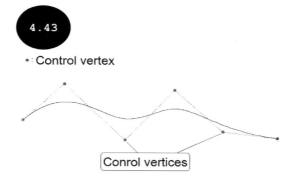

Procedure for Drawing a Spline by Using the Spline CV Tool

1. Expand the **Draw** panel by clicking on the down arrow available in the title bar of the **Draw** panel and then click on the **Spline CV** tool, see Figure 4.44. The **Spline CV** tool gets activated, and you are prompted to specify the first control point for creating spline.

   ```
   Specify first point or [Method Knots Objects]:
   ```

2. Click the left mouse button in the drawing area to specify the first control point of the spline. You are prompted to specify the next control point of the spline.

   ```
   Enter next point:
   ```

3. Click to specify the second control point of the spline. You are prompted to specify the next control point of the spline. Also, the preview of the spline appears such that it passes near the specified control points.

   ```
   Enter next point or [Undo]:
   ```

4. Click to specify the third control point of the spline. You are prompted to specify the next control point of the spline.

   ```
   Enter next point or [Close Undo]:
   ```

5. Similarly, you can continue specifying control points for creating spline. Once you have defined all the control points, press the ENTER key. The spline gets created in the drawing area.

   Note: You can also draw a closed spline. To draw a close spline whose end control point joins to the start control point, enter **C** in the Command Line window and then press ENTER.

   You can also undo/remove the last specified control point by entering **U** in the Command Line window and then press the ENTER key.

Drawing Donuts

A donut is a filled solid ring/circle, which is made up of two end-to-end joined polyarcs with width. The width of polyarc defined by specifying the inside and outside diameters, see Figure 4.45. If you specify the inside diameter as 0 (zero) then the donut will be drawn as a filled circle, see Figure 4.46. In AutoCAD, you can draw donuts by using the **Donut** tool, which is available in the expanded **Draw** panel. The procedure to draw donuts is discussed next.

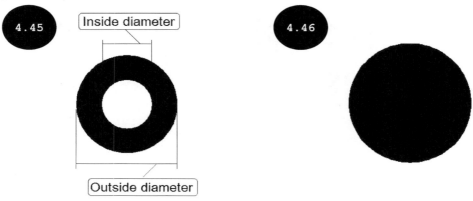

Procedure for Drawing Donuts

1. Expand the **Draw** panel of the **Home** tab and then click on the **Donut** tool, see Figure 4.47. You are prompted to specify the inside diameter of the donut. Alternatively, enter **DO** in the Command Line window and then press ENTER to activate the **Donut** tool.

    ```
    Specify inside diameter of donut <0.0000>:
    ```

2. Enter the inside diameter value of donut and then press ENTER. You are prompted to specify the outside diameter of the donut.

    ```
    Specify outside diameter of donut <current>:
    ```

3. Enter the outside diameter value of donut and then press ENTER. You are prompted to specify the center of the donut.

    ```
    Specify center of donut or <exit>:
    ```

4. Click the left mouse button in the drawing area or specify coordinates (X, Y) to define the center of the donut. A donut gets drawn with specified parameters in the drawing area. Also, an another donut of same parameters is attached to the cursor. It means you can draw multiple donuts one after another by specifying their centers in the drawing area.

5. Press ENTER to exit from creating donuts.

Note: By default, the fill mode set to 1. As a result, the resultant donut appears as solid ring/circle. However, if you change the fill mode to 0 (zero), the resultant donut will not be filled and appears similar to the one shown in Figure 4.48. To define the fill mode, enter **FILLMODE** in the Command Line window and then specify the fill value (0 or 1). Next, press ENTER.

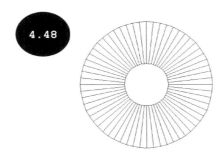

4.48

Drawing Construction and Ray lines

Construction lines and ray lines act as references lines for creating objects. A construction line is also known as XLINE. A construction line extended to infinite length in both the directions and passes through two specified points, see Figure 4.49. Whereas, a ray line is extended to infinite length in one direction only from the first specified point, see Figure 4.49. You can create a construction line (XLINE) by using the **Construction Line** tool and a ray line by using the **Ray** tool. Both the tools are available in the expanded **Draw** panel of the **Home** tab, see Figure 4.50. The procedures to draw construction line and ray line are discussed next.

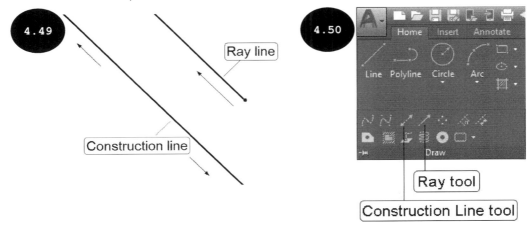

Procedure for Drawing Construction Lines

1. Expand the **Draw** panel of the **Home** tab and then click on the **Construction Line** tool, see Figure 4.50. The **Construction Line** tool gets activated, and you are prompted to specify a point in the drawing area. Alternatively, enter **XLINE** in the Command Line window and then press ENTER to activate the **Construction Line** tool.

   ```
   Specify a point or [Hor Ver Ang Bisect Offset]:
   ```

2. Click to specify a point (P1) in the drawing area, see Figure 4.51. You are prompted to specify a through point.

   ```
   Specify through point:
   ```

3. Click to specify a point (P2) in the drawing area, see Figure 4.51. A construction line of infinite length passing through the specified points (P1 and P2) is drawn in the drawing area. Also, the preview of another construction line appears in the drawing area such that it passes through the first specified point and is attached to the cursor. It means you can create multiple construction lines one after another by specifying points in the drawing area.

4. Click to specify another point (P3) in the drawing area, see Figure 4.51. An another construction line of infinite length passing through the points (P1 and P3) is drawn in the drawing area. Also, the preview of another construction line appears in the drawing area. Similarly, you can create multiple construction lines passing through a common point.

5. After creating the construction lines, press ENTER to exit the tool. Figure 4.51 shows two construction lines created in the drawing area.

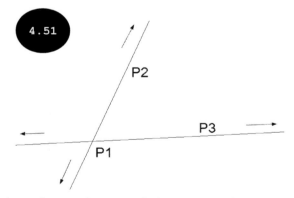

You can also create horizontal, vertical, at an angle, bisect, and offset construction lines by using the **Construction Line** tool. The procedures to create horizontal, vertical, and other construction lines are discussed next.

Procedure for Drawing Horizontal and Vertical Construction Lines

1. Expand the **Draw** panel of the **Home** tab and then click on the **Construction Line** tool. The **Construction Line** tool gets activated, and you are prompted to specify a point in the drawing area. Alternatively, you can enter **XLINE** in the Command Line window and then press ENTER to activate the **Construction Line** tool.

   ```
   Specify a point or [Hor Ver Ang Bisect Offset]:
   ```

2. Enter **H** in the Command Line window and then press ENTER. Alternatively, you can click on the **Hor** option in the command prompt. A horizontal construction line attached to the cursor is displayed, and you are prompted to specify a through point.

   ```
   Specify through point:
   ```

3. Click to specify a point in the drawing area. A horizontal construction line created such that it passes through the specified point, see Figure 4.52. Note that an another horizontal construction line attached to the cursor is displayed. As a result, you can create multiple horizontal construction lines one after another by specifying points in the drawing area.

4. Once you have created horizontal construction lines, press ENTER.

5. Similarly, you can create vertical construction lines by entering **V** in the Command Line window or by clicking on the **Ver** option in the command prompt, see Figure 4.52.

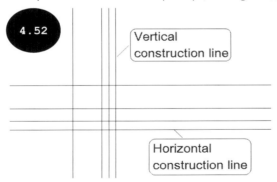

Procedure for Drawing Construction Lines at an Angle

1. Invoke the **Construction Line** tool. You are prompted to specify a point in the drawing area.

   ```
   Specify a point or [Hor Ver Ang Bisect Offset]:
   ```

2. Enter **A** in the Command Line window and then press ENTER. You are prompted to specify angle value for the construction line. Alternatively, you can click on the **Ang** option of the command prompt.

   ```
   Enter angle of xline (0) or [Reference]:
   ```

192 Chapter 4 > Creating Drawings - II

3. Enter the angle value and then press ENTER. A construction line at the specified angle is attached to the cursor. Also, you are prompted to specify a through point.

   ```
   Specify through point:
   ```

4. Click to specify a point in the drawing area. A construction line at the specified angle is created such that it passes through the specified point, see Figure 4.53. Also, an another construction line of specified angle is attached to the cursor. As a result, you can create multiple construction lines one after another by specifying points in the drawing area.

5. After creating the construction lines, press ENTER or right-click to exit.

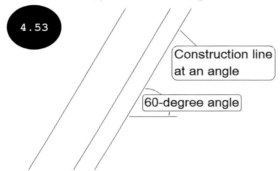

Procedure for Drawing Bisect Construction Lines

1. Invoke the **Construction Line** tool. You are prompted to specify a point in the drawing area.

   ```
   Specify a point or [Hor Ver Ang Bisect Offset]:
   ```

2. Enter **B** in the Command Line window and then press ENTER. You are prompted to specify vertex point. Alternatively, you can click on the **Bisect** option in the command prompt.

   ```
   Specify angle vertex point:
   ```

3. Click to specify vertex point (P1) in the drawing area, see Figure 4.54. You are prompted to specify angle start point.

   ```
   Specify angle start point:
   ```

4. Click to specify angle start point (P2) in the drawing area, see Figure 4.54. You are prompted to specify angle end point.

   ```
   Specify angle end point:
   ```

5. Click to specify angle end point (P3) in the drawing area, see Figure 4.54. A construction line created such that it passes through the vertex (P1) and bisects to the angle formed by specified points, see Figure 4.54. Next, press the ENTER key or right-click to exit.

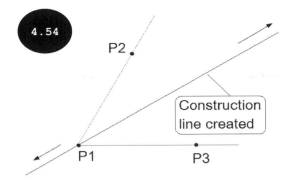

Procedure for Drawing Construction Lines at an Offset Distance

1. Invoke the **Construction Line** tool. You are prompted to specify a point in the drawing area.

   ```
   Specify a point or [Hor Ver Ang Bisect Offset]:
   ```

2. Enter **O** in the Command Line window and then press ENTER or click on the **Offset** option of the command prompt. You are prompted to specify offset distance for construction line.

   ```
   Specify offset distance or [Through] <0.0000>:
   ```

   Note: The **Offset** option is used to create construction line at an offset distance from an entity.

3. Enter offset distance value and then press ENTER. You are prompted to select a line. You can choose a line or a construction line as the reference line for measuring the offset distance.

   ```
   Select a line object:
   ```

4. Click to select a line or a construction line. You are prompted to specify the side to offset.

   ```
   Specify side to offset:
   ```

5. Click on either side of the selected line. The construction line created at the specified offset distance in the drawing area, see Figure 4.55.

Tip: In addition to defining offset value, you can also specify a point in the drawing area to define the offset distance. For doing so, click on the **Through** option in the command prompt or enter **T** in the Command Line window when you are prompted to specify offset distance. Next, click on the line as a reference line and then click in the drawing area to define offset distance. The construction line created in the drawing area.

Procedure for Drawing Ray Lines

A ray line is similar to construction lines (Xlines) with the only difference that it extends to infinite length in one direction only from the first specified point.

1. Expand the **Draw** panel of the **Home** tab and then click on the **Ray** tool. Alternatively, enter **RAY** in the Command Line window and then press ENTER. You are prompted to specify the start point.

   ```
   Specify start point:
   ```

2. Click to specify the start point of the ray line in the drawing area. You are prompted to specify a through point.

   ```
   Specify through point:
   ```

3. Click to specify a point in the drawing area. A ray line of infinite length in one direction from the start point is created in the drawing area. Also, the preview of another ray line appears in the drawing area whose origin fixed at the specified start point. You can create multiple ray lines one after another by specifying through points in the drawing area.

4. After creating the ray lines, press ENTER or right-click to exit. Figure 4.56 shows two ray lines sharing the same start point are created.

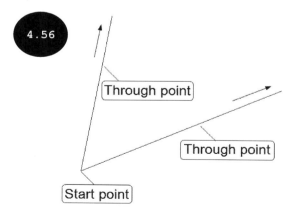

Drawing Points and Defining Point Style/Size

In AutoCAD, a point acts as reference geometry for creating other drawing objects, measuring distance, and so on. You can create points by using the **Multiple Points** tool, which is in the expanded **Draw** panel of the **Home** tab, see Figure 4.57. Alternatively, you can use the **POINT** command to create points. By default, the point style of a point is a simple dot which is relatively small. As the default size of a point is small and it's hard to visible on the screen. You can make the required changes in the point style and size by using the **Point Style** tool. The procedures to draw reference points, changing point style, and size are discussed next.

Procedure for Drawing Reference Points

1. Expand the **Draw** panel of the **Home** tab and then click on the **Multiple Points** tool, see Figure 4.57. The **Multiple Points** tool gets activated, and you are prompted to specify a point in the drawing area.

   ```
   Specify a point:
   ```

2. Click to specify a point in the drawing area. The point created with default point style (dot). You are prompted to specify another point.

   ```
   Specify a point:
   ```

   Note: The point created with default point style and size may not be visible easily in the drawing area due to its small size. You can change the point style and size by using the **Point Style** tool. The procedure to change the point style and size is discussed later in this chapter.

3. You can continue specifying points in the drawing area and create multiple points. Once you have drawn points, press ESC to exit.

Procedure for Defining the Point Style and Point Size

1. Expand the **Utilities** panel of the **Home** tab and then click on the **Point Style** tool, see Figure 4.58. The **Point Style** dialog box appears, see Figure 4.59. Alternatively, you can enter **DDPTYPE** in the Command Line window and then press ENTER to invoke the **Point Style** dialog box.

196 Chapter 4 > Creating Drawings - II

2. Select the required point style in the **Point Style** dialog box.

   After selecting the required point style, you can define the point size by using the **Set Size Relative to Screen** and **Set Size in Absolute Units** radio buttons of the **Point Style** dialog box. By default, the **Set Size Relative to Screen** radio button is selected. As a result, you can specify percentage relative to the screen for defining the point size in the **Point Size** field of the dialog box. To define the point size in absolute unit, click to select the **Set Size in Absolute Units** radio button and then enter the absolute unit of the point size in the **Point Size** field of the dialog box, see Figure 4.60.

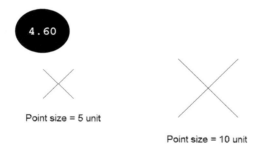

3. Click to select the required radio button: **Set Size Relative to Screen** or **Set Size in Absolute Units** in the **Point Style** dialog box for defining the point size.

4. Specify the point size in terms of percentage relative to the screen or absolute unit in the **Point Size** field of the **Point Style** dialog box, respectively.

5. Click on the **OK** button in the dialog box to accept the changes as well as to exit the dialog box.

Tutorial 1

Create the drawing shown in Figure 4.61. The dimensions shown in the figure are for your reference only.

Section 1: Starting AutoCAD

1. Double-click on the AutoCAD icon on your desktop to start AutoCAD. The initial screen of AutoCAD with the **Start** tab appears, see Figure 4.62.

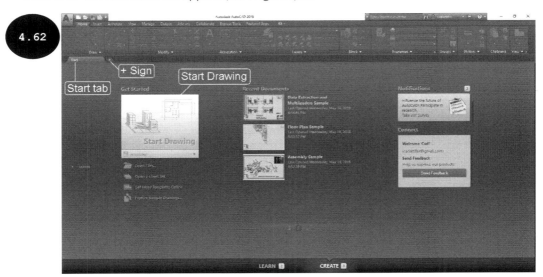

2. Click on the + sign next to the **Start** tab, see Figure 4.62. A new drawing file with the default drawing template invoked. Alternatively, click on **Start Drawing** in the **Get Started** section of the **Start** tab to start a new drawing file with default drawing template. You can also start a new drawing file by using the **New** tool of the **Quick Access Toolbar**, which is at the top left corner of AutoCAD.

Section 2: Selecting Workspace for Creating Drawing

1. Click on the **Workspace Switching** button in the Status Bar. A flyout appears, see Figure 4.63.

2. In this flyout, make sure that the **Drafting & Annotation** option is tick-marked to create drawing in the Drafting & Annotation workspace.

Section 3: Defining Drawing Limits

1. Define the drawing limits. You can define the drawing limits based on the overall dimensions of the drawing and keeping some extra space for placing dimension in the drawing area.

Section 4: Drawing Outer Loop of the Drawing

1. Click on the **Line** tool in the **Draw** panel of the **Home** tab. The **Line** tool gets activated, and you are prompted to specify the first point of the line. Alternatively, you can enter **L** in the Command Line window and then press ENTER to activate the **Line** tool.

   ```
   Specify first point:
   ```

2. Click on the **Ortho Mode** button of the Status Bar or press the F8 key to turn on the Ortho mode. Note that this is a toggle button.

3. Make sure that the Dynamic Input mode is activated. You can enable the Dynamic Input mode by clicking on the **Dynamic Input** button in the Status Bar.

4. Follow the command sequence given below for creating the drawing.

   ```
   Specify first point:
   ``` **0,0 (ENTER)**
   ```
   Specify next point or [Undo]:
   ``` *Move the cursor horizontally toward the right and then enter* **20** *in the Dynamic Input box* **(ENTER)**
   ```
   Specify next point or [Undo]:
   ``` *Move the cursor vertically upward and then enter* **5** **(ENTER)**
   ```
   Specify next point or [Undo]:
   ``` *Move the cursor horizontally toward the right and then enter* **50** **(ENTER)**
   ```
   Specify next point or [Undo]:
   ``` *Move the cursor vertically downward and then enter* **5** **(ENTER)**

```
Specify next point or [Close Undo]:
``` *Move the cursor horizontally toward the right and then enter* **20** (***ENTER***)

```
Specify next point or [Undo]:
``` *Move the cursor vertically upward and then enter* **20** (***ENTER***)

```
Specify next point or [Close Undo]:
``` *Move the cursor horizontally toward the left and then enter* **5** (***ENTER***)

```
Specify next point or [Undo]:
``` *Move the cursor vertically upward and then enter* **25** (***ENTER***)

```
Specify next point or [Close Undo]:
``` *Move the cursor horizontally toward the right and then enter* **5** (***ENTER***)

```
Specify next point or [Close Undo]:
``` *Move the cursor vertically upward and then enter* **20** (***ENTER***)

```
Specify next point or [Close Undo]:
``` *Move the cursor horizontally toward the left and then enter* **20** (***ENTER***)

```
Specify next point or [Close Undo]:
``` *Move the cursor vertically downward and then enter* **5** (***ENTER***)

```
Specify next point or [Close Undo]:
``` *Move the cursor horizontally toward the left and then enter* **50** (***ENTER***)

```
Specify next point or [Close Undo]:
``` *Move the cursor vertically upward and then enter* **5** (***ENTER***)

```
Specify next point or [Close Undo]:
``` *Move the cursor horizontally toward the left and then enter* **20** (***ENTER***)

```
Specify next point or [Close Undo]:
``` *Move the cursor vertically downward and then enter* **20** (***ENTER***)

```
Specify next point or [Close Undo]:
``` *Move the cursor horizontally toward the right and then enter* **5** (***ENTER***)

```
Specify next point or [Close Undo]:
``` *Move the cursor vertically downward and then enter* **25** (***ENTER***)

```
Specify next point or [Close Undo]:
``` *Move the cursor horizontally toward the left and then enter* **5** (***ENTER***)

```
Specify next point or [Close Undo]:
``` ***C*** *or* ***Close***   *(See Figure 4.64)*

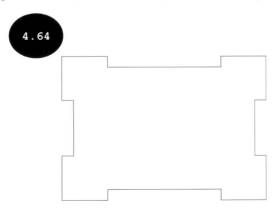

4.64

Section 5: Drawing Ellipse

1. Invoke the **Ellipse** flyout in the **Draw** panel and then click on the **Center** tool, see Figure 4.65. You are prompted to specify the center of the ellipse. Alternatively, you can enter **EL** in the Command Line window and then press ENTER. Next, enter **C** and then press ENTER to activate the tool.

   ```
   Specify center of ellipse:
   ```

2. Move the cursor to the midpoint of the left middle vertical line (P1) (see Figure 4.66) and then move the cursor to the midpoint of the upper middle horizontal line (P2), see Figure 4.66. Next, move the cursor vertically downward. A reference/tracking line appears.

3. Continue moving the cursor vertically downward and then click to specify the center point of the ellipse when the cursor snaps to the intersection of reference/tracking lines, which are passing through the points (P1 and P2), see Figure 4.66.

4. Move the cursor horizontally toward the right and then enter **25** in the Dynamic Input box. Next, press ENTER.

5. Move the cursor vertically upward to a small distance. Next, enter **15** in the Dynamic Input box and then press ENTER. An ellipse of major axis 50 and the minor axis 30 created in the drawing area, see Figure 4.67.

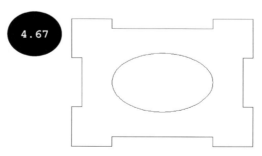

Section 6: Drawing Circles

In this section, you will draw the circles of the drawing with the help of construction lines.

1. Expand the **Draw** panel of the **Home** tab and then click on the **Construction Line** tool. You are prompted to specify the start point of the construction line (xline). Alternatively, you can enter **XLINE** in the Command Line window to activate the **Construction Line** tool.

    ```
    Specify a point or [Hor Ver Ang Bisect Offset]:
    ```

2. Click on the **Offset** option in the command prompt or enter **O** and then press ENTER. You are prompted to specify offset distance.

    ```
    Specify offset distance or [Through] <0.0000>:
    ```

3. Enter **10** as the offset distance value and then press ENTER. You are prompted to select a line object.

    ```
    Select a line object:
    ```

4. Click on the lower left vertical line (L1), see Figure 4.68. You are prompted to specify side to offset construction line (xline).

    ```
    Specify side to offset:
    ```

5. Click anywhere inside the outer closed loop of the drawing. A construction line (xline) at the offset distance of 10 units from the selected vertical line created. Also, you are prompted to choose a line object.

    ```
    Select a line object:
    ```

6. Click on the lower left horizontal line (L2), see Figure 4.68. You are prompted to specify side to offset construction line (xline).

    ```
    Specify side to offset:
    ```

7. Click anywhere inside the outer closed loop of the drawing. A construction line (xline) at the offset distance of 10 units from the selected horizontal line created, see Figure 4.69. Also, you are prompted to choose a line object.

    ```
    Select a line object:
    ```

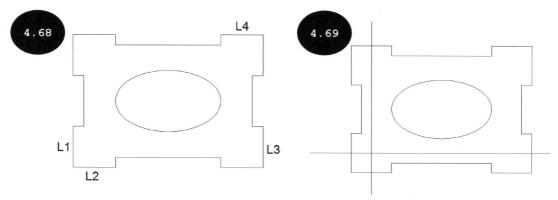

8. Similarly, select the lower right vertical line (L3) and the upper right horizontal line (L4) for creating other construction lines, refer to Figure 4.68. Figure 4.70 shows the drawing after creating all the construction lines.

9. Press ENTER or right-click to exit from the creation of construction lines.

   After creating the construction lines (xlines), you can use the intersection of the construction lines for specifying the center point of the circles.

10. Enter **C** in the Command Line window and then press ENTER to activate the **Center, Radius** tool. You can also click on the **Center, Radius** tool in the **Draw** panel. You are prompted to specify the center point of the circle.

    ```
    Specify center point for circle or [3P 2P Ttr (tan tan radius)]:
    ```

11. Move the cursor over the lower left intersection of the construction lines (P1), see Figure 4.70, and then click to specify the center point of the circle when the cursor snaps to the intersection (P1). You are prompted to specify the radius of the circle.

    ```
    Specify radius of circle or [Diameter] <0.0000>:
    ```

12. Enter **5** as the radius value of the circle and then press ENTER. A circle of radius 5 units created in the drawing area, see Figure 4.71.

13. Similarly, draw the other three circles of radius 5 units at the intersections (P2, P3, and P4) of construction lines, see Figure 4.72.

14. After drawing all the circles, you can delete the construction lines. However, it recommended that you create a layer and move all the construction lines to it. Next, hide the layer. Figure 4.73 shows the final drawing after hiding the construction lines.

Tip: To move a set of entities to a layer, select the entities to be moved. Next, invoke the **Layer** drop-down list in the **Layers** panel of the **Home** tab and then click on the layer in the drop-down list to which you want to move the selected set of entities.

Section 7: Saving the Drawing
After creating the drawing, you need to save it.

1. Click on the **Save** tool in the **Quick Access Toolbar**. The **Save Drawing As** dialog box appears.

2. Browse to the *AutoCAD* folder and then create a folder with the name *Chapter 4* inside the *AutoCAD* folder.

3. Enter **Tutorial 1** in the **File name** field of the dialog box and then click on the **Save** button. The drawing saved with the name Tutorial 1 in the *Chapter 4* folder.

Tutorial 2
Draw the drawing shown in Figure 4.74. The dimensions shown in the figure are for your reference only.

Section 1: Starting AutoCAD
1. Start AutoCAD and click on the **New** tool in the **Quick Access Toolbar**, which is at the top left corner of AutoCAD. The **Select template** dialog box appears.

2. In the **Select template** dialog box, click on the ***acad.dwt*** template and then click on the **Open** button. A new drawing file with the ***acad.dwt*** template gets invoked.

Section 2: Defining Drawing Limits
1. Define the drawing limits. You can define the drawing limits based on the overall dimensions of the drawing and keeping some extra space for placing dimension in the drawing area.

Section 3: Creating Drawing
1. Click on the **Rectangle** tool in the **Draw** panel of the **Home** tab. The **Rectangle** tool gets activated, and you are prompted to specify the first corner of the rectangle. Alternatively, you

can enter **REC** in the Command Line window and then press ENTER to activate the **Rectangle** tool.

```
Specify first corner point or [Chamfer Elevation Fillet Thickness Width]:
```

2. Click in the drawing area to specify the first corner of the rectangle. You are prompted to specify the other corner of the rectangle.

```
Specify other corner point or [Area Dimensions Rotation]:
```

You need to create a rectangle by specifying dimensions (length 60 units and width 10 units).

3. Click on the **Dimensions** option in the command prompt. You are prompted to specify the length of the rectangle. Alternatively, you can enter **D** and then press ENTER.

```
Specify length for rectangles <current>:
```

4. Enter **60** as the length of the rectangle and then press ENTER. You are prompted to specify the width of the rectangle.

```
Specify width for rectangles <current>:
```

5. Enter **10** as the width of the rectangle and then press ENTER. You are prompted to specify another corner of the rectangle.

```
Specify other corner point or [Area Dimensions Rotation]:
```

6. Click to specify the corner point of the rectangle in the drawing area. A rectangle of length 60 units and width 10 units is created in the drawing area, see Figure 4.75.

Now, you need to create the line entities of the drawing.

7. Click on the **Line** tool in the **Draw** panel. You are prompted to specify the first point of the line. Alternatively, you can enter **L** in the Command Line window and then press ENTER.

```
Specify first point:
```

8. Move the cursor over the upper left corner of the rectangle and then click to specify the start point of the line when the cursor snaps to it. You are prompted to specify the next point of the line.

```
Specify next point or [Undo]:
```

9. Move the cursor vertically upward and then enter **35** as the length of the line. Next, press ENTER. A line of length 35 units created, see Figure 4.76. Make sure that the Ortho mode and the Dynamic Input mode are activated.

10. Right-click and then select the **Enter** option from the shortcut menu appeared to exit from the **Line** tool.

11. Similarly, draw another vertical line of the same length starting from the upper right corner of the rectangle, see Figure 4.77.

After creating the line entities, you need to create the arc of radius 30 units.

12. Invoke the **Arc** flyout and then click on the **Start, End, Radius** tool. You are prompted to specify the start point of the arc.

    ```
    Specify start point of arc or [Center]:
    ```

13. Move the cursor over the endpoint of the right vertical line and then click to specify the start point of the arc when the cursor snaps to it. You are prompted to specify the endpoint of the arc.

    ```
    Specify end point of arc:
    ```

14. Move the cursor over the endpoint of the left vertical line and then click to specify the endpoint of the arc when the cursor snaps to it. You are prompted to specify the radius of the arc.

    ```
    Specify radius of arc:
    ```

15. Move the cursor vertically upward and then enter **30** as the radius of the arc. Next, press ENTER. An arc of radius 30 units created, see Figure 4.78.

After creating the arc, you need to create a circle such that it is concentric to the arc drawn.

16. Invoke the **Center, Radius** tool in the **Draw** panel. The **Center, Radius** tool gets activated, and you are prompted to specify the center point of the circle. Alternatively, you can enter **C** in the Command Line window and then press ENTER.

    ```
    Specify center point for circle or [3P 2P Ttr (tan tan radius)]:
    ```

17. Move the cursor over the circumference of the previously drawn arc and then move the cursor toward its center point. Next, click to specify the center point of the circle when the cursor snaps to the center point of the arc. You are prompted to specify the radius of the circle.

    ```
    Specify radius of circle or [Diameter]:
    ```

18. Enter **12** as the radius of the circle and then press ENTER. A circle of radius 12 units created, see Figure 4.79.

Now, you need to draw two inner vertical lines of the drawing with the help of construction lines (xlines).

19. Expand the **Draw** panel of the **Home** tab and then click on the **Construction Line** tool. You are prompted to specify the start point of the construction line (xline). Alternatively, you can enter XLINE in the Command Line window to invoke the tool.

    ```
    Specify a point or [Hor Ver Ang Bisect Offset]:
    ```

20. Click on the **Offset** option of the command prompt or enter **O** and then press ENTER. You are prompted to specify the offset distance.

    ```
    Specify offset distance or [Through] <0.0000>:
    ```

21. Enter **25** as the offset distance and then press ENTER. You are prompted to select a line object.

    ```
    Select a line object:
    ```

22. Click on the left vertical line. You are prompted to specify side to offset the construction line.

    ```
    Specify side to offset:
    ```

23. Click anywhere on the right side of the selected line. A construction line (xline) at an offset distance of 25 units from the left vertical line created, see Figure 4.80. Also, you are prompted to select a line object.

    ```
    Select a line object:
    ```

24. Click on the right vertical line. You are prompted to specify side to offset the construction line.

    ```
    Specify side to offset:
    ```

25. Click anywhere on the left side of the selected line. A construction line (xline) at the offset distance of 25 units from the right vertical line created, see Figure 4.81. Next, right-click to exit the tool.

After creating the construction lines (xlines), you can use them for creating vertical lines of the drawing.

26. Invoke the **Line** tool and then create a vertical line whose start point is at the intersection of P1 and endpoint is at the intersection of P2, refer to Figure 4.81.

27. Similarly, create another vertical line whose start point is at the intersection of P3 and endpoint is at the intersection of P4, refer to Figure 4.81.

28. After creating all the drawing entities, you can delete the construction lines. However, it recommended that you create a layer and name it as Construction and then move the construction lines to the Construction layer. Next, hide the Construction layer. Figure 4.82 shows the final drawing after hiding the construction lines.

Section 4: Saving the Drawing

After creating the drawing, you need to save it.

1. Click on the **Save** tool in the **Quick Access Toolbar**. The **Save Drawing As** dialog box appears.

2. Browse to the *Chapter 4* inside the *AutoCAD* folder. If the *Chapter 4* not created in the Tutorial 1 of this chapter, then you need first to create this folder.

3. Enter **Tutorial 2** in the **File name** field of the dialog box and then click on the **Save** button. The drawing saved with the name Tutorial 2 in the *Chapter 4* folder.

Tutorial 3

Draw the drawing shown in Figure 4.83. You need to create the drawing by using polylines and donut. The dimensions shown in the figure are for your reference only.

Section 1: Starting AutoCAD

1. Start a new drawing file in AutoCAD. Make sure that the Drafting & Annotation workspace is activated.

2. Define the drawing limits.

Section 2: Creating Drawing

1. Click on the **Polyline** tool in the **Draw** panel. You are prompted to specify the start point of the polyline. Alternatively, you can enter **PL** in the Command Line window.

   ```
   Specify start point:
   ```

2. Click in the drawing area to specify the start point of the polyline. You are prompted to specify the next point of the polyline.

   ```
   Specify next point or [Arc Halfwidth Length Undo Width]:
   ```

3. Click on the **Width** option in the command prompt or enter **W** and then press ENTER. You are prompted to specify the starting width of the polyline.

   ```
   Specify starting width <0.0000>:
   ```

4. Enter **20** as the starting width of the polyline and then press ENTER. You are prompted to specify the end width of the polyline.

   ```
   Specify ending width <20.0000>:
   ```

5. Enter **20** as the end width of the polyline and then press ENTER. You are prompted to specify the next point of the polyline.

   ```
   Specify next point or [Arc Halfwidth Length Undo Width]:
   ```

6. Make sure that the Ortho mode is activated. Next, move the cursor vertically upward a distance in the drawing area.

7. Enter **300** as the length of the polyline and then press ENTER. You are prompted to specify the next point of the polyline.

   ```
   Specify next point or [Arc Halfwidth Length Undo Width]:
   ```

   Now, you need to create a polyarc having starting width 20 units and end width 0.

8. Click on the **Arc** option in the command prompt or enter **A** in the Command Line window and then press ENTER. You are prompted to specify the end point of the arc.

   ```
   Specify endpoint of arc or [Angle CEnter Close Direction Halfwidth
   Line Radius Second pt Undo Width]:
   ```

9. Click on the **Width** option in the command prompt or enter **W** in the Command Line window and then press ENTER. You are prompted to specify the starting width of the arc.

   ```
   Specify starting width <20.0000>:
   ```

10. Enter **20** as the starting width of the arc and then press ENTER. You are prompted to specify the end width of the arc.

    ```
    Specify ending width <20.0000>:
    ```

11. Enter **0** (Zero) as the end width of the polyline and then press ENTER. You are prompted to specify the endpoint of the arc.

    ```
    Specify endpoint of arc or [Angle CEnter Close Direction Halfwidth
    Line Radius Second pt Undo Width]:
    ```

12. Move the cursor horizontally toward the right and then enter **300**. Next, press ENTER. A polyarc created, see Figure 4.84. Also, you are prompted to specify the endpoint of the arc.

    ```
    Specify endpoint of arc or [Angle CEnter Close Direction Halfwidth
    Line Radius Second pt Undo Width]:
    ```

13. Enter **L** and then press ENTER to invoke the Line mode of the polyline. You are prompted to specify the next point of the line.

    ```
    Specify next point or [Arc Close Halfwidth Length Undo Width]:
    ```

14. Move the cursor vertically downward and then enter **300** as the length of the line. Next, press ENTER. You are prompted to specify the next point of the line.

    ```
    Specify next point or [Arc Close Halfwidth Length Undo Width]:
    ```

15. Enter **C** in the Command Line window and then press ENTER or click on the **Close** option in the command prompt to close the polyline, see Figure 4.85.

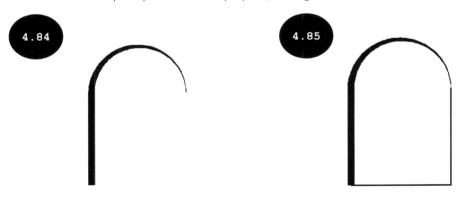

Section 3: Creating Donut

1. Expand the **Draw** panel of the **Home** tab and then click on the **Donut** tool. You are prompted to specify the inside diameter of the donut. Alternatively, enter **DO** in the Command Line window and then press ENTER.

   ```
   Specify inside diameter of donut <0.0000>:
   ```

2. Enter **90** as the inside diameter of the donut and then press ENTER. You are prompted to specify the outside diameter of the donut.

   ```
   Specify outside diameter of donut <0.0000>:
   ```

3. Enter **100** as the outside diameter of the donut and then press ENTER. A donut of the specified parameter attached to the cursor. Also, you are prompted to specify the center point of the donut.

   ```
   Specify center of donut or <exit>:
   ```

4. Make sure that Object Snap mode is activated.

5. Move the cursor over the circumference of the arc and then move the cursor toward the center point of the arc. Next, click to specify the center point of the donut when the cursor snaps to the center point of the arc. A donut created in the drawing area, see Figure 4.86.

6. Press ENTER or right-click to exit from the **Donut** tool. Figure 4.86 shows the final drawing.

Section 4: Saving the Drawing

After creating the drawing, you need to save it.

1. Click on the **Save** tool in the **Quick Access Toolbar**. The **Save Drawing As** dialog box appears.

2. Browse to the *Chapter 4* inside the *AutoCAD* folder.

3. Enter **Tutorial 3** in the **File name** field of the dialog box and then click on the **Save** button. The drawing saved with the name Tutorial 3 in the *Chapter 4* folder.

Hands-on Test Drive 1

Draw the drawing shown in Figure 4.87. The dimensions shown in the figure are for your reference only. You will learn about applying dimensions in later chapters.

Hands-on Test Drive 2

Draw the drawing shown in Figure 4.88. The dimensions shown in the figure are for your reference only.

Summary

In this chapter, you have learned how to create rectangles, polygons, polylines, ellipses, elliptical arcs, splines, donuts, construction lines, ray lines, and points. You have also learned how to define point style/size.

Questions

- The _____ tool is used to draw rectangles by using different methods.

- The value entered inside the _____ symbol in the command prompt is the last defined or default value of the command.

- AutoCAD allow you to draw polygons of equal sides in the range between _____ to _____ .

- In AutoCAD, you can draw two type of polygon: _____ and _____ .

- You can draw the polyline by using the _____ tool.

- A ellipse is drawn by defining its _____ and _____ axes.

- You can draw an elliptical arc by using the _____ tool.

- In AutoCAD, you can draw splines by using the _____ and _____ tools.

- The _____ tool is used to create a spline such that it passes through a set of fit points that influence the shape of the spline.

- A construction line is also known as _____ .

- A _____ line extended to infinite length in both the directions and passes through two specified points.

- You can draw donuts by using the _____ tool.

CHAPTER 5

Modifying and Editing Drawings - I

In this chapter, you will learn the following:

- Working with Object Selection Methods
- Invoking a Selection Method within a Command
- Trimming Drawing Entities
- Extending Drawing Entities
- Working with the Array
- Mirroring Drawing Entities
- Filleting Drawing Entities
- Chamfering Drawing Entities
- Offsetting Drawing Entities
- Moving Drawing Objects
- Copying Drawing Objects
- Rotating Drawing Objects
- Scaling Drawing Objects
- Stretching Drawing Objects
- Lengthening Drawing Objects

Performing editing and modifying operations in a drawing is imperative to complete the drawing as per the requirement. In AutoCAD, you can perform various editing operations such as trimming unwanted entities, extending entities, mirroring, creating array, moving, and rotating entities. The tools to perform various editing and modifying operations are in the **Modify** panel of the **Home** tab, see Figure 5.1.

Before you learn about various editing and modifying operations, it is important to understand about different object selection methods available in AutoCAD.

Working with Object Selection Methods

In AutoCAD, you can select drawing objects individually one by one by clicking the left mouse button. However, selecting objects individually one by one is time-consuming if you have to perform an editing operation on multiple objects of a drawing. For example, moving a group of objects from one location to another. AutoCAD is provided with various selection methods such as Window selection, Cross Window selection, Add, Crossing Polygon, Fence, and All. Out of all these, the Window selection and Cross Window selection methods are the most widely used methods. The different selection methods are discussed next.

Window Selection Method

The Window selection method is used for selecting a group of objects together by creating a rectangular window from left (P1) to the right (P2) around the objects to be selected, see Figure 5.2. Note that only the objects that are completely enclosed within the rectangular window will be selected and the objects that lie partially inside the rectangular window will not be selected. Also, the boundary of the rectangular window appears as solid outlines.

Cross Window Selection Method

The Cross Window selection method is used for selecting a group of objects together by creating a rectangular cross window from the right (P1) to left (P2) around the objects to be selected, see Figure 5.3. Note that all objects that are completely enclosed as well as the objects that touch the rectangular cross window will be selected. Means, the objects that lie partially inside the rectangular cross window will also be selected. Also, the boundary of the rectangular cross window appears as dashed outlines.

Invoking a Selection Method within a Command

In AutoCAD, you may have noticed that on invoking some of the tools/commands, you are prompted to select objects. When you are prompted to select objects, you can invoke different selection methods, as per your requirement. For example, on invoking the **Move** tool, you are prompted to select objects to be moved. Now, you can select objects by using different selection methods which are discussed next.

```
Tool/Command: M or MOVE (ENTER)
Select objects:
```

Window Selection Method

To invoke the Window selection method, when you are prompted to select objects in the command prompt, enter **W** in the Command Line window and then press ENTER. The method of selecting objects by using the Window selection method is discussed earlier.

For example,
```
    Tool/Command: M or MOVE (ENTER)
    Select objects: W (ENTER)
```

> **Note:** The M is the short form of the **MOVE** command. This command is used to move drawing objects from one location to another. You will learn more about the **MOVE** command later in this chapter.

Cross Window Selection Method

To invoke the Cross Window selection method, when you are prompted to select objects in the command prompt, enter **C** in the Command Line window and then press ENTER. The method of selecting objects by using the Cross Window selection method is discussed earlier.

```
Tool/Command: M or MOVE (ENTER)
Select objects: C (ENTER)
Specify first corner:
Specify opposite corner:
```

All Selection Method

The All selection method is used to select all drawing objects except the objects that assigned to the frozen or locked layers. To invoke the All selection method, enter **ALL** in the Command Line window and then press ENTER when you are prompted to select objects in the command prompt.

For example,
```
Tool/Command: M or MOVE (ENTER)
Select objects: ALL (ENTER)
```

Cross Polygon Selection Method

The Cross Polygon selection method is used to select a group of objects by drawing a cross polygon boundary around the objects to be selected, see Figure 5.4. Note that all the objects that are completely enclosed as well as the objects that touch the cross polygon boundary will be selected. Also, the cross polygon boundary appears as dashed outline.

To invoke this selection method, enter **CP** in the Command Line window and then press ENTER when you are prompted to select objects in the command prompt. After invoking the Cross Polygon selection method, click in the drawing area to specify the first polygon point (P1) followed by the endpoints of the polygon lines, as required, see Figure 5.4. After drawing a cross polygon boundary around the objects to be selected, press ENTER to exit. All the objects that are completely enclosed or touch the cross polygon boundary are selected.

Window Polygon Selection Method

The Window Polygon selection method is used to select a group of objects by drawing a polygon boundary around the objects to be selected, see Figure 5.5. Note that, only the objects that are completely enclosed within the polygon boundary will be selected. Also, the polygon boundary appears as a solid outline.

To invoke this selection method, enter **WP** in the Command Line window and then press ENTER when you are prompted to select objects in the command prompt. Next, you can click in the drawing area to specify the first polygon point (P1) followed by the endpoints of the polygon lines, as required, see Figure 5.5. After drawing a polygon boundary around the objects to be selected, press ENTER to exit. All the objects that completely enclosed within the polygon boundary are selected.

Fence Selection Method

The Fence selection method is used to select group of objects by drawing a series of continuous lines over the objects to be selected, see Figure 5.6. Note that the objects which come across the lines drawn will be selected.

To invoke this selection method, enter **F** in the Command Line window and then press ENTER when you are prompted to select objects in the command prompt. Next, you can click in the drawing area to specify the first point (P1) of the fence line followed by the continuous endpoints one after another, as required, see Figure 5.6. After drawing a series of continuous lines over the objects to be selected, press ENTER to exit. All the objects which come across the fence line are selected.

Last Selection Method

The Last selection method is used to select the last drawn object in the drawing. To invoke this selection method, enter **L** in the Command Line window and then press ENTER when you are prompted to select objects in the command prompt. The last drawn object gets selected.

Trimming Drawing Entities

In AutoCAD, you can trim the unwanted drawing entities of a drawing up to their nearest intersection or the intersection with cutting edges/boundaries. You can trim the entities by using the **Trim** tool of the **Modify** panel, see Figure 5.7. You can also invoke the **Trim** tool for trimming entities by entering TR in the Command Line window and then pressing ENTER. The procedure to trim the unwanted entities of a drawing is discussed next.

5.7

Procedure for Trimming Entities

1. Click on the **Trim** tool in the **Modify** panel, see Figure 5.7. You are prompted to select cutting edges/boundaries. Alternatively, enter TR in the Command Line window and then press ENTER to invoke the **Trim** tool.

   ```
   Select cutting edges ...
   Select objects or <select all>:
   ```

2. Click on the objects/entities to be used as the cutting edges/boundaries to trim entities, see Figure 5.8. You can select rectangles, lines, circles, polylines, or construction lines as the cutting edges to trim entities. Next, press ENTER. You are prompted to select objects to be trimmed.

   ```
   Select object to trim or shift-select to extend or
   [Fence Crossing Project Edge eRase Undo]:
   ```

   > **Note:** Instead of selecting the objects/entities as the cutting edges/boundaries, you can directly select the entities to be trimmed and skip the step 2 mentioned above. For doing so, press the ENTER key when you are prompted to select the cutting edges. Next, click on the entity to be trimmed. The portion of the selected entity is trimmed up to its nearest intersection.

3. Click on the entity to be trimmed, see Figure 5.8. The portion of the selected entity where you clicked the left mouse button trimmed up to the intersection with the cutting edges, see Figure 5.9. Also, you are prompted to select another object to be trimmed.

   ```
   Select object to trim or shift-select to extend or
   [Fence Crossing Project Edge eRase Undo]:
   ```

AutoCAD 2019: A Power Guide > 221

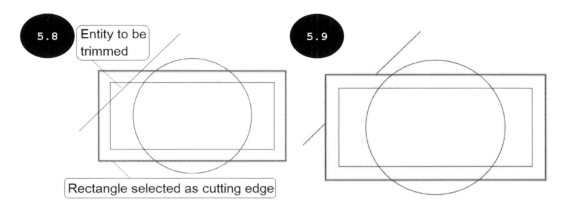

Tip: You can select the objects to be trimmed by clicking the left mouse button one by one or by using a selection method such as Window, Cross Window, or Fence, as discussed earlier.

4. Similarly, click on the other entities to be trimmed one by one, see Figure 5.10. The portion of the selected entities are trimmed up to the intersection with the cutting edges, see Figure 5.11.

5. Once you have trimmed all the unwanted entities of the drawing, press ENTER to exit.

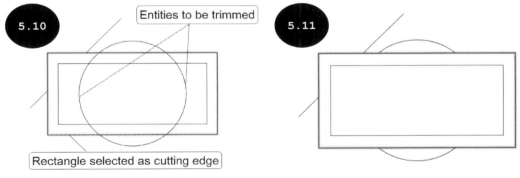

Note: You can also extend the entities up to the nearest intersection or at the intersection with cutting edges/boundaries by using the **Trim** tool. To extend the entities by using the **Trim** tool, press and hold the SHIFT key and then click on the entity to be extended. The selected entity, from the side you have chosen, is extended up to the intersection with cutting edges.

Extending Drawing Entities

You can extend the entities up to their nearest intersection or the intersection with boundaries by using the **Extend** tool of the **Trim** flyout in the **Modify** panel, see Figure 5.12. You can also invoke the **Extend** tool by entering **EX** in the Command Line window and then pressing ENTER. The procedure to extend drawing entities by using the **Extend** tool is discussed next.

Procedure for Extending Entities

1. Click on the down arrow next to the **Trim** tool in the **Modify** panel. A flyout appears, see Figure 5.12. In this flyout, click on the **Extend** tool. You are prompted to select boundary edges. Alternatively, enter **EX** in the Command Line window and then press ENTER to invoke the **Extend** tool.

   ```
   Select boundary edges ...
   Select objects or <select all>:
   ```

2. Click on the objects to be used as the boundary edges for extending entities, see Figure 5.13. You can select rectangles, lines, circles, polylines, or construction lines as the boundary edges. Next, press ENTER. You are prompted to select objects to be extended.

   ```
   Select object to extend or shift-select to trim or
   [Fence Crossing Project Edge Undo]:
   ```

   Note: If you want to extend entities up to their nearest intersection, skip the step 2 of selecting boundary edges as discussed above and then press ENTER. Next, directly click on the entity to be extended. The selected entity gets extended up to their nearest intersection.

3. Click on the entity to be extended, see Figure 5.13. The portion of the selected entity is extended up to the intersection with the boundary edges, see Figure 5.14. Also, you are prompted to select another object to be extended.

   ```
   Select object to extend or shift-select to trim or
   [Fence Crossing Project Edge Undo]:
   ```

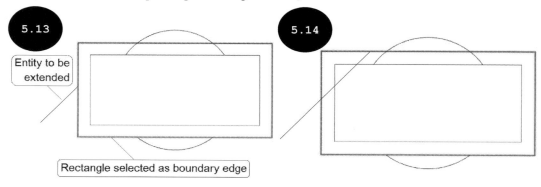

4. Similarly, click on the entities to be extended one by one, see Figure 5.15. The portion of the selected entities gets extended up to the intersection with the boundary edges, see Figure 5.16.

Tip: You can select the entities to be extended by clicking the left mouse button or by using a selection method such as Window, Cross Window, or Fence.

5. Once you have extended the required entities of a drawing, press ENTER or right-click to exit the **Extend** tool.

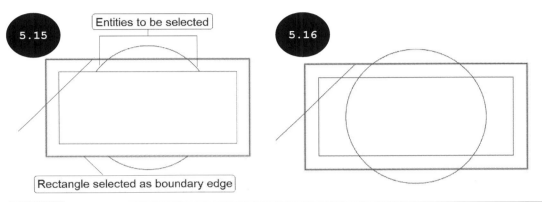

Note: You can also trim entities up to the nearest intersection or at the intersection of boundaries by using the **Extend** tool. To trim the entities by using the **Extend** tool, press and hold the SHIFT key and then click on the entity to be trimmed. The selected entity, from the side you have chosen, is trimmed up to the intersection.

Working with the Array

The Array is a very powerful feature of AutoCAD for creating multiple instances/duplicate copies of an existing geometry in rectangular fashion, circular fashion, or along a path, see Figures 5.17 through 5.19.

Rectangular array   Polar/Circular array

Path array

In AutoCAD, you can create rectangular array, polar/circular array, and path array by using the **Rectangular Array**, **Polar Array**, and **Path Array** tools of the **Array** flyout in the **Modify** panel, see Figure 5.20. The procedures to create various types of arrays are discussed next.

Procedure for Creating a Rectangular Array

1. Invoke the **Array** flyout in the **Modify** panel (see Figure 5.20) and then click on the **Rectangle Array** tool. You are prompted to select objects. Alternatively, enter **AR** in the Command Line window and then press ENTER to invoke the tool.

    ```
    Select objects:
    ```

2. Click on the object/objects in the drawing area, see Figure 5.21. Next, press ENTER or right-click. The preview of the rectangular array appears in the drawing area with default parameters, see Figure 5.22. Also, the **Array Creation** tab appears in the **Ribbon** which provides different options for controlling the array parameters, see Figure 5.23. Also, you are prompted to select array grips to edit array.

    ```
    Select grip to edit array or [ASsociative Base point COUnt Spacing
    COLumns Rows Levels eXit] <eXit>:
    ```

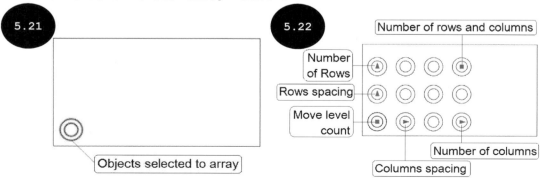

Tip: You can select the objects to be array by clicking the left mouse button or by using a selection method such as Window, Cross Window, or Fence, as discussed earlier.

Note: If you have invoked the array tool by entering AR in Command Line window then after selecting the objects to be array, you are prompted to select the type of array "`Enter array type [Rectangular PAth POlar] <Polar>:`". Click on the **Rectangular** option in the command prompt or enter **R** and then press ENTER to create the rectangular array.

3. Specify the columns count, rows count, column spacing, and row spacing for the rectangular array in the respective fields of the **Columns** and **Rows** panel in the **Array Creation** tab, see Figure 5.23.

Tip: You can also use the grips that appear in the preview of the rectangular array (refer to Figure 5.22) for specifying array parameters such as columns count, rows count, and column spacing. For example, to increase or decrease the number of array columns, click on the **Number of columns** grip (refer to Figure 5.22) and then move the cursor toward the right or left to change the array columns count and then click to specify the placement point.

4. After editing the array parameters, press ENTER to exit. The rectangular array created in the drawing area, see Figure 5.24.

Procedure for Creating a Polar/Circular Array

1. Invoke the **Array** flyout and then click on the **Polar Array** tool, see Figure 5.25. You are prompted to select objects. Alternatively, enter **AR** in the Command Line window and then press ENTER.

```
Select objects:
```

2. Select the objects in the drawing area. The selected objects get highlighted, see Figure 5.26. You can select one or more than one object to be array by clicking the left mouse button.

3. After selecting the objects, press ENTER or right-click. You are also prompted to specify the center point of the array.

    ```
    Specify center point of array or [Base point Axis of rotation]:
    ```

    Note: If you have invoked the array tool by entering **AR** in Command Line window then after selecting the objects to be array, you are prompted to select the type of array "`Enter array type [Rectangular PAth POlar] <Polar>:`". Click on the **POlar** option in the command prompt or enter **PO** in the Command Line window and then press ENTER to create the polar array.

4. Click to specify the center point of the array. The preview of circular/polar array appears in the drawing area with default parameters, see Figure 5.27. Also, the **Array Creation** tab appears in the **Ribbon** which provides different options for controlling the array parameters. Also, you are prompted to select array grips to edit array.

    ```
    Select grip to edit array or [ASsociative Base point Items Angle
    between Fill angle ROWs Levels ROTate items eXit] <eXit>:
    ```

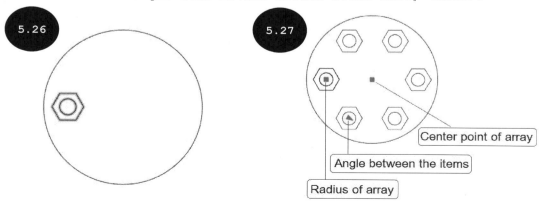

5. Specify the item count and angle between items for the circular array in the respective fields available in the **Items** panel of the **Array Creation** tab. Alternatively, use the grips, which appear in the preview of the array (refer to Figure 5.27) for specifying array parameters.

6. After editing the array parameters, press ENTER to exit. The circular/polar array created in the drawing area, see Figure 5.28.

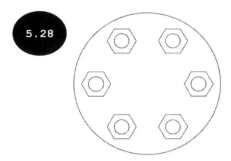

Procedure for Creating a Path Array

1. Invoke the **Array** flyout and then click on the **Path Array** tool. You are prompted to select objects. Alternatively, enter **AR** in the Command Line window and then press ENTER.

   ```
   Select objects:
   ```

2. Select the objects in the drawing area. The selected objects get highlighted, see Figure 5.29. For selecting multiple objects, you can use Window or Cross Window selection method. After selecting the objects to be array, press ENTER or right-click. You are also prompted to select path curve.

   ```
   Select path curve:
   ```

3. Click on the path curve along which you want to pattern the selected objects, see Figure 5.29. The preview of path array appears in the drawing area with default parameters, see Figure 5.30. Also, the **Array Creation** tab appears in the **Ribbon** which provides different options for controlling the array parameters. You are also prompted to select grips to edit array.

   ```
   Select grip to edit array or [ASsociative Method Base point
   Tangent direction Items Rows Levels Align items Z direction eXit]
   <eXit>:
   ```

4. Specify the item spacing for the path array in the respective field available in the **Items** panel of the **Array Creation** tab. Alternatively, use the grips which appear in the preview of path array for specifying the spacing between the items.

5. After editing the array parameters, press ENTER. The path array created in the drawing area, see Figure 5.31.

Mirroring Drawing Entities

In AutoCAD, you can create a mirror image of the drawing entities/objects about a mirroring line by using the **Mirror** tool of the **Modify** panel, see Figure 5.32. The procedure to mirror drawing objects is discussed next.

Procedure for Mirroring Entities

1. Click on the **Mirror** tool in the **Modify** panel. You are prompted to select objects. Alternatively, enter **MI** in the Command Line window and then press ENTER.

   ```
   Select objects:
   ```

2. Select objects to be mirrored and then press ENTER. You are prompted to select the first point of the mirror line. For selecting multiple objects, you can use the Window or Cross Window selection method.

   ```
   Specify first point of mirror line:
   ```

3. Click to specify the first point of the mirror line. You are prompted to select the second point of the mirror line.

   ```
   Specify first point of mirror line: Specify second point of mirror
   line:
   ```

4. Click to specify the second point of the mirror line. You are prompted to define whether to erase the source/original objects. By default, the **No** option is selected.

   ```
   Erase source objects? [Yes No] <N>:
   ```

> **Note:** The mirroring line is an imaginary line which can define by specifying two points in the drawing area.

5. Press ENTER to accept the default option (**No**) for keeping the source/original objects in the resultant drawing, see Figure 5.33 (a). The mirror image created in the drawing area.

> **Note:** If you do not want to keep the source/original objects in the resultant drawing, then enter Y in the Command Line window and then press ENTER, see Figure 5.33 (b).

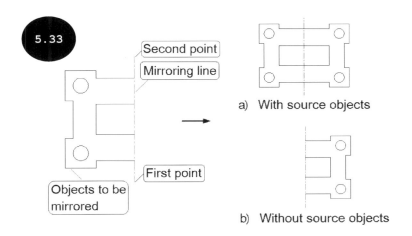

Filleting Drawing Entities

A fillet is a curved edge which is used to remove or eliminate sharp edges of the model that can cause injury while handling. Also, fillet distributes the stress of the model, which makes the model more durable and capable of withstanding larger loads. Figure 5.34 shows a drawing with fillets on its corners.

230 Chapter 5 > Modifying and Editing Drawings - I

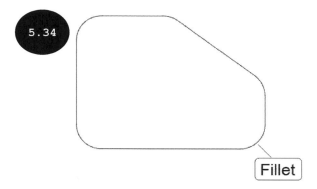

In AutoCAD, you can create fillet between two intersecting or non-intersecting entities/objects by using the **Fillet** tool of the **Modify** panel, see Figure 5.35. The procedure to create fillet is discussed next.

Procedure for Creating a Fillet

1. Click on the **Fillet** tool in the **Modify** panel, see Figure 5.35. You are prompted to select the first object. Alternatively, enter **F** in the Command Line window and then press ENTER to invoke the **Fillet** tool.

   ```
   Select first object or [Undo Polyline Radius Trim Multiple]:
   ```

   Before you select the first object for the fillet, it is recommended to specify the radius of the fillet. If you do not specify the fillet radius, then the default fillet radius will be applied.

2. Click on the **Radius** option in the command prompt or enter **R** in the Command Line window and then press ENTER. You are prompted to specify fillet radius.

   ```
   Specify fillet radius <current>:
   ```

3. Enter the radius value and then press ENTER. You are prompted to select the first object.

   ```
   Select first object or [Undo Polyline Radius Trim Multiple]:
   ```

4. Click on the first object of the fillet, see Figure 5.36. You are prompted to select the second object.

   ```
   Select second object or shift-select to apply corner or [Radius]:
   ```

5. Click on the second object of the fillet, see Figure 5.36. The fillet of the specified radius is created, see Figure 5.37.

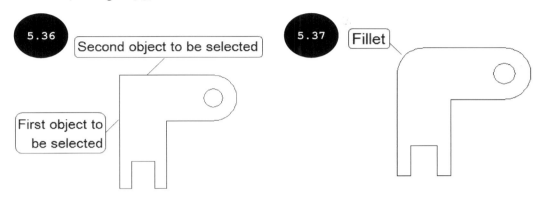

You can also fillet parallel or non-parallel entities, see Figures 5.38 and 5.39.

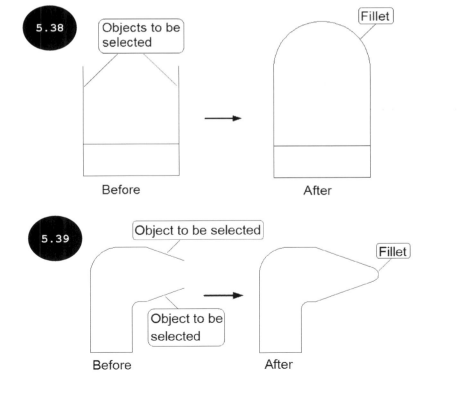

Note: You can fillet all the corners of a polyline object at a time, see Figure 5.40. To fillet all corners of a polyline object, click on the **Polyline** option in the command prompt when you are prompted to select the first object "`Select first object or [Undo Polyline Radius Trim Multiple]:`". Alternatively, enter **P** in the Command Line window and then press ENTER. Next, select the polyline object whose all corners are to fillet.

By default, when you create a fillet at a corner, an arc is created by trimming the selected objects, see Figure 5.41 (a). It is because the trim mode set to **Trim**. To set the trim mode to **No Trim**, click on the **Trim** option in the command prompt when you are prompted to select first object "`Select first object or [Undo Polyline Radius Trim Multiple]:`". Next, enter **N** in the Command Line window and then press ENTER. Now, on creating a fillet at a corner, an arc created without trimming the selected objects, see Figure 5.41 (b).

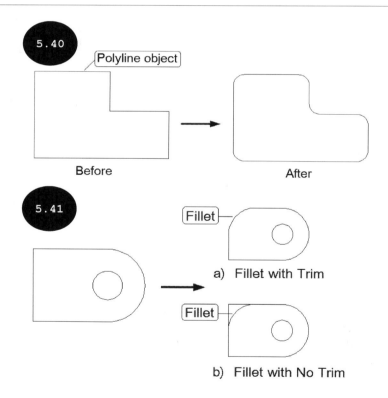

Chamfering Drawing Entities

A chamfer is a bevel edge that is non-perpendicular to its adjacent edges. In AutoCAD, you can create chamfer by using the **Chamfer** tool of the **Modify** panel, see Figure 5.42. Figure 5.43 shows a drawing with a chamfer at its upper left corner.

In AutoCAD, you can create chamfer by using two methods: **Distance distance** method and **Angle distance** method. The procedures to create chamfer by using these methods are discussed next.

Procedure for Creating a Chamfer by Distance distance Method

1. Click on the down arrow next to the **Fillet** tool in the **Modify** panel. A flyout appears. In this flyout, click on the **Chamfer** tool, see Figure 5.42. Alternatively, enter **CHA** in the Command Line window and then press ENTER. You are prompted to select the first line for creating a chamfer.

   ```
   Select first line or [Undo Polyline Distance Angle Trim mEthod
   Multiple]:
   ```

   Before you select the first line for the chamfer, it is recommended to define the type of method for creating the chamfer.

2. Click on the **Distance** option in the command prompt or enter **D** and then press ENTER to invoke the **Distance distance** method. You are prompted to specify first chamfer distance.

   ```
   Specify first chamfer distance <current>:
   ```

3. Enter the first chamfer distance value and then press ENTER. You are prompted to specify second chamfer distance.

   ```
   Specify second chamfer distance <current>:
   ```

4. Enter the second chamfer distance value and then press ENTER. You are prompted to select the first line for creating the chamfer.

   ```
   Select first line or [Undo Polyline Distance Angle Trim mEthod
   Multiple]:
   ```

5. Click on the first chamfer line, see Figure 5.44. You are prompted to select second chamfer line.

   ```
   Select second line or shift-select to apply corner or [Distance
   Angle Method]:
   ```

6. Click on the second chamfer line, see Figure 5.44. The chamfer of specified distance is created, see Figure 5.45.

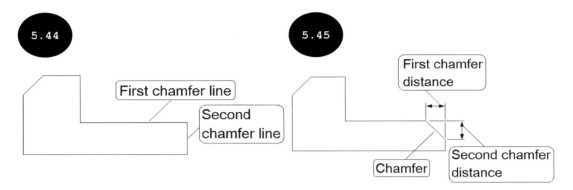

Procedure for Creating a Chamfer by Angle distance Method

1. Click on the down arrow next to the **Fillet** tool in the **Modify** panel. A flyout appears. In this flyout, click on the **Chamfer** tool. Alternatively, enter **CHA** in the Command Line window and then press ENTER. You are prompted to select the first line for creating a chamfer.

   ```
   Select first line or [Undo Polyline Distance Angle Trim mEthod
   Multiple]:
   ```

2. Click on the **Angle** option in the command prompt or enter **A** and then press ENTER to invoke the **Angle distance** method. You are prompted to specify the chamfer length on the first line.

   ```
   Specify chamfer length on  the first line <current>:
   ```

3. Enter the chamfer length value and then press ENTER. You are prompted to specify chamfer angle.

   ```
   Specify chamfer angle from the first line <0>:
   ```

4. Enter the chamfer angle value and then press ENTER. You are prompted to select chamfer first line.

   ```
   Select first line or [Undo Polyline Distance Angle Trim mEthod
   Multiple]:
   ```

5. Click on the first chamfer line, see Figure 5.46. You are prompted to select second chamfer line.

   ```
   Select second line or shift-select to apply corner or [Distance
   Angle Method]:
   ```

6. Click on the second chamfer line, see Figure 5.46. The chamfer of specified angle and distance is created, see Figure 5.47.

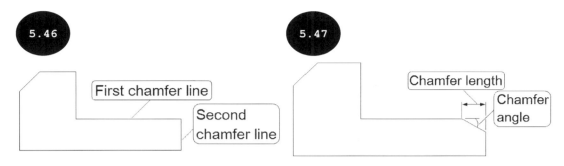

Offsetting Drawing Entities

In AutoCAD, you can offset an existing object/entity at a specified offset distance and create a new object, see Figure 5.48. Note that the shape of the newly created object is same and parallel to the existing object. You can offset an existing entity or entities by using the **Offset** tool of the **Modify** panel, see Figure 5.49. The procedure to create objects by offsetting existing entities is discussed next.

Procedure for Offsetting Objects/Entities

1. Click on the **Offset** tool in the **Modify** panel. You are prompted to specify offset distance. Alternatively, enter O in the Command Line window and then press ENTER.

   ```
   Specify offset distance or [Through Erase Layer] <current>:
   ```

2. Enter offset distance value and then press ENTER. You are prompted to select an object to offset.

   ```
   Select object to offset or [Exit Undo] <Exit>:
   ```

> **Note:** In addition to specifying the offset distance value, you can specify two points in the drawing area by clicking the left mouse button for defining the offset distance.

3. Click on the object to be offset, see Figure 5.50. The preview of the offset entity appears attached to the cursor, see Figure 5.50. You are prompted to specify a point for defining the offset side.

    ```
    Specify point on side to offset or [Exit Multiple Undo] <Exit>:
    ```

4. Click on either side of the selected entity for defining the offset side. The offset object is created, see Figure 5.51. Also, you are again prompted to select an object to offset.

    ```
    Select object to offset or [Exit Undo] <Exit>:
    ```

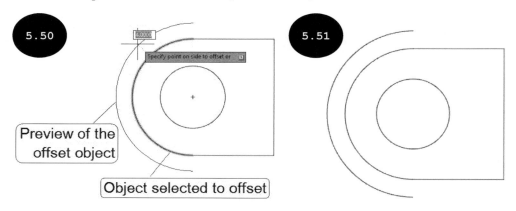

5. Similarly, you can select the other objects one by one to offset, see Figure 5.52.

6. After offsetting the objects, press ENTER to exit.

Note: By default, when you offset an entity, the original/parent selected entity remains available in the drawing area, and new offset entity gets created. It is because the erase mode is turned off, by default. To activate the erase mode, click on the **Erase** option in the command prompt when you are prompted to select the first object "`Specify offset distance or [Through Erase Layer] <current>:`". Next, enter **Y** and then press ENTER. Now, on offsetting an object, the original/parent object gets erased from the drawing area and a new offset object is created.

Moving Drawing Objects

While creating drawing in AutoCAD, sometimes you may need to move the drawing objects from their current location to the new location in the drawing area. In AutoCAD, you can move the drawing objects from one place to another by using the **Move** tool of the **Modify** panel, see Figure 5.53. The procedure to move the drawing objects is discussed next.

Procedure for Moving Objects/Entities

1. Click on the **Move** tool in the **Modify** panel (refer to Figure 5.53) or enter **M** in the Command Line window and then press ENTER. You are prompted to select objects to be moved.

   `Select objects:`

2. Click on the object to be moved in the drawing area, see Figure 5.54 (a). You can select one or more than one object to move. For selecting multiple objects, you can use the Window or Cross Window selection method.

3. After selecting the objects, press ENTER. You are prompted to specify a base point. Note that the base point acts as a reference point for moving the selected objects.

   `Specify base point or [Displacement] <Displacement>:`

4. Click to specify the base point in the drawing area, see Figure 5.54 (a). You are prompted to specify second/placement point for the selected objects. Also, the preview of selected objects is attached to the cursor.

   `Specify second point or <use first point as displacement>:`

238 Chapter 5 > Modifying and Editing Drawings - I

5. Click to specify the second point in the drawing area as the placement point, see Figure 5.54 (a). The selected objects are moved to the specified location, see Figure 5.54 (b).

5.54
a) Before   b) After

Copying Drawing Objects

While creating drawing in AutoCAD, you may need to create duplicate copies of an object. You can create multiple copies of an object by using the **Copy** tool of the **Modify** panel, see Figure 5.55. The procedure to copy objects is discussed next.

5.55

Procedure for Copying Objects/Entities

1. Click on the **Copy** tool in the **Modify** panel (refer to Figure 5.55) or enter **CO** in the Command Line window and then press ENTER. You are prompted to select objects to be copied.

   ```
   Select objects:
   ```

2. Click on the object to be copied, see Figure 5.56 (a). You can select one or multiple objects to be copied. For selecting multiple objects, you can use the Window or Cross Window selection method.

3. After selecting objects, press ENTER. You are prompted to specify a base point. Note that the base point acts as a reference point for copying the selected objects.

   ```
   Specify base point or [Displacement mOde] <Displacement>:
   ```

4. Click to specify the base point in the drawing area, see Figure 5.56 (a). You are prompted to specify second point for the selected objects. Also, the preview of selected objects is attached to the cursor.

```
Specify second point or [Array] <use first point as displacement>:
```

5. Click to specify second/placement point for the selected objects in the drawing area, see Figure 5.56 (a). The selected objects are copied to the specified location, see Figure 5.56 (b). Also, you are still prompted to specify the second point. Similarly, you can create multiple copies of the selected objects by specifying the placement points one after another.

a) Before   b) After

6. After copying the selected objects, press the ENTER key to exit.

Rotating Drawing Objects

While creating drawing in AutoCAD, you may need to rotate objects at an angle around a point. You can rotate an object or a set of objects at an angle by using the **Rotate** tool of the **Modify** panel, see Figure 5.57. The procedure to rotate objects is discussed next.

Procedure for Rotating Objects/Entities

1. Click on the **Rotate** tool in the **Modify** panel, refer to Figure 5.57 or enter RO in the Command Line window and then press ENTER. You are prompted to select objects.

```
Select objects:
```

2. Click on the object to be rotated, see Figure 5.58 (a). You can select one or multiple objects to be rotated. For selecting multiple objects, you can use the Window or Cross Window selection method.

3. After selecting objects, press ENTER. You are prompted to specify a base point. Note that the base point acts as a reference point for rotating the selected objects.

   ```
   Specify base point:
   ```

4. Click to specify the base point in the drawing area, see Figure 5.58 (a). You are prompted to specify the rotational angle. Also, the preview of selected objects is attached to the cursor.

   ```
   Specify rotation angle or [Copy Reference] <current>:
   ```

5. Enter rotational angle value and then press ENTER. The selected objects are rotated at the specified angle, see Figure 5.58 (b). Note that you can also specify the rotational angle by clicking the left mouse button in the drawing area.

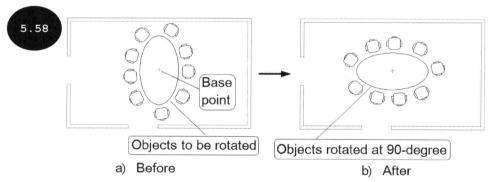

a) Before   b) After

Scaling Drawing Objects

In addition to moving, rotating, and copying drawing objects, you may need to increase or decrease the scale of the objects as well. Note that on increasing/decreasing the scale of a drawing object, the size of the object is enlarged/shrunk, respectively, by maintaining the aspect ratio of the object. You can scale an object or a set of objects by using the **Scale** tool of the **Modify** panel, see Figure 5.59. The procedure to scale objects is discussed next.

Procedure for Scaling Objects/Entities

1. Click on the **Scale** tool in the **Modify** panel or enter SC in the Command Line window and then press ENTER. You are prompted to select objects.

   ```
   Select objects:
   ```

2. Click on the object to be scaled, see Figure 5.60 (a). You can select one or multiple objects to be scaled. For selecting multiple objects, you can use the Window or Cross Window selection method.

3. After selecting objects, press ENTER. You are prompted to specify a base point. Note that the base point acts as a reference point for scaling the selected objects.

   ```
   Specify base point:
   ```

4. Click to specify a base point in the drawing area, see Figure 5.60 (a). You are prompted to specify a scale factor. Also, the preview of selected object is attached to the cursor. Note that as you move the cursor, the scale of the objects increases or decreases, accordingly.

   ```
   Specify scale factor or [Copy Reference]:
   ```

5. Enter scale factor and then press ENTER. The selected objects are scaled equally by maintaining the aspect ratio of the object to the specified base point, see Figure 5.60 (b). Note that to enlarge the selected object, you need to enter scale factor greater than 1 and to shrink the selected object, you need to enter scale factor smaller than 1.

a) Before   b) After

Note: You can also scale an object by specifying the current length and the new length of the object instead of specifying the scale factor. If you do so, the object gets scaled relative to the new specified length. To scale an object by specifying the current length and the new length, click on the **Reference** option in the command prompt when you are prompted to specify scale factor "`Specify scale factor or [Copy Reference]:`". Next, specify the current length value of the object and then press ENTER. You can also pick two points in the drawing area to specify the current length of the object. After specifying the current length, enter the new length of the object and then press ENTER. The selected object gets scaled relative to the new length specified. For example, if the current length of the object is 90 unit and you want it to 35 unit after scaling it then you need to enter 90 as the current length and 35 as the new length of the object.

Stretching Drawing Objects

In AutoCAD, you can stretch an object or a group of objects to change its shape and size. You can stretch objects by using the **Stretch** tool of the **Modify** panel, see Figure 5.61. The procedure to stretch objects is discussed next.

5.61

Procedure for Stretching Objects/Entities

1. Click on the **Stretch** tool in the **Modify** panel (refer to Figure 5.61) or enter **S** in the Command Line window and then press ENTER. You are prompted to select objects to be stretched.

   `Select objects:`

2. Select objects by drawing a Cross Window around them such that it partially encloses the objects to be stretched, see Figure 5.62 (a). You can select the objects to be stretched by using the Cross Window or Cross Polygon selection method.

   Note: You can only stretch objects that partially enclosed by the boundary of the Cross Window or Cross Polygon window. The objects that completely enclosed within the boundary can move rather than being stretched.

3. After selecting objects to be stretched, press ENTER. You are prompted to specify a base point.

   `Specify base point or [Displacement] <Displacement>:`

4. Click to specify the base point for stretching the selected objects in the drawing area, see Figure 5.62 (a). You are prompted to specify the second point.

   ```
   Specify second point or <use first point as displacement>:
   ```

5. Click to specify the second/placement point. The portion of the objects selected gets stretched by leaving the rest of the portion unchanged, see Figure 5.62 (b).

a) Before   b) After

Lengthening Drawing Objects

In AutoCAD, you can shorten or extend the line objects by using the **Lengthen** tool of the expanded **Modify** panel, see Figure 5.63. You can expand the **Modify** panel by clicking on the arrow available in the title bar of the **Modify** panel. You can shorten or extend the line object by entering the delta length, percentage, total length, or by dragging the object. The procedures to lengthen object are discussed next.

Procedure for Lengthening Object by Specifying Delta Value

1. Click on the **Lengthen** tool in the expanded **Modify** panel (see Figure 5.63) or enter **LEN** in the Command Line window and then press ENTER. You are prompted to select an object.

   ```
   Select an object or [DElta Percent Total DYnamic]:
   ```

2. Click on the **DElta** option in the command prompt or enter **DE** and then press ENTER. You are prompted to specify delta length of the object to lengthen.

   ```
   Enter delta length or [Angle]: <0.0000>:
   ```

244   Chapter 5 > Modifying and Editing Drawings - I

Note: The delta length is the length of the object by which the object is to be extended or shorten. On entering the positive delta value, the length of the object is increased (extended) and on entering the negative delta value, the length of the object is decreased (shorten).

3. Enter the delta length and then press ENTER. You are prompted to select an object.

    ```
    Select an object to change or [Undo]:
    ```

4. Select the object to be lengthened, see Figure 5.64 (a). The length of the object is increased/decreased by the length specified, see Figure 5.64 (b). You are prompted to select the object to be lengthened again.

    ```
    Select an object to change or [Undo]:
    ```

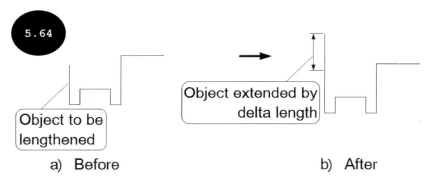

a) Before   b) After

5. You can select multiple objects one after another to be lengthened by the specified delta length. Once you have lengthened the objects, press ENTER to exit.

Procedure for Lengthening Object by Specifying Percentage

1. Click on the **Lengthen** tool in the expanded **Modify** panel or enter **LEN** in the Command Line window and then press ENTER. You are prompted to select an object.

    ```
    Select an object or [DElta Percent Total DYnamic]:
    ```

2. Click on the **Percent** option in the command prompt or enter **P** and then press ENTER. You are prompted to specify percentage length of the object.

    ```
    Enter percentage length <current>:
    ```

Note: The current length of the object taken as 100 percent. As a result, on entering the percentage value more than 100, the length of the object is increased, and on entering the percentage value less than 100, the length of the object is decreased. For example, by entering percentage as 200, the length of the object becomes double of the current length.

3. Enter percentage value for increasing or decreasing the length of the object and then press ENTER. You are prompted to select an object.

   ```
   Select an object to change or [Undo]:
   ```

4. Select the object to lengthen. The length of the object is increased/decreased by the specified percentage. You are prompted to select object again.

   ```
   Select an object to change or [Undo]:
   ```

5. You can select multiple objects one after another to increase/decrease their length as per the specified percentage value. Once you have lengthened the objects, press ENTER to exit.

Procedure for Lengthening Object by Specifying Total Length

1. Click on the **Lengthen** tool in the expanded **Modify** panel or enter **LEN** in the Command Line window and then press ENTER. You are prompted to select an object.

   ```
   Select an object or [DElta Percent Total DYnamic]:
   ```

2. Click on the **Total** option in the command prompt or enter **T** and then press ENTER. You are prompted to specify the total length of the object.

   ```
   Specify total length or [Angle] <current>:
   ```

   Note: The total length of an object is its overall length. You can specify total length less or greater than the current length of the object.

3. Enter the new total length value of the object and then press ENTER. You are prompted to select an object.

   ```
   Select an object to change or [Undo]:
   ```

4. Select the object. The current length of the object changed to the new specified length. You are prompted to select the object again.

   ```
   Select an object to change or [Undo]:
   ```

5. You can select objects one after another to increase or decrease their length. Once you have lengthened the objects, press ENTER to exit.

Procedure for Lengthening Object by Dragging

1. Click on the **Lengthen** tool in the expanded **Modify** panel or enter **LEN** in the Command Line window and then press ENTER. You are prompted to select an object.

   ```
   Select an object or [DElta Percent Total DYnamic]:
   ```

246 Chapter 5 > Modifying and Editing Drawings - I

2. Click on the **DYnamic** option in the command prompt or enter **DY** and then press ENTER. You are prompted to select an object.

   ```
   Select an object to change or [Undo]:
   ```

3. Select the object. The endpoint of the selected object is attached to the cursor. As you move the cursor, the length of the object is increased or decreased. Also, you are prompted to specify the new endpoint of the object.

   ```
   Specify new end point:
   ```

4. Click to specify the new endpoint of the object. The length of the object is increased/decreased as per the new endpoint specified. Next, press ENTER to exit.

Tutorial 1

Create the drawing shown in the Figure 5.65. The dimensions shown in the figure are for your reference only. You will learn about applying dimensions in later chapters.

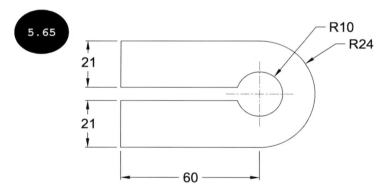

Section 1: Starting AutoCAD

1. Double-click on the AutoCAD icon on your desktop to start AutoCAD. The initial screen of AutoCAD appears with **Start** tab, see Figure 5.66.

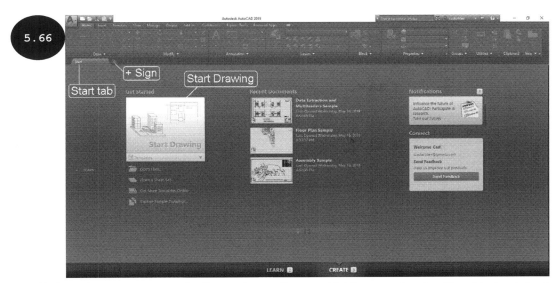

Figure 5.66

2. Click on the + sign next to the **Start** tab, see Figure 5.66. The new drawing file with the default drawing template invoked. Alternatively, click on **Start Drawing** in the **Get Started** section of the **Start** tab to start a new drawing file with default drawing template. You can also start a new drawing file by using the **New** tool of the **Quick Access Toolbar**, which is at the top left corner of AutoCAD screen.

Section 2: Selecting Workspace for Creating Drawing
1. Make sure that the **Drafting & Annotation** workspace selected as the workspace for creating the drawing.

Section 3: Defining the Drawing Limits
1. Follow the command sequence given below for defining the drawing limits.

   ```
   Command: LIMITS (ENTER)
   Specify lower left corner or [ON/OFF]<0.0000,0.0000>: 0,0 (ENTER)
   Specify upper right corner <12.0000,9.0000>: 150,110 (ENTER)
   ```

Section 4: Creating Drawing
1. Click on the arrow next to the circle tool in the **Draw** panel. The **Circle** flyout appears. In this flyout, click on the **Center, Radius** tool. Alternatively, enter C in the Command Line window and then press ENTER. You are prompted to specify the center point of the circle.

   ```
   Specify center point for circle or [3P 2P Ttr (tan tan radius)]:
   ```

2. Click in the drawing area to specify the center point of the circle. You are prompted to specify the radius of the circle.

   ```
   Specify radius of circle or [Diameter]:
   ```

248 Chapter 5 > Modifying and Editing Drawings - I

3. Enter **24** and then press ENTER. The circle of radius 24 unit is created, see Figure 5.67.

4. Invoke the **Center, Radius** tool again. You are prompted to specify the center point of the circle.

   ```
   Specify center point for circle or [3P 2P Ttr (tan tan radius)]:
   ```

5. Move the cursor toward the center point of the existing circle in the drawing area and then click to specify the center point of the circle when cursor snaps to it. You are prompted to specify the radius of the circle.

   ```
   Specify radius of circle or [Diameter]:
   ```

6. Enter **10** and then press ENTER. The circle of radius 10 created, see Figure 5.68.

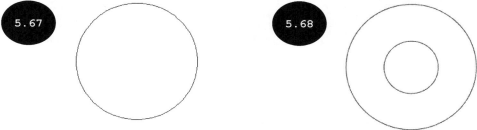

7. Click on the **Line** tool in the **Draw** panel and then move the cursor toward the top quadrant of the first drawn circle, see Figure 5.69.

8. Click to specify the first point of the line when cursor snaps to the top quadrant of the first drawn circle, see Figure 5.69. You are prompted to specify the second point of the line.

   ```
   Specify next point or [Undo]:
   ```

9. Make sure that the Ortho mode is turned on. Next, move the cursor horizontally toward the left and then enter **60** as the length of the line, see Figure 5.70. Next, press ENTER. The line of length 60 unit is drawn. Also, you are prompted to specify next point of the line.

   ```
   Specify next point or [Undo]:
   ```

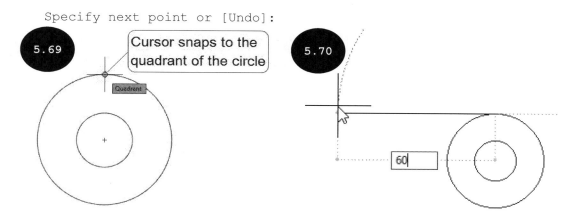

10. Move the cursor vertically downward and then enter **21** as the length of the line. Next, press ENTER. The line of length 21 unit is drawn, and you are prompted to specify next point of the line.

    ```
    Specify next point or [Undo]:
    ```

11. Move the cursor horizontally toward the right and then click to specify the end point of the line anywhere inside the smaller circle of diameter 20, see Figure 5.71. Next, press ENTER to exit.

12. Similarly, draw the other line entities of the drawing by using the **Line** tool, see Figure 5.72.

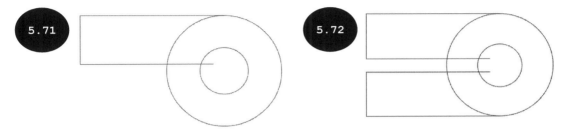

Section 5: Trimming the Drawing Entities

1. Click on the **Trim** tool in the **Modify** panel or enter **TR** in the Command Line window and then press ENTER. You are prompted to select cutting edges/boundaries.

    ```
    Select cutting edges ...
    Select objects or <select all>:
    ```

2. Press ENTER to skip the selection of cutting edges/boundaries. You are prompted to select objects to be trimmed.

    ```
    Select object to trim or shift-select to extend or
    [Fence Crossing Project Edge eRase Undo]:
    ```

3. Click on the line entity (1), see Figure 5.73. The selected line entity gets trimmed to its next nearest intersection, see Figure 5.74. Also, you are prompted to select objects to trim again.

    ```
    Select object to trim or shift-select to extend or
    [Fence Crossing Project Edge eRase Undo]:
    ```

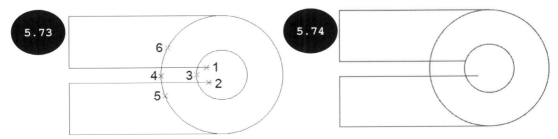

4. Similarly, click on the other entities (2, 3, 4, 5, and 6), refer to Figure 5.73 for trimming them to their nearest intersection. Figure 5.75 shows the drawing after trimming all the unwanted entities of the drawing.

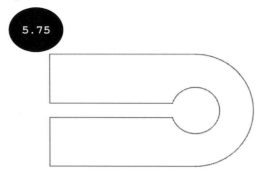

Section 6: Saving the Drawing
After creating the drawing, you need to save it.

1. Click on the **Save** tool in the **Quick Access Toolbar**. The **Save Drawing As** dialog box appears.

2. Browse to the *AutoCAD* folder and then create a folder with the name *Chapter 5* inside the *AutoCAD* folder.

3. Enter **Tutorial 1** in the **File name** field of the dialog box and then click on the **Save** button. The drawing gets saved with the name Tutorial 1 in the *Chapter 5* folder.

Tutorial 2

Create the drawing shown in the Figure 5.76. The dimensions shown in the figure are for your reference only. You will learn about applying dimensions in the later chapters.

Section 1: Starting AutoCAD

1. Start AutoCAD, if not started already. Next, click on the **New** tool in the **Quick Access Toolbar**, which is at the top left corner of AutoCAD screen. The **Select template** dialog box appears.

2. In the **Select template** dialog box, click on the *acad.dwt* template and then click on the **Open** button. A new drawing file with *acad.dwt* template invoked.

3. Specify the drawing limits.

Section 2: Creating Construction Lines

1. Click on the **Construction Line** tool in the expanded **Draw** panel of the **Home** tab. You are prompted to specify a point in the drawing area. You can also enter **XLINE** in the Command Line window and then press ENTER to invoke the **Construction Line** tool.

   ```
   Specify a point or [Hor Ver Ang Bisect Offset]:
   ```

2. Click on the **Hor** option in the command prompt or enter **H** and then press ENTER to create horizontal construction line. A horizontal construction line is attached to the cursor. Also, you are prompted to specify a through point.

   ```
   Specify through point:
   ```

3. Click in the drawing area to specify a point in the drawing area. A horizontal construction line created such that it passes through the specified point. Also, another horizontal construction line is attached to the cursor.

4. Press ENTER to exit the tool.

   Now, you need to create another horizontal construction line at the offset distance of 25 units from the existing horizontal construction line.

5. Invoke the **Construction Line** tool and then click on the **Offset** option of the command prompt or enter **O** and then press ENTER. You are prompted to specify the offset distance.

   ```
   Specify offset distance or [Through] <Through>:
   ```

6. Enter **25** and then press ENTER. You are prompted to select a line object.

   ```
   Select a line object:
   ```

7. Click on the existing horizontal construction line. You are prompted to specify the side to offset.

   ```
   Specify side to offset:
   ```

8. Click on the bottom side of the existing horizontal construction line. The horizontal construction line at the offset distance of 25 units is created, see Figure 5.77. Next, press ENTER to exit the tool.

252 Chapter 5 > Modifying and Editing Drawings - I

9. Similarly, create two vertical construction lines at the offset distance of 5 units from each other by using the **Construction Line** tool, see Figure 5.78.

Section 3: Creating Drawing

1. Invoke the **Circle** flyout of the **Draw** panel and then click on the **Circle, Radius** tool. Alternatively, enter **C** in the Command Line window and then press ENTER. You are prompted to specify the center point of the circle.

    ```
    Specify center point for circle or [3P 2P Ttr (tan tan radius)]:
    ```

2. Move the cursor toward the intersection point (P1) created between the upper horizontal and right vertical construction lines, refer to Figure 5.78.

3. Click to specify the center point of the circle when cursor snaps to the intersection point (P1). You are prompted to specify the radius of the circle.

    ```
    Specify radius of circle or [Diameter]:
    ```

4. Enter **60** as the radius of the circle. The circle of diameter 120 is created, see Figure 5.79.

5. Similarly, create a circle of radius 55 whose center point is at the intersection point (P1) and a circle of radius 35 whose center point is at the intersection point (P2), see Figure 5.80.

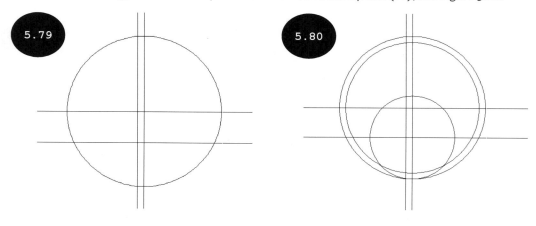

Section 4: Trimming Unwanted Drawing Entities

1. Click on the **Trim** tool in the **Modify** panel or enter **TR** in the Command Line window and then press ENTER. You are prompted to select cutting edges/boundaries.

   ```
   Select cutting edges ...
   Select objects or <select all>:
   ```

2. Press ENTER to skip the selection of cutting edges/boundaries. You are prompted to select objects to be trimmed.

   ```
   Select object to trim or shift-select to extend or
   [Fence Crossing Project Edge eRase Undo]:
   ```

3. Click on the entity (1), see Figure 5.81. The selected entity gets trimmed to its next nearest intersection, see Figure 5.82. Also, you are prompted to select objects to be trimmed again.

   ```
   Select object to trim or shift-select to extend or
   [Fence Crossing Project Edge eRase Undo]:
   ```

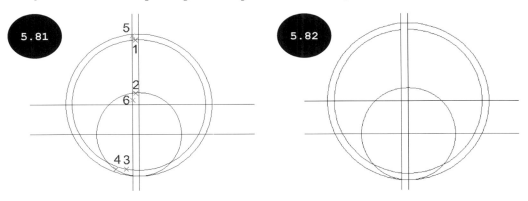

4. Similarly, click on the other entities (2, 3, 4, 5, and 6), see Figure 5.81. Figure 5.83 shows the drawing after trimming all the unwanted entities of the drawing. Next, press ENTER to exit.

Section 5: Deleting Unwanted Drawing Entities

1. Click on the entities to be deleted (four entities), see Figure 5.84. Next, press the DELETE key. The selected entities of the drawing get deleted, see Figure 5.85.

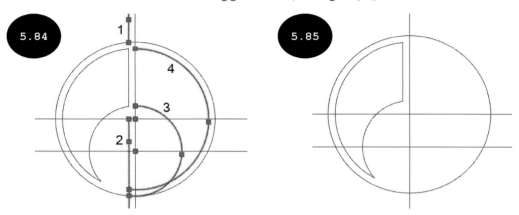

Section 6: Creating Fillets

1. Click on the **Fillet** tool in the **Modify** panel or enter **F** and then press ENTER. You are prompted to select the first object.

   ```
   Select first object or [Undo Polyline Radius Trim Multiple]:
   ```

2. Click on the **Radius** option of the command prompt or enter **R** and then press ENTER. You are prompted to specify the radius of the fillet.

   ```
   Specify fillet radius <0.0000>:
   ```

3. Enter **5** as the fillet radius and then press ENTER. You are prompted to select the first object.

   ```
   Select first object or [Undo Polyline Radius Trim Multiple]:
   ```

4. Click on the first object of the first corner to be filleted, see Figure 5.86. You are prompted to select the second object.

   ```
   Select object or shift-select to apply corner or [Radius]:
   ```

5. Click on the second object of the first corner, see Figure 5.86. The fillet of radius 5 created at the first corner of the drawing, see Figure 5.87.

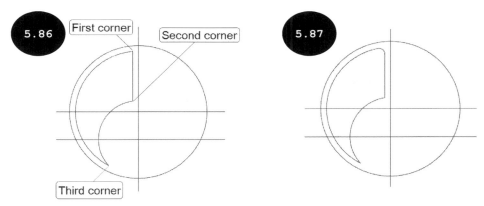

6. Similarly, create fillets of radius 5 on the second and third corners, see Figure 5.88.

Section 7: Mirroring Drawing Entities

1. Click on the **Mirror** tool in the **Modify** panel or enter **MI** and then press ENTER. You are prompted to select objects.

   ```
   Select objects:
   ```

2. Click on the entities (6 entities) of the drawing, see Figure 5.89. The selected entities get highlighted, see Figure 5.89. Next, press ENTER. You are prompted to specify the first point of the mirror line.

   ```
   Specify first point of mirror line:
   ```

256   Chapter 5 > Modifying and Editing Drawings - I

3. Click to specify the first point of the mirroring line anywhere on the vertical construction line. You are prompted to specify the second point of mirror line.

   ```
   Specify first point of mirror line: Specify second point of mirror line:
   ```

4. Move the cursor vertically upward and then click to specify the second point of the mirror line anywhere on the vertical construction line. You are prompted to specify whether you wanted to erase source objects.

   ```
   Erase source object? [Yes No] <N>:
   ```

5. Enter **N** and then press ENTER. The mirror image of the selected entities is created, see Figure 5.90.

Section 8: Creating Remaining Drawing Entities

1. Create two circles, one of diameter 60 and another of diameter 30 by using the **Circle, Diameter** tool, see Figure 5.91.

2. Create a layer named as **Construction Line** and then move the construction lines of the drawing to the **Construction Line** layer. Next, hide the **Construction Line** layer. Figure 5.92 shows the final drawing after hiding the construction lines.

Section 9: Saving the Drawing

1. Click on the **Save** tool in the **Quick Access Toolbar**. The **Save Drawing As** dialog box appears.

2. Browse to the *Chapter 5* folder inside the *AutoCAD* folder.

3. Enter **Tutorial 2** in the **File name** field of the dialog box and then click on the **Save** button. The drawing saved with the name Tutorial 2 in the *Chapter 5* folder.

Tutorial 3

Create the drawing shown in the Figure 5.93. The dimensions shown in the figure are for your reference only. You will learn about applying dimensions in later chapters.

Section 1: Starting AutoCAD

1. Start a new AutoCAD drawing file and then define the drawing limits.

258 Chapter 5 > Modifying and Editing Drawings - I

Section 2: Creating Reference Entities

1. Click on the **Construction Line** tool in the expanded **Draw** panel of the **Home** tab. You are prompted to specify a point in the drawing area. You can also enter **XLINE** in the Command Line window and then press ENTER to invoke the **Construction Line** tool.

   ```
   Specify a point or [Hor Ver Ang Bisect Offset]:
   ```

2. Click on the **Ver** option in the command prompt or enter **V** and then press ENTER. A vertical construction line is attached to the cursor. Also, you are prompted to specify a through point.

   ```
   Specify through point:
   ```

3. Click in the drawing area to specify the through point. A vertical construction line is created such that it passes through the specified point. Next, press ENTER to exit.

4. Similarly, create a horizontal construction line by using the **Construction Line** tool.

   Now, you need to create construction lines at an angle.

5. Invoke the **Construction Line** tool and then click on the **Ang** option in the command prompt or enter **A** and then press ENTER. You are prompted to specify an angle of construction line.
   ```
   Enter angle of xline (0) or [Reference]:
   ```

6. Enter **60** and then press ENTER. A construction line at the angle 60-degree, measured from the horizontal X-axis is attached to the cursor. Also, you are prompted to specify a through point.

   ```
   Specify through point:
   ```

7. Click on the intersection point created between the horizontal and vertical construction lines to specify the through point. The construction line of angle 60-degree is created, see Figure 5.94.

8. Similarly, create another construction line at the angle 120-degree from the horizontal X-axis, see Figure 5.95.

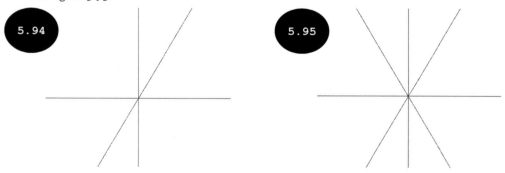

After creating the construction lines, you need to create a reference circle.

9. Invoke the **Circle, Diameter** tool in the **Draw** panel and then create a circle of diameter 90 whose center point is at the intersection of construction lines, see Figure 5.96.

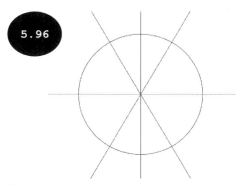

Section 3: Creating Reference Layer

1. Invoke the **LAYER PROPERTIES MANAGER** by clicking on the **Layer Properties** tool in the **Layers** panel of the **Home** tab. Alternatively, enter **LA** in the Command Line window and then press ENTER to invoke the **LAYER PROPERTIES MANAGER**.

2. Create a layer named as Reference in the **LAYER PROPERTIES MANAGER** and then assign the Red color and Center linetype to it, see Figure 5.97. Next, exit the **LAYER PROPERTIES MANAGER** by clicking on the cross mark .

After creating the Reference layer, you need to move construction lines and the circle of diameter 90 to this Reference layer.

3. Select all construction lines and the circle of diameter 90. Next, invoke the **Layer** drop-down list of the **Layer** panel, see Figure 5.98 and then click on the **Reference** layer to assign all the selected objects to it. Figure 5.99 shows the drawing after moving the construction lines and circle to the Reference layer.

260 Chapter 5 > Modifying and Editing Drawings - I

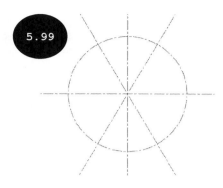

Section 4: Creating Drawing Circles

1. Make sure that the **0** layer is activated and selected in the **Layer** drop-down list of the **Layer** panel in the **Ribbon**.

2. Click on the **Circle, Diameter** tool in the **Circle** flyout in the **Draw** panel or enter C in the Command Line window and then press ENTER. You are prompted to specify the center point of the circle.

   ```
   Specify center point for circle or [3P 2P Ttr (tan tan radius)]:
   ```

3. Move the cursor toward the intersection point created between the construction lines and then click to specify the center point of the circle. You are prompted to specify the diameter of the circle.

   ```
   Specify radius of circle or [Diameter]:_d Specify diameter of circle:
   ```

4. Enter **120** as the diameter of the circle. The circle of diameter 120 is created, see Figure 5.100.

5. Similarly, create a circle of diameter 40 at the intersection of construction lines and a circle of diameter 16 whose center point is at the intersection of horizontal construction line and the reference circle, see Figure 5.101.

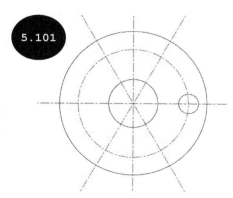

Section 5: Creating Reference Entities

1. Click on the **Offset** tool in the **Modify** panel. Alternatively, enter O and then press ENTER. You are prompted to specify the offset distance.

    ```
    Specify offset distance or [Through Erase Layer] <Through>:
    ```

2. Enter **5** as the offset distance and then press ENTER. You are prompted to select an object to offset.

    ```
    Select object to offset or [Exit Undo] <Exit>:
    ```

3. Click on the horizontal construction line and then click to specify the placement point on the upper side of the horizontal construction line. A construction line at the offset distance of 5 units from the horizontal construction line is created. Also, you are prompted to select an object to offset.

    ```
    Select object to offset or [Exit Undo] <Exit>:
    ```

4. Click on the horizontal construction line again and then click to specify the placement point on the lower side of the horizontal construction line. A construction line at the offset distance of 5 units from the horizontal construction line is created, see Figure 5.102.

Section 6: Creating Line Entities

1. Click on the **Line** tool in the **Draw** panel. Alternatively, enter L and then press ENTER. You are prompted to specify the first point of the line.

    ```
    Specify first point:
    ```

2. Move the cursor to the intersection point P1, refer to Figure 5.102. Next, click to specify the first point of the line when the cursor snaps to the intersection point P1. You are prompted to specify the next point of the line.

    ```
    Specify next point or [Undo]:
    ```

3. Move the cursor horizontally toward the left and then click to specify the end point of the line when the cursor snaps to the intersection point P2, refer to Figure 5.102. Next, press ENTER to exit the **Line** tool.

4. Similarly, create another line from the intersection point P3 to intersection point P4, refer to Figure 5.102. Figure 5.103 shows the resultant drawing after creating the line entities.

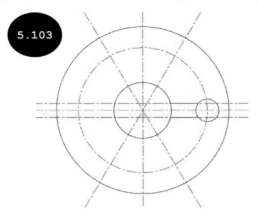

Section 7: Trimming Unwanted Entities

1. Click on the **Trim** tool in the **Modify** panel or enter **TR** in the Command Line window and then press ENTER. You are prompted to select cutting edges/boundaries.

   ```
   Select cutting edges ...
   Select objects or <select all>:
   ```

2. Press ENTER to skip the selection of cutting edges/boundaries. You are prompted to select objects to be trimmed.

   ```
   Select object to trim or shift-select to extend or
   [Fence Crossing Project Edge eRase Undo]:
   ```

3. Click on the unwanted entities (four entities) to be trimmed one by one, see Figure 5.104. Figure 5.105 shows the drawing after trimming the unwanted entities.

4. After trimming the unwanted entities, press ENTER to exit the **Trim** tool.

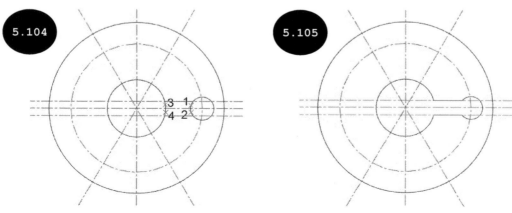

Section 8: Creating Circular/Polar Array

1. Invoke the **Array** flyout of the **Modify** panel and then click on the **Polar Array** tool, see Figure 5.106. You are prompted to select objects.

   ```
   Select objects:
   ```

2. Click on the circle of diameter 16 and two horizontal lines, see Figure 5.107. The selected objects get highlighted.

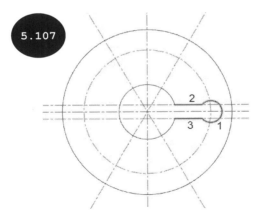

3. After selecting the objects, press ENTER. You are prompted to specify the center point of the array.

   ```
   Specify center point of array or [Base point Axis of rotation]:
   ```

4. Click to specify the center point of the array at the intersection of horizontal and vertical construction lines. The preview of the array with default parameters appears in the drawing area. Also, you are prompted to select the grip to edit array.

   ```
   Select grip to edit array or [ASsociative Base point Items Angle
   between Fill angle ROWs Levels ROTate items eXits] <eXit>:
   ```

5. Make sure that the **6** entered in the **Items** field and **360** in the **Fill** field of the **Items** panel in the **Array Creation** tab. Next, press ENTER. The circular/polar array is created, see Figure 5.108.

After creating the circular/polar array, you need to trim the remaining unwanted entities of the drawing by using the **Trim** tool.

6. Invoke the **Trim** tool and then trim the unwanted entities of the innermost circle of the drawing. Figure 5.109 shows the entities to be trimmed and Figure 5.110 shows the resultant drawing after trimming the entities.

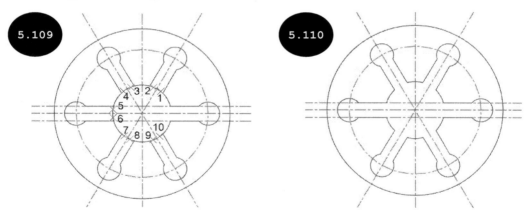

Section 9: Creating the Remaining Drawing Entities

1. Invoke the **Circle, Diameter** tool of the **Circle** flyout in the **Draw** panel and create a circle of diameter 240 whose center point is at the intersection of horizontal and vertical construction lines, see Figure 5.111. This circle will use as the reference circle for creating drawing entities.

2. Assign the newly created circle of diameter 240 to the Reference layer. For doing so, select the circle and then invoke the **Layer** drop-down list in the **Layers** panel. Next, click on the **Reference** layer in the **Layer** drop-down list and then press the ESC key to exit the selection set. Figure 5.112 shows the circle after assigning it to the Reference layer.

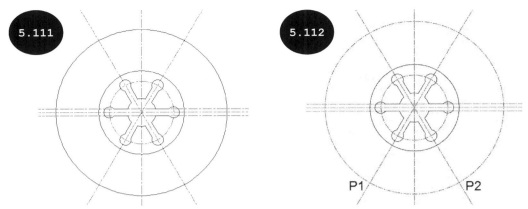

3. Invoke the **Circle, Diameter** tool and then create two circles of diameter 40 at the intersection points 'P1' and 'P2', refer to Figure 5.112. Figure 5.113 shows the drawing after creating two circles of diameter 40.

4. Similarly, create two more circles (one of diameter 200 and another of diameter 280) at the intersection of horizontal and vertical construction lines, see Figure 5.114.

5. Click on the **Trim** tool in the **Modify** panel and then press ENTER. Next, select the unwanted entities to be trimmed. Figure 5.115 shows the entities to be trimmed and Figure 5.116 shows the drawing after trimming the entities. Next, press ENTER to exit the **Trim** tool.

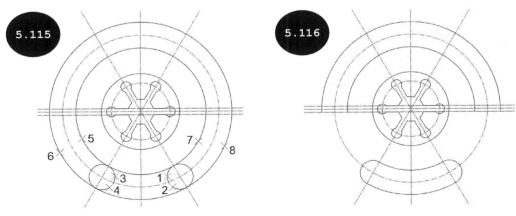

Now, you need to delete the unwanted entities of the drawing.

6. Click on the entities (two entities) to be deleted one by one, see Figure 5.117. Next, press the DELETE key. The selected entities get deleted, see Figure 5.118.

Now, you need to offset the slot entities at the offset distance of 5 units.

7. Click on the **Offset** tool in the **Modify** panel or enter **O** and then press ENTER. You are prompted to specify the offset distance.

    ```
    Specify offset distance or [Through Erase Layer] <current>:
    ```

8. Enter **5** as the offset distance and then press ENTER. You are prompted to select objects.

    ```
    Select object to offset or [Exit Undo] <Exit>:
    ```

9. Click on the lower larger arc of the slot and then move the cursor outside it, see Figure 5.119. You are prompted to specify the point to define the offset direction.

    ```
    Specify point on side to offset or [Exit Multiple Undo] <Exit>:
    ```

10. Click outside the slot to specify the position of the offset entity. The offset entity is created, see Figure 5.120. Also, you are prompted to select objects to offset again.

    ```
    Select object to offset or [Exit Undo] <Exit>:
    ```

11. Similarly, click on the other entities of the slot one by one and offset them at the offset distance of 5 units, see Figure 5.121. Next, press ENTER to exit the **Offset** tool.

Now, you need to create construction lines which help in creating other entities of the drawing.

12. Click on the **Construction Line** tool in the expanded **Draw** panel or enter **XLINE** and then press ENTER. You are prompted to specify a point in the drawing area for creating a construction line.

    ```
    Specify a point or [Hor Ver Ang Bisect Offset]:
    ```

13. Click on the **Offset** option in the command prompt or enter **O** and then press ENTER. You are prompted to specify the offset distance.

    ```
    Specify offset distance or [Through] <current>:
    ```

14. Enter **20** as the offset distance and then press ENTER. You are prompted to select the line object to offset.

    ```
    Select a line object:
    ```

15. Click on the vertical construction line and then click on its left side to specify the placement point for creating a new vertical construction line. The vertical construction line is created, see Figure 5.122. Also, you are prompted to select the object to offset.

16. Click on the vertical construction line again and then click on its right side. The vertical construction line is created on the right side of the existing construction line, see Figure 5.123. Next, press ENTER to exit the **Construction Line** tool.

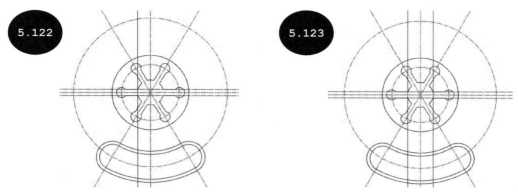

Now, you need to assign the newly created vertical construction lines to the Reference layer.

17. Click on the newly created vertical construction lines and then invoke the **Layer** drop-down list in the **Layers** panel. Next, click on the **Reference** layer in the **Layer** drop-down list and then press ESC. The selected objects are assigned to the Reference layer, see Figure 5.124.

18. Invoke the **Line** tool and then click to specify the start point and end point of the line at the intersection points 'P1' and 'P2', respectively, refer to Figure 5.124. Next, press ENTER to exit the tool.

19. Similarly, create a line whose start point and the end point is at the intersection points 'P3' and 'P4', respectively, refer to Figure 5.124. Figure 5.125 shows the drawing after creating the line entities at the intersection points. Next, press ENTER to exit the tool.

Now, you need to trim the unwanted entities of the drawing.

20. Invoke the **Trim** tool and then press ENTER. Next, trim the entities shown in Figure 5.126. Figure 5.127 shows the drawing after trimming the entities.

Now, you can hide the Reference layer.

21. Invoke the **Layer** drop-down list of the **Layer** panel, see Figure 5.128. Next, click on the **Turn a layer On or Off** icon of the Reference layer, see Figure 5.128. All the construction lines assigned to the Reference layer get hidden in the drawing area. Figure 5.129 shows the final drawing.

270   Chapter 5 > Modifying and Editing Drawings - I

Section 10: Saving the Drawing
After creating the drawing, you need to save it.

1. Click on the **Save** tool in the **Quick Access Toolbar**. The **Save Drawing As** dialog box appears.

2. Browse to the *Chapter 5* folder inside the *AutoCAD* folder.

3. Enter **Tutorial 3** in the **File name** field of the dialog box and then click on the **Save** button. The drawing saved with the name Tutorial 3 in the *Chapter 5* folder.

Hands-on Test Drive 1

Draw the drawing shown in the Figure 5.130. The dimensions shown in the figure are for your reference only. You will learn about applying dimensions in later chapters.

Hands-on Test Drive 2

Draw the drawing shown in the Figure 5.131.

Hands-on Test Drive 3

Draw the drawing shown in the Figure 5.132.

Summary

In this chapter, you have learned about various object selection methods, how to trim and extend drawing entities. You have also learned how to create an array, mirror, fillet, chamfer, offset, move, copy, rotate, scale, stretch, and lengthen drawing entities.

Questions

- In the _____ selection method, only the objects that completely enclosed within the rectangular window gets selected.

- In the _____ selection method, all objects that completely enclosed and touch the rectangular window gets selected.

- The _____ selection method is used to select group of objects by drawing a series of continuous lines over the objects to be selected.

- In AutoCAD, you can trim the unwanted drawing entities by using the _____ tool.

- In AutoCAD, you can create different types of arrays by using the _____ , _____ , and _____ tools.

- You can create a mirror image of the drawing entities about a mirroring line by using the _____ tool.

- A _____ is a curved edge which is used to remove or eliminate sharp edges of the model that can cause injury while handling the object.

- You can create chamfer by using the _____ tool.

- You can move the drawing objects from one location to another by using the _____ tool.

- You can stretch objects by using the _____ tool.

- You can rotate an object or set of objects at an angle by using the _____ tool.

CHAPTER 6

Working with Dimensions and Dimensions Style

In this chapter, you will learn the following:

- Working with Components of a Dimension
- Creating New Dimension Style
- Modifying Existing Dimension Style
- Overriding Dimension Style
- Applying Dimensions
- Applying the Linear Dimension
- Applying the Aligned Dimension
- Applying the Angular Dimension
- Applying the Arc Length Dimension
- Applying the Radius Dimension
- Applying the Diameter Dimension
- Applying the Jogged Radius Dimension
- Applying the Jogged Linear Dimension
- Applying the Ordinate Dimension
- Applying Baseline Dimensions
- Applying Continue Dimensions
- Applying Multiple Dimensions

After creating a drawing, it is imperative to dimension it. An excellent AutoCAD drawing with all needed dimensions conveys the complete information clearly and accurately. Note that the 2D drawings are the only source for manufacturing components. It is not only a drawing but a language for engineers to communicate with each other. By using drawings having proper dimensions, designers/engineers communicate the information about the components to be manufactured. Therefore, it is imperative to generate accurate and error-free drawings with all the needed dimensions and annotations for production. Any incorrect or missing information in drawings about a component can lead to the wrong production.

274 Chapter 6 > Working with Dimensions and Dimensions Style

AutoCAD is provided with various dimensioning tools in the **Dimension** flyout of the **Annotation** panel in the **Home** tab for applying dimensions quickly and easily, see Figure 6.1.

On adding dimensions to a drawing, the dimensions appear as per the default dimension style which is the Standard dimension style. The Standard dimension style is the current dimension style of a drawing which controls the appearance of dimensions such as the size of dimension text and arrows, the length of extension lines, and so on. In most of the drawings, the default dimension style may not meet your requirements. Therefore, AutoCAD allows you to modify the existing dimension style or create new dimension styles as per your requirement. In this chapter, you will learn about various components of dimensions that can be controlled by dimension style, creating new dimension style, and adding dimensions to a drawing.

Working with Components of a Dimension

In AutoCAD, each dimension has several components such as dimension line, dimension text, extension line, and so on, see Figure 6.2. You can control these dimension components by using the dimension style. You can modify the existing dimension style or create a new dimension style as required by using the **Dimension Style Manager** dialog box. Note that each industry follows different dimension style. Therefore, it is important to become familiar with the **Dimension Style Manager** dialog box for creating your industrial specific dimension style.

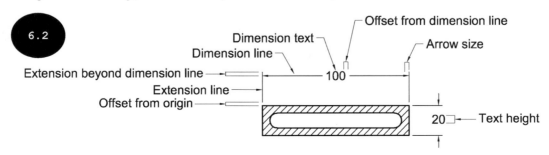

To invoke the **Dimension Style Manager** dialog box, enter **D** in the Command Line window and then press ENTER. Figure 6.3 shows the **Dimension Style Manager** dialog box. You can also invoke this dialog box by clicking on the **Dimension Style** tool in the expanded **Annotation** panel of the **Home** tab, see Figure 6.4. The options of the **Dimension Style Manager** dialog box are discussed next.

Styles
The **Styles** area is available on the left of the **Dimension Style Manager** dialog box. This area displays the list of all the available dimension styles. Note that the display of dimension styles in this area controlled by the option selected in the **List** drop-down list of the dialog box. The options of the **List** drop-down list discussed next.

List
The options in the **List** drop-down list control the display of dimension styles in the **Styles** area of the dialog box. By default, the **All styles** option is selected in this drop-down list. As a result, all the dimension styles available in the drawing are displayed in the **Styles** area of the dialog box. If you select the **Styles in use** option, only the dimension styles that are in use get listed in the **Styles** area of the dialog box.

Don't list styles in Xrefs
On selecting the **Don't list styles in Xrefs** check box, the Xref dimension styles will not display in the **Styles** area of the dialog box. If you uncheck this check box, all the Xref dimension styles display in the **Styles** area of the dialog box. Note that this check box is enabled if a Xref drawing is attached to the current drawing. The Xref is an external reference drawing which attached to the current drawing as a reference file. You can attach multiple external drawings to the current drawing. You will learn more about external reference drawings in later chapters.

Preview of
The **Preview of** area of the dialog box displays the preview of the currently selected dimension style in the **Style** area.

Set Current
The **Set Current** button of the dialog box is used to make a dimension style as the current dimension style of the drawing. Note that the current dimension style controls the dimensions applied in the drawing. To make a dimension style as the current style, select the dimension style in the **Styles** area of the dialog box and then click on the **Set Current** button. The selected dimension style becomes the current dimension style for the drawing.

The **New**, **Modify**, and **Override** buttons of the **Dimension Style Manager** dialog box are used to create new dimension style, modify existing dimension style, and override existing dimension style, respectively. All these are discussed next.

Creating New Dimension Style
In addition to the default dimension style, you can create new dimension styles by using the **New** button of the **Dimension Style Manager** dialog box. To create a new dimension style, invoke the **Dimension Style Manager** dialog box and then click on the **New** button. The **Create New Dimension Style** dialog box appears, see Figure 6.5.

In the **New Style Name** field of the **Create New Dimension Style** dialog box, you can specify a name for the dimension style. Next, select the base dimension style in the **Start With** drop-down list of the dialog box. Next, choose the type of dimension to which you want to apply this dimension style in the **Use for** drop-down list of the dialog box. By default, the **All dimensions** option is selected in this drop-down list. As a result, the new dimension style applies to all dimension types. If you want to apply the new dimension style only to a particular dimension type, then you need to select that dimension type in this drop-down list. For example, if you want to apply the new dimension style only to the radial dimensions then select the **Radius dimensions** option in this drop-down list. To make the annotative dimension style, select the **Annotative** check box. Next, click on the **Continue** button in the dialog box. The **New Dimension Style** dialog box appears, see Figure 6.6. In this dialog box, you can specify dimension parameters as required by using their respective options available under the respective tabs of the dialog box. The different tabs and options of this dialog box are discussed next.

Lines Tab

The options in the **Lines** tab of the dialog box are arranged in two areas: **Dimension lines** and **Extension lines**, refer to Figure 6.6. The options of both these areas are discussed next.

Dimension lines Area

The options of the **Dimension lines** area are used to control the appearance of dimension lines. The options of this area are discussed next.

Color

The **Color** drop-down list is used to select a color for the dimension lines. Figure 6.7 shows dimension lines in red color. Note that the color set for dimension lines also applied to dimension arrowheads.

Linetype

The **Linetype** drop-down list is used to select a linetype such as Continuous (solid line), Center, or Hidden for dimension lines. Figure 6.8 shows dimension lines with the DASHED linetype.

Lineweight

The **Lineweight** drop-down list is used to select a lineweight (thickness) for dimension lines. Figure 6.9 shows dimension lines with 0.80 mm lineweight.

Extend beyond ticks

The **Extend beyond ticks** field is used to specify the distance for the dimension line to extend beyond the extension lines. Figure 6.10 shows dimension lines with 0 (zero) distance beyond the extension lines and Figure 6.11 shows dimension lines with 3 units distance beyond the extension lines. By default, this field not enabled in the dialog box. It is activated only when the arrowhead style for dimension lines is set to architectural tick, integral, or similar in the **First** or **Second** drop-down lists of the **Arrowheads** area which is available in the **Symbols and Arrows** tab of the dialog box.

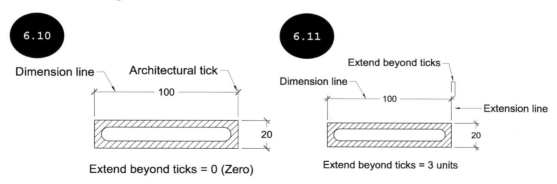

Baseline spacing

The **Baseline spacing** field is used to specify spacing between dimension lines of the baseline dimensions, see Figure 6.12. You will learn more about applying baseline dimensions later in this chapter.

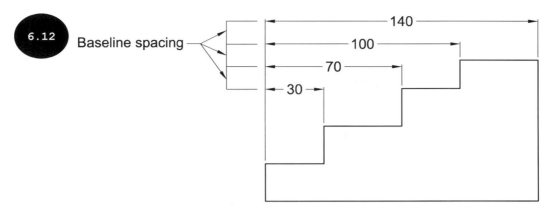

Suppress

The **Dim line 1** and **Dim line 2** check boxes are used to suppress first and second dimension lines, respectively. Figure 6.13 shows dimensions with the first dimension line is suppressed and Figure 6.14 shows dimensions with the second dimension line is suppressed. By default, these check boxes are unchecked. As a result, both the dimension lines of a dimension appeared in the drawing.

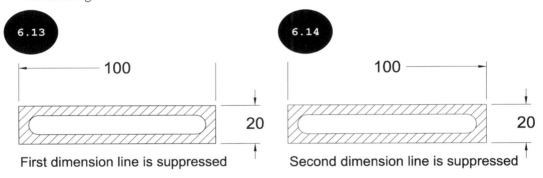

Extension lines Area

The options of the **Extension lines** area are used to control the appearance of extension lines of dimensions. The options are discussed next.

Color

The **Color** drop-down list of the **Extension lines** area is used to select the color for the extension lines. You can assign a different color to extension lines of dimensions.

Linetype ext line 1

The **Linetype ext line 2** drop-down list of this area is used to select a linetype such as Continuous (solid line), Center, or Hidden for the first extension lines of dimensions.

Linetype ext line 2

The **Linetype ext line 2** drop-down list of this area is used to select a linetype such as Continuous (solid line), Center, or Hidden for the second extension lines of dimensions.

Lineweight
The **Lineweight** drop-down list of this area is used to select a lineweight (thickness) for extension lines.

Extend beyond dim lines
The **Extend beyond dim lines** field is used to specify a distance value for the extension lines to extend beyond the dimension line, see Figure 6.15.

Offset from origin
The **Offset from origin** field is used to specify an offset distance for the extension lines from their origin, see Figure 6.16.

Fixed length extension lines
On selecting the **Fixed length extension lines** check box, the **Length** field which is available below this check box gets enabled. In the **Length** field, you can specify a fix distance for the extension line, starting from the dimension line, see Figure 6.17. By default, the **Fixed length extension lines** check box is unchecked. As a result, dimensions are applied with full-length extension lines. Figure 6.17 shows dimensions with a specified fixed length extension lines and Figure 6.18 shows dimensions with the full-length extension lines.

Suppress
The **Ext line 1** and **Ext line 2** check boxes of the **Extension lines** area are used to suppress first and second extension lines of dimensions, respectively.

Symbols and Arrows Tab
The options in the **Symbols and Arrows** tab of the dialog box are used to specify dimension arrowheads, arrow size, center marks, dimension break, and so on, see Figure 6.19. The options in the **Symbols and Arrows** tab are discussed next.

6.19

Arrowheads Area
The options in the **Arrowheads** area of the **Symbols and Arrows** tab are used to control the styles and parameters for arrowheads. The options are discussed next.

First and Second
The **First** and **Second** drop-down lists are used to specify the first and second arrowheads for dimension lines, respectively. By default, the same arrowhead styles (Closed filled) applied at both ends (first and second) of the dimension lines. Also, on selecting the first arrowhead style in the **First** drop-down list, the same arrowhead style gets selected automatically in the **Second** drop-down list. To apply different arrowhead style for the second arrowhead of the dimension lines, select the required arrowhead style in the **Second** drop-down list. Figure 6.20 shows dimensions with the **Closed filled** as the first arrowhead style and the **Architectural tick** as the second arrowhead style.

6.20

Note: In addition to selecting arrowhead styles from the **First** and **Second** drop-down lists, you can use custom/user-defined arrowhead styles for dimensions, as per your requirement. To define custom/user-defined arrowhead styles, you need to first create it as a block, and then you can select the **User Arrow** option from these drop-down lists. On selecting the **User Arrow** option, the **Select Custom Arrow Block** window appears, see Figure 6.21. The **Select from Drawing Blocks** drop-down list of this window displays a list of all blocks created in the drawing. You can select the required block as the arrowhead style in this drop-down list and then click on the **OK** button. You will learn about creating blocks in later chapters.

Leader
The **Leader** drop-down list is used to specify arrowhead style for leader lines.

Arrow size
The **Arrow size** field is used to specify a size of dimension arrowheads.

Center marks Area
The options in the **Center marks** area are used to control the display of the center marks for the radius and diameter dimensions, see Figure 6.22. By default, the **None** radio button selected in this area. As a result, no center mark displayed at the center of circles or arcs on applying diameter or radius dimensions. If you choose the **Mark** radio button, a cross mark appeared at the center of circles or arcs on applying diameter or radius dimensions, see Figure 6.23. If you select the **Line** radio button, the centerlines appeared at the center of circles or arcs on applying diameter or radius dimensions, see Figure 6.24. Note that as soon as you select the **Mark** or **Line** radio button, the **Size** field becomes enabled in this area. In this field, you can specify the size of the center mark or centerline to appear at the center of circles or arcs on applying diameter or radius dimensions.

Dimension Break Area

The **Break size** field of the **Dimension Break** area (see Figure 6.25) is used to specify the default break size for the dimension lines. Note that you can break dimension lines which are intersecting with each other or drawing objects to avoid overlapping or confusion by using the DIMBREAK command. When you break dimension lines by using the DIMBREAK command, the break size which specified in the **Break size** field will be applied, automatically. Figure 6.26 shows the intersecting dimension lines and Figure 6.27 shows the dimensions after breaking the dimension lines by using the DIMBREAK command.

Tip: To break dimension lines which are intersecting with other dimension or drawing object, enter DIMBREAK command and then press ENTER. You are prompted to select the dimension to add/remove break. Click on the dimension to be broken and then click on the object for breaking selected dimension. The object to break selected dimension can be a drawing entity or another dimension.

Arc length symbol Area

The options in the **Arc length symbol** area (see Figure 6.28) are used to control the position of the arc length dimension symbol. By default, the **Preceding dimension text** radio button selected in this area. As a result, on applying the arc length dimension, the arc length symbol appears before the dimension text, see Figure 6.29. On selecting the **Above dimension text** radio button, the arc length symbol appears above the dimension text. If you select the **None** radio button, the arc length symbol gets suppressed, and not appears in the dimension text. You will learn about applying arc length dimension later in this chapter.

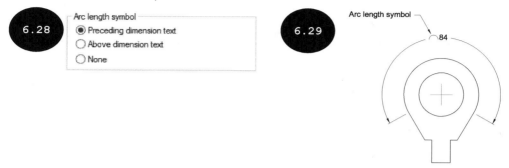

Radius jog dimension Area

The **Jog angle** field in the **Radius jog dimension** area (see Figure 6.30) is used to specify the jogging angle for the jogged dimension. By default, the 45-degree jog angle specified in this field. As a result, a jog with 45-degree angle is applied on applying the radius jog dimension to arcs or circles, see Figure 6.31. You will learn about applying jogged dimension later in this chapter.

Linear jog dimension Area

The **Jog height factor** field of the **Linear jog dimension** area is used to specify the jog factor which controls the jog height of the linear jog dimensions. A jog height is a distance between two vertices of the jog angles that make the jog, see Figure 6.32. Note that the value entered as the jog height factor in this field gets multiplied by the text height of the dimension to calculate the jog height. You will learn about applying linear jog dimensions later in this chapter.

Text Tab

The options in the **Text** tab of the dialog box are used to control the dimension text style and format, see Figure 6.33. The options are discussed next.

Figure 6.33

Text appearance Area

The options in the **Text appearance** area are used to control the appearance of the dimension text such as text style and color. The options are discussed next.

Text style

The **Text style** drop-down list is used to select the predefined text style for dimensions. You can also modify the predefined text style and create a new text style, as required. To edit the existing text style and create a new text style, click on the [...] button, which is available in front of the **Text style** drop-down list. The **Text Style** dialog box appears, see Figure 6.34. By using the options in this dialog box, you can modify the existing text style such as text font, font style, and height. Also, you can create a new text style by using the **New** button of this dialog box. To close the dialog box, click on the **Cancel** button.

6.34

Text color
The **Text color** drop-down list is used to select a color for the dimension text.

Fill color
The **Fill color** drop-down list is used to select a fill color which appears in the background of the dimension text in a box. Figure 6.35 shows a box around the dimension text which is filled with red color.

6.35

Text height
The **Text height** field is used to specify the dimension text height. Note that this field is enabled only when the text style is selected in the **Text style** drop-down list has text height set to 0 (zero) in the **Text Style** dialog box, refer to Figure 6.34. If the text height defined for the selected text style, then this field will not be enabled, and the specified text height overrides the current text height of the dimensions.

Fraction height scale
The **Fraction height scale** field is used to specify the scale for the fraction unit format. The value specified in this field multiplies by the text height to calculate the height for the fraction dimensions. Note that this field is enabled only when the unit format set to **Fractions** in the **Primary** tab of the dialog box.

Draw frame around text
On selecting the **Draw frame around text** check box, a frame box drawn around the dimension text. By default, this check box is cleared. As a result, the frame box is not drawn around the dimension text.

Text placement Area
The options in the **Text placement** area of the dialog box are used to control the dimension text placement, see Figure 6.36. The options are discussed next.

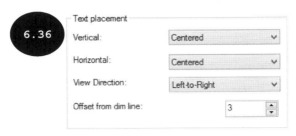

6.36

Vertical
The **Vertical** drop-down list of this area is used to control the vertical placement of dimension text on the dimension line. By default, the **Centered** option selected in this drop-down list. As a result, the dimension text is placed at the center of dimension line, see Figure 6.37 (a). On selecting the **Above** option, the dimension text is placed above the dimension line, see Figure 6.37 (b). On selecting the **Outside** option, the dimension text is placed on the side of the dimension line, see Figure 6.37 (c). On selecting the **Below** option, the dimension text is placed below the dimension line, see Figure 6.37 (d). On selecting the **JIS** option, the dimension text is set to conform to the JIS (Japanese Industrial Standards) representation.

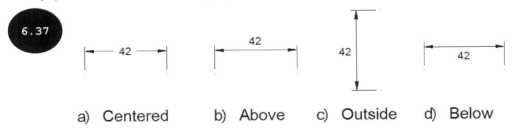

6.37

a) Centered   b) Above   c) Outside   d) Below

Horizontal
The **Horizontal** drop-down list is used to control the horizontal placement of the dimension text along the dimension line concerning the extension lines. By default, the **Centered** option selected in this drop-down list. As a result, the dimension text is placed at the center of extension lines along the dimension line, see Figure 6.38 (a). On selecting the **At Ext Line 1** option, the dimension text is placed near the first extension line, see Figure 6.38 (b). On selecting the **At Ext Line 2** option, the dimension text is placed near the second extension line, see Figure 6.38(c). On selecting the **Over Ext Line 1** option, the dimension text is placed over or along the first extension line, see Figure 6.38 (d). On selecting the **Over Ext Line 2** option, the dimension text is placed over or along the second extension line, see Figure 6.38 (e).

288　Chapter 6 > Working with Dimensions and Dimensions Style

a) Centered　　b) At Ext Line 1　　c) At Ext Line 2　　d) Over Ext Line 1　　e) Over Ext Line 2

View Direction
The **View Direction** drop-down list is used to control the viewing direction of the dimension text from left to right or right to left by selecting the respective options from this drop-down list.

Offset from dim line
The **Offset from dim line** field is used to specify the offset distance between the dimension text and the dimension line, see Figure 6.39.

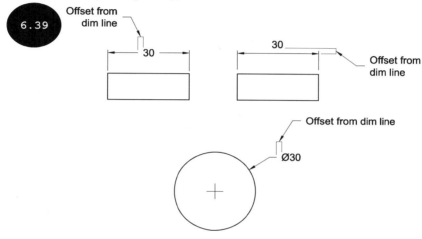

Text alignment Area
The options in the **Text alignment** area are used to control the orientation of the dimension text, see Figure 6.40. The options are discussed next.

Horizontal
By default, the **Horizontal** radio button is selected in the **Text alignment** area. As a result, the dimension text is placed horizontally to a dimension, see Figure 6.41.

Aligned with dimension line
On selecting the **Aligned with dimension line** radio button, the dimension text aligns with the dimension line, see Figure 6.41.

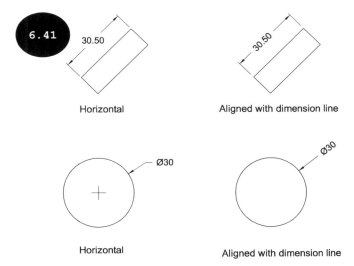

ISO standard

On selecting the **ISO standard** radio button, the dimension text aligns with the dimension line when the dimension text is placed inside the extension lines. If the dimension text is placed outside the extension lines then on selecting this radio button, the dimension text aligns horizontally.

Fit Tab

The options of the **Fit** tab in the dialog box are used to control the placement of dimension lines, arrowheads, leader lines, and scale of all dimension components, see Figure 6.42. The options are discussed next.

Fit options Area

The options in the **Fit options** area of the dialog box are used to control the placement of dimension text and arrowheads depending upon the availability of space between the extension lines. If space is available for the placement, then the text and arrowhead are placed between the extension lines. Whereas, if enough space is not available between the extension lines for the placement of dimension text then the dimension text and arrowheads get placed according to the fit option selected in this area. The options of the **Fit options** area are discussed next.

Either text or arrows (best fit)

By default, the **Either text or arrows (best fit)** radio button is selected in the **Fit options** area of the dialog box. As a result, either the dimension text or arrowheads move outside the extension lines based on the best fit. Note that if the enough space is available between the extension lines, then both text and arrowheads are placed between the extension lines. Otherwise, either the text, the arrowheads, or both move outside the extension lines based on the best fit.

Arrows

On selecting the **Arrows** radio button, the arrowheads move outside the extension lines first and then the dimension text. For example, if the space between the extension lines is available either for text or arrowheads, then the arrowheads move outside the extension lines.

Text

On selecting the **Text** radio button, the dimension text moves outside the extension lines first and then the arrowheads. For example, if the space between the extension lines is available either for text or arrowheads, then the text moves outside the extension lines.

Both text and arrows

On selecting the **Both text and arrows** radio button, the dimension text and arrowheads both move outside the extension lines when the enough space is not available between the extension lines.

Always keep text between ext lines

On selecting the **Always keep text between ext lines** radio button, the dimension text is always placed between the extension lines regardless of space available between them.

Suppress arrows if they don't fit inside extension lines

On selecting the **Suppress arrows if they don't fit inside extension lines** radio button, the arrowheads get suppressed, if the enough space is not available to place them inside the extension lines.

Text placement Area

The options in the **Text placement** area of the dialog box are used to control the placement of dimension text when it is not in the default position or moved from the default position, see Figure 6.43. These options are discussed next.

Beside the Dimension Line
The **Beside the Dimension Line** radio button is selected, by default. As a result, the dimension text is placed beside the dimension line or moves the dimension line whenever dimension text move.

Over the Dimension Line, with Leader
On selecting the **Over the Dimension Line, with Leader** radio button, the dimension line will not move on moving the dimension text. Whereas, on moving the dimension text away from the dimension line, a leader line is added to the dimension text which connects the dimension text to the dimension line, see Figure 6.44. Note that if the dimension text placed very close to the dimension line, then leader line cannot be added.

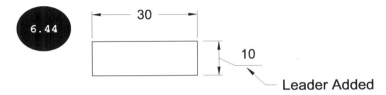

Over dimension line, without leader
On selecting the **Over dimension line, without leader** radio button, the dimension line will not move on moving the dimension text. However, you can move the dimension text freely or independent of the dimension line. Note that the moved dimension text will not be connected to the dimension line through a leader line if this radio button is selected.

Scale for dimension features Area
The options in the **Scale for dimension features** area of the dialog box are used to control the overall dimension scale value or the paper space scaling, see Figure 6.45. These options are discussed next.

Annotative
The **Annotative** check box is used to define whether the dimension style is annotative. To make the dimension style annotative, select the **Annotative** check box. You will learn about annotative dimension later in this chapter.

Scale dimensions to layout
On selecting the **Scale dimensions to layout** radio button, AutoCAD automatically calculates an acceptable scale factor for dimension components such as text height, arrow sizes, and so on based on the scaling between the current model space viewport and the paper space layout. You will learn about layouts in later chapters.

Use overall scale of
On selecting the **Use overall scale of** radio button, the **Scale** field gets enabled in front of it. By default, the scale value set to 1 (one). As a result, the dimension style such as text height, arrowhead size, and all other settings that specify size, distance, or spacing is plotted on a full

292 Chapter 6 > Working with Dimensions and Dimensions Style

scale. You can specify an overall scale for controlling all dimension styles in this field, as required. Note that the scale specified in this field will not change the dimension measurement.

Fine tuning Area

The options in the **Fine tuning** area provides additional options for the placement of dimension text, see Figure 6.46. These options are discussed next.

Place text manually

By default, the **Place text manually** check box is cleared. As a result, the dimension text is placed at the middle of the dimension line, if the enough space is available. However, on selecting this check box, you can position the dimension text anywhere on the dimension line. Also, while positioning the dimension text, it ignores the horizontal justification settings, if specified.

Draw dim line between ext lines

On selecting the **Draw dim line between ext lines** check box, the dimension line is drawn between the extension lines even if the dimension text and dimension lines placed outside the extension lines due to not having enough space.

Primary Units Tab

The options in the **Primary Units** tab are used to control the unit format, dimension precision, fraction format, measurement scale, zero suppression, and so on for linear and angular dimensions, see Figure 6.47. The options are discussed next.

Linear dimensions Area

The options in the **Linear dimensions** area of the dialog box are used to control the unit format, precision, and so on for linear dimensions. The options of this area are discussed next.

Unit format

The **Unit format** drop-down list is used to select the current unit format: Decimal, Scientific, Engineering, Architectural, Fractional, or Windows Desktop for all dimension types except angular dimensions.

Precision

The **Precision** drop-down list is used to specify the dimension precision (decimal places) for dimension text of the current/primary dimension units.

Fraction format

The **Fraction format** drop-down list is used to specify the fraction format: **Horizontal**, **Diagonal**, or **Not Stacked** for the fractional or architectural unit format. Note that this drop-down list is enabled only when the **Fractional** or **Architectural** unit format is selected in the **Unit format** drop-down list of this area.

Decimal separator

The **Decimal separator** drop-down list is used to specify the separator: '.'(Period), ','(Comma), ' '(Space) for decimal formats, see Figure 6.48.

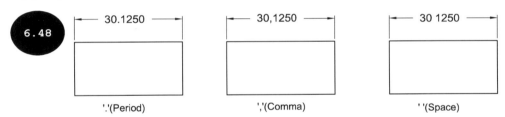

Round off

The **Round off** field is used to specify the nearest rounded value for dimension measurements of all dimension types except angular dimensions. For example, if you specify 0.5 in this field then the dimension having the measurement of 30.3 units gets round off to 30.5 units, and 30.8 units gets round off to 31.0 units. Note that the display of the number of digits after the decimal point depends on the precision setting.

Prefix

The **Prefix** field is used to specify a prefix for the dimension measurement. The prefix specified in this field placed in front of the dimension text. You can enter text or any control code as the prefix for the dimension measurement. For example, on entering the text "Cad" as the prefix in this field, the "Cad" gets placed in front of dimension text. Also, if you enter control code "%%c" as the prefix in this field, the diameter symbol gets placed in front of dimension text.

Suffix

Similar to specifying the prefix, you can specify the suffix for the dimension measurement. The suffix specified is placed after the dimension text. You can enter text or any control code as the suffix for the dimension measurement. For example, on entering the text "mm" as the suffix, the "mm" gets placed after the dimension text. Also, if you enter control code "%%d" as the suffix, then the symbol of degree gets placed after the dimension text.

Measurement scale Area

The **Scale factor** field of this **Measurement scale** area (see Figure 6.49) is used to specify a scale factor for linear dimension measurements which also includes radii, diameters, and coordinates measurements. By default, the scale factor defined as 1 (one) in this field. As a result, the two units segments are dimensioned as 2 units (2 X 1) only. However, if you specify 2 (two) as the scale factor in this field, then the two units segments are dimensioned as 4 units (2 X 2). Note that this scale factor does not apply to angular dimensions, round off values, and to the plus or minus tolerance values.

On selecting the **Apply to layout dimension only** check box of this area (see Figure 6.49), the specified measurement scale factor applies only to the dimensions created in the layout viewports.

Zero suppression Area

The options in the **Zero suppression** area of the dialog box are used to suppress or unsuppress the leading and trailing zeros in the dimension values, see Figure 6.50.

On selecting the **Leading** check box of this area, the leading zeros in all decimal dimensions get suppressed. For example, if the dimension is 0.800 unit then by selecting this check box it becomes .800. Similarly, on selecting the **Trailing** check box, the trailing zeros in all decimal dimensions get suppressed. For example, if the dimension is 15.500 units then by selecting this check box it becomes 15.5 and 15.000 units become 15.

By default, the **0 feet** and **0 inches** check boxes are not enabled in this area. These check boxes get enabled when the **Engineering** or **Architectural** format is selected in the **Unit format** drop-down list. If the feet and inches dimensions are less than one then on selecting the **0 feet** check box, the leading zero (feet portion) of the dimensions get suppressed. For example, if the **0 feet** check box is selected then the 0'-5 1/2" dimension becomes 5 1/2". Similarly, on selecting the **0 inches** check box, the trailing zeros (inches portion) of the feet and inches dimensions get suppressed. For example, if the **0 inches** check box is selected, the 5'-0" dimension becomes 5'.

The **Sub-units factor** field of this area is used to specify the sub-unit factor for dimensions. For example, if the current dimension is in meter (2 meters) then on entering 100 as the sub-unit factor, the dimension gets converted to centimeter (2 X 100 = 200 cm). You can also enter the suffix (cm) for the sub-unit in the **Sub-unit suffix** field of this area.

Angular dimensions Area

Similar to specifying the unit format, precision, and zero suppression for the linear dimensions, you can also specify the unit format, precision, and zero suppression for the angular dimensions by using the options in the **Angular dimensions** area of the dialog box, see Figure 6.51.

Alternate Units Tab

The options in the **Alternate Units** tab are used to display alternate unit for the dimension measurements and control the format and precision of the alternate unit, see Figure 6.52. The options of the **Alternate Units** tab are discussed next.

Display alternate units Check Box

By default, the **Display alternate units** check box is unchecked. As a result, the dimension display only in the primary unit. To display dimensions in the alternate unit as well, select the **Display alternate**

units check box. As soon as you select this check box, the preview area of the dialog box shows the alternate unit in bracket [ ] for all dimensions in addition to the primary unit. Also, the other options of the dialog box get enabled for defining the format and precision of the alternate unit. The options are discussed next.

Alternate units Area

The options in the **Alternate units** area are used to specify the format and precision for the alternate unit. All these options are same as those discussed in the **Primary Units** tab except the **Multiplier for alt units** field. The **Multiplier for alt units** field of this area is used to specify the multiplier as the conversion factor for the alternate unit. For example, if the inch unit is specified as the primary unit for the dimensions and you want to add millimeter as the alternate unit for the measurements. In such case, you can enter 25.4 as the conversion factor in this **Multiplier for alt units** field. On doing so, the dimensions display inch as well as millimeter measurements, see Figure 6.53. Note that the alternate unit is not applied to the angular dimensions, round off values, or the plus or minus tolerance values.

Zero suppression Area

The options in the **Zero suppression** area of the dialog box are used to suppress or unsuppress the leading and trailing zeros in the alternate dimension values, see Figure 6.54. These options are same as those discussed in the **Primary Units** tab with the only difference that these options affect the alternate dimension values.

Placement Area

The options in the **Placement** area of the dialog box are used to define the placement for the alternate unit, see Figure 6.55.

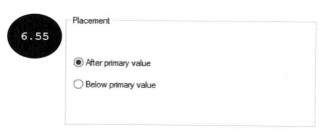

By default, the **After primary value** radio button is selected in the **Placement** area. As a result, the alternate unit is placed after the primary unit, refer to Figure 6.53. If you select the **Below primary value** radio button, then the alternate unit is positioned below the primary unit.

Tolerances Tab

The options in the **Tolerances** tab of the dialog box are used to specify the parameters that control the format and display of the tolerance in the dimension text, see Figure 6.56. The options are discussed next.

Tolerance format Area

The options in the **Tolerance format** area are used to control the tolerance format such as tolerance method, tolerance precision, scaling for height, position, and so on. The options are discussed next.

Method

The **Method** drop-down list is used to select the type of tolerance: Symmetrical, Deviation, Limits, or Basic. By default, the **None** option is selected in this drop-down list. As a result, the tolerance values are not added to the dimension text. The other options of this drop-down list are discussed next.

Symmetrical: On selecting the **Symmetrical** option, the symmetrical tolerances get added to the dimension texts with plus (+) and minus (-) expressions to the symmetric tolerance values, see

Figure 6.57. As soon as you select this tolerance type, the other respective options of the **Tolerance format** area are enabled. You can specify the precision and tolerance values for the symmetrical tolerance in the **Precision** drop-down list and **Upper value** field of this area, respectively.

Deviation: On selecting the **Deviation** option, the deviation tolerances get added to the dimension texts with the plus (+) and minus (-) expressions to the deviation tolerance values, see Figure 6.58. You can specify the plus (+) tolerance value in the **Upper value** field and minus (-) tolerance value in the **Lower value** field of this area.

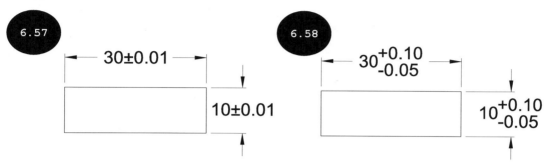

Limits: On selecting the **Limits** option, the maximum and minimum limit dimensions are applied by adding the upper limit value and subtracting the lower limit value to the actual dimension, respectively, see Figure 6.59. The maximum and minimum limit dimensions appear one above the other in the drawing area. In Figure 6.59, the maximum limit dimension is 30.10 (30 + 0.1) and the minimum limit dimension is 29.95 (30 - 0.05).

Basic: On selecting the **Basic** option, the basic dimensions are applied with the display of a box around the dimension text, see Figure 6.60. The basic dimension is also known as reference dimension.

Precision, Upper value, and Lower value
The **Precision** drop-down list, **Upper value** field, and **Lower value** field are used to specify the precision, upper value, and the lower value for the tolerances dimension values, respectively.

Scaling for height
The **Scaling for height** field is used to specify the scale factor for the tolerance text height

concerning the current height of the dimension text. By default, the scale factor for the tolerance text height is set to 1 (one). As a result, the height of the tolerance dimension is same as of the current dimension text height. If you want to set the tolerance dimension height as half of the current dimension text height, then you need to enter 0.5 in this field.

Vertical position
The **Vertical position** drop-down list is used to specify the position/text justification for the symmetrical and deviation tolerance dimension values. By default, the **Middle** option is selected in this drop-down list. As a result, the tolerance text value is aligned to the middle of the dimension text, see Figure 6.61 (a). On selecting the **Top** option, the tolerance text value gets aligned to the top of the dimension text, see Figure 6.61 (b). On selecting the **Bottom** option, the tolerance text value gets aligned to the bottom of the dimension text, see Figure 6.61 (c).

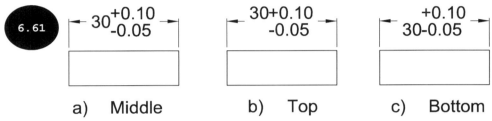

a) Middle b) Top c) Bottom

Tolerance alignment Area
The options in the **Tolerance alignment** area are used to control the alignment of upper and lower tolerance values when they are stacked. These options are available only when the **Deviation** or **Limits** tolerance type is selected. On selecting the **Align decimal separators** radio button of this area, the tolerance values get aligned vertically to the decimal separators (.), see Figure 6.62 (a). However, on selecting the **Align operational symbols**, the tolerance values get aligned to the operational symbols [plus (+) and minus (-)], see Figure 6.62 (b).

a) Align decimal separators   b) Align operational symbols

Zero suppression Area
The options in the **Zero suppression** area are used to suppress or unsuppress the leading and trailing zeros in the tolerance values, as discussed earlier.

Alternate unit tolerance Area
The options in the **Alternate unit tolerance** area are used to specify formats such as precision and zero suppression for the alternate tolerance units. Note that these options are enabled only when the display of alternate dimension units along with the primary dimension units are turned on.

Once you have specified all settings for creating the new dimension style, click on the **OK** button of the dialog box to accept the settings and to exit the **New Dimension Style** dialog box.

Modifying Existing Dimension Style

In AutoCAD, you can also modify existing dimension styles, as required by using the **Modify** button of the **Dimension Style Manager** dialog box. For doing so, invoke the **Dimension Style Manager** dialog box by entering **D** in the Command Line window and then pressing the ENTER key. Next, select the dimension style to be modified from the **Styles** area of the dialog box (see Figure 6.63) and then click on the **Modify** button. The **Modify Dimension Style** dialog box appears, see Figure 6.64.

6.63

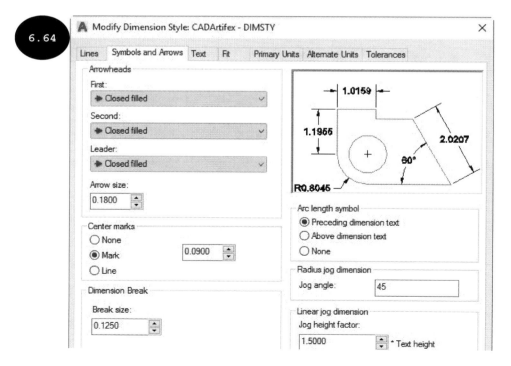

6.64

The options available in the **Modify Dimension Style** dialog box for modifying the selected dimension style are same as those discussed earlier while creating the new dimension style. By using these options, edit the dimension style settings and then click on the **OK** button to accept the modifications and to exit the dialog box. Next, click on the **Close** button in the **Dimension Stye Manager** dialog box to close it.

Overriding Dimension Style

In addition to creating new dimension style and modifying existing dimension style, you can also define overrides or change specific parameters of an existing dimension style. Most of the time the same dimension style is used throughout a drawing. However, sometimes you may need to make small changes in some of the dimension parameters/settings without altering the entire dimension style. In such a case, you can use dimension style overrides. For example, you can assign a different color to the extension line by overriding the color assigned to the parent dimension style. On creating a dimension style override, the sub-dimension style gets created that varies from its parent/original dimension style. When you create override for any of the dimension parameters, the original/parent dimension style will remain unchanged, and the new value for color stored in the DIMCLRE system variable. Note that all dimensions you apply include the overrides until you delete the overrides or set another style as the current dimension style.

To create a dimension override, invoke the **Dimension Style Manager** dialog box by entering **D** in the Command Line window and then pressing the ENTER key. Once the **Dimension Style Manager** dialog box is invoked, select the dimension style to be overridden from the **Styles** area of the dialog box and then click on the **Override** button. The **Override Current Style** dialog box appears, see Figure 6.65. In this dialog box, you can define overrides for the required dimension style parameters/settings.

6.65

The options of the **Override Current Style** dialog box are the same as those discussed earlier while creating the new dimension style. Once you have defined overrides, click on the **OK** button. The **Override Current Style** dialog box gets closed, and a sub-dimension style <*style overrides*> is created and appears under the parent dimension style in the **Styles** area of the dialog box, see Figure 6.66.

After learning about various dimension components, making a dimension style current, creating new dimension style, modifying existing dimension style, and overriding dimension style, you will now learn about applying the various type of dimensions in a drawing.

Applying Dimensions

As discussed earlier, a good AutoCAD drawing is the one that has all dimensions which convey the complete information about the drawing clearly and accurately, see Figure 6.67.

Note: When you apply dimensions, a new layer named as "Defpoints" is created automatically. This "Defpoints" layer stores the dimension properties and cannot be deleted or renamed.

AutoCAD is provided with various dimensioning tools in the **Dimension** flyout of the **Annotation** panel in the **Home** tab which help you quickly and easily dimension a drawing, see Figure 6.68.

Additionally, you can access dimensioning tools from the **Dimensions** panel of the **Annotate** tab, see Figure 6.69; **Dimension** toolbar, see Figure 6.70; **Dimension** Menu Bar, see Figure 6.71; and by using the DIM command.

304 Chapter 6 > Working with Dimensions and Dimensions Style

6.71

> **Note:** By default, the display of the Menu Bar and **Dimension** toolbar are turned off. To display the Menu Bar, enter **MENUBAR** in the Command Line window and then press ENTER. You are prompted to enter a new value for MENUBAR. Enter **1** (one) to turn on the display and **0** (zero) to turn off the display of Menu Bar, respectively.
>
> To display the **Dimension** toolbar, click on the **Tools** > **Toolbars** > **AUTOCAD** > **Dimension** in the Menu Bar.

You can apply different types of dimensions such as linear, aligned, angular, radius, diameter, arc length, and ordinate by using their respective tool. Moreover, you can apply different types of dimensions by using the **Dimension** tool of the **Annotation** panel in the **Home** tab. The **Dimension** tool is a smart tool, which applies dimension depending on the selected entity. For example, if you select a horizontal entity, the horizontal dimension is applied, and if you select a vertical entity, the vertical dimension is applied. The method of applying different types of dimensions are discussed next.

Applying the Linear Dimension

A linear dimension is a most widely used dimension type which measures the length and width of an object. You can apply horizontal or vertical linear dimensions to horizontal, vertical, or aligned objects, by using the **Linear** tool or **Dimension** tool, see Figure 6.72. You can either select an object or two points to apply dimension.

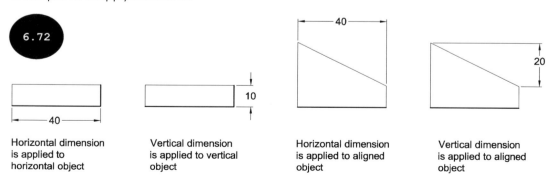

6.72

Horizontal dimension is applied to horizontal object

Vertical dimension is applied to vertical object

Horizontal dimension is applied to aligned object

Vertical dimension is applied to aligned object

Procedure for Applying the Linear Dimension

1. Click on the **Dimension** tool in the **Annotation** panel in the **Home** tab. You are prompted to select objects to be dimensioned or specify the origin for the first extension line. Alternatively, invoke the **Dimension** flyout in the **Annotation** panel and then click on the **Linear** tool for applying the linear dimension. You can also invoke the **Linear** tool by using the DIMLINEAR command.

   ```
   Select objects or specify first extension line origin or [Angular
   Baseline Continue Ordinate aliGn Distribute Layer Undo]:
   ```

2. Move the cursor over the object to be dimensioned. The object gets highlighted, and the preview of dimension appears in the drawing area, see Figure 6.73.

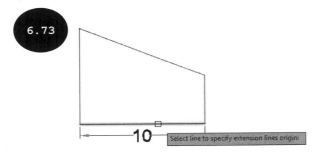

3. Click on the object to be dimensioned. The extension lines of the dimension are attached to the object, and the dimension line is attached to the cursor. Also, you are prompted to specify the location of the dimension line.

   ```
   Specify dimension line location or second line for angle [Mtext
   Text text aNgle Undo]:
   ```

4. Click in the drawing area to specify the location of the dimension line.

Note: In addition to selecting the object to be dimensioned, you can specify the origin for the first and second extension line of the dimension by clicking the left mouse button on the end points (P1 and P2) one by one, see Figure 6.74. To select the end points of the object, make sure that the **Object Snap** mode is turned on.

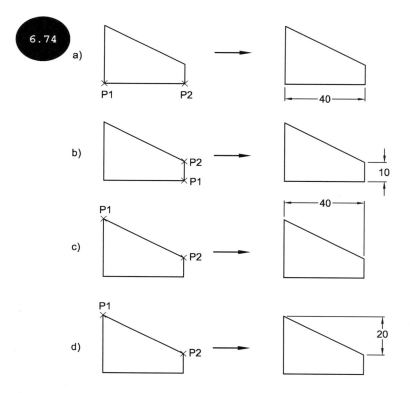

6.74

> **Note:** If you invoke the **Linear** tool or the DIMLINEAR command for applying the linear dimension, then you will be prompted to specify the origin of the first extension line "`Specify first extension line origin or <select object>:`". Click on the end points (P1 and P2) of the object to be dimensioned one by one (refer to Figure 6.74) as the origin of the first and second extension lines of the dimension and then specify the placement point for the dimension line. You can also select the object to be dimensioned instead of specifying the origin of the extension lines. For doing so, press the ENTER key when you are prompted to specify the origin of the first extension line.
>
> The dimension parameters such as dimension text, text height, text font, arrow height, and arrow style are displayed in the drawing area based on the current dimension style.

Applying the Aligned Dimension

An aligned dimension is used to measure the true distance of an inclined object, see Figure 6.75. You can apply aligned dimension by using the **Dimension** tool, **Aligned** tool, or DIMALIGNED command. To apply the aligned dimension, you can select the object or the end points of the object to dimension.

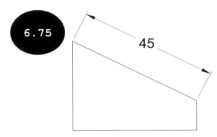

Procedure for Applying the Aligned Dimension

1. Click on the **Dimension** tool in the **Annotation** panel in the **Home** tab. You are prompted to select objects to be dimensioned or specify the origin for the first extension line. Alternatively, invoke the **Dimension** flyout in the **Annotation** panel and then click on the **Aligned** tool for applying the aligned dimension. You can also invoke the **Aligned** tool by using the DIMALIGNED command.

   ```
   Select objects or specify first extension line origin or [Angular
   Baseline Continue Ordinate aliGn Distribute Layer Undo]:
   ```

2. Move the cursor over the aligned object to be dimensioned. The object gets highlighted, and the preview of aligned dimension appears in the drawing area, see Figure 6.76.

3. Click on the object to be dimensioned. The extension lines of the dimension are attached to the end points of the object, and the dimension line is attached to the cursor. Also, you are prompted to specify the location of the dimension line.

   ```
   Specify dimension line location or second line for angle [Mtext
   Text text aNgle Undo]:
   ```

4. Press the SHIFT key and then move the cursor perpendicular to the selected object. The aligned dimension appears attached to the cursor.

5. Click in the drawing area to specify the location of the dimension line. The aligned dimension is applied.

   Note: In addition to selecting the object to be dimensioned, you can specify the origin for the first and second extension line of the dimension by clicking the left mouse button on the end points (P1 and P2) of the object one by one, see Figure 6.77. To select the end points of the object, make sure that the **Object Snap** mode is turned on.

308 Chapter 6 > Working with Dimensions and Dimensions Style

Note: If you invoke the **Aligned** tool or the DIMALIGNED command for applying the aligned dimension, then you will be prompted to specify the origin of the first extension line "`Specify first extension line origin or <select object>:`". Click on the end points (P1 and P2) of the aligned object to be dimensioned one by one (refer to Figure 6.77) as the origin of the first and second extension lines of the dimension and then specify the placement point for the dimension line. You can also select the object to be dimensioned instead of specifying the origin of the extension lines. For doing so, press the ENTER key when you are prompted to specify the origin of the first extension line.

The dimension parameters such as dimension text, text height, text font, arrow height, and arrow style are displayed in the drawing area based on the current dimension style.

Applying the Angular Dimension

An angular dimension is used to measure the angle between two non-parallel line objects, see Figure 6.78. In addition to measuring the angle between two non-parallel line objects, you can also apply angular dimensioning to an arc or a circle, see Figure 6.79. In AutoCAD, you can apply angular dimension by using the **Angular** tool.

Procedure for Applying the Angular Dimension between Line Objects

1. Invoke the **Dimension** flyout in the **Annotation** panel and then click on the **Angular** tool. You are prompted to select an arc, circle, or line. You can also invoke the **Angular** tool by using the DIMANGULAR command.

   `Select arc, circle, line, or <specify vertex>:`

2. Click on the first line object. You are prompted to select the second line object.

   ```
   Select second line:
   ```

3. Click on the second line object. The angular dimension is attached to the cursor and you are prompted to specify the location of the dimension in the drawing area.

   ```
   Specify dimension arc line location or [Mtext Text Angle Quadrant]:
   ```

4. Click in the drawing area to specify the location of the angular dimension. The angular dimension is applied.

Procedure for Applying the Angular Dimension to an Arc

1. Click on the **Angular** tool in the **Dimension** flyout of the **Annotation** panel. You are prompted to select an arc, circle, or line. Alternatively, enter DIMANGULAR in the Command Line window and then press ENTER to invoke the **Angular** tool.

   ```
   Select arc, circle, line, or <specify vertex>:
   ```

2. Click on the arc to be dimensioned (P1), see Figure 6.80. The angular dimension is attached to the cursor, and you are prompted to specify the location of the dimension in the drawing area.

   ```
   Specify dimension arc line location or [Mtext Text Angle Quadrant]:
   ```

3. Click to specify the location for the angular dimension in the drawing area (P2), see Figure 6.80. The angular dimension is applied to the arc and placed at the specified location (P2).

Arc

Procedure for Applying the Angular Dimension to a Circle

1. Invoke the **Angular** tool. You are prompted to select an arc, circle, or line.

   ```
   Select arc, circle, line, or <specify vertex>:
   ```

2. Click on the circumference of the circle to be dimensioned (P1), see Figure 6.81. The specified point (P1) on the circle used as the origin for the first extension line of the angular dimension.

310 Chapter 6 > Working with Dimensions and Dimensions Style

Also, you are prompted to specify the second angle endpoint (origin for the second extension line).

```
Specify second angle endpoint:
```

3. Click to specify a point (P2) on the circumference of the circle as the origin for the second extension line, see Figure 6.81. The angular dimension is attached to the cursor, and you are prompted to specify the location of the dimension in the drawing area.

```
Specify dimension arc line location or [Mtext Text Angle Quadrant]
```

4. Click to specify the location for the angular dimension (P3) in the drawing area, see Figure 6.81.

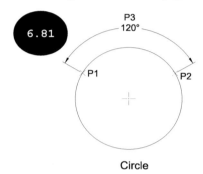

Circle

Procedure for Applying the Angular Dimension by using Three Points

1. Invoke the **Angular** tool. You are prompted to select an arc, circle, or line.

```
Select arc, circle, line, or <specify vertex>:
```

2. Press the ENTER key to apply the angular dimension by using three points. You are prompted to specify the angle vertex (first point).

```
Specify angle vertex:
```

3. Click to specify the angle vertex (V1), see Figure 6.82. You are prompted to specify the first angle endpoint.

```
Specify first angle endpoint:
```

4. Click to specify the first angle endpoint (P1), see Figure 6.82. You are prompted to specify the second angle endpoint.

```
Specify second angle endpoint:
```

5. Click to specify the second angle endpoint (P2), see Figure 6.82. The angular dimension is attached to the cursor and you are prompted to specify the location of the dimension in the drawing area.

```
Specify    dimension    arc    line    location    or    [Mtext    Text    Angle
Quadrant]:
```

6. Click to specify the location for the angular dimension in the drawing area, see Figure 6.82.

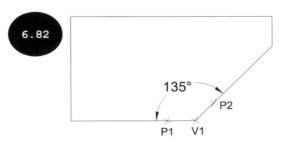

Applying the Arc Length Dimension
An arc length dimension is used to measure the length of an arc or polyline arc segment, see Figure 6.83. You can apply arc length dimension by using the **Arc Length** tool of the **Dimension** flyout.

Procedure for Applying the Arc Length Dimension
1. Invoke the **Dimension** flyout in the **Annotation** panel and then click on the **Arc Length** tool. You are prompted to select arc or polyline arc segment. You can also invoke this tool by using the DIMARC command.

```
Select arc or polyline arc segment:
```

2. Click on an arc or a polyline to be dimensioned. The arc length dimension is attached to the cursor. Also, you are prompted to specify the location of the dimension in the drawing area.

```
Specify   arc   length   dimension   location,   or   [Mtext   Text   Angle
Partial]:
```

3. Click to specify the location of the arc length dimension in the drawing area.

Applying the Radius Dimension
A radius dimension is used to measure the distance from the center to a point on the circumference of a circle/arc, see Figure 6.84. You can apply radius dimension to an arc or a circle by using the **Radius** tool of the **Dimension** flyout.

Procedure for Applying the Radius Dimension

1. Invoke the **Dimension** flyout and then click on the **Radius** tool. You are prompted to select arc or circle. You can also invoke this tool by using the DIMRAD command.

    ```
    Select arc or circle:
    ```

2. Click on an arc or a circle for applying radius dimension. The radius dimension is attached to the cursor. Also, you are prompted to specify the location for the radius dimension in the drawing area.

    ```
    Specify dimension line location or [Mtext Text Angle]:
    ```

3. Click to specify the location for the radius dimension in the drawing area.

Applying the Diameter Dimension

A diameter dimension is used to measure the distance from one point to another (diametrically opposite) on the circumference of a circle or an arc which passes through the center, see Figure 6.85. You can apply diameter dimension to an arc or a circle by using the **Diameter** tool.

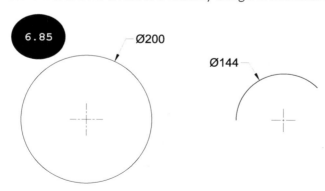

Procedure for Applying the Diameter Dimension

1. Invoke the **Dimension** flyout and then click on the **Diameter** tool. You are prompted to select arc or circle. You can also invoke this tool by using the DIMDIA command.

    ```
    Select arc or circle:
    ```

2. Click on an arc or a circle for applying diameter dimension. The diameter dimension is attached to the cursor. Also, you are prompted to specify the location for the diameter dimension in the drawing area.

   ```
   Specify dimension line location or [Mtext Text Angle]:
   ```

3. Click to specify the location for the diameter dimension in the drawing area.

Applying the Jogged Radius Dimension

A jogged dimension is used to apply jogged radius dimension to a circle or an arc whose center is not displayed in the drawing area or the current viewport, see Figure 6.86. You can apply jogged radius dimension to an arc or a circle by using the **Jogged** tool.

Procedure for Applying the Jogged Radius Dimension

1. Invoke the **Dimension** flyout and then click on the **Jogged** tool. You are prompted to select arc or circle. You can also invoke this tool by using the DIMJOGGED command.

   ```
   Select arc or circle:
   ```

2. Click on an arc or a circle for applying the jogged radius dimension (P1), see Figure 6.87. You are prompted to specify the override center location.

   ```
   Specify center location override:
   ```

3. Click to specify override center location (P2) for the selected object (arc or circle), see Figure 6.87. The preview of jogged dimension is attached to the cursor and you are prompted to specify the dimension line location.

   ```
   Specify dimension line location or [Mtext Text Angle]:
   ```

4. Click to specify dimension line location (P3), see Figure 6.87. You are prompted to specify jog location.

   ```
   Specify jog location:
   ```

5. Click to specify the jog location (P4), see Figure 6.87. The jogged radius dimension is applied, see Figure 6.87.

314 Chapter 6 > Working with Dimensions and Dimensions Style

Applying the Jogged Linear Dimension
A linear jogged dimension is applied to an object having the high length to width ratio, see Figure 6.88. You can apply linear jogged dimension by using the **Jogged Linear** tool.

Procedure for Applying the Jogged Linear Dimension
1. Invoke the **Jogged Linear** tool by clicking on the **Dimension > Jogged Linear** in the Menu Bar. You can also invoke this tool by using the DIMJOGLINE command. You are prompted to select the dimension to add jog.

   ```
   Select dimension to add jog or [Remove]:
   ```

2. Click on a linear dimension to add jog, see Figure 6.89. You are prompted to specify the jog location.

   ```
   Specify jog location (or press ENTER):
   ```

3. Click to specify a location for adding jog in the selected linear dimension, see Figure 6.89. The jog gets added to the linear dimension at the specified location, see Figure 6.89.

Note: Instead of specifying the jog location, you can press ENTER to add jog in the default location of the linear dimension, automatically.

Applying the Ordinate Dimension

Ordinate dimensions are used to dimension machine parts for maintaining the accuracy. The ordinate dimensions measure the perpendicular distance from the specified origin and are described as X and Y ordinate dimensions, see Figure 6.90. Note that the X ordinate dimensions measure the distance from the origin along the X axis and Y ordinate dimensions measure the distance from the origin along the Y axis, see Figure 6.90.

Procedure for Applying the Ordinate Dimension

Before you start applying ordinate dimension, it is important to define the origin for measuring the dimensions.

1. Enter **UCS** in the Command Line window and then press ENTER. You are prompted to specify the origin of the UCS.

   ```
   Specify origin of UCS or [Face NAmed OBject Previous View World X
   Y Z ZAxis] <World>: no
   ```

316   Chapter 6 > Working with Dimensions and Dimensions Style

2. Click on the required location to specify the origin (P1), see Figure 6.91. You can also enter coordinates (X, Y) for specifying the origin location. As soon as you specify the origin of the UCS, you are prompted to specify a point on X-axis.

   Specify point on X-axis or <accept>:

3. Click to specify a point for defining the X-axis of the UCS. Similarly, define the Y-axis of the UCS. Note that to specify the X-axis and Y-axis direction of the UCS, it is recommended to turn on the Object snap mode. Next, press ENTER. A UCS is created at the specified origin in the drawing area.

   After specifying the origin location by using the UCS, you can apply the ordinate dimensions.

4. Invoke the **Dimension** flyout of the **Annotation** panel in the **Home** tab and then click on the **Ordinate** tool. You can also use the DIMORD command to invoke this tool. You are prompted to specify the feature location.

   Specify feature location:

5. Click on a point/feature (P2) for applying the X ordinate dimension, see Figure 6.91. You are prompted to specify the leader endpoint location.

   Specify leader endpoint or [Xdatum Ydatum Mtext Text Angle]:

6. Move the cursor vertically upward and then click to specify the leader endpoint location for the X ordinate dimension in the drawing area. The X ordinate dimension is applied.

7. Similarly, invoke the **Ordinate** tool again from the **Dimension** flyout and then click on the point/feature (P2) for applying the Y ordinate dimension, see Figure 6.91.

8. Move the cursor horizontally toward the right and then click to specify the leader endpoint location for the Y ordinate dimension. The Y ordinate dimension is applied.

9. Similarly, invoke the **Ordinate** tool again and apply the remaining ordinate dimensions concerning the specified origin (P1), see Figure 6.91.

Applying Baseline Dimensions

Baseline dimensions are the series of parallel linear dimensions that share the same base point, see Figure 6.92. The baseline dimensions used to eliminate cumulative errors that can occur due to the rounded dimension values between consecutive adjacent dimensions or due to the upper and lower dimension limits. In AutoCAD, you can apply baseline dimensions by using the **Baseline** tool or by using the DIMBASE command.

Procedure for Applying Baseline Dimensions

Before you start applying the baseline dimensions, you need to apply a linear/angular dimension which will use as the base dimension.

1. Apply a linear dimension in the drawing as the base dimension by using the **Linear** tool, see Figure 6.93.

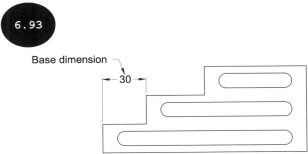

After applying the base dimension, you can apply the baseline dimensions by using the **Baseline** tool.

2. Click on **Dimension > Baseline** in the Menu Bar. The preview of the baseline dimension appears whose origin of the first extension line fixed at the first extension line of the base dimension and you are prompted to specify the origin of the second extension line. You can also invoke this tool by using the DIMBASE command.

   ```
   Specify a second extension line origin or [Undo Select] <Select>:
   ```

318   Chapter 6 > Working with Dimensions and Dimensions Style

Note: If the linear, angular, or ordinate dimensions are present in the current drawing, then the last applied dimension will select as the base dimension, automatically. Also, you are prompted to specify the origin of the second extension line. If you want to skip the automatic selection of base dimension, then press the ENTER key. On doing so, you will be prompted to select the base dimension.

3. Move the cursor toward a point (P1) of the drawing which is to select as the origin of the second extension line, see Figure 6.94.

4. Click to specify the origin of the second extension line when the cursor snaps to the point in the drawing area. The baseline dimension is placed by maintaining the default baseline spacing, which specified in the current dimension style. Also, the preview of another baseline dimension is attached to the cursor whose origin of the first extension line is fixed at the first extension line of the base dimension and you are prompted to specify the origin of the second extension line.

```
Specify a second extension line origin or [Undo Select]
<Select>:
```

Note: The default spacing between the baseline dimensions controlled by the current dimension style parameters. You can modify the spacing between the baseline dimensions by entering the new value in the **Baseline spacing** field of the **Lines** tab in the **Modify Dimension Style** dialog box, as discussed earlier in this chapter.

5. Move the cursor toward a point (P2) in the drawing which is to select as the origin of the second extension line, see Figure 6.94.

6. Click to specify the origin of the second extension line when the cursor snaps to the point. The second baseline dimension is applied (see Figure 6.94), and the preview of another baseline dimension is attached to the cursor, and you are prompted to specify the origin of the second extension line.

```
Specify a second extension line origin or [Undo Select] <Select>:
```

7. Similarly, you can continue to specify the origin of the second extension line and apply multiple baseline dimensions. After applying the baseline dimensions, press the ENTER key twice to exit the tool.

Applying Continue Dimensions

Similar to applying baseline dimensions, you can apply continue dimensions in a drawing, see Figure 6.95. Continue dimensions are the chain of linear dimensions which are placed end to end (second extension line of the first linear dimension used as the first extension line for the next linear dimension). In AutoCAD, you can apply the continue dimensions by using the **Continue** tool or by using the DIMCONT command.

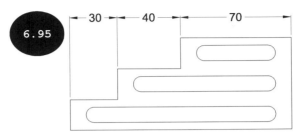

Procedure for Applying Continue Dimensions

Before you start applying the continue dimensions, you need to apply a linear/angular dimension as the base dimension.

1. Apply a linear dimension in the drawing as the base dimension by using the **Linear** tool, see Figure 6.96.

   After applying the base dimension, you can apply the continue dimensions by using the **Continue** tool.

2. Click on **Dimension > Continue** in the Menu Bar. The preview of the continue dimension is attached to the cursor whose first extension line is fixed at the second extension line of the base dimension and you are prompted to specify the origin of the second extension line. You can also invoke this tool by using the DIMCONT command.

   ```
   Specify a second extension line origin or [Undo Select] <Select>:
   ```

   Note: If the linear, angular, or ordinate dimensions are present in the current drawing, then the last applied dimension is selected as the base dimension, automatically. Also, you are prompted to specify the origin of the second extension line. If you want to skip the automatic selection of base dimension, then press the ENTER key. On doing so, you are prompted to select the base dimension.

320 Chapter 6 > Working with Dimensions and Dimensions Style

3. Move the cursor toward a point (P1) which is to select as the origin of the second extension line, see Figure 6.97.

4. Click to specify the origin of the second extension line when the cursor snaps to the point in the drawing area. The continue linear dimension is placed in the drawing area and the preview of another linear dimension is attached to the cursor

5. Move the cursor toward a point (P2) which is to select as the origin of the second extension line, see Figure 6.97.

6. Click to specify the origin of the second extension line when the cursor snaps to the point. The second linear dimension is applied, and the preview of another linear dimension is attached to the cursor.

```
Specify  a  second  extension  line  origin  or  [Undo  Select]
<Select>:
```

6.97

7. Similarly, you can continue to specify the origin of the second extension line and apply multiple continue linear dimensions. After applying all the required continue dimensions, press the ENTER key twice to exit the tool.

Applying Multiple Dimensions

In addition to applying individual dimension one by one, as discussed, AutoCAD allows you to apply multiple dimensions together by using the **Quick Dimension** tool or QDIM command. You can apply multiple dimensions such as radius, diameter, baseline, or continue.

Procedure for Applying Multiple Dimensions

1. Click on **Dimension > Quick Dimension** in the Menu Bar. Alternatively, enter QDIM in the Command Line window and then press ENTER. You are prompted to select geometry.

```
Select geometry to dimension:
```

2. Select geometries to be dimensioned by using the Window or Cross Window selection method, see Figure 6.98.

6.98

3. After selecting geometries, press ENTER. The preview of continue dimensions attached to the cursor and you are prompted to specify the position in the drawing area.

```
Specify dimension line position, or [Continuous Staggered Baseline
Ordinate Radius Diameter datumPoint Edit SeTtings] <Continuous>:
```

 By default, the continue dimension applied to the selected geometries. To apply baseline dimensions, click on the **Baseline** option in the command prompt or enter **B**. Similarly, to apply radius or diameter dimensions, click on the **Radius** or **Diameter** option in the command prompt or enter **R** or **D** in the Command Line window.

4. Select the required type of dimensions to be applied by using the options available in the command prompt. For example, to apply multiple diameter dimensions, click on the **Diameter** option in the command prompt or enter **D**.

5. After specifying the type of dimensions to be applied, click to define the placement point in the drawing area. The selected type of dimensions are applied to the geometries. Figure 6.99 shows a drawing in which multiple diameter dimensions are applied.

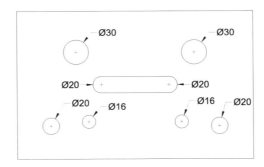

6.99

322   Chapter 6 > Working with Dimensions and Dimensions Style

Tutorial 1

Create the drawing and apply dimensions as shown in Figure 6.100. You need to apply dimensions as per the new dimension style having following dimension parameters.

New Dimension Style Parameters	
Text font	Arial
Text font style	Regular
Text height	4.75
Text placement - Offset from dimension line	2.5
Arrowheads style	Closed filled
Arrow size	4.5
Center marks	Mark - 1
Dimension break size	3.5
Extension lines - Extend beyond dimension lines	2
Extension lines - Offset from origin	1.75
Linear dimensions - Precision	0
Angular dimensions - Precision	0

6.100

Section 1: Starting a new AutoCAD Drawing
1. Start AutoCAD and then open a new drawing file. Next, set the drawing limits.

Section 2: Creating Drawing
1. Click on the **Line** tool in the **Draw** panel of the **Home** tab. You are prompted to specify the first point of the line. Alternatively, enter **L** in the Command Line window and then press ENTER to invoke the **Line** tool.

```
Specify first point:
```

2. Click to specify the start point of the line in the drawing area. You are prompted to specify the next point of the line.

3. Make sure that the Dynamic Input mode and the Ortho mode are turned on.

4. Follow the command sequence given below for creating the drawing.

```
Specify next point or [Undo]:
```
Move the cursor horizontally toward the right and then enter 126 in the Dynamic Input box (***ENTER***)
```
Specify next point or [Undo]:
```
Move the cursor vertically upward and then enter 76 (***ENTER***)
```
Specify next point or [Undo]:
```
Move the cursor horizontally toward the left and then enter 14 (***ENTER***)
```
Specify next point or [Undo]:
```
Move the cursor vertically downwards and enter 24 (***ENTER***)
```
Specify next point or [Close Undo]:
```
Move the cursor horizontally toward the left and then enter 2 (***ENTER***)
```
Specify next point or [Undo]:
```
Move the cursor vertically upward and then enter 24 (***ENTER***)
```
Specify next point or [Close Undo]:
```
Move the cursor horizontally toward the left and then enter 14 (***ENTER***)
```
Specify next point or [Undo]:
```
Move the cursor vertically downward and then enter 40 (***ENTER***)
```
Specify next point or [Close Undo]:
```
Move the cursor horizontally toward the left and then enter 48 (***ENTER***)
```
Specify next point or [Close Undo]:
```
Move the cursor vertically downward and then enter 18 (***ENTER***)
```
Specify next point or [Close Undo]:
```
Move the cursor horizontally toward the left and then enter 24 (***ENTER***)
```
Specify next point or [Close Undo]:
```
Move the cursor vertically upward and then enter 28 (***ENTER***)
```
Specify next point or [Close Undo]:
```
Move the cursor horizontally toward the left and then enter 24 (***ENTER***)
```
Specify next point or [Close Undo]:
```
C or Close (***ENTER***) *(See Figure 6.101)*

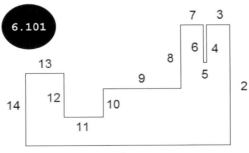

> **Note:** In Figure 6.101, the entities are numbered for your reference to create other entities of the drawing.

After creating the line entities of the drawing, you need to create circle entities.

5. Click on the **Circle, Radius** tool in the **Circle** flyout of the **Draw** panel or enter C in the Command Line window and then press ENTER. You are prompted to specify the center point of the circle.

   ```
   Specify center point for circle or [3P 2P Ttr (tan tan radius)]:
   ```

6. Move the cursor toward the midpoint of the horizontal line (13), refer to Figure 6.101.

7. Click to specify the center point of the circle when cursor snaps to the midpoint of the horizontal line (13), see Figure 6.102. You are prompted to specify the radius of the circle.

   ```
   Specify radius of circle or [Diameter]:
   ```

8. Enter **12** as the radius of the circle and then press ENTER. The circle of radius 12 units is created in the drawing area, see Figure 6.103.

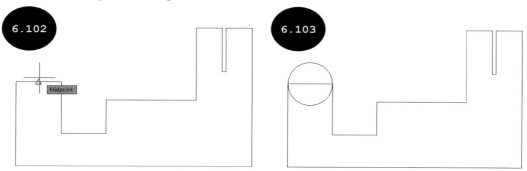

9. Similarly, create another two circles of radius 9 units and 7 units, see Figure 6.104. The center point of the circle having radius 9 units is at the midpoint of the line (5), and the center point of the circle having radius 7 units is at the midpoint of the line (13), see Figure 6.104.

Now, you need to create a vertical line at the offset distance of 45 units from the vertical line (2).

10. Click on the **Offset** tool in the **Modify** panel of the **Home** tab or enter O in the Command Line window and then press ENTER. You are prompted to specify the offset distance.

    ```
    Specify offset distance or [Through Erase Layer] <Through>:
    ```

11. Enter **45** as the offset distance and then press ENTER. You are prompted to select an object to offset.

    ```
    Select object to offset or [Exit Undo] <Exit>:
    ```

12. Click on the vertical line (2) as the object to offset, refer to Figure 6.101. You are prompted to specify a point on the side to offset.

    ```
    Specify point on side to offset or [Exit Multiple Undo] <Exit>:
    ```

13. Move the cursor toward left and then click to specify a point on the left side of the selected vertical line (2). The vertical line at the offset distance of 45 units is created, see Figure 6.105.

14. Press ENTER to exit the tool.

15. Similarly, create another vertical line at the offset distance of 25 units from the newly created vertical line, see Figure 6.106.

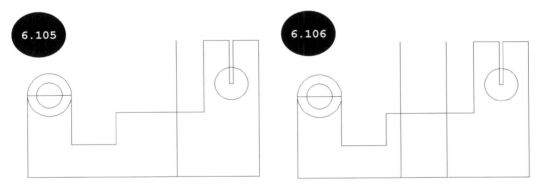

Now, you need to trim the unwanted portions of the entities.

Section 3: Trimming the Drawing Entities

1. Click on the **Trim** tool in the **Modify** panel or enter TR in the Command Line window and then press ENTER. You are prompted to select cutting edges/boundaries.

    ```
    Select cutting edges ...
    Select objects or <select all>:
    ```

326   Chapter 6 > Working with Dimensions and Dimensions Style

2. Press ENTER to skip the selection of cutting edges/boundaries. You are prompted to select an object to trim.

   ```
   Select object to trim or shift-select to extend or
   [Fence Crossing Project Edge eRase Undo]:
   ```

3. Click on the unwanted entity (1) to be trimmed, see Figure 6.107. The selected entity is trimmed to its nearest intersection, see Figure 6.108. Also, you are prompted to select an object to trim.

   ```
   Select object to trim or shift-select to extend or
   [Fence Crossing Project Edge eRase Undo]:
   ```

4. Similarly, click on the other unwanted entities (2, 3, 4, 5, 6, 7, and 8), refer to Figure 6.107. Figure 6.109 shows the drawing after trimming all the unwanted entities.

5. After trimming the entities, press the ENTER key to exit the tool.

Section 4: Deleting the Unwanted Entities

1. Click on the horizontal entities inside the circles of radius 7 units and 9 units as the objects to be deleted from the drawing area, see Figure 6.110.

2. Press the DELETE key. The selected entities get removed from the drawing, see Figure 6.111.

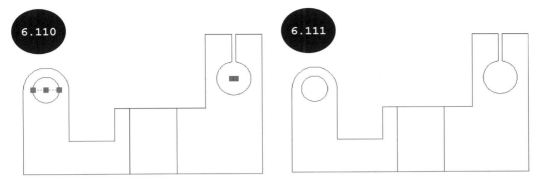

Section 5: Creating Fillet

1. Click on the **Fillet** tool in the **Modify** panel or enter **F** in the Command Line window and then press ENTER. You are prompted to select the first object of the fillet.

   ```
   Select first object or [Undo Polyline Radius Trim Multiple]:
   ```

2. Click on the **Radius** option in the command prompt or enter **R** and then press ENTER. You are prompted to specify the fillet radius.

   ```
   Specify fillet radius <0.0000>:
   ```

3. Enter **15** as the fillet radius and then press ENTER. You are prompted to select the first object of the fillet.

   ```
   Select first object or [Undo Polyline Radius Trim Multiple]:
   ```

4. Click on the right-most vertical line of the drawing as the first object of the fillet. You are prompted to select the second object of the fillet.

   ```
   Select second object or shift-select to apply corner or [Radius]:
   ```

5. Click on the bottom horizontal line as the second object of the fillet. The fillet of radius 15 is created, see Figure 6.112.

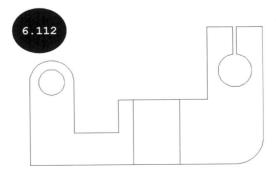

328   Chapter 6 > Working with Dimensions and Dimensions Style

Section 6: Creating Layers

Now, you need to create layers: Object, Hidden, and Dimension. After creating the layers, assign different drawing objects to the respective layers such as hidden objects to the Hidden layer.

1. Click on the **Layer Properties** tool in the **Layers** panel of the **Home** tab or enter **LA** in the Command Line window and then press ENTER. The **LAYER PROPERTIES MANAGER** appears, see Figure 6.113.

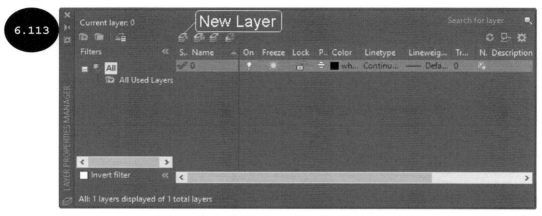

6.113

2. Click on the **New Layer** button in the **LAYER PROPERTIES MANAGER** or press ALT + N key. A new layer with default name "**Layer 1**" is created.

3. Enter **Object** as the name of the newly created layer in the **LAYER PROPERTIES MANAGER**. Accept the default parameters for the newly created Object layer.

4. Similarly, create two more layers: Hidden and Dimension. Also, assign the HIDDEN linetype to the Hidden layer and accept the default parameters for Dimension layer, see Figure 6.114.

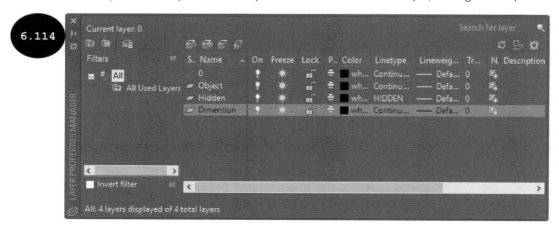

6.114

5. After creating all the layers, close the **LAYER PROPERTIES MANAGER**.

Section 7: Assigning Drawing Objects to the Layers

1. Select all the drawing objects except two vertical lines (hidden lines), see Figure 6.115.

2. Invoke the **Layer** drop-down list in the **Layers** panel of the **Home** tab, see Figure 6.116.

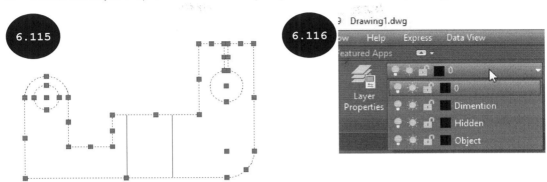

3. Move the cursor over the **Object** layer in the **Layer** drop-down list and then click on it to assign the selected objects to the **Object** layer. Next, press the ESC key to exit the selection.

4. Select two vertical lines to assign them to the Hidden layer, see Figure 6.117.

5. Invoke the **Layer** drop-down list, refer to Figure 6.116, and then click on the **Hidden** layer. The selected vertical lines are assigned to the **Hidden** layer, see Figure 6.118. Next, press the ESC key to exit the selection.

Note: If the entities of the Hidden layer appear as continuous linetype in the drawing area, then you may need to increase or decrease its linetype scale by using the **Properties** panel. To increase or decrease the linetype scale, enter **PR** in the Command Line window and then press ENTER. The **Properties** panel appears on the left of the drawing area. Next, select the entities of the Hidden layer in the drawing area whose linetype scale has to change and then enter the scale value in the **Linetype scale** field of the **Properties** panel. You can try any value as the linetype scale to match the display of the hidden line, as required.

330   Chapter 6 > Working with Dimensions and Dimensions Style

After creating the drawing, you need to apply dimensions. As mentioned in the tutorial description, you need to apply dimensions as per the new dimension style. Therefore, you need first to create a new dimension style.

Section 8: Creating New Dimension Style

1. Enter **D** in the Command Line window and then press ENTER. The **Dimension Style Manager** dialog box appears, see Figure 6.119.

2. Click on the **Standard** dimension style in the **Styles** area of the dialog box as the base dimension style for creating the new dimension style.

3. Click on the **New** button in the **Dimension Style Manager** dialog box. The **Create New Dimension Style** dialog box appears.

4. Enter **C06_TUT** as the name of the new dimension style in the **New Style Name** field of the dialog box.

5. Click on the **Continue** button of the **Create New Dimension Style** dialog box. The **New Dimension Style** dialog box appears, see Figure 6.120.

6. Make sure that the **Text** tab is activated in this dialog box, see Figure 6.120.

7. Make sure that the **Standard** option is selected in the **Text style** drop-down list in the **Text** tab of the dialog box, see Figure 6.120.

6.120

8. Click on the [...] button available next to the **Text style** drop-down list. The **Text Style** dialog box appears.

9. Make sure that the **Arial** option is selected in the **Font Name** drop-down list, and the **Regular** option is selected in the **Font Style** drop-down list in this **Text Style** dialog box.

10. Click on the **Cancel** button to exit the **Text Style** dialog box.

11. Enter **4.75** in the **Text height** field of the **Text appearance** area in the **Text** tab of the dialog box.

12. Enter **2.5** in the **Offset from dim line** field of the **Text placement** area in the **Text** tab.

13. Click on the **Symbols and Arrows** tab in the **New Dimension Style** dialog box.

14. Make sure that the **Closed filled** option is selected in the **First**, **Second**, and **Leader** drop-down lists of the **Arrowheads** area in the **Symbols and Arrows** tab.

15. Enter **4.5** in the **Arrow size** field of the **Arrowheads** area.

16. Make sure that the **Mark** radio button is selected in the **Center marks** area.

17. Enter **1** in the field available in front of **Mark** radio button of the **Center marks** area.

332 Chapter 6 > Working with Dimensions and Dimensions Style

18. Enter **3.5** in the **Break size** field of the **Dimension Break** area of the dialog box.

19. Click on the **Lines** tab in the **New Dimension Style** dialog box.

20. Enter **2** in the **Extend beyond dim lines** field of the **Extension lines** area in the **Lines** tab.

21. Enter **1.75** in the **Offset from origin** field of the **Extension lines** area in the **Lines** tab.

22. Click on the **Primary Units** tab in the dialog box.

23. Select the **0** option in the **Precision** drop-down list of the **Linear dimensions** area.

24. Select the **0** option in the **Precision** drop-down list of the **Angular dimensions** area.

25. Accept the remaining default settings and then click on the **OK** button in the **New Dimension Style** dialog box. The new dimension style named as C06_TUT is created and listed in the **Styles** area of the **Dimension Style Manager** dialog box.

26. Click on the newly created dimension style "C06_TUT" in the **Styles** area of the **Dimension Style Manager** dialog box.

27. Click on the **Set Current** button in the dialog box to make the newly created dimension style as the current dimension style of the drawing.

28. Click on the **Close** button in the **Dimension Style Manager** dialog box to exit the dialog box.

    After creating the dimension style and making it the current style of the drawing, you need to apply dimensions to the drawing.

Section 9: Applying Dimensions

1. Click on the **Linear** tool in the **Dimension** flyout of the **Annotation** panel in the **Home** tab or enter **DIMLIN** in the Command Line window and then press ENTER. You are prompted to specify the origin for the first extension line.

    ```
    Specify first extension line origin or <select object>:
    ```

2. Press ENTER to select the object to be dimensioned directly. You are prompted to select the object to be dimensioned.

    ```
    Select object to dimension:
    ```

3. Click on the bottom horizontal line of the drawing. The linear dimension of the selected line is attached to the cursor. Also, you are prompted to specify the dimension line location.

    ```
    Specify dimension line location or
    [Mtext Text Angle Horizontal Vertical Rotated]:
    ```

4. Move the cursor vertically downward to a small distance and then click to specify the location for the attached dimension, see Figure 6.121.

5. Click on the **Linear** tool in the **Dimension** flyout again. You are prompted to specify the origin for the first extension line.

   ```
   Specify first extension line origin or <select object>:
   ```

6. Move the cursor toward the upper right corner of the drawing (P1), see Figure 6.122. Next, click on it to specify the origin of the first extension line when the cursor snaps to the point (P1). You are prompted to specify the origin of the second extension line.

   ```
   Specify second extension line origin:
   ```

7. Move the cursor toward the center point of the right circle (P2), see Figure 6.122. Next, click to specify the origin of the second extension line when the cursor snaps to it. The linear dimension between the selected points (P1 and P2) is attached to the cursor. Also, you are prompted to specify the dimension location.

   ```
   Specify dimension line location or
   [Mtext Text Angle Horizontal Vertical Rotated]:
   ```

8. Move the cursor horizontally toward the right to a small distance and then click to specify the location for the attached dimension, see Figure 6.122.

9. Similarly, apply the remaining linear (horizontal and vertical) dimensions to other entities of the drawing, see Figure 6.123. You can apply dimension by selecting the object to be dimensioned or by selecting points. Make sure that the Object snap mode is turned on for selecting points. Figure 6.123 shows the drawing after applying all the linear dimensions.

    After applying the linear dimensions, you need to apply radius dimensions to the arc entities.

10. Click on the **Dimension** tool in the **Annotation** panel. You are prompted to select the object to be dimensioned. Alternatively, click on the **Radius** tool in the **Dimension** flyout of the **Annotation** panel or enter DIMRAD in the Command Line window and then press ENTER.

    ```
    Select objects or specify first extension line origin or [Angular
    Baseline Continue Ordinate aliGn Distribute Layer Undo]:
    ```

11. Move the cursor toward the upper left arc (A1), see Figure 6.124 and then click on it. The radius dimension is attached to the cursor, and you are prompted to specify the dimension location.

    ```
    Specify dimension line location or [Mtext Text Angle]:
    ```

12. Click to specify the dimension location on the upper left side of the selected arc (A1). The radius 12 units applied to the arc, see Figure 6.124.

13. Similarly, apply the radius dimension to the arc (A2), see Figure 6.124. Note that the **Dimension** tool is still activated.

After applying the radius dimension to the arcs, you need to apply diameter dimension to the circle.

14. Move the cursor toward the circle (C1), see Figure 6.125 and then click on it. The diameter dimension attached to the cursor, and you are prompted to specify the dimension location.

    Note: You can also apply diameter dimensions to circles by using the **Diameter** tool of the **Dimension** flyout or by using the DIMDIA command.

15. Click to specify the dimension location above the selected circle (C1). The diameter dimension is applied, see Figure 6.125.

After applying all the dimensions to the drawing entities, you need to move them to the Dimension layer.

16. Select all the dimensions and then invoke the **Layer** drop-down list of the **Layers** panel in the **Home** tab. Next, click on the **Dimension** layer to assign all the selected dimensions to it.

Section 10: Saving the Drawing

After creating the drawing, you need to save it.

1. Click on the **Save** tool in the **Quick Access Toolbar**. The **Save Drawing As** dialog box appears.

2. Browse to the *AutoCAD* folder and then create a folder with the name *Chapter 6* inside the *AutoCAD* folder.

3. Enter **Tutorial 1** in the **File name** field of the dialog box and then click on the **Save** button. The drawing gets saved with the name *Tutorial 1* in the *Chapter 6* folder.

336 Chapter 6 > Working with Dimensions and Dimensions Style

Hands-on Test Drive 1

Create the drawing and apply dimensions as shown in Figure 6.126. You need to modify the default dimension style "Standard" for applying the dimensions. Below are the dimension parameters to be modified in the Standard dimension style.

Dimension Style Parameters	
Text font	Arial
Text font style	Regular
Text height	4.5
Text placement - Offset from dimension line	1.75
Arrowheads style	Closed filled
Arrow size	4.25
Dimension break size	3
Extension lines - Extend beyond dimension lines	1.25
Extension lines - Offset from origin	1
Linear dimensions - Precision	0
Angular dimensions - Precision	0

6.126

Hands-on Test Drive 2

Create the drawing and apply dimensions as shown in Figure 6.127. You need to modify the default dimension style "Standard" for applying the dimensions. The dimension parameters to be modified in the Standard dimension style are same as mentioned in the Hands-on Test Drive 1 description.

6.127

Hands-on Test Drive 3

Create the drawing and apply Continue dimensions as shown in Figure 6.128. You need to create the new dimension style for applying the Continue dimensions. The dimension parameters for creating the new dimension style are discussed next.

New Dimension Style Parameters	
Text font	Arial
Text font style	Regular
Text height	2.75
Text placement - Offset from dimension line	1.5
Arrowheads style	Closed filled
Arrow size	2.5

Chapter 6 > Working with Dimensions and Dimensions Style

Dimension break size	3.5
Extension lines - Extend beyond dimension lines	1.25
Extension lines - Offset from origin	1
Linear dimensions - Precision	0
Angular dimensions - Precision	0

6.128

Hands-on Test Drive 4

Create the drawing and apply dimensions as shown in Figure 6.129. You need to modify the default dimension style "Standard" for applying the dimensions. The dimension parameters to be modified in the Standard dimension style are same as mentioned in the Hands-on Test Drive 3 description.

6.129

Summary

In this chapter, you have learned about various components of a dimension, how to create a new dimension style, modify existing dimension style, and override dimension style. You have also learned how to apply various types of dimensions such as linear, aligned, angular, diameter, and radius.

Questions

- You can create a new dimension style by using the _____ dialog box.

- You can break dimension lines which are intersecting with other dimension or drawing object by using the _____ command.

- You can invoke the **Dimension Style Manager** dialog box by entering the _____ in the Command Line window and then pressing the ENTER key.

- When you apply a dimension, a new layer named as _____ created, automatically.

- A _____ dimension is used to measure the angle between two non-parallel objects.

- A _____ dimension is used to measure the length of an arc or a polyline arc segment.

- The _____ tool is used to apply the jogged radius dimension to a circle or an arc whose center not displayed in the drawing area.

- The _____ tool is used to apply the linear dimension to an object having a high length to width ratio.

- The _____ dimensions are the series of parallel linear dimensions that share the same base point.

- AutoCAD allows you can apply multiple dimensions together by using the _____ tool or _____ command.

CHAPTER 7

Editing Dimensions and Adding Text

In this chapter, you will learn the following:

- Editing Dimensions by using DIMEDIT Command
- Editing Dimensions by using DIMTEDIT Command
- Editing Dimensions by using DDEDIT Command
- Editing Dimensions by using Dimension Grips
- Editing Dimensions by using PROPERTIES Palette
- Editing Dimensions by using Editing Tools
- Adding Text/Notes
- Creating and Modifying a Text Style
- Adding Text by using the Single Line Tool
- Adding Text by using the Multiline Text Tool
- Editing the Single Line and Multiline Text
- Converting the Single line Text to the Multiline Text

In this chapter, you will learn about editing and modifying dimensions. As the drawing process involves several design revisions, the editing and modifying dimensions become imperative. AutoCAD provided with various tools/commands which make the editing and modification process faster and easy. You can edit the dimension text/value, add a prefix or suffix to the dimension value, modify dimension text format, dimension position, dimension text justification, and so on by using the DIMEDIT command, DIMTEDIT command, DDEDIT command, Dimension grips, or by using the Properties palette. Moreover, you can edit the dimensions by using the editing tools such as **Trim**, **Extend**, and **Stretch**. In addition to editing dimensions by using various tools/commands, in this chapter, you will also learn about annotating drawings.

Editing Dimensions by using DIMEDIT Command

The DIMEDIT command is used to edit dimension text/value such that you can rotate, modify, restore, and specify new dimension text/value. Moreover, you can change the oblique angle of extension lines by using this command. The procedures to specify new dimension text/value, rotate and restore dimension text, change the oblique angle of dimension text are discussed next.

Procedure for Specifying the New Dimension Text/Value

1. Enter DIMEDIT in the Command Line window and then press ENTER. You are prompted to enter the editing type.

   ```
   Enter  type  of  dimension  editing  [Home  New  Rotate  Oblique]
   <Home>:
   ```

2. Click on the **New** option in the command prompt or enter **N** and then press ENTER. An edit field appears in the drawing area.

3. Enter new dimension text/value in the edit field and then click the left mouse button anywhere in the drawing area. You are prompted to select objects. You can also enter a prefix or suffix to the dimension text/value.

   ```
   Select objects:
   ```

4. Click on the dimension for specifying the new dimension text/value. Next, press ENTER. The dimension text/value of the selected dimension is changed.

   Note: The newly specified dimension text/value is an override dimension value and it does not affect the original size of the object.

Procedure for Rotating the Dimension Text

1. Enter DIMEDIT in the Command Line window and then press ENTER. You are prompted to enter the editing type.

   ```
   Enter  type  of  dimension  editing  [Home  New  Rotate  Oblique]
   <Home>:
   ```

2. Click on the **Rotate** option in the command prompt or enter **R** and then press ENTER. You are prompted to specify the rotational angle for dimension text.

   ```
   Specify angle for dimension text:
   ```

3. Enter a rotational angle for dimension text and then press ENTER. You are prompted to select objects to rotate.

   ```
   Select objects:
   ```

4. Click on the dimension whose dimension text to be rotated and then press ENTER. The dimension text of the selected dimension gets rotated to the specified angle, see Figure 7.1.

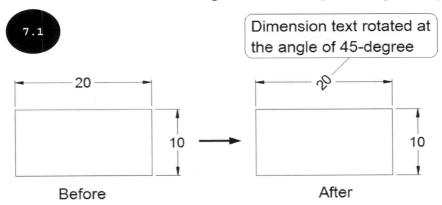

Procedure for Restoring the Dimension Text to Original Position
1. Enter DIMEDIT in the Command Line window and then press ENTER.

   ```
   Enter type of dimension editing [Home New Rotate Oblique]
   <Home>:
   ```

2. Click on the **Home** option in the command prompt or enter H and then press ENTER. You are prompted to select objects.

   ```
   Select objects:
   ```

3. Click on the dimension whose dimension text to be restored to its original position and then press ENTER. The dimension text of the selected dimension is restored to its original position.

Procedure for Changing the Oblique Angle of Extension Lines
1. Enter DIMEDIT in the Command Line window and then press ENTER.

   ```
   Enter type of dimension editing [Home New Rotate Oblique]
   <Home>:
   ```

2. Click on the **Oblique** option in the command prompt or enter O and then press ENTER. You are prompted to select objects.

   ```
   Select objects:
   ```

3. Click on dimensions whose oblique angle of extension lines to be changed and then press ENTER. You are prompted to enter an oblique angle.

   ```
   Enter obliquing angle (press ENTER for none):
   ```

344   Chapter 7 > Editing Dimensions and Adding Text

4. Enter the oblique angle and then press ENTER. The oblique angle of extension lines is changed, see Figure 7.2.

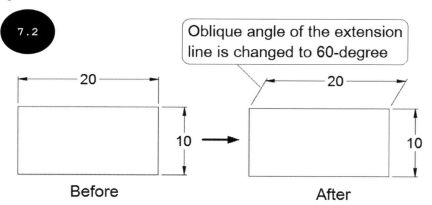

Editing Dimensions by using DIMTEDIT Command

The DIMTEDIT command is used to change the dimension text justification and angle. The procedure to change dimension text justification and angle is discussed next.

Procedure for Changing the Dimension Text Justification and Angle

1. Enter DIMTEDIT in the Command Line window and then press ENTER. You are prompted to select dimension.

   ```
   Select dimension:
   ```

2. Click on the dimension to be edited. The dimension text is attached to the cursor and you are prompted to specify a new location for the dimension text.

   ```
   Specify new location for dimension text or [Left Right Center Home Angle]:
   ```

3. Click on the **Left**, **Right**, or **Center** option in the command prompt for left, right, or center justification of the dimension text, respectively. Alternatively, enter L, R, or C in the Command Line window and then press ENTER. The dimension text is placed in the drawing area as per the option selected, see Figure 7.3.

> **Note:** By using the **Angle** option of the command prompt, you can change the angle/orientation of the dimension text. Also, you can restore the dimension text to the previous position or orientation by using the **Home** option of the command prompt.

Editing Dimensions by using DDEDIT Command

The DDEDIT command is used to add a prefix or suffix to the dimension text/value or specify a new dimension value. You can also edit the single and multiline annotations of a drawing by using the DDEDIT command. You will learn about adding annotations in this chapter. The procedure to edit dimension text/value by using the DDEDIT command is discussed next.

Procedure for Editing the Dimension text/Value

1. Enter DDEDIT in the Command Line window and then press ENTER. You are prompted to select an annotation object to be edited.

   ```
   Select an annotation object:
   ```

2. Click on the dimension text or annotation to be edited. The selected dimension text or annotation appears in an edit box, see Figure 7.4. You will learn about adding annotation later in this chapter.

3. Enter a new dimension text/value in the edit box. You can also add a prefix or suffix to the dimension text/value, see Figure 7.5. For example, to add a diameter symbol to a linear diameter dimension, enter '%%c' followed by the diameter value.

4. Click anywhere in the drawing area. The dimension text/value of the selected dimension is changed or override to the new dimension text/value.

Editing Dimensions by using Dimension Grips

You can also edit dimensions by using dimension grips. Grips of a dimension appear in the drawing area when you select it, see Figure 7.6. By using grips, you can change the position of the dimension text, the spacing between the dimension line and the object, and the position of extension lines.

Procedure for Changing the Position of Dimension Text

1. Click on the dimension to be edited in the drawing area. The grips of the selected dimension appear in the drawing area, see Figure 7.6.

2. Click on the grip near the dimension text. The dimension text with the dimension line attached to the cursor. Now, as you move the cursor, the dimension text along with the dimension line moves in the drawing area, accordingly. Move the cursor and then click the left mouse button anywhere in the drawing area to position the dimension text.

Note: When you click on the grip near the dimension text, the dimension text with the dimension line gets attached to the cursor. It is because the default option for the movement of dimension text set to the **Move with Dim Line** option. To change the default option or access other options for editing the dimension text, move the cursor over the grip near the dimension text. A menu appears, see Figure 7.7. In this menu, click on the **Move Text Only** option to move only the dimension text. Now, on moving the cursor, only the dimension text moves in the drawing area. Next, click in the drawing area to specify the new position for the dimension text. You can specify the position of the dimension text along the dimension line or anywhere in the drawing area, as required. To move the dimension text with leader, click on the **Move with Leader** option in the menu. As soon as you click on the **Move with Leader** option, the dimension text gets attached to the cursor such that it connected to the dimension line with a leader. Now, click to specify the position of the dimension text. The dimension text is placed to the specified position with a leader, which is connected to the dimension line, see Figure 7.8.

To place the dimension text above the dimension line, click on the **Above Dim Line** option in the menu appeared. To move the dimension text at the center of dimension line, click on the **Center Vertically** option of the menu. To reset the text position, click on the **Reset Text Position** option.

Procedure for Changing the Space between Dimension Line and Object

1. Click on the dimension to be edited in the drawing area. The grips of the selected dimension appear in the drawing area, refer to Figure 7.6.

2. Click on the grip near the endpoint of an extension line, refer to Figure 7.6. The dimension line is attached to the cursor. Next, move the cursor away or near the object, perpendicularly. On moving the cursor, the distance between the dimension line and the object changes. Next, click on the left mouse button in the drawing area to define the new position of the dimension line.

Procedure for Changing the Position of Extension Lines

1. Click on the dimension to be edited in the drawing area. The grips of the selected dimension appear in the drawing area, see Figure 7.9.

2. Click on the grip near the origin of an extension line to be edited, refer to Figure 7.6. The respective extension line is attached to the cursor. Now, as you move the cursor, the extension line moves in the drawing area, and the dimension text/value gets modified, accordingly. Next, click to specify the new position for the extension line. The position of the extension line is defined and the dimension text/value is modified, see Figure 7.9.

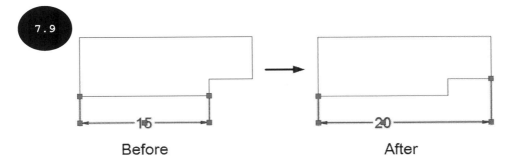

Editing Dimensions by using PROPERTIES Palette

You can also edit dimensions properties such as dimension text size, arrowhead size, linetype, lineweight, and so on by using the PROPERTIES palette. To invoke the PROPERTIES palette, click on the **View** tab in the **Ribbon**. The tools of the **View** tab appear, see Figure 7.10. Next, click on the **Properties** tool in the **Palettes** panel of the **View** tab. The PROPERTIES palette appears on the left of the drawing area, refer to Figure 7.11.

After invoking the PROPERTIES palette, click on the dimension to be edited. The properties of the selected dimension appear in the different categories of the PROPERTIES palette, see Figure 7.11. You can modify the properties of the selected dimension by using the options in the different categories of the PROPERTIES palette. The options are discussed next.

General

The options in the **General** category of the PROPERTIES palette are used to edit the properties such as color, layer, linetype, linetype scale, lineweight, transparency, and hyperlink of the selected dimension. You can modify these properties by using the options available in the **General** category.

Misc

The options in the **Misc** category are used to change the dimension style and the annotative property of the selected dimension. You can modify the dimension style and the annotative property by using the options available in this category.

Lines & Arrows
The options in the **Lines & Arrows** category are used to edit the arrowheads style, arrow size, dimension line lineweight, extension line lineweight, dimension line color, and so on. You can modify these parameters by using the options available in this category.

Text
The options in the **Text** category are used to edit the dimension text properties such as dimension text color, text height, text offset, text style, text horizontal position, text vertical position, text rotation, text override, and so on. You can edit these parameters by using the options available in this category.

Fit
The options in the **Fit** category are used to edit the fit parameters of the selected dimension such as the position of the dimension text inside extension line on/off, text movement, overall dimension scale, and so on. You can edit the fit parameters by using the options available in this category.

Primary Units
The options in the **Primary Units** category are used to edit the unit format, dimension precision, dimension prefix/suffix, dimension scale factor, zero suppression, and so on for the selected dimension.

Alternate Units
The options in the **Alternate Units** category are used to edit the unit format, unit precision, prefix/suffix, unit scale factor, and so on of the alternate unit. Note that by default, the options of this category not enabled. To enable the options of this category, select the **On** option in the **Alt enabled** drop-down list of this category.

Tolerances
The options in the **Tolerances** category are used to edit parameters that control the format and display of the tolerance in the dimension text.

Editing Dimensions by using Editing Tools
You can also edit the dimensions by using the editing tools such as **Trim**, **Extend**, and **Stretch**. The procedures to edit dimensions by using the editing tools are discussed next.

Procedure for Editing Dimensions by using the Trim Tool
1. Click on the **Trim** tool in the **Modify** panel of the **Home** tab. You are prompted to select cutting edges/boundaries objects. Alternatively, enter **TR** in the Command Line window and then press ENTER.

   ```
   Select cutting edges ...
   Select objects or <select all>:
   ```

350 Chapter 7 > Editing Dimensions and Adding Text

2. Click on an object as the cutting edge to trim the dimension, see Figure 7.12. Next, press ENTER. You are prompted to select objects to be trimmed.

   ```
   Select object to trim or shift-select to extend or
   [Fence Crossing Project Edge eRase Undo]:
   ```

3. Click on the dimension to be trimmed, see Figure 7.12. The portion of the selected dimension is trimmed and the dimension value of the dimension is modified accordingly, see Figure 7.13.

4. Press ENTER to exit the tool.

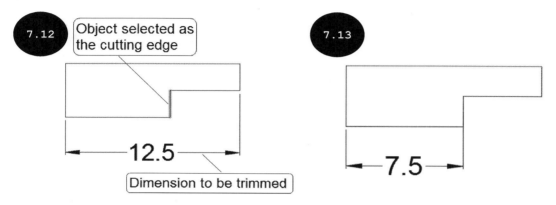

Procedure for Editing Dimensions by using the Extend Tool

1. Click on the down arrow next to the **Trim** tool in the **Modify** panel. A flyout appears. In this flyout, click on the **Extend** tool. You are prompted to select boundary edges objects. Alternatively, enter **EX** in the Command Line window and then press ENTER to invoke the **Extend** tool.

   ```
   Select boundary edges ...
   Select objects or <select all>:
   ```

2. Click on the object as the boundary edge for extending dimension, see Figure 7.14. Next, press ENTER. You are prompted to select objects to be extended.

   ```
   Select object to extend or shift-select to trim or
   [Fence Crossing Project Edge Undo]:
   ```

3. Click on the dimension to be extended, see Figure 7.14. Next, press ENTER. The selected dimension is extended up to the boundary edge and the dimension value of the dimension is modified, see Figure 7.15.

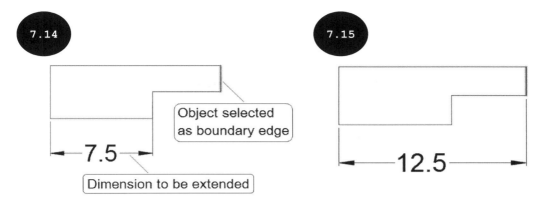

Procedure for Editing Dimensions by using the Stretch Tool

1. Click on the **Stretch** tool in the **Modify** panel or enter **S** in the Command Line window and then press ENTER. You are prompted to select objects to be stretched.

   ```
   Select objects:
   ```

2. Draw a cross window by defining first and second corner points around the objects to be stretched such that the boundary of the cross window encloses the objects partially, see Figure 7.16. You can select the objects to be stretched by using the Cross Window or Cross Polygon selection method.

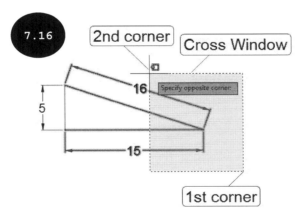

3. Press ENTER. You are prompted to specify the base point for stretching the objects.

   ```
   Specify base point or [Displacement] <Displacement>:
   ```

4. Click to specify the base point in the drawing area, see Figure 7.17. Next, move the cursor in the drawing area. The selected objects get stretched, dynamically. Also, the dimension values get modified, dynamically. You are prompted to specify the second point.

   ```
   Specify second point or <use first point as displacement>:
   ```

352   Chapter 7 > Editing Dimensions and Adding Text

5. Click to specify the second point in the drawing area as the placement point for the objects. The objects get stretched, and dimensions are modified, see Figure 7.18.

Adding Text/Notes

Text/notes used in drawings to convey additional information that is not available in drawings. In AutoCAD, you can add text by using the **Single Line** and **Multiline Text** tools. Before you learn about adding text in drawings, it is important to understand how to set a text style. A text style stores all information about text such as text height and font. When you open a new AutoCAD drawing file with the default template, the Annotative and Standard text styles are available, by default. You can edit the default text styles or create a new text style as per the requirement. Creating a new text style and adding text to a drawing are discussed next.

Creating and Modifying a Text Style

To create a new text style, enter **ST** in the Command Line window and then press ENTER. The **Text Style** dialog box appears, see Figure 7.19. Alternatively, expand the **Annotation** panel of the **Home** tab and then click on the **Text Style** tool to invoke the **Text Style** dialog box, see Figure 7.20.

In the **Text Style** dialog box, click on the **New** button. The **New Text Style** window appears, see Figure 7.21.

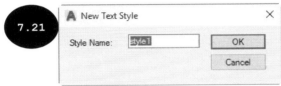

In this window, enter the name of the text style to be created and then click on the **OK** button. A new style created, and its name gets listed in the **Styles** area of the **Text Style** dialog box. Make sure that the newly created text style is selected in the **Styles** area of the dialog box. Next, specify the text font in the **Font Name** drop-down list, font style in the **Font Style** drop-down list, text height in the **Height** field, and so on for the text style. After specifying the properties for the text style, click on the **Apply** button and then click on the **Set Current** button in the dialog box to make the newly added text style as the current text style for the drawing. Next, click on the **Close** button to exit the dialog box.

Similar to creating a new text style, you can modify the existing text style parameters as per the requirement. To modify the existing text style, invoke the **Text Style** dialog box by using the ST command. Next, select the text style to be modified in the **Styles** area of the **Text Style** dialog box. The parameters of the selected text style appear on the right of the dialog box. You can modify the parameters such as text font, font style, and text height of the text style by using the options of the dialog box. Once you have made the changes, click on the **Apply** button in the dialog box and then click on the **Close** button to exit the dialog box.

After creating a new text style or modifying the existing text style, you can start with adding text/note in the drawing area. You can add text/notes in a drawing by using the **Single Line** and **Multiline Text** tools. Both these tools are discussed next.

Adding Text by using the Single Line Tool

The **Single Line** tool is used for adding single line text such as labels and notes in a drawing. You can add one or more lines of the text by using the **Single Line** tool, where each text line is an independent object which can move, format, or modify, individually. The procedure to add a single line text is discussed next.

354 Chapter 7 > Editing Dimensions and Adding Text

Procedure for Adding a Single Line Text

1. Invoke the **Text** flyout in the **Annotation** panel of the **Home** tab, see Figure 7.22. Next, click on the **Single Line** tool in the **Text** flyout, see Figure 7.22. Alternatively, enter **TEXT** in the Command Line window and then press ENTER to invoke the **Single Line** tool. You are prompted to specify the start point of the text.

    ```
    Specify start point of text or [Justify Style]:
    ```

7.22

> **Note:** You can also specify the justification and style for the text to add in the drawing area. To specify the text justification, click on the **Justify** option in the command prompt when you are prompted to 'Specify start point of text or [Justify Style]:'. Next, select the required text justification such as left, center, right, or middle in the command prompt. Similarly, to specify the text style, click on the **Style** option in the command prompt and then enter the name of the style in the Command Line window and then press ENTER.

2. Click in the drawing area to specify the start point of the text, see Figure 7.23. You are prompted to specify text height.

    ```
    Specify height <0.2000>:
    ```

> **Note:** If you have specified the text height in the text style by using the **Text Style** dialog box, then you will not be prompted to specify the text height. In such case, the text height defined in the text style will use for the text, and you will be directly prompted to specify the rotation angle of the text.

3. Enter a value of the text height, see Figure 7.23 and then press ENTER. Alternatively, click in the drawing area to specify the text height. You are prompted to specify the rotation angle of the text.

    ```
    Specify rotation angle of text <0>:
    ```

4. Enter a rotation angle of the text, see Figure 7.23 and then press ENTER. A blinking cursor appears in a text window, and you are prompted to write the text in the drawing area.

5. Write a text in the text window, as required. For writing multiple text lines, press ENTER at the end of each line. Figure 7.24 shows the text window with multiple text lines written. After writing the text, click anywhere in the drawing area and then press the ESC key to exit the tool.

Note: The multiple text lines written by using the **Single Line** tool/**TEXT** command act as independent objects which can be selected, moved, formatted, or edited individually.

Adding Text by using the Multiline Text Tool

The **Multiline Text** tool is used to write multiline text such as a paragraph of information, a block of text, and longer notes in a paragraph form in a drawing. In AutoCAD, writing multiline text is similar to writing text in a word document, where you can select words and change their properties such as height, color, and font. The procedure to add multiline text is discussed next.

Procedure for Adding a Multiline Text

1. Invoke the **Text** flyout in the **Annotation** panel of the **Home** tab, refer to Figure 7.22. Next, click on the **Multiline Text** tool. Alternatively, enter **MTEXT** in the Command Line window and then press ENTER to invoke the **Multiline Text** tool. You are prompted to specify the first corner of the text window.

        Specify first corner:

356 Chapter 7 > Editing Dimensions and Adding Text

2. Click to specify the first corner of the text window in the drawing area, see Figure 7.25. You are prompted to specify the opposite corner of the text window.

   ```
   Specify opposite corner or [Height Justify Line spacing Rotation
   Style Width Columns]:
   ```

   Note: You can change the default text height by using the **Height** option of the command prompt, text justification by using the **Justify** option, text style by using the **Style** options of the command prompt, and so on. For example, to change the default text height, click on the **Height** option in the command prompt when you are prompted to specify the opposite corner. You can also enter **H** in the Command Line window and then press ENTER to change the default text height. Next, enter new text height and then press ENTER.

3. Click to specify the opposite corner of the text window in the drawing area, see Figure 7.25. The **Text Editor** tab appears in the **Ribbon**, see Figure 7.26. Also, the **In-Place Text Editor** window appears with the tab and indent ruler in the drawing area for writing the text, see Figure 7.27.

7.25

7.26

Note: The options in the **Text Editor** tab are used to control the text parameters such as text style, text height, text font, layer, bold, italic, underline, text justification, bullets and numbering, columns, symbol, and so on. The **Text Editor** allows you to control the text parameters similar to a word document.

4. Write a text in the text window, as required, see Figure 7.27. Next, click anywhere in the drawing area. The text appears in the area which defined by specifying the corners of the text window.

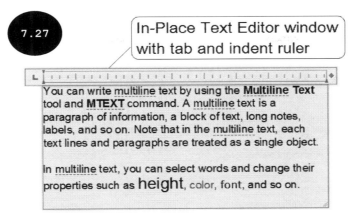

Note: You can change the width and height of the **In-Place Text Editor** window. To change the width of the window, move the cursor either over the right end of the text frame or the ruler until the cursor changes to a double arrow, see Figure 7.28. Next, drag the cursor to adjust the width. Similarly, to change the height, move the cursor over the bottom of the text frame and then drag the cursor to set the height of the window.

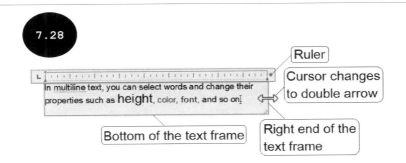

Editing the Single Line and Multiline Text

You can edit the single line and multiline text by using the DDEDIT command. For doing so, enter DDEDIT in the Command Line window and then press ENTER. Alternatively, double-click on the text to edit in the drawing area. You are prompted to select an annotation object to be edited.

    Select an annotation object:

Next, click on the text/annotation in the drawing area. The **In-Place Text Editor** window appears. Now, you can edit the text, as required. Once you have made the necessary modifications, click anywhere in the drawing area to exit the command.

358 Chapter 7 > Editing Dimensions and Adding Text

Converting the Single line Text to the Multiline Text

In a drawing, you may need to combine several individual single line text objects into a single multiline text object. You can convert one or more than one single line text objects to a multiline text object by using the TXT2MTXT command. For doing so, enter **TXT2MTXT** in the Command Line window and then press ENTER. You are prompted to select the objects to be converted into the multiline text object. Alternatively, click on the **Convert to Mtext** tool in the **Text** panel of the **Express Tools** tab of the **Ribbon** to invoke this command.

```
Select objects:
```

Click on the single line text objects to be converted into a multiline text one by one in the drawing area. Next, press ENTER. All the selected single line text objects get converted into a single multiline text object.

Tutorial 1

Create the drawing shown in Figure 7.29. Apply dimensions as illustrated in Figure 7.29. You need to edit the linear diameter dimensions of the drawing to add diameter symbols as a prefix to them, see Figure 7.29.

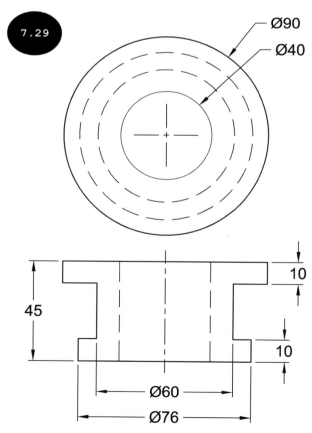

7.29

Section 1: Starting AutoCAD
1. Start AutoCAD and then open a new drawing file. Next, set the drawing limits.

Section 2: Creating the Front View
1. Click on the **Line** tool in the **Draw** panel of the **Home** tab. You are prompted to specify the first point of the line. Alternatively, enter **L** in the Command Line window and then press ENTER.

   ```
   Specify first point:
   ```

2. Click to specify the first point of the line in the drawing area. You are prompted to specify the next point of the line.

3. Make sure that the Dynamic Input mode and the Ortho mode are turned on.

4. Follow the command sequence given below for creating the drawing.

   ```
   Specify next point or [Undo]:
   ```
   Move the cursor horizontally toward the right and then enter **76** *in the Dynamic Input box* (**ENTER**)
   ```
   Specify next point or [Undo]:
   ```
   Move the cursor vertically upward and then enter **10** (**ENTER**)
   ```
   Specify next point or [Undo]:
   ```
   Move the cursor horizontally toward the left and then enter **8** (**ENTER**)
   ```
   Specify next point or [Undo]:
   ```
   Move the cursor vertically upward and then enter **25** (**ENTER**)
   ```
   Specify next point or [Close Undo]:
   ```
   Move the cursor horizontally toward the right and then enter **15** (**ENTER**)
   ```
   Specify next point or [Undo]:
   ```
   Move the cursor vertically upward and then enter **10** (**ENTER**)
   ```
   Specify next point or [Close Undo]:
   ```
   Move the cursor horizontally toward the left and then enter **90** (**ENTER**)
   ```
   Specify next point or [Undo]:
   ```
   Move the cursor vertically downward and then enter **10** (**ENTER**)
   ```
   Specify next point or [Close Undo]:
   ```
   Move the cursor horizontally toward the right and then enter **15** (**ENTER**)
   ```
   Specify next point or [Close Undo]:
   ```
   Move the cursor vertically downward and then enter **25** (**ENTER**)
   ```
   Specify next point or [Close Undo]:
   ```
   Move the cursor horizontally toward the left and then enter **8** (**ENTER**)
   ```
   Specify next point or [Close Undo]:
   ```
   C *or* **Close** (**ENTER**) *(See Figure 7.30)*

7.30

After creating the line entities of the drawing, you need to create hidden and centerline entities.

5. Click on the **Offset** tool in the **Modify** panel. You are prompted to specify the offset distance. Alternatively, enter **O** in the Command Line window and then press ENTER.

    ```
    Specify offset distance or [Through Erase Layer] <Through>:
    ```

6. Enter **10** as the offset distance and then press ENTER. You are prompted to select an object to offset.

    ```
    Select object to offset or [Exit Undo] <Exit>:
    ```

7. Click on the left middle vertical line as the object to offset, see Figure 7.31. You are prompted to specify a point on side to offset.

    ```
    Specify point on side to offset or [Exit Multiple Undo] <Exit>:
    ```

8. Click the left mouse button to the right of the vertical line selected. The offset entity is created, see Figure 7.31. You are prompted to select an object to offset again.

    ```
    Select object to offset or [Exit Undo] <Exit>:
    ```

9. Click on the right middle vertical line as the object to offset, see Figure 7.32. Next, click on the left of the vertical line selected. The offset entity is created, see Figure 7.32.

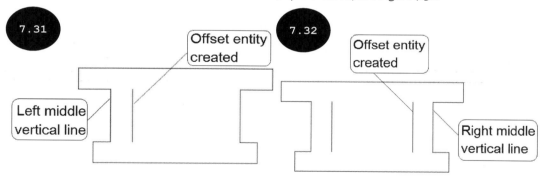

10. Press ENTER to exit the **Offset** tool.

    Now, you need to extend the offset entities up to their next intersection.

11. Enter **EX** in the Command Line window and then press ENTER. The **Extend** tool gets invoked, and you are prompted to select boundary edges. Alternatively, click on the **Extend** tool in the **Modify** panel of the **Home** tab to invoke the tool.

    ```
    Select boundary edges ...
    Select objects or <select all>:
    ```

12. Press ENTER to skip the selection of boundary edges. You are prompted to select the object to be extended.

    ```
    Select object to extend or shift-select to trim or
    [Fence Crossing Project Edge Undo]:
    ```

13. Click on the upper side of the left offset entity in the drawing area. The top portion of the offset entity gets extended up to the next intersection, see Figure 7.33. Next, click on the lower side of the left offset entity. The bottom portion of the entity gets extended, see Figure 7.34.

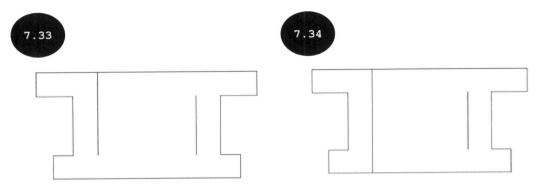

14. Similarly, click on both sides of the right offset entity to extend one by one. Figure 7.35 shows the drawing after extending the entities. Next, press ENTER to exit the **Extend** tool.

    Now, you need to draw centerline of the drawing.

15. Click on the **Line** tool in the **Draw** panel or enter **L** and then press ENTER. The **Line** tool gets invoked and you are prompted to specify the first point of the line.

    ```
    Specify first point:
    ```

16. Make sure that the Object Snap mode is activated.

362 Chapter 7 > Editing Dimensions and Adding Text

17. Move the cursor to the midpoint of the upper horizontal line and when the cursor snaps to it, see Figure 7.36, move the cursor vertically upward to a small distance. Next, click the left mouse button to specify the first point of the line. You are prompted to specify the next point of the line.

   ```
   Specify next point or [Undo]:
   ```

18. Move the cursor vertically downward and click to specify the end point of the line outside the bottom horizontal line of the drawing. The line is created, see Figure 7.37. Next, press ENTER to exit the **Line** tool.

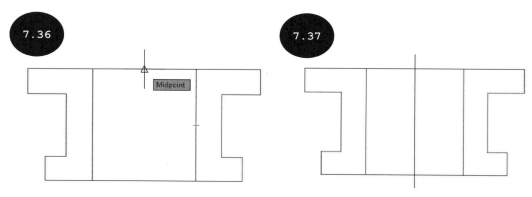

Section 3: Creating Layers and Assigning Objects to Layers

1. Click on the **Layer Properties** tool in the **Layers** panel of the **Home** tab. The **LAYER PROPERTIES MANAGER** appears.

2. Create four layers with the name Object, Hidden, Center, and Dimension in the **LAYER PROPERTIES MANAGER**, see Figure 7.38. Note that you need to assign the HIDDEN linetype to the Hidden layer, the CENTER linetype to the Center layer, and accept the remaining default properties of the layers, see Figure 7.38. Next, exit the **LAYER PROPERTIES MANAGER**.

3. After creating the layers, assign the hidden line entities (2 line entities) of the drawing to the Hidden layer, centerline entity (1 line entity) to the Center layer, and the remaining line entities

of the drawing to the Object layer. Figure 7.39 shows the drawing after assigning the drawing entities to the respective layers.

7.39

Note: If the hidden lines and the centerline of the drawing appear as continuous/solid lines in the drawing area, then you need to change the linetype scale of the entities. For doing so, enter **PR** in the Command Line window and then press ENTER. The **PROPERTIES** palette appears. Alternatively, click on the **Properties** tool in the **Palettes** panel of the **View** tab to invoke the **PROPERTIES** palette. Next, select the entity whose scale has to change. The current properties of the selected entity appear in the **PROPERTIES** palette. Next, enter a new linetype scale value for the selected entity in the **Linetype** field of the palette. You can try with different scale values to match your requirement.

Section 4: Creating the Top View

1. Create a vertical construction line passing through the center of the Front view by using the **Construction Line** tool or the XL command, see Figure 7.40.

2. Create a circle of diameter 40 units whose center point is on the newly created vertical construction line, anywhere above the Front view, see Figure 7.40.

7.40

364   Chapter 7 > Editing Dimensions and Adding Text

3. Similarly, create the remaining circles of diameter 60, 76, and 90 units, see Figure 7.41.

4. Assign two circles of diameter 60 and 76 units to the Hidden layer and two circles of diameter 40 and 90 units to the Object layer. Next, delete the construction line, see Figure 7.42. Note that if the circles that are assigned to the Hidden layer appear as continuous/solid lines in the drawing area, then you need to change their linetype scale.

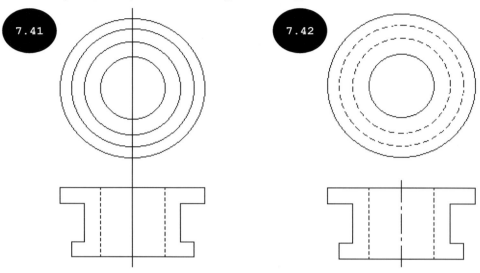

7.41

7.42

Section 5: Applying Dimensions
1. Apply dimensions to the drawing by using the **Dimension** tool, see Figure 7.43.

7.43

> **Note:** By default, dimensions appear as per the default dimension style properties, which may not fit the requirement and dimensions may appear either very small or large in the drawing. In such a case, you may need to create a new dimension style or edit the existing dimension style to match the dimension properties as per the requirement. You can create a new dimension style or modify an existing dimension style by using the **Dimension Style Manager** dialog box. You can invoke this dialog box by using the **D** command.

2. Select all the dimensions and assign them to the Dimension layer.

Section 6: Editing Dimensions

Now, you need to edit the linear diameter dimensions of the drawing to add diameter symbols as a prefix to them.

1. Enter **DDEDIT** in the Command Line window and then press ENTER. You are prompted to select an annotation object to be edited. Alternatively, double-click on the dimension to edit. You can also use the DIMEDIT command to edit a dimension text.

   ```
   You are prompted to select an annotation object:
   ```

2. Click on the dimension measuring 76 units in the drawing area. The dimension text of the selected dimension appears in an edit box, see Figure 7.44.

3. Enter '%%c' as the prefix to the dimension text '76 units' in the edit box. Next, click anywhere in the drawing area. The diameter symbol is added to the selected dimension, see Figure 7.45.

4. Similarly, add the diameter symbol to the dimension measuring 60 units in the drawing. Figure 7.46 shows the final drawing.

7.46

Section 7: Saving the Drawing
After creating the drawing, you need to save it.

1. Click on the **Save** tool in the **Quick Access Toolbar**. The **Save Drawing As** dialog box appears.

2. Browse to the *AutoCAD* folder and then create a folder with the name *Chapter 7* inside the *AutoCAD* folder.

3. Enter **Tutorial 1** in the **File name** field of the dialog box and then click on the **Save** button. The drawing saved with the name Tutorial 1 in the *Chapter 7* folder.

Tutorial 2

Create the drawing shown in Figure 7.47. Apply dimensions as illustrated in Figure 7.47. Also, you need to add labels in the different areas of the drawing, see Figure 7.47.

Section 1: Starting AutoCAD
1. Start AutoCAD and then open a new drawing file. Next, set the drawing limits.

Section 2: Specifying Unit System
You need to change the default unit system to the Architectural unit system.

1. Enter **UN** in the Command Line window and then press ENTER. The **Drawing Units** dialog box appears.

2. Select the **Architectural** unit system in the **Type** drop-down list of the **Length** area in the **Drawing Units** dialog box.

3. Make sure that the **0'-0 1/16"** option selected in the **Precision** drop-down list of the **Length** area in the dialog box.

4. Click on the **OK** button to accept the change and to exit the dialog box. The Architectural unit system is set for the current drawing.

368 Chapter 7 > Editing Dimensions and Adding Text

Section 3: Creating Drawing

1. Create the drawing as shown in Figure 7.48. To create the drawing, you can use various drawing tools such as **Line**, **Offset**, **Trim**, and **Extend**. For dimensions, refer to Figure 7.47.

Note: To enter feet dimension values, use the single quote (') and to enter inches values, use the double quotes (") as the suffix to the dimension values. You can specify the inches values with or without double quotes ("). For example, 15 feet can define as 15' and 10 feet 6 inches can define either as 10'6" or 10'6.

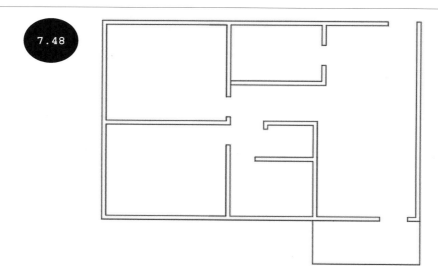

7.48

Section 4: Editing Dimension Style and Applying Dimensions

Now, you need to edit the dimension style of the drawing.

1. Enter **D** in the Command Line window and then press ENTER. The **Dimension Style Manager** dialog box appears.

2. Select the **Standard** dimension style in the **Styles** area of the dialog box and then click on the **Modify** button. The **Modify Dimension Style** dialog box appears.

3. Click on the **Symbols and Arrows** tab in the dialog box. Next, select the **Architectural tick** option in the **First** and **Second** drop-down lists of the **Arrowheads** area in the dialog box.

4. Click on the **Primary Units** tab of the dialog box and then select the **Architectural** option in the **Unit format** drop-down list of the **Linear dimensions** area in the dialog box.

5. Similarly, specify the other properties such as arrow size, text height, offset from dimension line, extend beyond dimension lines, and offset from the origin in the respective fields.

6. Click on the **OK** button to accept the change and to exit the **Modify Dimension Style** dialog box. Next, click on the **Close** button in the **Dimension Style Manager** dialog box.

After modifying the dimension style, you can apply dimensions in the drawing area.

7. Apply dimensions to the drawing by using the **Linear** tool, see Figure 7.49.

Section 5: Adding the Annotation/Text

1. Enter **TEXT** in the Command Line window and then press ENTER. The **Single Line** text tool gets invoked, and you are prompted to specify the start point of the text. Alternatively, click on the **Single Line** tool in the **Text** flyout of the **Annotation** panel in the **Home** tab.

   ```
   Specify start point of text or [Justify Style]:
   ```

2. Click in the kitchen area of the drawing to specify the start point of the text. You are prompted to specify the height of the text.

   ```
   Specify height <1'0">:
   ```

3. Enter **1'** as the height of the text and then press ENTER.

   ```
   Specify rotation angle of text <0>:
   ```

4. Enter **0** as the rotation angle of the text and then press ENTER. A blinking cursor appears in a text window, and you are prompted to enter text in the drawing area.

5. Enter **Kitchen** in the text window and then click anywhere in the drawing area. Next, press ESC key. The Kitchen label is added to the kitchen area of the drawing, see Figure 7.50.

6. Similarly, add labels to the other area of the drawing. Figure 7.51 shows the final drawing after adding all the labels/text to the drawing.

Section 6: Saving the Drawing
1. Save the drawing with the name Tutorial 2 inside the *Chapter 7* folder.

Hands-on Test Drive 1

Create the drawing and add multiline text to the drawing, see Figure 7.52.

DESIGN SPECIFICATION
Design pressure = 800 psi
Design temperature = 700 F
Material:
    Shell SA-516 Gr. 70
    Head SA-181 Class 70
    Nozzle SA-106 Gr. B
Weld efficiency factor = 1.0 = E
(Full radiographic examination)

Summary

In this chapter, you have learned to edit dimensions by using the DIMEDIT command, DIMTEDIT command, DDEDIT command, dimension grips, **Properties** palette, and editing tools such as **Trim**, **Extend**, and **Stretch**. You have also learned about adding text/notes to drawings, creating and modifying text style, and writing text by using the **Single Line** and **Multiline Text** tools. Besides, in this chapter, you have learned about modifying the single line text and the multiline text. Also, you have learned how to convert one or more than one single line text to the multiline text.

Questions

- The _____ command is used to edit the dimension text/value such that you can rotate, modify, restore, and specify a new dimension text/value.

- The _____ command is used to change the dimension text justification and angle.

- The _____ command is used to add a prefix or suffix to the dimension text/value or specify a new dimension value.

- By using the _____ of a dimension, you can change the position of the dimension text, the spacing between the dimension line and the object, and the position of extension lines.

- In AutoCAD, you can add text by using the _____ and _____ tools.

- The _____ command is used to invoke the **Text Style** dialog box.

- The _____ tool used for writing single line text such as labels and notes in a drawing.

- The _____ tool is used to write multiline text such as a paragraph of information or a block of text.

- You can convert one or more than one single line text objects to a multiline text object by using the _____ command.

CHAPTER 8

Modifying and Editing Drawings - II

In this chapter, you will learn the following:

- Editing Objects by using Grips
- Editing Objects by using PROPERTIES Palette
- Matching Properties of an Object
- Identifying Coordinates of a Point

In Chapter 5, you have learned about various editing operations such as trim, extend, mirror, array, move, and rotate. In this chapter, you will learn about some advanced editing operations such as editing objects by using grips, editing objects properties, matching objects properties, and so on.

Editing Objects by using Grips

In AutoCAD, all objects have grips, which appear when you select them in the drawing area, see Figure 8.1. A grip is a small square blue symbol. The number of grips varies object to object. For example, a line object has three grips, an arc object has four grips, and a circle object has five grips, see Figure 8.1. By using these grips, you can perform various editing operations such as stretch, move, rotate, scale, and mirror. The methods of editing objects by using the grips are discussed next.

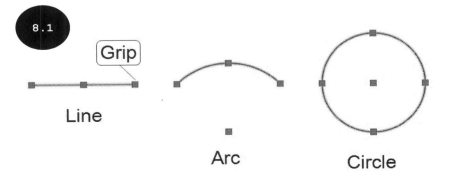

Stretching Objects by using Grips

To stretch objects by using grips, select them. The grips of the selected objects appear in the drawing area, see Figure 8.2. In this figure, the horizontal and inclined lines of the drawing are selected. Next, click on a grip as the base point to stretch objects, see Figure 8.2. As soon as you click on a grip, the **Stretch** command gets activated, automatically. Next, move the cursor to a required distance in the drawing area. As you move the cursor, the objects stretch, dynamically in the drawing area. Next, click to specify the placement point for the objects in the drawing area. The objects get stretched, see Figure 8.3.

You can select one or more than one grips to stretch multiple objects, simultaneously. To select multiple grips, press the SHIFT key and then click on the grips one by one. After selecting the grips, release the SHIFT key and then click on a grip as the base point to stretch objects, simultaneously. Next, move the cursor to a required distance and then click to specify the placement point. The selected objects get stretched. Figure 8.4 shows six objects and four grips selected to stretch. Figure 8.5 shows the resultant drawing after stretching the objects.

Moving Objects by using Grips

To move objects by using grips, select them. The grips of the selected objects appear in the drawing area, see Figure 8.6. Next, click on a grip as the base point to move objects, see Figure 8.6. The **Stretch** command gets activated, by default. Next, press ENTER or SPACEBAR to activate the **Move** command. Alternatively, right-click to invoke a shortcut menu and then click on the **Move** option to invoke the **Move** command. Next, move the cursor in the drawing area. As you move the cursor, the objects move, dynamically. Next, click to specify the placement point in the drawing area, see Figure 8.6. The objects are moved to the new specified location, see Figure 8.7. Next, press the ESC key to exit the selection of objects.

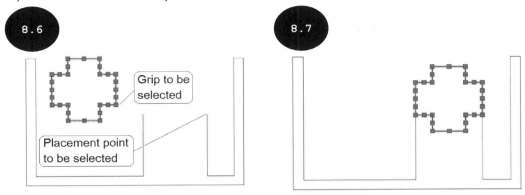

Note: By pressing the ENTER or SPACEBAR key after selecting a grip, you can cycle through the **Stretch, Move, Rotate, Scale,** and **Mirror** commands.

Tip: If you press and hold the CTRL key and then specify the placement point, a copy of the selected objects will be created in the new specified location.

Rotating Objects by using Grips

To rotate objects by using grips, select them. The grips of the selected objects appear in the drawing area, see Figure 8.8. Next, click on a grip as the base point to rotate objects, see Figure 8.8. The **Stretch** command gets activated, by default. Press the ENTER or SPACEBAR key twice to activate the **Rotate** command. You can cycle through the **Stretch, Move, Rotate, Scale,** and **Mirror** commands by pressing the ENTER key. Alternatively, right-click to invoke a shortcut menu and then click on the **Rotate** option to invoke the **Rotate** command. Next, enter the value of the rotation angle and then press ENTER. You can also click in the drawing area to specify the rotation angle. The selected objects are rotated around the base point at the specified rotation angle, see Figure 8.9. Next, press the ESC key to exit the selection of objects.

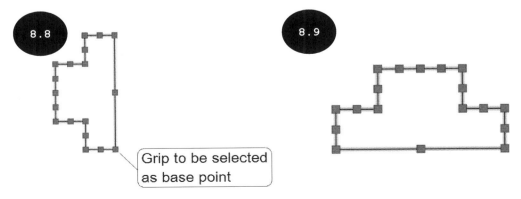

Scaling Objects by using Grips

To scale objects by using grips, select them. The grips of the selected objects appear in the drawing area, see Figure 8.10. Next, click on a grip as the base point to scale objects, see Figure 8.10. The **Stretch** command gets activated, by default. Press the ENTER key until the **Scale** command gets activated. Next, enter the scale factor and then press ENTER. The selected objects get scaled, see Figure 8.11. Note that to enlarge the selected objects, you need to enter scale factor greater than 1 and to shrink them, you need to enter scale factor smaller than 1. Next, press the ESC key to exit the selection of objects.

Mirroring Objects by using Grips

To mirror objects by using grips, select them. The grips of the selected objects appear in the drawing area, see Figure 8.12. Next, click on a grip as the start point of the mirroring line, see Figure 8.12. The **Stretch** command gets activated, by default. Press the ENTER key until the **Mirror** command gets activated, and the command prompt appears "`Specify second point or [Base point Copy Undo eXit]:`". Next, click on the **Copy** option in the command prompt to keep the original or source objects in the resultant drawing. Next, click in the drawing area to specify the second point of the mirroring line. The selected objects get mirrored, and the original or source objects are retained in the drawing area, see Figure 8.13. If you do not want to keep or retain the original or source objects, then you can skip the selection of **Copy** option in the command prompt and directly specify the second point of the mirroring line. After mirroring the objects, press the ESC key to exit the selection.

Editing Objects by using PROPERTIES Palette

You can edit object properties such as color, linetype, lineweight, layer, angle, and coordinates by using the PROPERTIES palette. To invoke the PROPERTIES palette, enter **PR** in the Command Line window and then press ENTER. Alternatively, click on the **Properties** tool in the **Palettes** panel of the **View** tab in the **Ribbon**. The PROPERTIES palette appears on the left of the drawing area. Next, select the object whose properties to be edited. The properties of the selected object appear in the PROPERTIES palette, see Figure 8.14. Next, change the properties of the selected object as required by using the respective fields or drop-down lists of the PROPERTIES palette. For example, to modify the color of the selected object, click on the **Color** field, see Figure 8.15. An arrow appears. Next, click on the arrow. The **Color** drop-down list appears, see Figure 8.15. In this drop-down list, you can select the required color for the selected object. Similarly, to edit the linetype scale, click on the **Linetype scale** field of the palette and then enter the new linetype scale value in it.

Note: By using the PROPERTIES palette, you can also edit the properties of the text/annotation, dimensions, and so on. Also, the availability of options in the PROPERTIES palette depends upon the type of object selected.

Matching Properties of an Object

In AutoCAD, you can match or copy the properties such as color, linetype, linetype scale, lineweight, and the layer of an object to other objects by using the **Match Properties** tool. For example, if you have assigned a particular set of properties such as color, linetype, linetype scale, lineweight to an object of a drawing then you can transfer the same properties of this object to the other objects in the drawing. You can also control the settings of match properties such that only a particular set of properties of the source object should transfer or copy to other objects. The procedure to match properties and control the settings of the properties is discussed next.

Procedure for Matching Properties and Controlling Settings

1. Click on the **Match Properties** tool in the **Properties** panel of the **Home** tab. The **Match Properties** tool gets invoked, and you are prompted to select the source object. Alternatively, enter **MA** in the Command Line window and then press ENTER to invoke the **Match Properties** tool.

   ```
   Select source object:
   ```

2. Click on the source object whose properties are to be transferred to the desired objects in the drawing. You are prompted to select the destination objects.

   ```
   Select destination object(s) or [Settings]:
   ```

3. Click on an object as the destination object to transfer the properties of the source object. The properties of the source object are transferred to the destination object.

4. Similarly, click on other objects as the destination objects to match the properties one by one. You can also select destination objects by using the Window or Cross Window selection method. Next, press ENTER to exit the **Match Properties** tool.

> **Note:** To change the settings of match properties, click on the **Settings** option in the command prompt when you are prompted to select destination objects "`Select destination object(s) or [Settings]:`". Alternatively, enter **S** and then press ENTER. The **Property Settings** dialog box appears, see Figure 8.16. In this dialog box, select the check boxes for the properties which you want to transfer and uncheck the remaining check boxes. Next, click on the **OK** button of the dialog box. The settings of the match properties get changed.

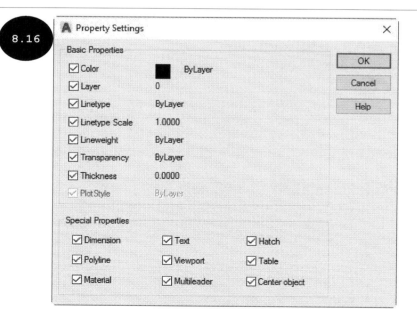

8.16

Identifying Coordinates of a Point

In AutoCAD, you can identify location/coordinates of a point in a drawing by using the **ID Point** tool. For doing so, click on the **ID Point** tool in the expanded **Utilities** panel of the **Home** tab, see Figure 8.17. Alternatively, enter **ID** and then press ENTER to invoke this tool.

8.17

As soon as you invoke the **ID Point** tool, you are prompted to specify a point. Click on the point whose coordinates are to be identified. The coordinates (X, Y, Z) of the specified point appears on the screen as well as in the command prompt.

Note: The identified coordinates of the point stored in the LASTPOINT system variable, which can use as the start point for creating new entities of the drawing by entering @ in the Command Line window and then pressing ENTER. For example, while creating a line by using the **Line** tool when you are prompted to specify the start point of the line, enter @ in the Command Line window and then press ENTER. The start point of the line gets specified to the last identified point in the drawing area.

380   Chapter 8 > Modifying and Editing Drawings - II

Tutorial 1

Create the drawing shown in the Figure 8.18. In this tutorial, you need to set the dimension properties for a dimension and then use the **Match Properties** tool to transfer the specified properties to other dimensions of the drawing.

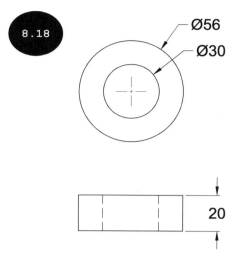

Section 1: Starting AutoCAD
1.   Start AutoCAD and then open a new drawing file.

Section 2: Creating Drawing
1.   Create the Front and Top views of the drawing by using the drawing tools, as shown in Figure 8.19. In this figure, the construction lines are used for creating the drawing views. Also, the color of the construction lines are changed for the clarity of the image. You can delete the construction lines after creating the drawing.

Section 3: Assigning Properties to Hidden Line

Now, you need to assign the HIDDEN linetype to the hidden lines of the drawing by using the **PROPERTIES** palette. However, you first need to load the HIDDEN linetype in the drawing.

1. Click on the **Layer Properties** tool in the **Layers** panel of the **Home** tab. The **LAYER PROPERTIES MANAGER** window appears, see Figure 8.20.

2. Click on the **Linetype** field of the **0** layer, see Figure 8.20. The **Select Linetype** dialog box appears.

3. In the **Select Linetype** dialog box, click on the **Load** button. The **Load or Reload Linetype** dialog box appears.

4. Select the HIDDEN linetype in the **Load or Reload Linetype** dialog box and then click **OK** button. The HIDDEN linetype gets loaded in the dialog box.

5. Click on the **Cancel** button in the **Select Linetype** dialog box and then close the **LAYER PROPERTIES MANAGER** window.

   After loading the HIDDEN linetype in the drawing, you can assign it to the required drawing entities by using the **PROPERTIES** palette.

6. Enter **PR** in the Command Line window and then press ENTER. The **PROPERTIES** palette appears. Alternatively, click on the **Properties** tool in the **Palettes** panel of the **View** tab in the **Ribbon** to invoke the **PROPERTIES** palette.

7. Click on an inner vertical line of the Front view to be converted into the hidden line, see Figure 8.21. The current properties of the selected line appear in the **PROPERTIES** palette.

8. Click on the **Linetype** field of the **PROPERTIES** palette. An arrow appears. Next, click on the arrow. The **Linetype** drop-down list appears, see Figure 8.22.

382 Chapter 8 > Modifying and Editing Drawings - II

9. Click on the HIDDEN linetype in the **Linetype** drop-down list. The HIDDEN linetype is assigned to the selected line of the drawing.

10. Click on the **Linetype scale** field of the **PROPERTIES** palette and then enter **10** as the linetype scale of the selected line. Next, press the ESC key. The selected line appears similar to the one shown in Figure 8.23.

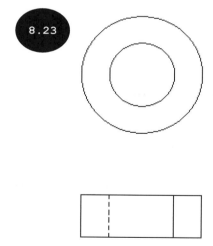

Section 4: Matching the Hidden Line Properties

Now, you need to match the properties of the left hidden line to the right hidden line.

1. Click on the **Match Properties** tool in the **Properties** panel of the **Home** tab. You are prompted to select the source object.

```
Select source object:
```

2. Click on the left hidden line of the drawing as the source object. You are prompted to select the destination objects.

   ```
   Select destination object(s) or [Settings]:
   ```

3. Click on the right inner vertical line of the drawing as the destination object, see Figure 8.24. The properties of the selected line are matched with the source object, see Figure 8.24.

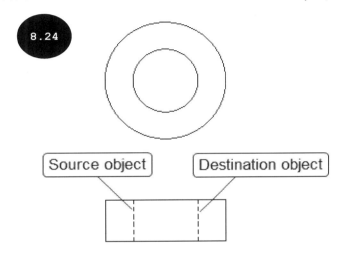

Section 5: Applying Dimensions

Now, you need to apply dimensions in the drawing and then set the dimension properties by using the **PROPERTIES** palette.

1. Click on the **Dimension** tool in the **Annotation** panel of the **Home** tab. You are prompted to select the object to be dimensioned.

   ```
   Select object or specify first extension line origin or [Angular
   Baseline Continue Ordinate aliGn Distribute Layer Undo]:
   ```

2. Move the cursor over the right most vertical line of the Front view and then click on the line when it highlights in the drawing area. The linear dimension is attached to the cursor.

3. Move the cursor horizontally toward right and then click to specify the placement point for the dimension in the drawing area. The linear dimension is applied and placed in the specified location, see Figure 8.25. Note that the dimension text and the arrowheads of the applied dimension may appear very small in size in the drawing area because of the dimension properties of the current dimension style, see Figure 8.25. You will modify the dimension properties later in this tutorial.

4. Similarly, apply the diameter dimensions in the drawing, see Figure 8.26.

384 Chapter 8 > Modifying and Editing Drawings - II

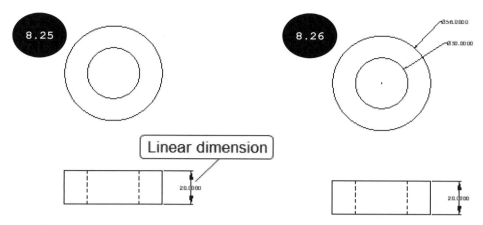

Section 6: Assigning and Matching Dimension Properties

Now, you need to assign the dimension properties to a dimension of the drawing by using the **PROPERTIES** palette and then match these properties to other dimensions of the drawing.

1. Click on the linear dimension of the drawing and then invoke the **PROPERTIES** palette.

2. Click on the **Arrow size** field in the **PROPERTIES** palette and then enter **5** as the arrow size of the dimension.

3. Similarly, enter **5.5** as the text height in the **Text height** field, **1.5** in the **Ext line ext** field, **1.5** in the **Ext line offset** field, and **1.5** in the **Text offset** field of the **PROPERTIES** palette. The selected dimension appears similar to the one shown in Figure 8.27.

   Now, you need to set the precision value of the dimension to 0.

4. In the **Primary Units** category of the **PROPERTIES** palette, click on the **Precision** field. An arrow appears. Next, click on the arrow. The **Precision** drop-down list appears. In this drop-down list, select the **0** option as the precision for the selected dimension, see Figure 8.28. Alternatively, right-click on the dimension in the drawing area. A shortcut menu appears. In this shortcut menu, click on the **Precision > 0** to set the precision for the selected dimension. Next, press the ESC key. The dimension properties of the selected dimension are modified, see Figure 8.28.

Now, you need to match the properties of this dimension to other dimensions of the drawing.

5. Click on the **Match Properties** tool in the **Properties** panel of the **Home** tab. You are prompted to select the source object.

    ```
    Select source object:
    ```

6. Click on the linear dimension as the source object. You are prompted to select the destination objects.

    ```
    Select destination object(s) or [Settings]:
    ```

7. Click on the diameter dimensions of the drawing one by one to match with the properties of the source dimension. Figure 8.29 shows the drawing after matching all the dimension properties.

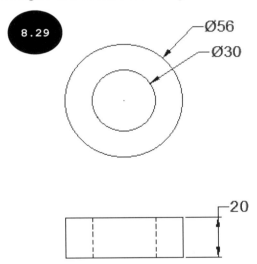

Section 7: Saving the Drawing

After creating the drawing, you need to save it.

1. Click on the **Save** tool in the **Quick Access Toolbar**. The **Save Drawing As** dialog box appears.

2. Browse to the *AutoCAD* folder and then create a folder with the name *Chapter 8* inside the *AutoCAD* folder.

3. Enter **Tutorial 1** in the **File name** field of the dialog box and then click on the **Save** button. The drawing gets saved with the name Tutorial 1 in the *Chapter 8* folder.

386 Chapter 8 > Modifying and Editing Drawings - II

Hands-on Test Drive 1

Create the drawing shown in the Figure 8.30. Modify dimension properties of the dimension style and then apply dimensions to the drawing. You can assume the values of dimension properties.

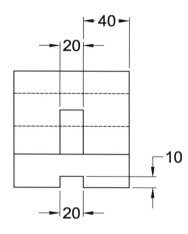

Hands-on Test Drive 2

Create the drawing shown in the Figure 8.31. Modify dimension properties of the dimension style and then apply dimensions to the drawing. You can assume the values of dimension properties such as dimension height and arrow size.

8.31

Summary

In this chapter, you have learned how to edit drawing objects/entities by using the grips and the **PROPERTIES** palette. You have also learned about matching the properties of an object with the other drawing objects. Also, in this chapter, you have learned how to identify coordinates of a point in the drawing.

Questions

- A line object has _____ number of grips and an arc object has _____ number of grips.

- After selecting a grip of an object, when you press the _____ or _____ key, you cycle through the **Stretch**, **Move**, **Rotate**, **Scale**, and **Mirror** commands.

- When you click on a grip of an object, the _____ command gets activated, by default.

- Click on a grip of an object and then press the ENTER or SPACEBAR key twice to activate the _____ command.

- You can edit object properties such as color, linetype, lineweight, layer, angle, and coordinates by using the _____ palette.

- To invoke the PROPERTIES palette, enter _____ in the Command Line window and then press ENTER.

- The _____ tool is used to match or copy the properties of an object such as color, linetype, linetype scale, lineweight, and layer with other objects of the drawing.

- The _____ tool is used to identify the location/coordinates of a point in the drawing.

CHAPTER 9

Hatching and Gradients

In this chapter, you will learn the following:

- Creating the Hatches
- Creating the Gradients

In mechanical drawings, the hatches are used to represent the cross-sectional shape and material of components. The cross-sectional shape of a part is created by cutting the component by using an imaginary cutting plane and then viewing it from the direction normal to the cutting plane, see Figure 9.1. The view that represents the cross-sectional shape of a component is known as section view.

It is evident from the above figure that the hatching created by filling enclosed areas of drawing views with hatch patterns. A hatch pattern is composed of hatch lines or solid fill. AutoCAD provided with various hatch patterns that can be used to represent the cross-sectional shape and material of components. In architectural drawings, the hatches are used to describe the type of material of the object such as brick, stone, wood, and sand. Figure 9.2 shows some of the hatch patterns available in AutoCAD.

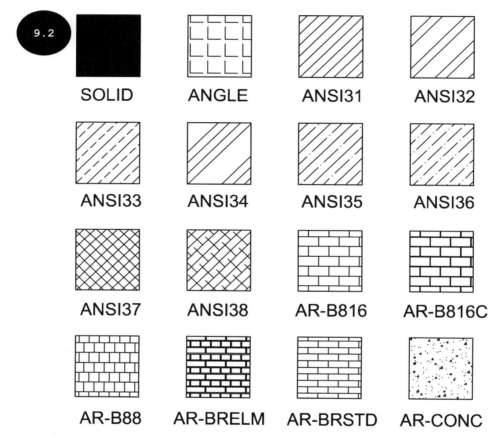

Creating the Hatches

You can create the hatching in an enclosed area of a drawing view by using the **Hatch** tool or HATCH command. To create a hatch, click on the **Hatch** tool in the **Draw** panel of the **Home** tab. The **Hatch Creation** tab appears in **Ribbon**, see Figure 9.3. Also, you are prompted to pick an internal point. Alternatively, enter **H** in the Command Line window and then press ENTER to invoke this tool.

```
Pick internal point or [Select object Undo seTtings]:
```

In the **Hatch Creation** tab, you can specify the pattern type and properties such as pattern angle, scale, and transparency. Click on the pattern to be created in the **Pattern** panel and then specify the pattern properties in the respective fields of the **Properties** panel of the **Hatch Creation** tab. Next, click on a close area of a drawing view to create hatch pattern. The hatch pattern gets created in the specified enclosed area of the drawing view, see Figure 9.4. Next, press the ESC key to exit the creation of hatch pattern. The options of the **Hatch Creation** tab are discussed next.

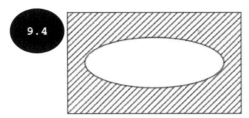

Boundaries Panel

The options in the **Boundaries** panel of the **Hatch Creation** tab are used to defined enclosed areas of drawing views to create hatch patterns, see Figure 9.5. The options are discussed next.

Pick Points

The **Pick Points** tool is used to select a pick point in an enclosed area of a drawing view to create the hatch pattern. By default, this tool is activated in the **Boundaries** panel. As a result, you are prompted to specify a pick point. Click to specify a pick point in an enclosed area of a drawing view. The hatch pattern is created in the enclosed area, which is defined by the pick point, see Figure 9.6. You can specify multiple pick points in a drawing to create hatch patterns.

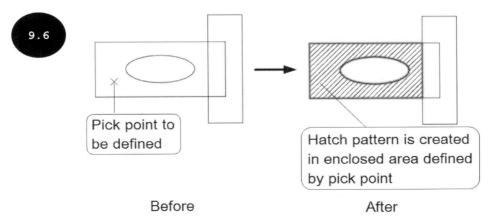

Select

The **Select** tool of the **Boundaries** panel is used to choose the object for creating hatch pattern. When you click on the **Select** tool in the **Boundaries** panel, you are prompted to select objects for creating the hatch pattern. Click on an enclosed object of a drawing. The enclosed area of the selected object filled with a hatch pattern, see Figure 9.7. You can select multiple enclosed objects of the drawing to create hatch pattern.

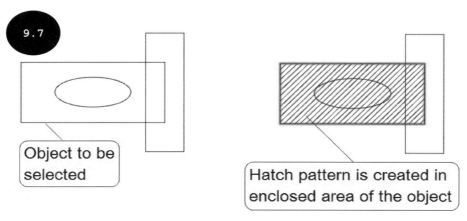

Remove

The **Remove** tool is used to select the previously selected object for removing the hatch pattern created in it.

Pattern Panel

The options in the **Pattern** panel are used to select the type of hatch pattern to be created. AutoCAD provided with various hatch patterns. Figure 9.8 shows the expanded **Pattern** panel with the display of different hatch patterns. You can expand the **Pattern** panel by clicking on the down arrow on the lower right of the panel.

Properties Panel

The **Properties** panel is used to specify the hatch pattern properties such as hatch pattern color, hatch background color, hatch transparency, hatch angle, and hatch scale in the respective fields of the panel, see Figure 9.9.

Options Panel

The **Associative** tool of the **Options** panel is used to make the hatch pattern associative to the object selected. An associative hatch pattern is updated automatically on modifying the object. To create an associative hatch pattern, click on the **Associative** tool in the **Options** panel to activate it and then create hatch patterns on enclosed objects. The **Annotative** tool is used to make the hatch pattern annotative such that the scale of the hatch pattern adjusts automatically concerning the scale of the viewport.

After specifying the hatch pattern properties, click to specify an enclosed area or object to create the hatch pattern. The hatch pattern is created in the enclosed area selected.

Creating the Gradients

Similar to creating the hatches by filling the boundary or enclosed area of a drawing view with a hatch pattern, you can also fill boundaries or enclosed areas with gradient having one or more gradient color, see Figure 9.10. Applying gradients are very useful to make the drawing presentable and give a realistic appearance to the drawing views. Gradients are also used to represent the section area and distinguish between two or more objects or enclosed areas of drawing views.

394 Chapter 9 > Hatching and Gradients

To apply a gradient to an enclosed area of a drawing view, click on the down arrow next to the **Hatch** tool in the **Draw** panel. A flyout appears, see Figure 9.11. In this flyout, click on the **Gradient** tool. The **Hatch Creation** tab appears, see Figure 9.12. Also, you are prompted to pick an internal point.

```
Pick internal point or [Select object Undo seTtings]:
```

The options in **Hatch Creation** tab are used to specify a gradient pattern and its properties. All these options are same as those discussed earlier while creating the hatch patterns. Select a gradient pattern to create in the **Pattern** panel and then specify its properties such as gradient color 1 and gradient color 2 in the respective fields of the **Properties** panel of the **Hatch Creation** tab. Next, click on a close area of a drawing view to create the gradient pattern. The gradient pattern gets created in the specified enclosed area of the drawing view, see Figure 9.13. You can specify multiple enclosed areas one by one to create gradient patterns. Next, press the ESC key to exit the creation of gradient pattern.

Tutorial 1

Create the drawing, as shown in the Figure 9.14. You need to apply the ANSI31 hatch patterns to the drawing at different hatch angles.

9.14

Section 1: Starting AutoCAD
1. Start AutoCAD and then open a new drawing file.

Section 2: Creating Drawing and Applying Dimensions
1. Create the drawing, as shown in Figure 9.15.

9.15

2. Invoke the **Modify Dimension Style** dialog box and then modify the Standard dimension style: Text height = 3.5, Offset from dim line = 1, Arrow size = 3.25, Extend beyond dim lines = 1, Offset from origin = 1, and Precision = 0. To invoke this dialog box, enter D in the Command Line window and then press ENTER. Next, select the **Standard** dimension style in the **Dimension Style Manager** dialog box appeared and then click on the **Modify** button.

396 Chapter 9 > Hatching and Gradients

3. Apply dimensions to the drawing by using the dimension tools, see Figure 9.16.

9.16

Section 3: Creating Hatches

1. Click on the **Hatch** tool in the **Draw** panel of the **Home** tab, see Figure 9.17. The **Hatch Creation** tab appears in the **Ribbon**. Also, you are prompted to pick an internal point. Alternatively, enter **H** in the Command Line window and then press ENTER.

   ```
   Pick internal point or [Select objects Undo seTtings]:
   ```

2. Click on the upper left enclosed area of the drawing, see Figure 9.18. The hatching created in the selected enclosed area, see Figure 9.18.

3. Make sure that the ANSI31 is selected as the hatch pattern in the **Pattern** panel of the **Hatch Creation** tab in the **Ribbon**.

   It is evident from the Figure 9.18 that the scale of the hatch pattern is minuscule. Therefore, you need to change the scale of the hatch pattern.

4. Enter **12** in the **Hatch Pattern Scale** field of the **Properties** panel of the **Hatch Creation** tab and then press ENTER. The scale of the hatch pattern changes, see Figure 9.19.

5. Click on the right enclosed area of the upper part of the drawing. The hatch gets created, see Figure 9.20.

6. Press ENTER to exit the creation of Hatch. The hatch is created on the upper part of the drawing.

   Now, you need to create the hatch on the lower part of the drawing.

7. Click on the **Hatch** tool in the **Draw** panel of the **Home** tab again. The **Hatch Creation** tab appears. Also, you are prompted to pick an internal point. Alternatively, enter **H** in the Command Line window and then press ENTER.

   ```
   Pick internal point or [Select objects Undo seTtings]:
   ```

8. Click on the lower left enclosed area of the drawing, see Figure 9.21. The hatching is created, see Figure 9.21. Make sure that the scale of the hatch specified as 12 in the **Hatch Pattern Scale** field of the **Properties** panel. Now, you need to change the angle of hatch pattern.

9. Enter **90** as the angle of hatch pattern in the **Angle** field of the **Properties** panel of the **Hatch Creation** tab. The angle of the hatch pattern is changed as specified, see Figure 9.22.

398   Chapter 9 > Hatching and Gradients

10. Click on the right enclosed area of the lower part of the drawing. The hatch pattern is created, see Figure 9.23. Next, press ENTER. Figure 9.23 shows the final drawing after creating the hatch patterns.

9.23

Section 4: Saving the Drawing

1. Click on the **Save** tool in the **Quick Access Toolbar**. The **Save Drawing As** dialog box appears.

2. Browse to the *AutoCAD* folder and then create a folder with the name *Chapter 9* inside the *AutoCAD* folder. Next, enter **Tutorial 1** in the **File name** field of the dialog box.

3. Click on the **Save** button. The drawing is saved with the name Tutorial 1 in the *Chapter 9* folder.

Hands-on Test Drive 1

Create the drawing shown in the Figure 9.24. You need to apply ANSI31 hatch patterns to the drawing at different hatch angles as shown in the Figure 9.24.

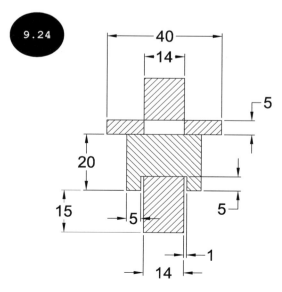

9.24

Hands-on Test Drive 2

Create the drawing shown in the Figure 9.25. You need to apply ANSI35 hatch patterns to the drawing at different hatch angles as shown in the Figure 9.25.

Summary

In this chapter, you have learned how to create different types of hatch patterns and gradients in enclosed areas of a drawing.

Questions

- A drawing view which represents the cross-section of a part is known as _____.

- You can create hatching in an enclosed area of a drawing view by using the _____ tool or the _____ command.

- The _____ tool is used to select a pick point in an enclosed area of a drawing view to create hatch pattern.

- The _____ tool is used to select the previously selected object for removing the hatch pattern created in it.

- The _____ tool is used to make the hatch pattern associative to the object selected.

- The _____ tool is used to create a gradient in an enclosed area of a drawing view.

CHAPTER 10

Working with Blocks and Xrefs

In this chapter, you will learn the following:

- Creating a Block
- Inserting a Block in the Drawing
- Creating a WBlock
- Inserting a WBlock in the Drawing
- Editing a Block
- Making a Dynamic Block
- Working with External References (Xrefs)

Block is a very powerful feature of AutoCAD, which helps designers to speed up the creation of design, increases efficiency, and saves time. For example, in a drawing, you often find some repetitive objects such as symbols and fasteners. Instead of creating the same objects, again and again, you can create its block and use it several times in a drawing. A block is a collection of objects that are combined and act as a single object. Figure 10.1 shows a geometry having multiple objects and Figure 10.2 shows the same geometry after converting it into a block, in which all its objects treated as a single object.

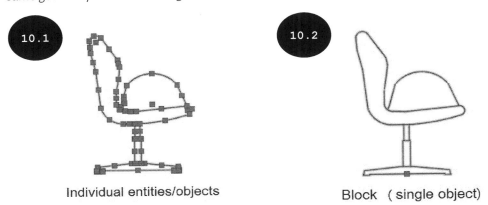

Individual entities/objects   Block (single object)

Chapter 10 > Working with Blocks and Xrefs

In AutoCAD, you can create two types of blocks: internal block (Block) and external block (WBlock). An internal block is a group of objects that is saved internally in a drawing and can be used several times within the drawing. An internal block is created by using the BLOCK command and is known as Block. Whereas an external block is a group of objects or entire drawing that is saved as an external file and can use several times in any drawing. An external block is created by using the WBLOCK command and is known as WBlock.

Creating a Block

In AutoCAD, you can create a block either by using the **Create Block** tool or the BLOCK command. To create a block, click on the **Create Block** tool in the **Block Definition** panel of the **Insert** tab in the **Ribbon**, see Figure 10.3. The **Block Definition** dialog box appears, see Figure 10.4. Alternatively, enter B in the Command Line window and then press ENTER. The B is the shortcut of BLOCK command. The options in the **Block Definition** dialog box are used to define the block definition such as block name, insertion point, and objects to convert into the block. The options are discussed next.

Name

The **Name** field of the dialog box is used to specify the name of the block. You can write up to 255 characters in a block name, which includes letters, numbers, blank spaces, and any special characters. Note that all the existing blocks created in the current drawing is listed in the **Name** drop-down list of this dialog box. To display the **Name** drop-down list, click on the arrow in the **Name** field of the dialog box, see Figure 10.5.

Base Point

The **Base point** area of the dialog box is used to specify a base/insertion point of the block. A base point of the block is used as a reference point while inserting it in the drawing. You can define a base point by specifying a point in the drawing area or by entering the coordinates (X, Y, Z). To define a base point by specifying a point in the drawing area, click on the **Pick point** button in the **Base point** area. The **Block Definition** dialog box gets closed, and you are prompted to specify the insertion base point.

```
_block Specify insertion base point:
```

Click to specify a point in the drawing area as the base/insertion point of the block, see Figure 10.6. Generally, a corner point or a center point of the geometry is specified as the base point. As soon as you define the base point of the block, the **Block Definition** dialog box appears again, and the coordinates (X, Y, Z) of the selected base point displayed automatically in the **X, Y**, and **Z** fields of the **Base point** area in the dialog box, respectively. Alternatively, you can enter the X, Y, and Z coordinates of the base point in the respective fields of the **Base point** area of the dialog box.

Note: If you do not specify the base point for the block, then the origin point (0,0,0) is used as the base/insertion point of the block, by default.

Objects

The **Objects** area of the dialog box is used for selecting the objects of the drawing to be converted into a block. To select objects, click on the **Select objects** button in the **Objects** area. The **Block Definition** dialog box gets closed, and you are prompted to select objects to be converted into the block.

```
Select objects:
```

Select objects of the drawing to be converted into a block, see Figure 10.7. You can select the objects by clicking the left mouse button or by using the Window selection or Cross Window selection method. After selecting the objects, press ENTER. The **Block Definition** dialog box appears again and displays the information about the number of objects selected at the bottom of the **Objects** area in the dialog box, see Figure 10.8. The remaining options of the **Objects** area of the dialog box are discussed next.

Retain

On selecting the **Retain** radio button in the **Objects** area, the objects that are selected for converting into a block are retained in the drawing area as individual entities and a new block is created, which gets saved internally in the drawing, automatically.

Convert to block

By default, the **Convert to block** radio button is selected in the dialog box. As a result, the selected objects are converted into a block in the drawing area and treated as a single object. Also, a copy of the block gets saved internally in the drawing.

Delete

On selecting the **Delete** radio button, the objects selected for converting into block get removed from the drawing area, and the block is created, which gets saved internally in the drawing.

Behavior

The options in the **Behavior** area of the dialog box are used for define the behavior of the block, see Figure 10.9. The options are discussed next.

Annotative

On selecting the **Annotative** check box, the selected objects get converted into an annotative block. An annotative block can be used several times with different scales in a drawing. Also, the size/scale of an annotative block gets adjusted to the appropriate scale of the viewport.

Match block orientation to layout

The **Match block orientation to layout** check box is enabled, if the **Annotative** check box is selected in the **Behavior** area of the dialog box. On selecting this check box, the orientation of the block in the paper space viewports matches to the orientation of the layout.

Scale uniformly

On selecting the **Scale uniformly** check box, the block maintains uniform scale such that it can stretch in all directions evenly. When this check box is unchecked, the block can stretch with different scales in different directions.

Allow exploding

By default, the **Allow exploding** check box is selected in this area. As a result, you can explode the block objects into individual objects.

Settings

The options in the **Settings** area of the dialog box are used to specify settings for the block, see Figure 10.10. The options are discussed next.

Block unit

The **Block unit** drop-down list is used to specify the insertion unit for the block. When you insert a block in a drawing, the block will scale as per the insertion unit defined in this drop-down list. By default, the current unit of the drawing is used as the insertion unit for the block and is selected in this drop-down list.

Hyperlink

The **Hyperlink** button is used to assign a hyperlink to the block. When you click on the **Hyperlink** button, the **Insert Hyperlink** dialog box appears. In this dialog box, you can select the file or specify a web page address (URL) to hyperlink with the block.

Description

The **Description** area of the dialog box is used add a brief description about the block.

Open in block editor

On selecting the **Open in block editor** check box, the block is created as per the specified block definitions and opened in the Block Editor when you click on the **OK** button in the dialog box. The Block Editor is used to edit the block definitions. You will learn about editing blocks by using the Block Editor later in this chapter.

After specifying the block definitions such as block name, insertion/base point, and objects to be converted into the block, click on the **OK** button in the dialog box. The block is created and saved internally in the current drawing for further use in the drawing.

Procedure for Creating a Block

1. Click on the **Create Block** tool in the **Block Definition** panel of the **Insert** tab. The **Block Definition** dialog box appears. Alternatively, enter **B** in the Command Line window and then press ENTER.

2. Click on the **Pick point** button in the **Base point** area of the dialog box. The **Block Definition** dialog box gets closed, and you are prompted to specify the insertion base point. Note that the **Pick point** button is enabled when the **Specify On-screen** check box is unchecked in the **Base point** area of the dialog box.

   ```
   Specify insertion base point:
   ```

3. Click to specify a base point for the block in the drawing area. The **Block Definition** dialog box appears again, and the base point is specified.

4. Click on the **Select objects** button in the **Objects** area of the dialog box. The **Block Definition** dialog box gets closed, and you are prompted to select objects.

   ```
   Select objects:
   ```

5. Select the objects to convert into the block. The **Block Definition** dialog box appears again, and the objects are selected.

6. Specify remaining block definitions such as annotative, block unit, and hyperlink by using the options of the dialog box. You can also accept the remaining default definitions and skip this step.

7. Click on the **OK** button. The block is created and saved internally in the current drawing.

Inserting a Block in the Drawing

The blocks created in the current drawing can be inserted in the drawing several times by using the **Insert** tool of the **Block** panel in the **Insert** tab. To insert a block in the drawing, click on the **Insert** tool in the **Block** panel of the **Insert** tab. The **Insert** flyout appears which contains a list of all the blocks created in the current drawing, see Figure 10.11. Next, click on the block to be inserted into the drawing. The selected block gets attached to the cursor with its base/insertion point, which specified while creating the block. Also, you are prompted to specify the insertion point in the drawing area for placing the attached block.

    Specify insertion point or [Basepoint Scale X Y Z Rotate]:

Click in the drawing area to specify the insertion point for the block. The attached block gets inserted at the specified location in the drawing. You can also control the block parameters such as scale and angle of rotation before specifying the insertion point by using the options available in the command prompt or by using the **Insert** dialog box. The **Insert** dialog box provides additional options for controlling the block parameters. To invoke the **Insert** dialog box, click on the **More Options** button in the **Insert** flyout, refer to Figure 10.11.

When you click on the **More Options** button in the **Insert** flyout, the **Insert** dialog box appears, see Figure 10.12. Alternatively, enter **I** in the Command Line window and then press ENTER to invoke the **Insert** dialog box. The options in the **Insert** dialog box are used to select the block to be inserted into the drawing area and specify parameters for the block such as scale, the angle of rotation, and insertion point. The options are discussed next.

408 Chapter 10 > Working with Blocks and Xrefs

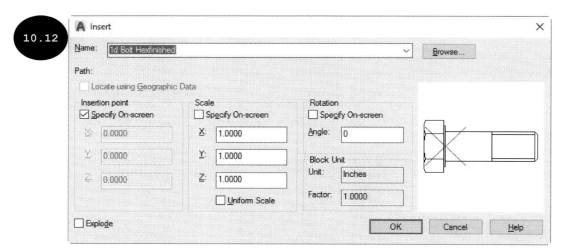

10.12

Name

The **Name** drop-down list of the **Insert** dialog box is used to select the block to be inserted into the drawing. To invoke the **Name** drop-down list, click on the down arrow, see Figure 10.13. The **Name** drop-down list displays a list of all the blocks created or available in the current drawing. You can also enter the name of the block to insert in the drawing here.

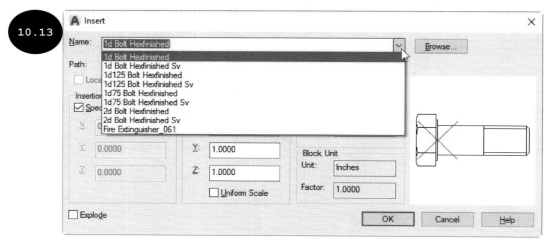

10.13

Insertion point

By default, the **Specify On-screen** check box is selected in the **Insertion point** area of the **Insert** dialog box. As a result, you can specify insertion point in the drawing area. To specify insertion point in the drawing area, select the **Specify On-screen** check box and then click on the **OK** button. You are prompted to specify the insertion point. Click to specify the insertion point in the drawing. The selected block is inserted in the drawing area and placed in the specified insertion point location.

If you uncheck the **Specify On-screen** check box, the **X**, **Y**, and **Z** fields of the **Insertion point** area are enabled. In these fields, you can specify the X, Y, and Z coordinates of the insertion point.

Scale

The **Scale** area of the dialog box is used to specify the scale of the block. By default, the 1 value is specified as the scale value in the **X**, **Y**, and **Z** fields. As a result, the block gets inserted in the drawing in its original size. You can specify scale in the X, Y, and Z axes of the block in the respective fields. On selecting the **Uniform Scale** check box, the block can be scaled uniformly in all axes. If you select the **Specify On-screen** check box in this area, then you are prompted to specify the scale for the block in the drawing area when you exit the dialog box by clicking on the **OK** button.

Rotation

The **Rotation** area of the dialog box is used to specify the rotational angle for the block. By default, **0** is specified in the **Angle** field of the **Rotation** area. You can specify the rotational angle for the block, as required in the **Angle** field. You can also specify the rotational angle for the block in the drawing area by selecting the **Specify On-screen** check box.

After specifying all the parameters for inserting the block, click on the **OK** button in the dialog box. The selected block gets attached to the cursor with its base/insertion point, which is specified while creating the block, see Figure 10.14. Also, you are prompted to specify the insertion point in the drawing area. Click to specify an insertion point for the block. The block gets inserted at the specified insertion point, see Figure 10.15. In this figure, the block is inserted by specifying the insertion point at the location 1 as marked in the Figure 10.14. Similarly, you can insert the same block several times in the drawing. Figure 10.16 shows the drawing in which 6 instances of the block are inserted in the drawing.

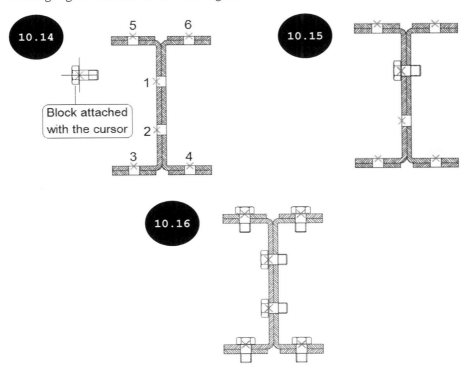

Creating a WBlock

A WBlock is a group of objects or entire drawing that is saved as an external file and acts as a single object. In AutoCAD, the WBlocks are same as the Blocks with the only difference that the WBlocks are saved as external files and can be inserted several times in any drawing, whereas the Blocks can only insert into the drawing in which they are created. You can create a WBlock either by using the **Write Block** tool or by using the WBLOCK command. To create a WBlock, click on the **Write Block** tool in the **Block** flyout of the **Block Definition** panel in the **Insert** tab, see Figure 10.17. The **Write Block** dialog box appears, see Figure 10.18. Alternatively, enter **W** in the Command Line window and then press ENTER. The W is the shortcut of the WBLOCK command. The **Write Block** dialog box has two areas: **Source** and **Destination**. The options of both these areas are discussed next.

Source
The options in the **Source** area of the dialog box are used to specify whether the block, entire drawing, or objects of the drawing to be converted into a WBlock. The options are discussed next.

Block
The **Block** radio button is used to select an existing block for converting into a WBlock. On selecting the **Block** radio button, the **Block** drop-down list gets enabled in front of this radio button. In this drop-down list, select the required Block to be converted into a WBlock. Note that the **Block** radio button is enabled only when the current drawing has existing Blocks available.

Entire drawing
The **Entire drawing** radio button is used to convert the whole drawing into a WBlock.

Objects
The **Objects** radio button is used to select a group of objects of the drawing for converting into a WBlock. By default, this radio button is selected in the **Source** area of the dialog box. As a result, the options in the **Base point** area and the **Objects** area of the dialog box are enabled, see Figure 10.19. The options of the **Base point** area and the **Objects** area are discussed next.

Base Point
The options of the **Base point** area are used to select a base point for the WBlock. You can specify a base point either by specifying a point in the drawing area or by entering its X, Y, and Z coordinates in the **X**, **Y**, and **Z** fields of the dialog box, respectively. To specify a base point in the drawing area, click on the **Pick point** button in the **Base point** area of the dialog box. The **Write Block** dialog box gets closed, and you are prompted to specify an insertion base point. Click in the drawing area to specify the base point. The **Write Block** dialog box appears again, and the base point is specified.

Objects
The options of the **Objects** area are used to select a group of objects to be converted into a WBlock. To select objects, click on the **Select objects** button of this area. The **Write Block** dialog box gets closed, and you are prompted to select objects. Select objects in the drawing area by clicking the left mouse button or by using the Window/Cross Window selection method. After selecting the objects, press ENTER. The **Write Block** dialog box appears again, and the information about the number of objects selected appears at the bottom of this area, see Figure 10.19. Similar to this, the other options such as **Retain**, **Convert to block**, and **Delete from drawing** of this area are same as those discussed earlier while creating the Blocks using the **Create Block** tool.

Destination

After specifying the source (block, entire drawing, or objects) for creating a WBlock, you need to define the name and the destination where you want to save the WBlock. You can specify a name and the destination for the WBlock by using the options in the **Destination** area of the dialog box. The options area discussed next.

File name and path

The **File name and path** field is used to specify a name and the location where the WBlock has to be saved. To specify a name and a location for the WBlock, click on the [...] button on the right of this field. The **Browse for Drawing File** dialog box appears. In this dialog box, browse to the location where you want to save the WBlock and then enter a new name for the WBlock in the **File name** field of this dialog box. Next, click on the **Save** button. The **Browse for Drawing File** dialog box gets closed, and the specified location and the name appear in the **File name and path** field of the **Write Block** dialog box.

Insert units

The **Insert units** drop-down list is used to select the unit for the WBlock.

After specifying the source and destination, click on the **OK** button. The **Write Block** dialog box gets closed, and the WBlock is saved in the specified location.

Inserting a WBlock in the Drawing

You can insert a WBlock in any drawing by using the **Insert** tool of the **Block** panel in the **Insert** tab or by using the INSERT command. To insert a WBlock in a drawing, enter I in the Command Line window and then press ENTER. The **Insert** dialog box appears, see Figure 10.20. Alternatively, you can use the **Insert** tool of the **Block** panel in the **Insert** tab to invoke the **Insert** dialog box.

In the **Insert** dialog box, click on the **Browse** button. The **Select Drawing File** dialog box appears. In this dialog box, browse to the location where the WBlock has been saved and then click on the WBlock to insert in the drawing. Next, click on the **Open** button in the dialog box. The **Select Drawing File** dialog box gets closed, and the name of the selected WBlock appears in the **Name** field of the **Insert** dialog box. Next, specify other parameters such as scale and angle of rotation in the respective fields of the **Insert** dialog box. The options in the **Insert** dialog box are the same as those discussed earlier. Next, click on the **OK** button. The selected WBlock gets attached to the cursor with the base point which specified while creating it. Next, click to specify the insertion point in the drawing area. The WBlock gets inserted at the specified insertion point. Similarly, you can insert the WBlock several time in the drawing.

Editing a Block

In a drawing, you may need to edit or modify existing blocks. In AutoCAD, you can edit the existing blocks either by using the **Block Editor** tool or BEDIT command. To edit a block, click on the **Block Editor** tool in the **Block Definition** panel of the **Insert** tab, see Figure 10.21. The **Edit Block Definition** dialog box appears, see Figure 10.22. It displays a list of all the blocks available in the current drawing. Alternatively, enter **BE** in the Command Line window and then press ENTER (BE is the shortcut of BEDIT command).

414   Chapter 10 > Working with Blocks and Xrefs

Click on the block to be edited in the **Edit Block Definition** dialog box. The preview of the selected block appears in the **Preview** area of the dialog box. Next, click on the **OK** button. The selected block is opened in the Block Editor, and the **Block Editor** tab appears in the **Ribbon**, see Figure 10.23. Now, you can make the changes in the block such as add new entities, delete existing entities, stretch, rotate, and so on by using the tools of the **Home** tab in the **Ribbon**. The tools in the **Block Editor** tab are used to make the block dynamic. You will learn more about making dynamic block later in this chapter. After making the necessary changes in the block, click on the **Save Block** tool in the **Open/Save** panel of the **Block Editor** tab. The changes made in the block get saved. Next, click on the **Close Block Editor** tool in the **Close** panel of the **Block Editor** tab to close the Block Editor. Note that if you have not saved the block after making the changes then by clicking the **Close Block Editor** tool, the **Block - Changes Not Saved** window appears, see Figure 10.24.

In the **Block - Changes Not Saved** window, click on **Save the changes to** *'the name of the block'* option to save the changes made in the Block Editor. To discard the changes made, click on **Discard the changes and close the Block Editor** option.

Making a Dynamic Block

A dynamic block is a block that can be modified dynamically in the drawing area. You can make a block dynamic by specifying the required parameters and actions using the tools in the **Block Editor** tab. To make a dynamic block, click on the **Block Editor** tool in the **Block Definition** panel of the **Insert** tab, see Figure 10.25. The **Edit Block Definition** dialog box appears. Alternatively, enter **BE** in the Command Line window and then press ENTER (BE is the shortcut of BEDIT command).

In the **Edit Block Definition** dialog box, select the block to be edited or converted into a dynamic block and then click on the **OK** button. The selected block gets opened in the Block Editor, and the **Block Editor** tab appears in the Ribbon, see Figure 10.26. In this figure, a rectangular block representing a table appears in the Block Editor.

Once the block is opened in the Block Editor, you can make the block dynamic by specifying required parameters and actions. To specify parameters for creating a dynamic block, click on the **Parameters** tab in the **BLOCK AUTHORING PALETTES**. The tools to specify parameters appear, see Figure 10.27. By using the tools of the **Parameters** tab, you can specify the parameters for the dynamic block.

416 Chapter 10 > Working with Blocks and Xrefs

For example, to specify a linear parameter, click on the **Linear** tool in the **Parameters** tab. You are prompted to specify the start point.

```
Specify start point or [Name Label Chain Description Base Palette
Value set]:
```

Next, click to specify the start point for the linear parameter, see Figure 10.28. In this figure, the midpoint of the upper horizontal line of the rectangle is defined as the start point. As soon as you specify the start point, a label is attached to the cursor, and you are prompted to specify the endpoint, see Figure 10.28.

```
Specify endpoint:
```

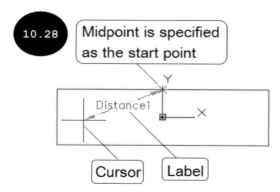

Next, click to specify the endpoint of the label, see Figure 10.29. You are prompted to specify the label location.

```
Specify label location:
```

Click to specify the label location. The label is placed in the specified location and the linear parameter is defined. Also, the grips appear at the specified midpoints, see Figure 10.30. The linear parameter allows you to modify the block in the linear fashion, dynamically by using the grips in the drawing area. However, only specifying the linear parameter does not make the block dynamic. You also need to specify the action such as stretch, scale, or move for the linear parameter.

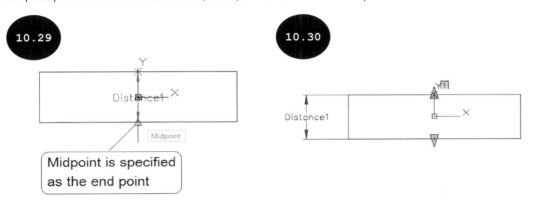

To specify the action for the parameter, click on the **Actions** tab in the BLOCK AUTHORING PALETTES. The tools to specify actions for the parameter such as **Move**, **Scale**, **Stretch**, and **Flip** appear in the **Actions** tab, see Figure 10.31.

418 Chapter 10 > Working with Blocks and Xrefs

For example, to specify a stretch action for the linear parameter, click on the **Stretch** tool in the **Actions** tab of the **BLOCK AUTHORING PALETTES**. You are prompted to select a parameter for specifying the action.

```
Select parameter:
```

Click on the parameter (linear parameter) for specifying the action. You can click on the label of the parameter to select it. As soon as you select the parameter (linear parameter), you are prompted to specify the parameter point to associate the action.

```
Specify parameter point to associate with action or enter [sTart
point Second point] <Second>:
```

Move the cursor over the grip, which is displayed at the midpoint of the upper horizontal line. The cursor snaps to the midpoint and a circle with cross mark appears, see Figure 10.32. Next, click on the midpoint of the upper horizontal line as the parameter point to associate the action. You are prompted to specify the first corner of the stretch frame. Note that the stretch frame is used to define the objects to stretch by using the grips in the drawing area, dynamically. You can create stretch frame by specifying its two diagonally opposite corners.

```
Specify first corner of stretch frame or [CPolygon]:
```

Click to specify the first corner of the stretch frame, see Figure 10.33. You are prompted to specify the opposite corner of the stretch frame.

```
Specify opposite corner:
```

Move the cursor diagonally and then click to specify the second corner of the stretch frame, see Figure 10.33. You are prompted to select objects to be stretched.

```
Select objects:
```

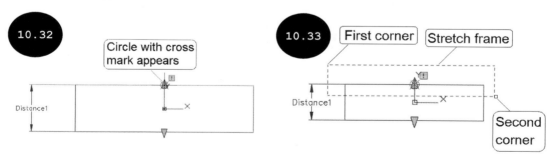

Click on the rectangle as the object to be stretched. Next, press ENTER. The stretch action is assigned to the upper selected grip of the rectangle. Similarly, assign the stretch action to the grip, which appears at the midpoint of the lower horizontal line of the block (rectangle). After assigning the parameter and the required action to it, click on the **Close Block Editor** tool in the **Close** panel of the **Block Editor** tab. The **Block - Changes Not Saved** window appears, see Figure 10.34. Click on **Save the changes to** *'name of the block'* in the **Block - Changes Not Saved** window. The changes made in the Block Editor are saved and the Block Editor gets closed. Also, the block becomes a dynamic block.

Now, if you select the block (dynamic block) in the drawing area, the grips of the dynamic block appears, see Figure 10.35. By using these grips, you can stretch the block, dynamically in the drawing.

Working with External References (Xrefs)

In AutoCAD, external references (Xrefs) are the drawings that are linked or attached to the current drawing, externally. External references (Xrefs) drawings are not the permanent part of the drawing and are connected externally to the drawing. The external references (Xrefs) drawings are most widely used in large assembly drawings, which have multiple parts. You can create drawings of all parts as individual drawings and then assemble them in the main drawing as external references (Xrefs).

External references also allow multiple users (CAD Engineers or Operators) to work on a single project (drawing) and then assemble all the drawings created by different users as external references to the main drawing. You can attach external references to a drawing by using the EXTERNAL REFERENCES Palette. To invoke the EXTERNAL REFERENCES Palette, click on the **External References Palette** tool in the **Palettes** panel of the **View** tab, see Figure 10.36. The EXTERNAL REFERENCES palette appears, see Figure 10.37. Alternatively, enter XREF in the Command Line window and then press ENTER to invoke this palette.

The **EXTERNAL REFERENCES** palette is used to attach a new Xref, detach existing Xref, unload the attached Xref, reload the unload Xref, and so on. Also, the **EXTERNAL REFERENCES** Palette displays the current status of each Xref that is attached in the current drawing.

To attach a Xref in the current drawing, click on the arrow in the **Attach** tool of the **EXTERNAL REFERENCES** palette. The **Attach** flyout appears, see Figure 10.38. By using the tools of this flyout, you can attach DWG, Image, DWF, DGF, PDF, Point Cloud, and Coordinate Model files. For example, to attach a DWG file, click on the **Attach DWG** tool in the **Attach** flyout. The **Select Reference File** dialog box appears. In this dialog box, browse to the location where the file to be attached is saved. Next, select the DWG file and then click on the **Open** button. The **Attach External Reference** dialog box appears, see Figure 10.39.

In the **Attach External Reference** dialog box, specify the parameters such as scale, insertion point, reference type, and rotation for attaching the external reference. Next, click on the **OK** button. The selected DWG file is attached to the cursor at its base point and you are prompted to specify the insertion point.

```
Specify insertion point or [Scale X Y Z Rotate PScale PX PY PZ
PRotate]:
```

Click to specify the insertion point in the drawing area. The selected drawing (DWG) is attached to the current drawing and placed at the specified insertion point. Also, the name of the attached drawing is listed in the **EXTERNAL REFERENCES** palette. Similarly, you can attach multiple files to the current drawing.

To detach a Xref, unload the attached Xref, reload the unload Xref, and so on, click on the Xref in the **EXTERNAL REFERENCES** palette and then right-click. A shortcut menu appears, see Figure 10.40. In this shortcut menu, click on the required option. For example, if you want to unload the Xref, click on the **Unload** option. The selected file gets unloaded and disappeared from the current drawing. Also, a symbol of cross mark appears in front of the file name in the **EXTERNAL REFERENCES** palette. You can reload the unloaded file. For doing so, click on the name of the drawing file to be reloaded in the current drawing and then right-click. A shortcut menu appears. In this shortcut menu, click on the **Reload** option. The file gets reloaded and is visible in the drawing area. Similarly, you can detach the existing Xrefs, change the Xref type, and so on. The **Details** area of the EXTERNAL REFERENCES palette displays the status of the selected Xref file.

Tutorial 1

Create the objects: arrow, condenser, exchanger, boiler, pump, Flux drum, and valve as shown in Figure 10.41, and then convert them into blocks. After creating the blocks, create the process flow diagram and insert the blocks in it, see Figure 10.42. Do not apply dimensions in the blocks. Also, you can assume the missing dimensions. You also need to add single line text in the flow diagram, see Figure 10.42.

10.41

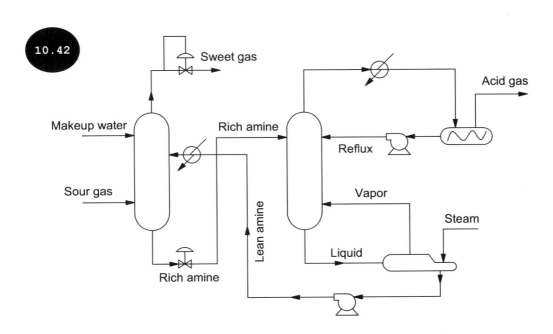

10.42

424 Chapter 10 > Working with Blocks and Xrefs

Section 1: Starting AutoCAD
1. Start AutoCAD and then open a new drawing file.

Section 2: Creating Blocks
1. Create the drawing of an arrow as shown in Figure 10.43 by using the **Line** tool. For overall size of the arrow, refer to Figure 10.41.

2. Fill the enclosed area of the arrow with a solid hatch pattern by using the **Hatch** tool, see Figure 10.44.

After creating the arrow, you need to convert it into a block.

3. Click on the **Insert** tab in the **Ribbon**. The tools of the **Insert** tab of the **Ribbon** appears, see Figure 10.45.

4. Click on the **Create Block** tool in the **Block Definition** panel of the **Insert** tab. The **Block Definition** dialog box appears, see Figure 10.46.

5. Enter **Arrow** as the name of the block in the **Name** field of the dialog box.

6. Click on the **Pick point** button in the **Base point** area of the dialog box. The dialog box disappears, and you are prompted to specify the insertion base point.

   ```
   _block specify insertion base point:
   ```

7. Click on the tip of the arrow as the insertion base point of the block, see Figure 10.47. The base point is defined and the **Block Definition** dialog box appears again.

8. Click on the **Select objects** button in the **Objects** area of the dialog box. The dialog box disappears, and you are prompted to select objects.

   ```
   Select objects:
   ```

9. Select all the entities of the arrow object including the hatch pattern in the drawing area by using the Window selection method, see Figure 10.48.

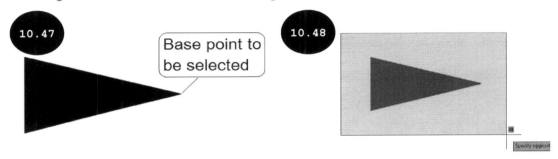

10. After selecting the all the entities of the object, press ENTER. The entities are selected and the **Block Definition** dialog box appears again.

11. Select the **Delete** radio button in the **Objects** area of the dialog box to delete the selected entities (arrow) in the drawing area and to create the block in the drawing.

12. Click on the **OK** button in the **Block Definition** dialog box. The Arrow block is created and saved internally in the drawing. Also, it is deleted from the drawing area.

13. Similarly, create the remaining objects: condenser, exchanger, boiler, pump, flux drum, and valve and then convert them into blocks, see Figure 10.49. In this figure, the cross mark indicates the base point of the objects.

426   Chapter 10 >   Working with Blocks and Xrefs

After creating the blocks, you can create the drawing and insert the blocks in it.

Section 3: Creating Drawing and Inserting Blocks

1. Click on the **Insert** tab in the **Ribbon**. The tools of the **Insert** tab of the **Ribbon** appears.

2. Click on the **Insert** tool in the **Block** panel of the **Insert** tab. The **Block** flyout appears with the display of all the blocks created in the drawing, see Figure 10.50. In this flyout, you may need to scroll the list to select the required block.

3. Click on the Exchanger block in the flyout appeared. The Exchanger block is attached to the cursor at its specified base point. Also, you are prompted to specify the insertion point.

   ```
   Specify insertion point or [Basepoint Scale X Y Z Rotate]:
   ```

4. Click anywhere in the drawing area to specify the insertion point of the Exchanger block. The Exchanger block is placed at the specified location in the drawing area.

5. Similarly, insert another instance of the Exchanger block in the drawing area, see Figure 10.51. Note that you need to place the second instance of the Exchanger block inline with the first inserted Exchanger block by keeping some space between them, see Figure 10.51.

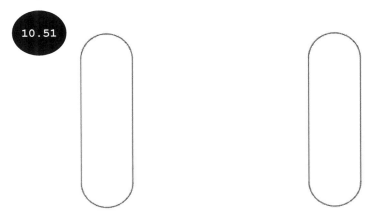

6. Invoke the **Line** tool and then create the line entities of the drawing as shown in Figure 10.52. You can assume the length of the lines. In the figure, the cross marks (P1 through P6) indicate the insertion points for the blocks in the drawing and are for your reference only.

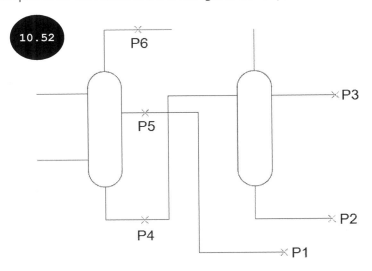

428 Chapter 10 > Working with Blocks and Xrefs

7. Click on the **Insert** tool in the **Block** panel of the **Insert** tab. The **Block** flyout appears. In this flyout, click on the Pump block. The Pump block is attached to the cursor at its specified base point. Also, you are prompted to specify an insertion point.

   ```
   Specify insertion point or [Basepoint Scale X Y Z Rotate]:
   ```

8. Move the cursor toward the insertion point "P1" in the drawing, refer to Figure 10.52. Next, click to specify the insertion point for the Pump block. The Pump block is placed at the specified insertion point in the drawing area, see Figure 10.53.

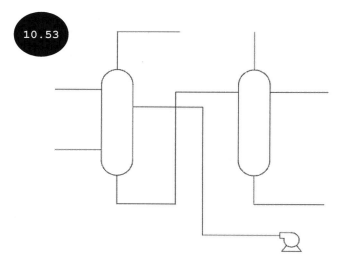

9. Similarly, insert a Boiler block at the insertion point "P2", a Pump block at the insertion point P3, a Valve block at the insertion point P4, a Condenser block at the insertion point P5, and a Valve block at the insertion point P6, see Figure 10.54.

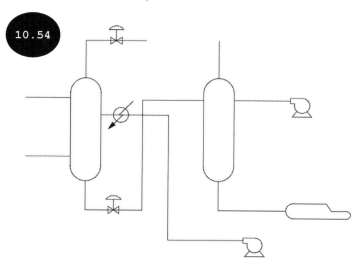

10. Create the line entities (L1 through L10) of the drawing by using the **Line** tool, see Figure 10.55. You can assume the length of the lines. Note that the Figure 10.55 numbered for your reference only.

11. Insert the Flux drum block at the end point of the line "L7", see Figure 10.56.

12. Create the line entities (L11 through L14) of the drawing by using the **Line** tool, see Figure 10.57. You can assume the length of the lines. Note that the Figure 10.57 numbered for your reference only.

13. Insert the Condenser block at the midpoint of the Line "L11", see Figure 10.58.

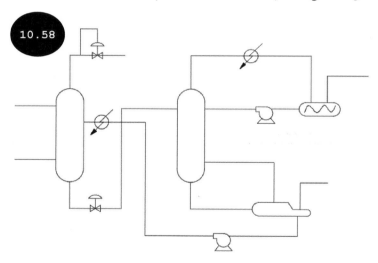

Now, you need to insert the Arrow blocks in the drawing to define the flow of the process in the drawing.

14. Click on the **Insert** tool in the **Block** panel of the **Insert** tab. The **Block** flyout appears. In this flyout, click on the Arrow block. The Arrow block gets attached to the cursor at its base point. Also, you are prompted to specify an insertion point.

    ```
    Specify insertion point or [Basepoint Scale X Y Z Rotate]:
    ```

15. Move the cursor to the end point of the line "L14", refer to Figure 10.57. Next, click to specify the insertion point of the Arrow block when the cursor snaps to it. The Arrow block is inserted and placed at the specified insertion point, see Figure 10.59.

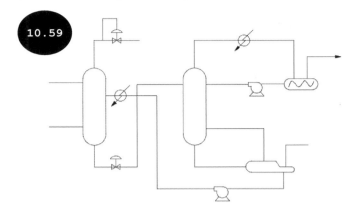

16. Again, invoke the **Block** flyout and then click on the Arrow block. The Arrow block gets attached to the cursor at its specified base point. Also, you are prompted to specify an insertion point.

    ```
    Specify insertion point or [Basepoint Scale X Y Z Rotate]:
    ```

17. Click on the **Rotate** option in the command prompt. You are prompted to specify a rotation angle. Alternatively, enter **R** in the Command Line window and then press ENTER.

    ```
    Specify rotation angle <0>:
    ```

18. Enter **-90** in the Command Line window and then press ENTER. The rotation angle of the attached Arrow block has changed.

19. Move the cursor to the end point of the Line "L12", refer to Figure 10.57. Next, click to specify the insertion point of the Arrow block when the cursor snaps to it. The Arrow block is inserted and placed at the specified insertion point, see Figure 10.60.

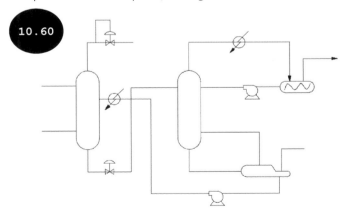

432 Chapter 10 > Working with Blocks and Xrefs

20. Similarly, insert the Arrow blocks at the remaining locations of the drawing, see Figure 10.61.

Section 4: Adding Single Line Text
1. Add the single line text in the drawing area by using the **Single Line** tool, see Figure 10.62.

Section 5: Saving the Drawing
1. Click on the **Save** tool in the **Quick Access Toolbar**. The **Save Drawing As** dialog box appears.

2. Browse to the *AutoCAD* folder and then create a folder with the name *Chapter 10* inside the *AutoCAD* folder. Next, enter **Tutorial 1** in the **File name** field of the dialog box.

3. Click on the **Save** button. The drawing saved with the name Tutorial 1 in the *Chapter 10* folder.

Hands-on Test Drive 1

Create the drawing template, as shown in Figure 10.63 and then convert it into WBlock (external block) by using the WBLOCK command so that you can insert the drawing template in any drawing as a block. Dimensions are for your reference only. You can assume the missing dimensions.

Summary

In this chapter, you have learned how to create and insert Blocks and WBlocks in a drawing. You have also learned how to edit Blocks and make Dynamic Blocks. Also, you have learned how to work with external reference files (Xrefs).

Questions

- In AutoCAD, you can create a Block either by using the _____ tool or _____ command.

- The _____ is the shortcut of the BLOCK command.

- The blocks created in the current drawing can be inserted in the drawing several times by using the _____ tool.

- You can create a WBlock either by using the _____ tool or _____ command.

- In AutoCAD, you can edit blocks either by using the _____ tool or _____ command.

- A _____ block can be modified dynamically in the drawing area.

- In AutoCAD, external reference files are known as _____ .

- You can attach external reference files to a drawing by using the _____ palette.

- To invoke the EXTERNAL REFERENCES Palette, click on the _____ tool.

CHAPTER 11

Working with Layouts

In this chapter, you will learn the following:

- Getting Started with Paper Space/Layout
- Understanding Different Components of a Layout
- Setting up the Sheet/Paper Size of a Layout
- Adding, Renaming, and Deleting a Layout
- Working with Viewports
- Accessing the Model Space within a Viewport
- Clipping a Viewport
- Locking the Object Scale in a Viewport
- Controlling the Display of Objects in a Viewport
- Controlling Layers Properties for Viewports
- Switching to the Model Space
- Creating Viewports in the Model Space
- Joining Two Viewports
- Restoring Viewports

So far in this textbook, you have learned about creating drawings in Model space. AutoCAD provided with two distinct working environments: Model space and Paper space. By default, when you start AutoCAD, the Model space is the activated environment for creating drawings. The drawing created in the Model space is in 1:1 scale and it represents the real world size of the model, whereas the Paper space is used for plotting drawings and generating different drawing views. In the Paper space, you can create multiple viewports, which represent different drawing views. Paper space is nothing but a sheet of paper on which the final drawing can print or plot. The Paper space is also known as the layout. You can switch between the Model space and Paper space by using the tabs: **Model**, **Layout1**, and **Layout2** available at the lower left corner of the drawing area, see Figure 11.1. By default, two layouts: **Layout1** and **Layout2** are available as the Paper space. In these layouts, you can prepare your drawing for plotting and generate different drawing views. In addition to the default layouts, you can add multiple layouts, as required. You will learn about adding layouts later in this chapter.

11.1

Getting Started with Paper Space/Layout

As discussed, the Paper space is a sheet of paper, which is used to prepare drawing for plotting and printing. Drawings are used to fully and clearly communicate the requirement for manufacturing the end product. It is a language that communicates ideas and information about the product with each other. You can either take the printout of the drawing on paper or create an electronic file to communicate the information about the product. The Design Web Format (DWF) is the most commonly used electronic file format to communicate the information about the product. In AutoCAD, you can plot a drawing in both the working environments: Model space and Paper space (layout). However, it is recommended to use Paper space (layout) for plotting a drawing. It is because the Paper space/layout gives you more flexibility to control the drawing for printing and allows you to generate different drawing views with different scales. Also, it gives the same appearance of the drawing as it is on the sheet of paper. By default, two layouts: **Layout1** and **Layout2** are available for plotting a drawing. In addition to the default layouts, you can add multiple layouts to generate different drawing views of an object on different layouts. In AutoCAD, each layout represents a sheet of paper having a standard size. You will learn about adding layouts later in this chapter.

To activate the Paper space, click on the **Layout1** tab in the lower left corner of the drawing area, see Figure 11.2. The Paper space gets activated, and the drawing created in the Model space appears in a default viewport. Also, the **Layout** tab appears in the **Ribbon**. You can create multiple viewports, delete the existing viewports, and modify the viewports in a layout. However, before you learn about creating, deleting, and editing viewports, it is important to understand the different components of a layout and to set up the sheet size for a layout.

Understanding Different Components of a Layout

In AutoCAD, a layout has several components such as paper/sheet, plot area, viewport, and layout icon, see Figure 11.3. The paper of a layout has a standard size. By default, the paper size of a layout1 is 8.5" X 11.0", which is ISO A4 sheet. You can define the paper/sheet size of a layout, as required. You will learn about setting up the sheet size later in this chapter. The plot area of a layout is the maximum area of printing the drawing, and it represented as dotted lines, see Figure 11.3. The viewports of a layout are used to create different drawing views of a model. You can create multiple viewports in a layout. You will learn about creating viewports later in this chapter.

11.3

Setting up the Sheet/Paper Size of a Layout

In AutoCAD, the default layouts (Layout1 and Layout2) have default paper/sheet size assigned. You can change the default paper/sheet size of a layout, as per the requirement. For doing so, activate the layout whose paper/sheet size is to change by clicking on its tab available at the lower right corner of the drawing area. Next, right-click on the activated layout tab. A flyout appears, see Figure 11.4. In this flyout, click on the **Page Setup Manager** option. The **Page Setup Manager** dialog box appears, see Figure 11.5. Alternatively, click on the **Page Setup** tool in the **Layout** panel of the **Layout** tab in the **Ribbon**. Note that the **Layout** tab appears in the **Ribbon** only when a layout is activated.

11.4

438 Chapter 11 > Working with Layouts

11.5

In the **Page Setup Manager** dialog box, the current activated layout is selected in the **Current page setup** area. Also, the details of the selected layout such as plot size and description are displayed in the **Selected page setup details** area of the dialog box. Click on the **Modify** button in the dialog box to modify the default page size of the selected layout. The **Page Setup** dialog box appears, see Figure 11.6.

11.6

By using the **Paper size** drop-down list of the **Page Setup** dialog box, you can select the required paper size for the layout. You can also choose the orientation of the sheet: portrait or landscape by using the respective radio buttons in the **Drawing orientation** area of the dialog box. After selecting the required paper size and orientation of the layout, click on the **OK** button in the dialog box. The paper/sheet size for the selected layout is modified. Now, you can close the **Page Setup Manager** dialog box by clicking the **Close** button in the dialog box.

Adding, Renaming, and Deleting a Layout

As discussed, by default, two layouts: **Layout1** and **Layout2** are provided as Paper space to prepare the drawing for plotting and printing. Each layout represents a sheet of paper. However, in some of the drawing, these two layouts are not enough, you may need to add additional layouts for generating drawing views of a drawing in various layouts. In AutoCAD, you can add multiple layouts for a drawing as required. To add additional layouts, right-click on a layout tab in the lower left corner of the drawing area. A flyout appears, see Figure 11.7. In this flyout, click on the **New Layout** option, see Figure 11.7. A new layout with a default name gets added, see Figure 11.8. In this figure, the **Layout3** is the newly added layout. Alternatively, you can click on the +sign available on the right of the last layout tab to add a layout in the drawing, refer to Figure 11.8. You can also click on the **New** tool in the **Layout** panel of the **Layout** tab in the **Ribbon** to add a layout, see Figure 11.9.

As discussed, on adding a layout, a default name is assigned to the newly added layout such as Layout3, Layout4, or Layout5. You can change the default assigned name of the newly added or an existing layout of the drawing. For doing so, right-click on the layout tab whose name has to be changed. A flyout appears. In this flyout, click on the **Rename** option. The default name of the selected layout is displayed in an edit field, see Figure 11.10. In this edit field, enter the new name for the layout as required and then press ENTER. The name of the layout is changed as specified.

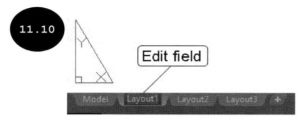

You can also delete a layout which added by mistake or is no longer required to be the part of the drawing. To delete a layout, right-click on the layout tab which is to be deleted. A flyout appears. In this flyout, click on the **Delete** option. The selected layout gets deleted and is no longer the part of the current drawing.

Working with Viewports

When you activate a layout by clicking on its respective tab (Layout1 or Layout2) available at the lower left corner of the drawing area, the drawing created in the Model space appears in a default viewport, see Figure 11.11. A viewport is a rectangular area which displays the drawing created in the Model space. You can fit the entire drawing in a single viewport or create multiple viewports in the layout for displaying different views of the model at various scales. Also, you can perform various editing operations on a viewport such as a move, copy, rotate, scale, and stretch. Moreover, you can also delete an existing viewport of a drawing. The method of editing, deleting, and creating viewports are discussed next.

Editing a Viewport

In AutoCAD, similar to performing various editing operations on an entity such as line, rectangle, and circle, you can perform editing operations such as move, copy, rotate, scale, and stretch on a viewport of a layout. For example, to stretch a viewport, click on the viewport boundary to be stretched. The viewport boundary gets highlighted with the display of grips, see Figure 11.12. Now, by using the grips of the viewport boundary, you can stretch the viewport as required. Alternatively, you can also use the **Stretch** tool. Figure 11.13 shows a shrinking view of the viewport. Note that in this figure, after shrinking the viewport, the drawing view is not displayed completely inside the viewport. In such cases, you can access the model space within the viewport of a layout to zoom or pan the drawing such that it fits inside the viewport. You will learn about accessing the model space within the viewport of a layout later in this chapter.

In AutoCAD 2019, you can also move and scale the viewport by using the square and triangular grips, respectively that appear at the center of the viewport boundary, refer to Figures 11.12 and 11.13. When you click on the triangular grip, a list of predefined scale factor appears, see Figure 11.14. In this list, you can select the required scale factor for the layout. Note that on changing the scale of the viewport, the boundary of the viewport as well as the drawing gets scaled, accordingly. To move the viewport, click on the square grip that appears at the center of the viewport boundary and then click to specify the new position of the viewpoint in the drawing sheet.

Deleting a Viewport

In AutoCAD, similar to deleting an entity such as line, rectangle, and circle, you can delete a viewport. To delete a viewport, click on it. Its boundary gets highlighted with the display of grips, refer to Figure 11.12. Next, press the DELETE key. The selected viewport gets deleted.

Creating Viewports

In addition to the default viewports, you can create multiple viewports in a layout for displaying different views of a model, see Figure 11.15. The viewports created in a layout are known as floating viewports. It is because you can create viewports of any shape and size. Moreover, the viewports in a layout can be overlapped and edited.

The tools to create viewports are in the **Layout Viewports** panel of the **Layout** tab in the **Ribbon**, see Figure 11.16. You can create different types of viewports by using these tools. The methods of creating viewports are discussed next.

Creating a Rectangular Viewport

To create a rectangular shape viewport, click on the **Rectangular** tool in the **Layout Viewports** panel of the **Layout** tab, refer to Figure 11.16. You are prompted to specify the first corner of the viewport. Alternatively, enter **-VPORTS** in the Command Line window and then press ENTER to create a rectangular viewport.

```
Specify corner of viewport or [ON OFF Fit Shadeplot Lock Object
Polygonal Restore LAyer 2 3 4] <Fit>:
```

Click to specify a corner of the viewport in the paper area of the layout, see Figure 11.17. You are prompted to specify the opposite corner of the viewport.

```
Specify opposite corner:
```

Click to specify the diagonally opposite corner of the viewport, see Figure 11.17. A rectangular viewport is created, and the drawing created in the Model space fits entirely inside the viewport, see Figure 11.17. Similarly, you can create multiple rectangular viewports in a layout. You can zoom, pan, or change the scale of the drawing view in a viewport by accessing the Model space within the viewport of a layout. You will learn about accessing the Model space within the viewport later in this chapter.

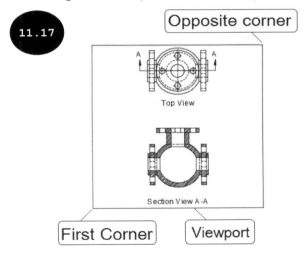

Note: You can also create rectangular viewports by using the MVIEW command. For doing so, enter MV in the Command Line window and then press ENTER. You are prompted to specify the first corner of the viewport. Specify the first and second/opposite corner of the viewport in a layout. A rectangular viewport is created. You can also create two, three, or four viewports together by using this command. For doing so, enter 2, 3, or 4, respectively and then press ENTER when you are prompted to specify the first corner of the viewport. Next, you are prompted to specify the arrangement of the viewports "`Enter viewport arrangement [Horizontal Vertical Above Below Left Right] <Right>:`" Specify the arrangement for the viewports by clicking on their respective option in the command prompt. Next, specify the first and second/opposite corner that defines the overall area/boundary for the viewports. The viewports are created.

Creating a Polygonal Viewport

To create a polygonal viewport, click on the **Layout** tab in the **Ribbon** and then click on the down arrow in the **Rectangular** tool of the **Layout Viewports** panel, see Figure 11.18. The **Viewport** flyout appears, see Figure 11.18. In the **Viewport** flyout, click on the **Polygonal** tool. You are prompted to specify the start point. Alternatively, enter **-VPORTS** in the Command Line window and then click on the **Polygonal** option in the command prompt.

```
Specify start point:
```

Click to specify the start point of the polygonal viewport in the paper/sheet area of the layout, see Figure 11.19. You are prompted to specify the next point for creating the polygonal viewport.

```
Specify next point or [Arc Length Undo]:
```

Click to specify the second point of the polygonal viewport, see Figure 11.19. You can also specify the length of the line or coordinates (X, Y) of the second point. As soon as you specify the second point, you are prompted to specify the third point for creating the polygonal viewport.

```
Specify next point or [Arc Close Length Undo]:
```

Similarly, you can continue to specify points in the paper/sheet area of the layout for creating a polygonal viewport. To close the viewport, either click on the **Close** option in the command prompt or enter **C** and then press ENTER. The closed polygonal viewport is created and the drawing views created in the Model space appear in it, see Figure 11.19. Note that the drawings views created in the Model space may not fit entirely inside the viewport. You can fit the drawings views in the viewport as well as zoom, pan, or change the scale by accessing the Model space within the viewport. You will learn about accessing the Model space within the viewport later in this chapter.

You can create a polygonal viewport having line entities or the combination of line and arc entities. To create a polygonal viewport having arc entities, you need to activate the arc mode either by clicking on the **Arc** option in the command prompt or by entering **A** in the Command Line window and then pressing ENTER. Note that once the arc mode is activated, you can create a chain of arc entities by specifying the arc end points. To activate the line mode again, either click on the **Line** option in the command prompt or enter **L** and then press ENTER. Figure 11.20 shows a polygonal viewport created by line and arc entities.

Creating a Viewport by using a Closed Object or Geometry

In addition to creating rectangular and polygonal viewports, you can convert an existing closed geometry into a viewport. Note the all entities of the closed geometry to be converted into a viewport must act as a single object. You can convert a rectangle created by using the **Rectangle** tool, a circle, an ellipse, a closed spline, or a group of closed polyline entities created by using the **Polyline** tool into a viewport. Note that the polylines entities must close by using the **Close** option of the command prompt to convert into a viewport. Figure 11.21 shows a closed spline and a group of polyline entities.

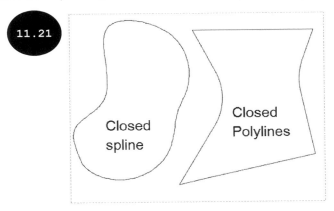

446 Chapter 11 > Working with Layouts

To convert a closed geometry into a viewport, click on the **Layout** tab in the **Ribbon** and then click on the down arrow in the **Rectangular** tool of the **Layout Viewports** panel, see Figure 11.22. The **Viewport** flyout appears, see Figure 11.22. In this flyout, click on the **Object** tool. You are prompted to select an object to convert into a viewport. Alternatively, enter -VPORTS in the Command Line window and then click on the **Object** option in the command prompt.

```
Specify corner of viewport or [ON OFF Fit Shadeplot Lock Object
Polygonal Restore LAyer 2 3 4] <Fit>:_o Select object to clip
viewport:
```

Click on the object to be converted into a viewport. The selected object gets converted into a viewport, and the drawing views created in the Model space appear inside the viewport, see Figure 11.23. Similarly, you can again invoke the **Object** tool and convert another closed object into a viewport, see Figure 11.24.

Creating Pre-Define Standard Viewports

You can create pre-defined standard viewports in a layout by using the **Viewport** dialog box. For doing so, click on the down arrow on the right of the **Layout Viewports** panel in the **Layout** tab, see Figure 11.25. The **Viewports** dialog box appears. In this dialog box, click on the **New Viewports** tab to display the list of standard viewports, see Figure 11.26. Alternatively, enter +VPORTS in the Command Line window and then press ENTER twice to invoke the **Viewports** dialog box.

AutoCAD 2019: A Power Guide > 447

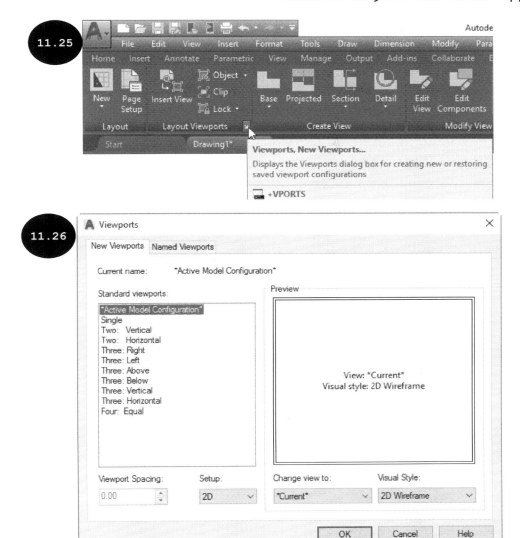

In the **Standard viewports** area of the dialog box, you can select the required standard viewports to be created. For example to create four rectangular viewports of equal sizes, select the **Four: Equal** option in the **Standard viewports** area. The preview of the selected standard viewports appears in the **Preview** area of the dialog box. After selecting the required standard viewports, click on the **OK** button in the dialog box. You are prompted to specify the first corner of a window which encloses the viewports.

```
Specify first corner or [Fit] <Fit>:
```

Click to specify the first corner of the window in the paper area of the layout, see Figure 11.27. You are prompted to specify the opposite corner of the window.

```
Specify opposite corner:
```

Click to specify the diagonally opposite corner of the window, see Figure 11.27. The viewports are created, see Figure 11.27. In this figure, four viewports of equal sizes are created in the layout.

Accessing the Model Space within a Viewport

In AutoCAD, you can access the Model space within a viewport of a layout to perform the editing operations and changing the drawing display. For doing so, double-click inside the viewport. The Model space gets activated, and the UCS icon appears inside the viewport, which indicates that the Model space is activated, see Figure 11.28.

After accessing the Model space, you can zoom or pan the drawing to fit the drawing view inside the viewport. Also, you can change the scale of the drawing view by using the **Scale of the selected viewport** drop-down list in the Status Bar. To invoke the **Scale of the selected viewport** drop-down list, click on the **Scale of the selected viewport** button in the Status Bar, see Figure 11.29. Moreover, you can edit the properties of the drawing entities such as linetype scale, lineweight, and linetype in the Model space.

Alternatively, you can also access the Model space within a viewport by clicking on the **PAPER** button in the Status Bar (see Figure 11.30) or by using the MSPACE command. Note that if only one viewport is available in the layout then on clicking the **Paper** button or by entering the MSPACE command, the Model space gets activated within the available viewport. However, if more than one viewports are available in the layout, then the Model space gets activated within the last created or activated viewport of the layout. You can also click on the required viewport of the layout to access the Model space in it.

After making the necessary changes in the Model space, you need to switch back to the Paper space. To switch back to the Paper space, double-click anywhere outside the viewport. Alternatively, click on the **MODEL** button in the Status Bar (see Figure 11.31) or enter PSPACE and then press ENTER.

Clipping a Viewport

You can clip a viewport of a layout by using the **Clip** tool of the **Layout Viewports** panel in the **Layout** tab. For doing so, you need to first create a closed object as the clipping object for clipping the viewport. The objects that can use as clipping objects includes a rectangle created by using the **Rectangle** tool, a circle, an ellipse, a closed spline, or a group of closed polyline entities created by using the **Polyline** tool (the polylines entities must close by using the **Close** option of the command prompt).

To clip a viewport, click on the **Clip** tool in the **Layout Viewports** panel in the **Layout** tab, see Figure 11.32. You are prompted to select the viewport to be clipped. Alternatively, enter VPCLIP in the Command Line window and then press ENTER to invoke the **Clip** tool.

```
Select viewport to clip:
```

After invoking the **Clip** tool, click on the viewport to be clipped, see Figure 11.33. You are prompted to select a clipping object.

```
Select clipping object or [Polygonal] <Polygonal>:
```

Click on the clipping object, see Figure 11.33. The selected viewport gets clipped, see Figure 11.34.

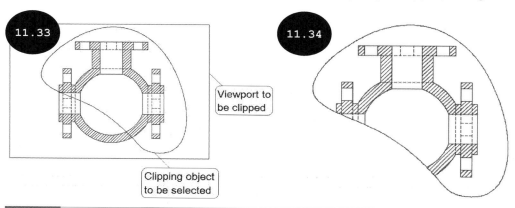

Note: You can also create a group of closed polyline entities by using the **Polyline** tool as the clipping object after invoking the **Clip** tool. For doing so, press the ENTER key when you are prompted to select the clipping object in the command prompt. As soon as you press ENTER, you are prompted to specify the start point of the polylines. After specifying all the points of the polylines, click on the **Close** option in the command prompt to create a closed loop of polylines. The selected viewport gets clipped by the polyline object created.

Locking the Object Scale in a Viewport

In AutoCAD, you can lock or unlock the scale (display) of objects in a viewport by using the **Lock** or **Unlock** tool of the **Layout Viewports** panel in the **Layout** tab, respectively. Note that once the objects of a viewport are locked, you cannot perform operations such as zoom and pan after accessing the Model space in the layout. Locking the scale of objects is useful if you want to prevent any modification by mistake.

To lock the scale of objects in a viewport, click on the **Lock** tool in the **Layout Viewports** panel of the **Layout** tab, see Figure 11.35. You are prompted to select objects to be locked.

    Select objects:

Click on the viewport whose objects/drawing views to be locked. You can select multiple viewports one by one. Next, press ENTER. The display of the objects of the selected viewport is locked. Note that you can access the Model space within the locked viewport but cannot modify the display/scale of the objects. However, you can edit the properties of the objects such as linetype scale, linetype, and lineweight. Also, you can add or delete the entities in the locked viewport. To unlock the viewport, click on the arrow in the **Lock** tool of the **Layout Viewports** panel. A flyout appears, refer to Figure 11.35. In this flyout, click on the **Unlock** tool. Next, click on the viewport to be unlocked.

Alternatively, to lock the display or scale of objects of a viewport, click on the viewport to be locked and then right-click. A shortcut menu appears. In this shortcut menu, click on the **Display Locked > Yes**. Similarly, click on the **Display Locked > No** to unlock the display of objects of the selected viewport.

Controlling the Display of Objects in a Viewport

You can turn on or off the display of objects in a viewport. To turn off the display of objects in a viewport, click on the viewport and then right-click. A shortcut menu appears. In this shortcut menu, click on the **Display Viewport Objects > No**. The display of objects of the selected viewport turns off. To turn on the display of objects again, click on the viewport and then right-click. Next, click on the **Display Viewport Objects > Yes** in the shortcut menu appeared.

Controlling Layers Properties for Viewports

In AutoCAD, you can control the layer properties for viewports such as freeze/thaw the newly created viewports, freeze all viewports, viewport color, viewport linetype, and viewport lineweight by using the **LAYER PROPERTIES MANAGER**. The concept and working with layers has discussed in chapter 3.

452 Chapter 11 > Working with Layouts

To control the layer properties for a viewport, double-click inside the viewport to access the Model space. Next, invoke the **LAYER PROPERTIES MANAGER** either by clicking on the **Layer Properties** tool in the **Layers** panel of the **Home** tab or by entering the **LA** in the Command Line window, see Figure 11.36. Most of the options of the **LAYER PROPERTIES MANAGER** have been discussed in chapter 3. The options that not discussed in chapter 3 are discussed next.

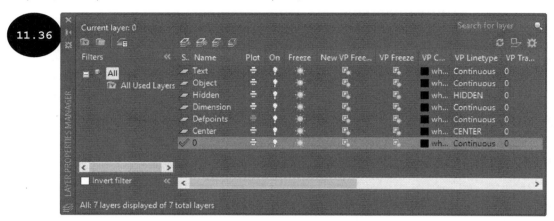

Viewport Freeze

The **Viewport Freeze** field of the **LAYER PROPERTIES MANAGER** is used to freeze the objects of the current viewport. To freeze objects of the current viewport, click on the **VP Freeze** field of the layer, see Figure 11.37. The layer gets frozen, and the objects assigned to the frozen layer become invisible in the currently active viewport. For example, if you click on the **VP Freeze** field of the Dimension layer (see Figure 11.37) then the Dimension layer gets frozen, and all dimensions assigned to the layer become invisible in the currently active viewport.

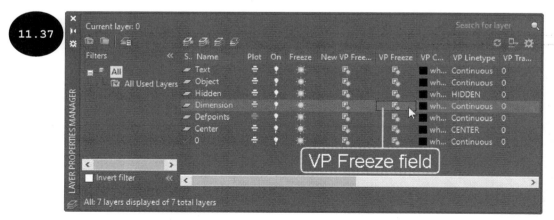

Viewport Color

You can change the color of the objects in the current viewport by using the **VP Color** field of a layer. To change the object's color in the current viewport, click on the **VP Color** field of a layer, see Figure 11.38. The **Select Color** dialog box appears. In this dialog box, select the required color to be assigned to the respective objects of the layer. Next, click on the **OK** button to accept the change and to close the dialog box. The color of the objects of the selected layer gets changed in the current viewport. For example, to change the color of the dimensions in the current viewport, click on the **VP Color** field of the Dimension layer (see Figure 11.38) and then select the required color in the **Select Color** dialog box that appears. Next, click **OK** in the **Select Color** dialog box. The color of the dimensions gets changed in the current viewport.

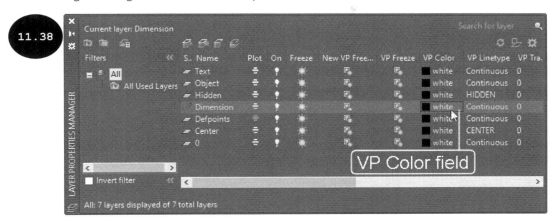

Similarly, you can change the linetype, lineweight, and transparency of the objects of a layer in the current viewport by using the VP Linetype, VP Lineweight, and VP Transparency fields of the layer, respectively in the **LAYER PROPERTIES MANAGER**.

Note: If none of the viewports is activated then on changing the viewport color, viewport linetype, viewport lineweight, and so on, only the boundary of the viewports in the layout gets affected by the change.

Switching to the Model Space

As discussed, you can switch between the Model space and Paper space (layout) anytime by using the tabs (**Model**, **Layout1**, and **Layout2**) available at the lower left corner of the drawing area, see Figure 11.39. The **Model** tab represents the Model space, and **Layout** tab represents the Paper space (layout) of a drawing.

Creating Viewports in the Model Space

In AutoCAD, you can also create viewports in the Model space. The viewports created in the Model space are known as Tiled viewports. By default, when you start AutoCAD, a single viewport is displayed in the Model space. You can create multiple viewports in the Model space to display the different drawing views of an object. Creating viewports in the Model space is same as dividing the work/drawing area into multiple areas. You can only create rectangular space viewports in the Model space by using the tools available in the **Model Viewports** panel of the **View** tab in the **Ribbon**, see Figure 11.40. The tools are discussed next.

Viewport Configuration

The **Viewport Configuration** drop-down list of the **Model Viewports** panel of the **View** tab is used to select the pre-defined viewport configurations, see Figure 11.41. You can select the required viewport configuration in this drop-down list such as **Two: Vertical**, **Two: Horizontal**, **Three: Right**, **Three: Left**, and **Four: Equal**. Depending upon the viewport configuration selected, the drawing area of the Model space gets divided, and the drawing appears in all viewports.

Similarly, you can create viewports in the Model space by using the **Named** tool in the **Model Viewports** panel of the **View** tab.

Joining Two Viewports

You can also merge or join two viewports by using the **Join** tool of the **Model Viewports** panel in the **View** tab. To join two viewports, click on the **Join** tool in the **Model Viewports** panel. You are prompted to select the dominant viewport.

```
Select dominant viewport <current viewport>:
```

Click on a viewport as the dominant viewport in the drawing area. You are prompted to select the viewport to be joined to the dominant viewport selected.

```
Select viewport to join:
```

Click on the viewport to be joined. The selected viewport joined to the selected dominant viewport.

Restoring Viewports

You can restore the multiple viewport configuration to the default single viewport in the Model space by using the **Restore** tool of the **Model Viewports** panel in the **View** tab. The **Restore** tool is used to toggle between a single viewport and the last multiple viewport configuration.

Tutorial 1

Create the drawing in the Model space, see Figure 11.42. After creating the drawing, create an elliptical viewport in a layout and set the drawing scale in the viewport to 1:40, see Figure 11.43. The major axis of the elliptical viewport is 8 inches (203.20 mm), and minor axis of the elliptical viewport is 5 inches (127 mm) for your reference.

11.43

Section 1: Starting AutoCAD
1. Start AutoCAD and then open a new drawing file.

Section 2: Creating Drawing and Applying Dimensions
1. Create the drawing as shown in Figure 11.44. You can refer to Figure 11.42 for dimensions. Also, you can assume the missing dimensions.

2. Apply the ANSI31 hatch pattern in the required enclosed areas of the drawing by using the **Hatch** tool in the **Draw** panel of the **Home** tab, see Figure 11.45. Note that you may need to adjust the hatch pattern scale so that the pattern appears similar to the one shown in Figure 11.45.

11.44   11.45

3. Apply dimensions to the drawing by using the dimension tools, see Figure 11.46. Note that you need to modify the dimension style properties such as text height, arrow size, extend beyond dimension lines, and offset from the origin by using the DIMSTYLE command.

11.46

Section 3: Creating Elliptical Shaped Viewport in a Layout

1. Click on the **Layout1** tab in the lower left corner of the drawing area. The **Layout1** is activated, and the drawing created in the Model space appears in a default viewport, see Figure 11.47.

11.47

2. Click on the rectangular boundary of the viewport and then press the DELETE key to delete the default viewport.

   Now, you need to draw an ellipse as the boundary of the viewport.

3. Create an ellipse having the major axis of 8 inches (203.20 mm) and minor axis of 5 inches (127 mm) on the sheet, see Figure 11.48. You can create an ellipse by using the **Center** tool of the **Ellipse** flyout in the **Draw** panel of the **Home** tab, see Figure 11.49 or by entering **EL** in the Command Line window. The EL is the shortcut of the ELLIPSE command.

458 Chapter 11 > Working with Layouts

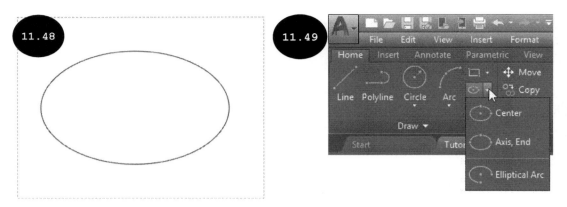

After creating the ellipse, you can convert it into a viewport.

4. Click on the **Layout** tab in the **Ribbon** to display the tools and panels of the **Layout** tab.

5. Click on the down arrow in the **Rectangular** tool of the **Layout Viewports** panel in the **Layout** tab, see Figure 11.50. The **Viewport** flyout appears, see Figure 11.50. In this flyout, click on the **Object** tool. You are prompted to select the object to be converted into a viewport. Alternatively, enter -**VPORTS** in the Command Line window and then click on the **Object** option in the command prompt.

```
Specify corner of viewport or [ON OFF Fit Shadeplot Lock Object
Polygonal Restore LAyer 2 3 4] <Fit>:_o Select object to clip
viewport:
```

6. Click on the ellipse drawn on the sheet as the object to convert into a viewport. The ellipse gets converted into a viewport, and the drawing created in the Model space is displayed inside it with the default scale, see Figure 11.51.

7. Double-click inside the elliptical viewport to access the Model space in the Layout. Next, select the **1:40** as the scale of the viewport in the drop-down list which appears on clicking the **Scale of the selected viewport** tool in the **Status Bar**, see Figure 11.52.

11.52

8. Double-click anywhere outside the elliptical viewport to switch back to the Paper space (layout). The scale of the selected viewport is changed to 1:40, see Figure 11.53.

11.53

Section 4: Saving the Drawing

1. Click on the **Save** tool in the **Quick Access Toolbar**. The **Save Drawing As** dialog box appears.

2. Browse to the *AutoCAD* folder and then create a folder with the name *Chapter 11* inside the *AutoCAD* folder. Next, enter **Tutorial 1** in the **File name** field of the dialog box.

3. Click on the **Save** button. The drawing is saved with the name Tutorial 1 in the *Chapter 11* folder.

460 Chapter 11 > Working with Layouts

Hands-on Test Drive 1

Create the drawing in the Model space, see Figure 11.54. After creating the drawing, create two rectangular viewports in a layout, see Figure 11.55. In the first viewport, fit the drawing completely inside the viewport, see Figure 11.55 (a). In the second viewport, zoom the object such that it appears similar to the one shown in the Figure 11.55 (b).

11.54

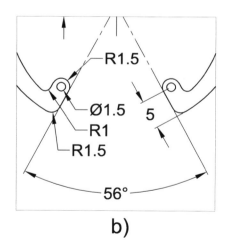

11.55

a)   b)

Hands-on Test Drive 2

Open the drawing created in Tutorial 2 of Chapter 7 and then create four rectangular viewports of equal sizes in a layout, see Figure 11.56. In these four viewports, adjust the drawing similar to the one shown in Figure 11.56.

11.56

Summary

In this chapter, you have learned about the Paper space/layout and different components of a layout (Paper space). You have also learned how to set up sheet/paper size of a layout and how to add, rename, and delete a layout. Besides, you have learned how to work with viewports, access the Model space within a viewport, clip an existing viewport, lock the object scale in a viewport, control the display of objects in a viewport, and control layer properties of a viewport. Moreover, you have learned how to switch between the Model space and the Paper space (layout). Also, you have learned how to create viewports in the Model space.

Questions

- AutoCAD is provided with two distinct working environments: _____ and _____ .

- The _____ working environment of AutoCAD is used for plotting/printing drawings and generating different drawing views.

- The _____ tool in the **Layout** panel of the **Layout** tab is used to invoke the **Page Setup Manager** dialog box.

- A viewport created in a layout is known as _____ viewport.

- The _____ tool is used to create rectangular viewports in a layout.

- The _____ tool is used to create polygonal viewports in a layout.

- The _____ tool is used to convert a closed object into a viewport.

- The _____ tool is used to clip the existing viewports of a layout.

- The _____ and _____ tools are used to lock and unlock the scale (display) of objects in a viewport, respectively.

- The viewports created in the Model space are known as _____ viewports.

- The _____ tool is used to merge or join two viewports in the Model space.

CHAPTER 12

Printing and Plotting

In this chapter, you will learn the following:

- Configuring a Plotter (Output Device)
- Creating a Plot Style
- Setting up a Default Plot Style
- Plotting a Drawing

Printing/Plotting is a process of getting a hard-copy output of a drawing. The hard-copy of a drawing is imperative to communicate ideas and information about the end product to the engineers working on the site. However, before you learn about plotting/printing a drawing in AutoCAD, it is important to understand how to configure a plotter (output device) and to set up a plot style.

Configuring a Plotter (Output Device)

In AutoCAD, a plotter is used to send the output information to the system printer for getting the hard-copy of a drawing. To configure a plotter, click on the **Plotter Manager** tool in the **Plot** panel of the **Output** tab, see Figure 12.1. The **Plotters** system window appears, which displays the list of AutoCAD plotters, see Figure 12.2. Alternatively, enter PLOTTERMANAGER in the Command Line window and then press ENTER.

464 Chapter 12 > Printing and Plotting

In the **Plotters** system window, double-click on the **Add-A-Plotter Wizard**. The **Add Plotter** dialog box is displayed with its **Introduction Page**, see Figure 12.3.

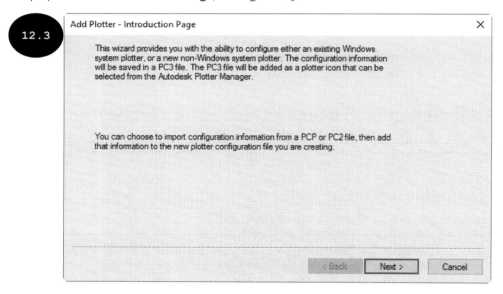

Next, in the **Add Plotter** dialog box, click on the **Next** button. The **Begin** page of the **Add Plotter** dialog box appears, see Figure 12.4.

In the **Begin** page of the **Add Plotter** dialog box, select the **System Printer** radio button and then click on the **Next** button. The **System Printer** page of the **Add Plotter** dialog box appears, which displays the list of system printers installed on your system, see Figure 12.5. In Figure 12.5, the **HP OfficeJet Pro 6960 is** listed as the system printer installed in the system. In your case, the listed printers may differ depending on which printer drivers have installed in your system. Note that if none of the printers installed on your computer, then you need first to install the printer to add it as a plotter and to take the printout of the drawing. Select the system printer from the list of printers in the dialog box and then click on the **Next** button. The **Import Pcp or Pc2** page of the dialog box appears. This page is used to import a legacy PCP or PC2 file from older versions of AutoCAD.

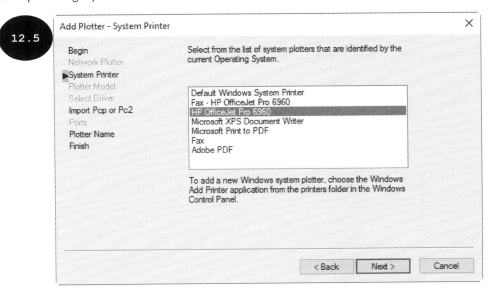

In the **Import Pcp or Pc2** page of the dialog box, click on the **Next** button. The **Plotter Name** page of the dialog box appears, see Figure 12.6. Enter the name for the plotter in the **Plotter Name** field of the **Plotter Name** page. By default, the name of the printer selected appears in this field. You can accept the default name or enter a new name for the plotter in this field. After entering the name of the plotter, click on the **Next** button. The **Finish** page of the **Add Plotter** dialog box appears. This page of the dialog box informs you that the plotter has been installed successfully with the default configuration settings. You can modify the default configuration settings of the installed plotter by using the **Edit Plotter Configuration** button of this page. Accept the default configuration settings for the plotter and then click on the **Finish** button in the dialog box. The dialog box is closed and the plotter is added in the AutoCAD.

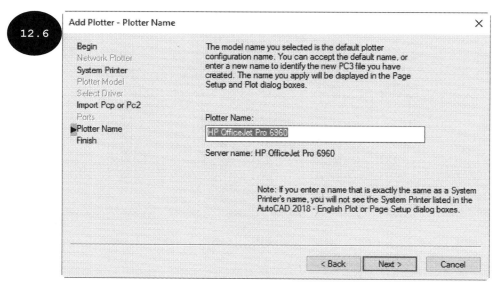

After adding the plotter and connecting the system printer with your computer through USB or wifi, you can take printouts of the drawing. However, before you start taking the printouts, it is important to understand how to create plot styles for plotting a drawing.

Creating a Plot Style

A plot style is used to define the appearance of drawing objects which include color, linetype, lineweight, line end style, and so on. Note that the plot style overrides the layer properties of the drawing objects. For example, if the red color is assigned to a layer and the blue color is assigned to the plot style then on plotting the drawing, the objects will be plotted in blue color. However, if no plot style has been assigned then the objects will be plotted in red color, which is assigned to the layer.

To create a plot style, enter **STYLESMANAGER** in the Command Line window and then press ENTER. The **Plot Styles** system window appears, which displays the list of predefined plot style files, see Figure 12.7.

In this **Plot Styles** system window, double-click on the **Add-A-Plot Style Table Wizard**. The **Add Plot Style Table** dialog box appears, see Figure 12.8. Read the given information and then click on the **Next** button in the **Add Plot Style Table** dialog box. The **Begin** page of the **Add Plot Style Table** dialog box appears, see Figure 12.9.

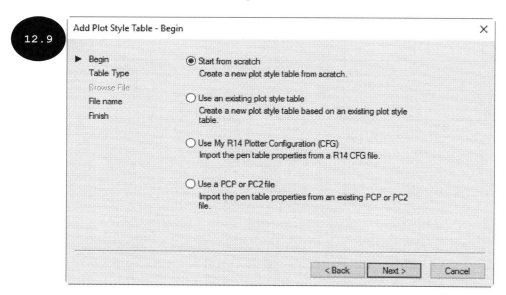

Figure 12.9

In the **Begin** page of the **Add Plot Style Table** dialog box, the **Start from scratch** radio button is selected by default. This radio button is used to create a new plot style from scratch. On selecting the **Use an existing plot style table** radio button, you can select an existing plot style as the base style to create the new plot style. On selecting the **Use My R14 Plotter Configuration (CFG)** radio button, the Release 14 *acad.cfg* (R14 CFG) file is used as the base style to create the new plot style. On selecting the **Use a PCP or PC2** radio button, the Release 14 PCP or PC2 file is used as the base style to create the new plot style. Select the **Start from scratch** radio button in the dialog box and then click on the **Next** button. The **Pick Plot Style Table** page of the dialog box appears, see Figure 12.10.

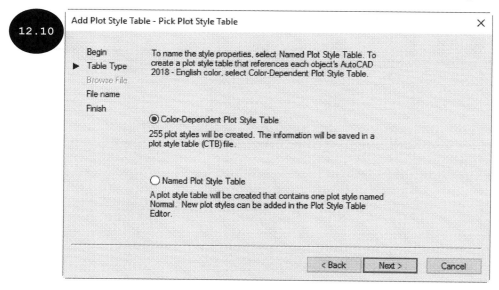

Figure 12.10

The **Pick Plot Style Table** page of the dialog box is used to select the type of plot style to be created. You can create two types of plot style: color-dependent and named plot style by choosing the respective radio buttons in the dialog box. The color-dependent plot style allows you to assign plot styles to the individual AutoCAD colors. For example, you can assign 0.5 mm width to the red objects of the drawing and 0.75 mm width to the blue objects of the drawing. In such a case, all red objects will plot with 0.5 mm width (pen) and the blue objects will plot with 0.75 mm width (pen). The color-dependent plot style is similar to the older method of highlighting the drawing objects with particular physical pen whereas, the named plot style allows you to assign plot style directly to objects or layers of the drawing instead of color only.

Select the required type of plot style in the dialog box by choosing the respective radio button (**Color-Dependent Plot Style Table** or **Named Plot Style Table**) and then click on the **Next** button. The **File name** page of the dialog box appears. Enter the name of the plot style in the **File name** field of the dialog box and then click on the **Next** button. The **Finish** page of the **Add Plot Style Table** dialog box appears, see Figure 12.11. Note that the **Finish** page of the dialog box appears based on the type of plot style selected in the **Pick Plot Style Table** page of the dialog box. Figure 12.11 shows the **Finish** page when the **Color-Dependent Plot Style Table** radio button selected as the plot style. The **Finish** page of the dialog box informs you that the plot style is created with the default settings. You can edit the default settings of the added plot style by using the **Plot Style Table Editor** button of the **Finish** page. When you click on the **Plot Style Table Editor** button, the **Plot Style Table Editor** dialog box appears. Note that the display of the **Plot Style Table Editor** dialog box depends on the type of plot style selected. Figure 12.12 shows the **Plot Style Table Editor** dialog box when the color-dependent plot style is selected, and Figure 12.13 shows the **Plot Style Table Editor** dialog box when the named plot style is selected.

470 Chapter 12 > Printing and Plotting

12.12

12.13

The **Plot Style Table Editor** dialog box has three tabs: **General**, **Table View**, and **Form View**. By using these tabs, you can edit all the properties of the plot style. The **General** tab of the dialog box displays the information such as the name, path, scale factor, and description of the plot style. In this tab, all the provided information are read only except the description.

The **Table View** tab of the dialog box displays all existing styles created in the plot style with their properties. In the case of a color-dependent plot style, the different color styles (**Color 1**, **Color 2**, **Color 3**, ... and **Color 255**) displayed in the **Table View** tab of the dialog box. You can select a color style such as **Color 1**, **Color 2**, or **Color 3** in this tab of the dialog box and then edit its properties by using the respective fields or drop-down lists of the **Table View** tab in the dialog box. Whereas, in the case of a named plot style, the Normal style is the default created style and displayed in the **Table View** tab of the dialog box. You can edit the default style or add new styles by using the **Add Style** button of the dialog box, refer to Figure 12.13. On clicking the **Add Style** button in the **Table View** tab of the dialog box, a new column with the default style name "**Style 1**" is added in the dialog box. By using the fields or drop-down lists of the newly added column (Style 1), you can change the style name, edit the style properties such as object color, linetype, lineweight, screening, and line end style.

The **Form View** tab of the **Plot Style Table Editor** dialog box displays the list of all the available styles. The available styles displayed in the **Plot Styles** area of the dialog box and the properties of the selected style displayed in the **Properties** area of the dialog box. You can select any style in the **Plot Styles** area and then edit its properties in the **Properties** area of the dialog box.

After editing the properties of the existing styles or creating new styles for the plot style in the **Plot Style Table Editor** dialog box, click on the **Save & Close** button to save the changes made and to close the dialog box. Next, click on the **Finish** button in the **Add Plot Style Table** dialog box. The plot style is created and saved as *.ctb or *.stb file in the **Plot Styles** directory of the local drive on your system. Note that the color-dependent plot style is saved with *.ctb file extension, whereas the named plot style is saved with *.stb file extension.

Setting up a Default Plot Style

After creating a plot style: color-dependent or named, you need to add the plot style in the drawing for plotting. You can add plot style by using the **Options** dialog box. To add a plot style for plotting the drawing, enter **OP** in the Command Line window and then press ENTER. The **Options** dialog box appears, see Figure 12.14. In the **Options** dialog box, click on the **Plot and Publish** tab. The options related to plotting and publishing the drawing appear in the dialog box, see Figure 12.14. Next, click on the **Plot Style Table Settings** button in the lower right of the dialog box. The **Plot Style Table Settings** dialog box appears, see Figure 12.15.

472   Chapter 12 > Printing and Plotting

12.14

12.15

In the **Plot Style Table Settings** dialog box, the **Use color dependent plot styles** radio button is selected in the **Default plot style behavior for new drawings** area, and the **None** option is selected in the **Default plot style table** drop-down list, by default. As a result, the no color-dependent style is used as the default plot style for plotting the drawing. You can select a color-dependent plot style in the **Default plot style table** drop-down list as the default plot style. To define the named plot style as the default plot style, select the **Use named plot styles** radio button in the **Default plot style behavior for new drawings** area of the dialog box. Next, select a required named plot style in the **Default plot style table** drop-down list. Also, you can select the default plot style for the objects of the layer 0 in the **Default plot style for layer 0** drop-down list and the default style for the drawing objects in the **Default plot style for objects** drop-down list of the dialog box. After specifying the default plot style (color-dependent or named), click on the **OK** button in the **Plot Style Table Settings** dialog box and then click on the **OK** button in the **Options** dialog box. The default plot style is specified. Note that the changes made in the **Plot Style Table Settings** dialog box reflects in the new drawing only (not in the current drawing).

Plotting a Drawing

After adding the plotter and creating the plot style, as required, you can plot the drawing on a sheet of paper. You can plot drawings in the Model space as well as in the Paper space (layout). Plotting drawings in Model space is usually done to create a test plot. Whereas, the Paper space (layout) is the recommended environment for plotting drawings where you can display multiple scaled drawing views in different viewports. The methods of plotting a drawing in both the environments (Model space and Paper space) are same.

To plot a drawing, activate the required environment (Model space or Paper space) for plotting the drawing. To activate the Model space, click on the **Model** tab, whereas to activate the Paper space, click on the required layout tab (**Layout1**, **Layout2**, ...) in the lower left corner of the drawing area. Next, click on the **Plot** tool in the **Plot** panel of the **Output** tab, see Figure 12.16. The **Plot** dialog box appears, see Figure 12.17. Alternatively, press CTRL+ P to invoke the **Plot** dialog box. You can also right-click on the active **Model** tab or the active layout tab and then click on the **Plot** option in the shortcut menu that appears to invoke the **Plot** dialog box.

The options in the **Plot** dialog box are used to specify plot settings such as a plotter, page size, plot area, plot scale, plot style, and drawing orientation. Some of the options of the **Plot** dialog box are discussed next.

Page setup Area

The **Page setup** area of the dialog box is used to select an already saved page setup. A page setup consists of plot settings such as a plotter, page size, plot area, plot scale, plot style, and drawing orientation. You can select an already saved page setup in the **Name** drop-down list of this area. You can also add a new page setup in the drawing by using the **Add** button in this area. To add a new page setup, first specify the plot settings such as a plotter, page size, plot area, and plot scale in the dialog box and then click on the **Add** button. The **Add Page Setup** dialog box appears, see Figure 12.18. In this dialog box, enter the name of the page setup and then click on the **OK** button. The new page setup with the specified plot settings gets added and selected in the **Name** drop-down list of the dialog box.

Printer/plotter Area
The **Name** drop-down list of the **Printer/plotter** area is used to select a configured plotting device for plotting the drawing. Choose the plotter in the **Name** drop-down list of the **Printer/plotter** area. After choosing the plotter, you can also edit or review its properties. For doing so, click on the **Properties** button in the **Printer/plotter** area of the dialog box. The **Plotter Configuration Editor** dialog box appears. This dialog box displays the information about the selected plotter. You can edit the plotter properties by using the options in the **Device and Document Settings** tab of the dialog box. Next, click on the **OK** button to exit the dialog box.

By default, the **Plot to file** check box of the **Printer/plotter** area is unchecked. As a result, the drawing will print by using the selected plotter. On selecting the **Plot to file** check box, the output can plot to a file such as .dwf, .plt, .jpg, or .png depending upon the plotter chosen. You can also plot the output to a .pdf file. For doing so, select the **Microsoft Print to PDF** option in the **Name** drop-down list and then specify the remaining plot settings. The options to specify the plot settings is discussed next.

Paper size
The **Paper size** drop-down list is used to select the standard paper size for the selected plotter. This drop-down list displays the list of standard paper sizes. Note that the availability of paper sizes in this drop-down list depends upon the plotter selected in the **Name** drop-down list of the **Printer/Plotter** area in the dialog box. If the **None** option is selected in the **Name** drop-down list, then all the standard paper sizes are listed in this drop-down list.

Number of copies
The **Number of copies** field is used to specify the number of copies to print. Note that if the **Plot to file** check box is selected in the **Printer/plotter** area, then the **Number of copies** field is not enabled.

Plot area
The options in the **What to plot** drop-down list of the **Plot area** are used to specify the portion of the drawing to print. The options in the **What to plot** drop-down list are displayed depending upon whether you are plotting in Model space or Paper space (layout). Figure 12.19 shows the **What to plot** drop-down list when you are in Model space, and Figure 12.20 shows the **What to plot** drop-down list when you are in Paper space (layout). The options are discussed next.

Display
The **Display** option of the **What to plot** drop-down list is used to plot the portion of the drawing that currently displayed on the screen.

Extents
The **Extents** option is used to plot the portion of the drawing that contains objects. By using this option, you can plot the entire drawing even if some of its objects not currently displayed on the screen.

Limits
The **Limits** option is used to plot the complete area that is defined by the drawing limits. Note that this option is available only if you are plotting the drawing in the Model space.

Layout
The **Layout** option is used to plot the drawing that lies within the printable area of the active layout. Note that this option is available only if you are plotting the drawing in the Paper space (layout).

Window
The **Window** option is used to define a window around the area/portion of the drawing to print. On selecting the **Window** option, the **Plot** dialog box disappears, and you are prompted to specify the first corner of the window. Click to specify the first corner. You are prompted to specify the opposite corner of the window. Click to specify the opposite corner. The area to be plotted is defined by the window drawn, and the **Plot** dialog box appears again.

Plot offset (origin set to printable area)
The options in the **Plot offset (origin set to printable area)** area are used to specify offset distances from the origin (0,0) to define the lower left corner of the printable area. By default, the origin (0,0) is defined as the lower left corner of the printable area, see Figure 12.21. You can specify the X and Y offset distances from the origin (0,0) to define the lower left corner of the printable area in the **X** and **Y** fields of this area, respectively.

On selecting the **Center the plot** check box, AutoCAD automatically calculates the X and Y offset values to center the plot on the paper. Note that the **Center the plot** check box is not enabled when the **Layout** option is selected in the **What to plot** drop-down list of the **Plot** area.

Plot scale
The options in the **Plot scale** area are used to control the scale of the drawing concerning the plot area. By default, the scale is set to 1:1 in the **Scale** drop-down list, see Figure 12.22. You can specify a scale for the plot in the **Scale** drop-down list, as required. When the **Fit to paper** check box is selected, see Figure 12.23, AutoCAD automatically fits the entire drawing on the paper. Note that the **Fit to paper** check box is not enabled when the **Layout** option is selected in the **What to plot** drop-down list.

On selecting the **Scale lineweights** check box of this area, the lineweights of the objects to be plotted get scaled in proportion to the specified plot scale. Note that this **Scale lineweights** check box is not enabled when you are plotting in the Model space.

Plot style table (pen assignments)

The **Plot style table (pen assignments)** area is used to select a plot style of plotting the drawing. The **Plot style table** drop-down list in this area displays the list of already created plot styles. You can select the required plot style in this drop-down list. By default, the **None** option is selected in the **Plot style table** drop-down list. As a result, no plot style is used for plotting the drawing and the drawing will plot as per the layers properties of the drawing objects. As discussed, a plot style overrides the layer properties of the drawing objects. Note that when you select a plot style in this drop-down list, the **Question** window may appear. In this window, click on the **Yes** button to assign the selected plot style to all the layouts of the drawing. If you want to assign the selected plot style only to the currently active layout, then click on the **No** button is this window.

Note: If you are working with default drawing template (*acad.dwt*), then the **Plot style table** drop-down list of the **Plot style table (pen assignments)** area displays the list of color-dependent plot styles. To display the default specified plot styles: named or color-dependent specified in the **Plot Style Table Settings** dialog box, then you need to open the drawing without the default template. For doing so, click on the **New** tool in the **Quick Access Toolbar**. The **Select template** dialog box appears, see Figure 12.24. In this dialog box, select the **acad.dwt** template file and then click on the arrow next to the **Open** button in the dialog box. A flyout appears, see Figure 12.24. In this flyout, either click on the **Open with no Template - Imperial** or the **Open with no Template - Metric** option, as required. The new drawing file with no default template gets opened.

12.24

You can also edit or modify the properties of the selected plot style by using the **Edit** button available next to the **Plot style table** drop-down list in the **Plot style table (pen assignments)** area of the dialog box. On clicking the **Edit** button, the **Plot Style Table Editor** dialog box appears, which is used to edit the properties of the selected plot style. After making the changes in the selected plot style, you can click on the **Save & Close** button in the **Plot Style Table Editor** dialog box to save the changes made and to exit the dialog box.

Shaded viewport options
The options in the **Shaded viewport options** area of the dialog box are used to plot a shaded or a rendered image of the drawing. By default, the **As displayed** option is selected in the **Shade plot** drop-down list, see Figure 12.25. As a result, the drawing objects are plotted same as they appeared on the screen. Note that the **Shade plot** drop-down list of this area is enabled if you are plotting the drawing in Model space.

On selecting the **Legacy wireframe** option in the **Shade plot** drop-down list, the drawing gets plotted in wireframe. On selecting the **Legacy hidden** option, the drawing gets plotted with hidden lines removed display style. On selecting the **Conceptual** option, the drawing objects get plotted with the conceptual visual style. On selecting the **Hidden** option, the drawing objects get plotted with hidden lines removed display style. On selecting the **Realistic** option, the drawing objects get plotted with the realistic visual style. On selecting the **Shaded** option, the drawing objects get plotted with the shaded visual style. On selecting the **Shaded with edges** option, the drawing objects get plotted with shaded with edges visual style. On selecting the **Shades of Gray** option, the drawing objects get plotted with the shades of gray visual style. On selecting the **Sketchy** option, the drawing objects get plotted with the sketchy visual style. On selecting the **Wireframe** option, the drawing objects get plotted in wireframe. On selecting the **X-Ray** option, the drawing objects get plotted with the x-ray visual style. On selecting the **Rendered** option, the drawing objects get plotted as rendered.

The options in the **Quality** drop-down list of the **Shaded viewport options** area are used to select the printing quality/resolution at which shaded and rendered drawing objects are to be plotted. You can select the **Draft**, **Preview**, **Normal**, **Presentation**, **Maximum**, or **Custom** option in the drop-down list as the plot quality of the drawing objects.

Plot options
The **Plot options** area is provided with additional options to control the display of drawing objects in print, see Figure 12.26. The options are discussed next.

Plot in background
On selecting the **Plot in background** check box, the process of plotting the drawing take place in the background only.

Plot object lineweights
By default, the **Plot object lineweights** check box is selected in this area. As a result, the objects are plotted as per the lineweights assigned to the objects and layers.

Plot transparency
On selecting the **Plot transparency** check box, the objects are plotted with specified transparency.

Plot with plot styles
By default, the **Plot with plot styles** check box is selected in this area. As a result, the objects are plotted with the specified plot style.

Plot paperspace last
The **Plot paperspace last** check box is enabled if you are plotting the drawing in a layout. By default, this check box is selected. As a result, the Model space geometry is plotted first followed by the Paper space geometry.

Hide Paperspace Objects
The **Hide Paperspace Objects** check box is enabled if you are working on a layout. On selecting the **Hide Paperspace Objects** check box, the 3D model drawn in a layout is plotted with hidden lines removed display style. You can copy and paste the 3D model drawn in Model space to a layout.

Plot stamp on
On selecting the **Plot stamp on** check box, the display of plot stamp is turned on in the plot. The plot stamp settings can specify in the **Plot Stamp** dialog box. A plot stamp is used to add a logo or additional information about the current drawing such as drawing name, layout name, date and time, and paper size. To invoke the **Plot Stamp** dialog box, click on the **Plot stamp on** check box. The **Plot Stamp Settings** button appears, see Figure 12.27. Next, click on this button to invoke the **Plot Stamp** dialog box. Alternatively, you can invoke the **Plot Stamp** dialog box for specifying the plot stamp settings by clicking on the **Plot Stamp Settings** button in the **Plot and Publish** tab of the **Options** dialog box.

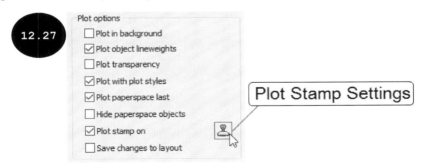

Save changes to layout
On selecting the **Save changes to layout** check box, the changes made in the **Plot** dialog box get saved with the current layout.

Drawing orientation

The options in the **Drawing orientation** area are used to specify the orientation (portrait or landscape) of the drawing on the paper, see Figure 12.28. You can select the **Portrait** or **Landscape** radio button as per the requirement to specify the orientation of the drawing. The **Plot upside-down** check box is used to flip the orientation of the plot upside down depending upon whether the **Portrait** or **Landscape** radio button is selected.

OK

After specifying all the plot settings/parameters in the **Plot** dialog box, click on the **OK** button. The **Plot Job Progress** window appears, which indicates that the process of plotting the drawing is in progress. Once the process of plotting the drawing is completed, the **Plot Job Progress** window gets closed, and you get the plotter output of the drawing.

Tutorial 1

Create the drawing in the Model space, see Figure 12.29. After creating the drawing, take the printout of the drawing on a sheet of paper with the default settings.

Section 1: Starting AutoCAD
1. Start AutoCAD and then open a new drawing file.

Section 2: Creating Drawing
1. Create the drawing and apply dimensions, see Figure 12.30.

Note: To create the drawing, you need to create different layers for hidden lines, centerlines, object entities, and dimensions. Also, for dimensions, you need to change the dimension settings such that the dimension text, dimension arrow, and so on are visible clearly in the drawing area. You can control the dimension settings either by creating the new dimension style or by editing the existing dimension style. You can create or edit the dimension style by using the **Dimension Style Manager** dialog box, as discussed in earlier chapters.

12.30

Section 3: Configuring/Adding Plotter

1. Make sure that a plotter is configured in your system. Before configuring a plotter, ensure that the system printer (output device) is installed on your computer.

   To configure a plotter, enter **PLOTTERMANAGER** in the Command Line window and then press ENTER. The **Plotters** system window appears. Alternatively, click on the **Plotter Manager** tool in the **Plot** panel of the **Output** tab in the **Ribbon**. Next, double-click on **Add-A-Plotter Wizard** in the **Plotters** system window. The **Introduction Page** of the **Add Plotter** dialog box appears, see Figure 12.31.

12.31

Next, read the information given in the **Introduction Page** of the **Add Plotter** dialog box and then click on the **Next** button. The **Begin** page of the dialog box appears. In the **Begin** page, select the **System Printer** radio button and then click on the **Next** button. The **System Printer** page of the dialog box appears. In this page, choose the system printer. If the system printer is not listed on this page, then you need first to install the printer drivers in your system. After selecting the system printer, click on the **Next** button. The **Import Pcp or Pc2** page appears. Click on the **Next** button in the **Import Pcp or Pc2** page. The **Plotter Name** page appears. Enter the name of the plotter in this page and then click on the **Next** button. The **Finish** page of the dialog box appears. Next, click on the **Finish** button. The plotter gets configured in the system.

2. Make sure that the system printer is connected with your computer through USB, Wifi, or any other mode.

Section 4: Plotting/Printing Drawing

1. Click on the **Layout1** tab in the lower left corner of the drawing area. The **Layout1** tab gets activated, and the drawing created in the Model space appears in the default viewport of the layout, see Figure 12.32. You can also delete the default viewport and create a new viewport as per your requirement by using the MV command or by using the tools in the **Layout Viewports** panel of the **Layout** tab in the **Ribbon**.

12.32

2. Click on the **Plot** tool in the **Plot** panel of the **Output** tab in the **Ribbon**. The **Plot** dialog box appears, see Figure 12.33. Alternatively, press the CTRL + P to invoke the **Plot** dialog box. Note that if the multiple drawings/layouts are opened in the current session of AutoCAD then on clicking the **Plot** tool, the **Batch Plot** window appears. In this window, click on the **Continue to plot a single sheet** button to invoke the **Plot** dialog box.

3. Select the plotter in the **Name** drop-down list of the **Printer/plotter** area in the dialog box, see Figure 12.33. In this figure, **HP OfficeJet Pro 6960** potter is selected.

4. Select the **A4** paper size in the **Paper size** drop-down list of the dialog box.

AutoCAD 2019: A Power Guide > 483

5. Select the **Window** option in the **What to plot** drop-down list of the **Plot area** in the dialog box. The **Plot** dialog box disappears, and you are prompted to specify the first corner of the plot window.

   ```
   Specify first corner:
   ```

6. Click to specify the first corner of the plot window. Note that the plot window defines the area of the drawing to be printed. You are prompted to specify the opposite corner of the window.

   ```
   Specify first corner: <Osnap off> Specify opposite corner:
   ```

7. Click to specify the opposite corner of the plot window. The plottable area is defined, and the **Plot** dialog box appears again.

8. Make sure that the **Center the plot** and **Fit to paper** check boxes of the dialog box are selected.

9. Accept the remaining default plot settings in the dialog box and then click on the **OK** button. The **Plot Job Progress** window appears, and the process of plotting starts. Once the process of plotting the drawing is completed, the **Plot Job Progress** window disappears, and the drawing gets plotted on a sheet of paper. Make sure that your printer device is connected to your computer through USB or wifi before taking the printout of the drawing. To view the preview of the plot before taking the print, click on the **Preview** button of the dialog box.

484 Chapter 12 > Printing and Plotting

Section 5: Saving the Drawing

1. Click on the **Save** tool in the **Quick Access Toolbar**. The **Save Drawing As** dialog box appears.

2. Browse to the *AutoCAD* folder and then create a folder with the name *Chapter 12* inside the *AutoCAD* folder. Next, enter **Tutorial 1** in the **File name** field of the dialog box and then click on the **Save** button. The drawing is saved with the name Tutorial 1 in the *Chapter 12* folder.

Tutorial 2

Create the drawing in the Model space, see Figure 12.34. You need to assign blue color to hidden lines, magenta color to dimensions, black color to objects entities, and cyan color to the reference lines of the drawing. You can assign these different colors to the drawing entities by creating different layers. Note that in Figure 12.34, the reference lines are turned off. After creating the drawing with different colors, you need to take a printout of the drawing by creating a color-dependent plot style named 'My Color Plot Style' such that all drawing entities printed in black color on a sheet of paper. Also, assign the 0.8 mm lineweight to the object entities, 0.65 mm lineweight to the dimensions, 0.53 mm lineweight to hidden lines in the color-dependent plot style for taking the printout of the drawing.

Section 1: Starting AutoCAD

1. Start AutoCAD and then open a new drawing file.

Section 2: Creating Layers

1. Invoke the **LAYER PROPERTIES MANAGER** and then create four layers with the names: **Object**, **Dimension**, **Hidden**, and **Reference**. Next, assign the magenta color to the **Dimension** layer, blue color to the **Hidden** layer, and cyan color to the **Reference** layer. Also, assign the

CENTER linetype to the **Reference** layer, the HIDDEN linetype to the **Hidden** layer, and accept the remaining default parameters of the layers, see Figure 12.35.

2. Double-click on the **Object** layer to make it the current layer of the drawing. A green color tick mark appears in front of the name of the **Object** layer in the **LAYER PROPERTIES MANAGER**, which indicates that the **Object** layer is now the current layer of the drawing, see Figure 12.35.

3. After creating the layers, close the **LAYER PROPERTIES MANAGER**.

Now, you can create the drawing.

Section 3: Creating Drawing

1. Create five circles as the Top view of the drawing, see Figure 12.36. For diameter dimensions of the circles, refer to Figure 12.34.

2. After creating the Top view of the drawing, activate the **Reference** layer by selecting it in the **Layer** drop-down list of the **Layers** panel in the **Home** tab, see Figure 12.37. Next, create vertical construction lines passing through the left and right quadrants, and the center of the circles as the reference entities to create the Front view of the drawing, see Figure 12.38.

3. Create the Front view of the drawing by taking reference from the vertical construction lines, see Figure 12.39.

4. Assign the hidden entities of the drawing to the Hidden layer, see Figure 12.40. Next, hide the Reference layer, see Figure 12.41.

Now, you need to apply dimensions to the drawing.

5. Make the **Dimension** layer as the current layer of the drawing and then apply dimensions to the drawing, see Figure 12.42. Note that you need to change the dimension settings such that the dimension text, dimension arrow, and other dimension components are visible clearly in the drawing area either by creating the new dimension style or by editing the existing dimension style. You can create or edit the dimension style by using the **Dimension Style Manager** dialog box as discussed in earlier chapters.

Section 4: Configuring/Adding Plotter

1. Make sure that a plotter configured in your system. Note that before configuring a plotter, you need to ensure that the system printer (output device) drivers are installed on your computer.

   To configure a plotter, enter **PLOTTERMANAGER** in the Command Line window and then press ENTER. The **Plotters** system window appears. Alternatively, click on the **Plotter Manager** tool in the **Plot** panel of the **Output** tab in the **Ribbon**. Next, double-click on **Add-A-Plotter Wizard** in the **Plotters** system window. The **Introduction Page** of the **Add Plotter** dialog box appears, see Figure 12.43.

   Next, read the information given in the **Introduction Page** of the **Add Plotter** dialog box and then click on the **Next** button. The **Begin** page of the dialog box appears. In the **Begin** page, select the **System Printer** radio button and then click on the **Next** button. The **System Printer** page of the dialog box appears. In this page, choose the system printer. If the system printer is not listed on this page, then you need first to install the printer drivers in your system. After selecting the system printer, click on the **Next** button. The **Import Pcp or Pc2** page appears. Click on the **Next** button in the **Import Pcp or Pc2** page. The **Plotter Name** page appears. Enter the name of the plotter in this page and then click on the **Next** button. The **Finish** page of the dialog box appears. Next, click on the **Finish** button. The plotter gets configured in the system.

2. Make sure that the system printer is connected to your computer through USB, or Wifi.

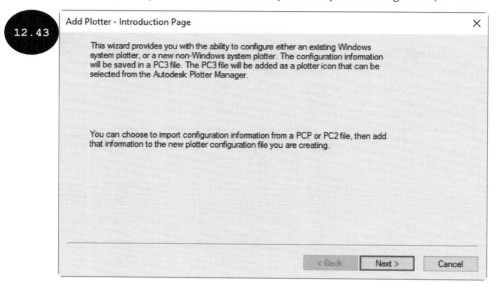

Section 5: Creating Color-Dependent Plot Style

1. Enter STYLESMANAGER in the Command Line window and then press ENTER. The **Plot Styles** system window appears, which displays the list of predefined plot style files.

2. Double-click on **Add-A-Plot Style Table Wizard** in the **Plot Styles** system window. The **Add Plot Style Table** dialog box appears. Read the information on this page and then click on the **Next** button. The **Begin** page of the **Add Plot Style Table** dialog box appears, see Figure 12.44.

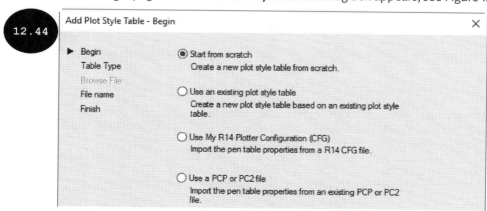

3. Make sure that the **Start from scratch** radio button is selected in the **Begin** page of the dialog box, see Figure 12.44. Next, click on the **Next** button. The **Pick Plot Style Table** page of the dialog box appears.

4. Make sure that the **Color-Dependent Plot Style Table** radio button is selected in the **Pick Plot Style Table** page of the dialog box. Next, click on the **Next** button. The **File name** page of the dialog box appears, see Figure 12.45.

5. Enter **My Color Plot Style** in the **File name** field as the name of the plot style, see Figure 12.45. Next, click on the **Next** button. The **Finish** page of the dialog box appears.

6. Click on the **Plot Style Table Editor** button in the **Finish** page of the dialog box. The **Plot Style Table Editor** dialog box appears, see Figure 12.46.

7. Make sure that the **Form View** tab of the **Plot Style Table Editor** dialog box is activated, see Figure 12.47.

8. Select the **Color 5** (blue color) in the **Plot styles** area of the dialog box. All the properties of the **Color 5** plot style appear in the **Properties** area of the dialog box, see Figure 12.47.

9. Select the **Black** color in the **Color** drop-down list and the **0.5300 mm** in the **Lineweight** drop-down list of the **Properties** area of the dialog box, see Figure 12.47.

12.47

10. Similarly, change the properties of the **Color 6** (magenta color) and **Color 7** (black color) plot styles. For the **Color 6** plot style, select the black color as the print color of the objects and the 0.65 mm as the print lineweight of the objects. For the **Color 7** (black color) plot style, select the black color as the print color of the objects and the 0.8 mm as the print lineweight of the objects.

11. After editing the plot style properties, click on the **Save & Close** button of the **Plot Style Table Editor** dialog box. The dialog box gets closed, and the plot style properties are modified.

12. Click on the **Finish** button in the **Add Plot Style Table** dialog box. The color-dependent plot style with the name **My Color Plot Style** is created.

   After creating the plot style, you can print the drawing as per the newly created plot style.

Section 6: Plotting/Printing Drawing

1. Click on the **Layout1** tab in the lower left corner of the drawing area. The **Layout1** tab gets activated and the drawing created in the Model space appears in the default viewport in the layout, see Figure 12.48.

12.48

2. Click on the **Plot** tool in the **Plot** panel of the **Output** tab in the **Ribbon**. The **Plot** dialog box appears, see Figure 12.49. Alternatively, press the CTRL + P to invoke the **Plot** dialog box. Note that if the multiple drawings/layouts are opened in the current session of AutoCAD then on clicking the **Plot** tool, the **Batch Plot** window appears. In this window, click on the **Continue to plot a single sheet** button to invoke the **Plot** dialog box.

3. Select the plotter from the **Name** drop-down list of the **Printer/plotter** area of the dialog box, see Figure 12.49. In this figure, the **HP OfficeJet Pro 6960** potter is selected.

12.49

4. Make sure that the **Letter** option is selected in the **Paper size** drop-down list and the **Layout** option is selected in the **What to plot** drop-down list of the **Plot** area in the dialog box, see Figure 12.49.

5. Select the *My Color Plot Style.ctb* plot style in the **Plot style table** drop-down list of the **Plot style table (pen assignments)** area.

6. Make sure that the **Plot with plot styles** check box is selected in the **Plot options** area of the dialog box.

7. Accept the remaining default settings and then click on the **Preview** button in the dialog box. The plot preview of the drawing appears in the **Preview** window, see Figure 12.50.

8. Right-click in the **Preview** window. A shortcut menu appears. In this shortcut menu, click on the **Plot** option. The **Plot Job Progress** window appears, and the process of plotting gets started. Once it completed, the **Plot Job Progress** window disappears and the drawing gets plotted on a sheet of paper.

Section 7: Saving the Drawing

1. Click on the **Save** tool in the **Quick Access Toolbar**. The **Save Drawing As** dialog box appears.

2. Browse to the *Chapter 12* folder inside the *AutoCAD* folder and then enter **Tutorial 2** in the **File name** field of the dialog box. Next, click on the **Save** button. The drawing is saved with the name Tutorial 2 in the *Chapter 12* folder.

Hands-on Test Drive 1

Open the drawing created in the Hands-on Test Drive 2 of Chapter 6, see Figure 12.51 and the take two copies of print on the A4 size sheets.

Hands-on Test Drive 2

Open the drawing created in Tutorial 1 of Chapter 9, see Figure 12.52 and the take the printout of the drawing in the Model space.

Summary

In this chapter, you have learned how to configure plotter (output device) in AutoCAD, how to create plot style and set up default plot style for plotting/printing. Also, you have also learned how to plot/print drawings in AutoCAD.

Questions

- The _____ tool and the _____ command are used to invoke the **Plotters** system window for configuring a plotter in AutoCAD.

- The _____ command is used to invoke the **Plot Styles** system window for creating a plot style.

- In AutoCAD, you can create two types of plot style: _____ and _____ .

- The _____ tool is used to invoke the **Plot** dialog box for plotting/printing a drawing.

- The options in the _____ drop-down list of the **Plot** area in the **Plot** dialog box are used to specify the portion of the drawing to print.

- The _____ option is used to plot the portion of the drawing that currently displayed on the screen.

- The _____ option is used to define a window around the portion of the drawing to print.

- The _____ style is used to override the layer properties of the drawing objects while plotting/printing.

- The _____ radio button in the **Begin** page of the **Add Plot Style Table** dialog box is used to create a new plot style from scratch.

- The _____ plot style allows you to assign plot styles to the individual AutoCAD colors.

- The _____ plot style allows you to assign plot style directly to objects or layers of a drawing.

- The _____ dialog box is used to setup a default plot style for plotting/printing a drawing.

CHAPTER 13

Introducing 3D Basics and Creating 3D Models

In this chapter, you will learn the following:

- Invoking the 3D Modeling/3D Basics Workspace
- Creating 3D Primitives
- Creating 3D Models
- Working with World Coordinate System (WCS)
- Working with User Coordinate System (UCS)
- Setting Work Plane to Predefined Orthographic View
- Working with Dynamic UCS
- Controlling the Display of the UCS
- Creating an Extrude Feature
- Converting a Closed Sketch into a Region
- Creating a Revolve Feature
- Creating a Sweep Feature
- Creating a Loft Feature
- Working with Presspull Tool
- Creating a 3D Wall-like Polysolid
- Performing Boolean Operations
- Checking Interference between Bodies
- Copying Edges of a Solid Feature
- Performing Modifying Operations

In this chapter, you will learn about creating 3D models. In AutoCAD, you can create three types of 3D models: solid, surface, and mesh. A solid model is filled with material and have mass properties, see Figure 13.1. It represents a real-world component. A surface model is a thin shell model that does not have mass or volume, see Figure 13.2. It is mainly used to achieve complex shape of the design. A mesh model is a polygonal representation of a 3D shape that does not have mass properties, see Figure 13.3. In this chapter, you will learn about creating 3D solid models. In AutoCAD, you can create 3D models in the **3D Modeling** or **3D Basics** workspace. The method of invoking the **3D Modeling** or **3D Basics** workspace is discussed next.

496 Chapter 13 > Introducing 3D Basics and Creating 3D Models

Invoking the 3D Modeling/3D Basics Workspace

To create 3D models in AutoCAD, you need to switch to the **3D Modeling** or **3D Basics** workspace. The **3D Modeling** workspace consists of all the tools that are required to create a 3D model, whereas the **3D Basics** workspace consists only the important or basic tools for creating a 3D model. To switch to the **3D Modeling** workspace, click on the **Workspace Switching** button in the Status Bar. The **Workspace Switching** flyout appears, see Figure 13.4. It displays a list of all the available workspaces. Next, click on the **3D Modeling** workspace in this flyout. The **3D Modeling** workspace is invoked and the startup user interface appears, see Figure 13.5. Now, you can create a 3D model by using the various 3D modeling tools available in the **Ribbon**. Alternatively, you can directly start a new drawing file in the **3D Modeling** workspace by using the *acad3D.dwt, acadiso3D.dwt, acad -Named Plot Styles3D.dwt,* or *acadISO -Named Plot Styles3D.dwt* template. For doing so, click on the **New** tool in the **Quick Access Toolbar**. The **Select template** dialog box appears. In this dialog box, select the required template to invoke the **3D Modeling** workspace and then click on the **Open** button.

Creating 3D Primitives

In AutoCAD, you can create various predefined 3D solid primitives such as Box, Cylinder, Cone, Sphere, Pyramid, and Torus. The tools to create various primitives are available in the **Primitive** flyout of the **Modeling** panel in the **Home** tab, see Figure 13.6. You can also access these tools in the **Primitive** panel of the **Solid** tab in the **Ribbon**, see Figure 13.7. The methods of creating various 3D primitives are discussed next.

498 Chapter 13 > Introducing 3D Basics and Creating 3D Models

Creating a 3D Solid Box
You can create a 3D solid box by using the **Box** tool, which is discussed next.

1. Click on the **Box** tool in the **Modeling** panel of the **Home** tab, see Figure 13.8. You are prompted to specify the first corner of the box. Alternatively, you can enter **BOX** in the Command Line window and then press ENTER to activate this tool.

    ```
    Specify first corner or [Center]:
    ```

2. Change the orientation of the drawing view to isometric by click on the **Home** icon of the ViewCube.

3. Click to specify the first corner of the box in the drawing area. You are prompted to specify the other corner of the box. You can also enter X and Y coordinates to specify the first corner of the box.

    ```
    Specify other corner or [Cube Length]:
    ```

4. Click to specify the diagonally opposite corner of the box in the drawing area. The preview of the 3D solid box appears, see Figure 13.9 and you are prompted to specify its height. You can also specify the length and width values of the box to specify the second corner of the box.

    ```
    Specify height or [2Point] <2.0000>:
    ```

5. Enter height of the box and then press ENTER. The 3D solid box of the specified height is created, see Figure 13.10.

Note: By default, the visual style for the 3D model is defined as 2D Wireframe. As a result, the 3D model appears in the 2D Wireframe visual style in the drawing area, see Figure 13.10. You can change the visual style of the model to Conceptual, Hidden, Shaded, Shaded with Edges, Shades of Gray, Wireframe, and so on by using the **Visual Styles** flyout of the **View** panel in the **Home** tab, see Figure 13.11.

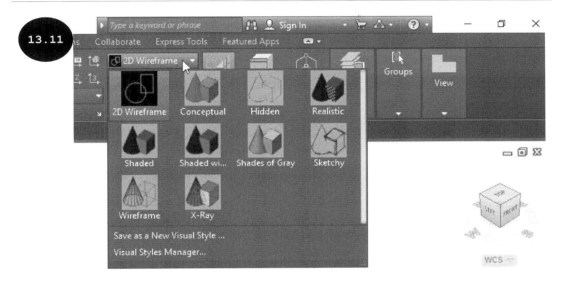

6. Change the visual style of the model to the "shades of gray" visual style by clicking on the **Shades of Gray** tool in the **Visual Styles** flyout of the **View** panel in the **Home** tab, see Figure 13.12.

Creating a 3D Solid Cylinder
You can create a 3D solid cylinder by using the **Cylinder** tool, which is discussed next.

1. Invoke the **Primitive** flyout in the **Modeling** panel of the **Home** tab and then click on the **Cylinder** tool, see Figure 13.13. You are prompted to specify the center point of the cylinder

base. Alternatively, you can enter CYL in the Command Line window and then press ENTER to activate this tool.

```
Specify center point of base or [3P 2P Ttr Elliptical]:
```

2. Click to specify the center point of the cylinder base in the drawing area. The center point is specified and you are prompted to specify its radius. You can also specify the coordinates (X,Y) to specify the center point of the cylinder base.

```
Specify base radius or [Diameter]:
```

3. Enter the radius value of the cylinder and then press ENTER. The preview of the cylinder appears in the drawing area, see Figure 13.14 and you are prompted to specify the height of the cylinder.

```
Specify height or [2Point Axis endpoint] <1.0000>:
```

4. Enter height of the cylinder and then press ENTER. The 3D solid cylinder of the specified height is created, see Figure 13.15.

Note: In Figures 13.14 and 13.15, the default visual style of the model is changed to "shades of gray" visual style.

Creating a 3D Solid Cone

You can create a 3D solid cone by using the **Cone** tool, which is discussed next.

1. Invoke the **Primitive** flyout and then click on the **Cone** tool. You are prompted to specify the center point of the cone base. Alternatively, you can enter **CONE** in the Command Line window and then press ENTER to activate this tool.

   ```
   Specify center point of base or [3P 2P Ttr Elliptical]:
   ```

2. Click to specify the center point of the cone base in the drawing area. The center point is specified and you are prompted to specify its radius. You can also specify the coordinates (X,Y) to specify the center point of the cone base.

   ```
   Specify base radius or [Diameter] <1.0000>:
   ```

3. Enter the radius value of the cone base and then press ENTER. The preview of the cone appears in the drawing area, see Figure 13.16 and you are prompted to specify the height of the cone.

   ```
   Specify height or [2Point Axis endpoint Top radius] <4.0000>:
   ```

4. Enter height of the cone and then press ENTER. The 3D solid cone of the specified height is created, see Figure 13.17.

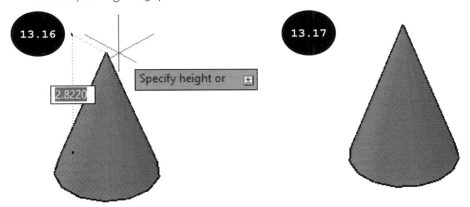

Creating a 3D Solid Sphere

1. Invoke the **Primitive** flyout and then click on the **Sphere** tool. You are prompted to specify the center point of the sphere. Alternatively, you can enter **SPHERE** in the Command Line window and then press ENTER to activate this tool.

   ```
   Specify center point or [3P 2P Ttr]:
   ```

502 Chapter 13 > Introducing 3D Basics and Creating 3D Models

2. Click to specify the center point of the sphere in the drawing area. The center point is specified and you are prompted to specify its radius. You can also specify the coordinates (X,Y) to specify the center point of the sphere.

   ```
   Specify radius or [Diameter] <1.0000>:
   ```

3. Enter the radius value of the sphere and then press ENTER. The 3D solid sphere of the specified radius is created, see Figure 13.18.

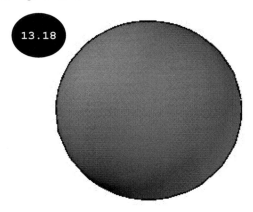

13.18

Creating a 3D Solid Pyramid
You can create a 3D solid pyramid by using the **Pyramid** tool, which is discussed next.

1. Invoke the **Primitive** flyout and then click on the **Pyramid** tool. You are prompted to specify the center point of the pyramid base. Alternatively, you can enter **PYR** in the Command Line window and then press ENTER to activate this tool.

   ```
   Specify center point of base or [Edge Sides]:
   ```

2. Click to specify the center point of the pyramid base in the drawing area. The center point is specified and you are prompted to specify the radius of an imaginary circle to create circumscribed pyramid base. You can also specify the coordinates (X,Y) to specify the center point of the pyramid base.

   ```
   Specify base radius or [Inscribed] <1.0000>:
   ```

   Note: You can create circumscribed or inscribed pyramid base. The circumscribed pyramid base is created outside an imaginary circle such that the midpoints of the pyramid sides touch the imaginary circle. The inscribed pyramid base is created inside an imaginary circle such that its vertices touch the imaginary circle. By default, you are prompted to specify the radius of an imaginary circle to create the circumscribed pyramid base. To create the inscribed pyramid base, click on the **Inscribed** option in the command prompt.

3. Enter the radius value of an imaginary circle to create circumscribed pyramid base and then press ENTER. The preview of the pyramid appears and you are prompted to specify the height of the pyramid.

   ```
   Specify height or [2Point Axis endpoint Top radius] <1.0000>:
   ```

4. Enter height of the pyramid and then press ENTER. The 3D solid pyramid of the specified height is created, see Figure 13.19.

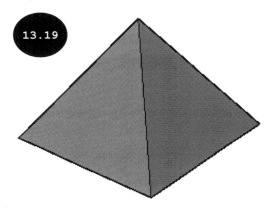

Creating a 3D Solid Wedge
You can create a 3D solid wedge by using the **Wedge** tool, which is discussed next.

1. Invoke the **Primitive** flyout and then click on the **Wedge** tool. You are prompted to specify the first corner of the wedge. Alternatively, you can enter **WE** in the Command Line window and then press ENTER to activate this tool.

   ```
   Specify first corner or [Center]:
   ```

2. Click to specify the first corner of the wedge in the drawing area. You are prompted to specify the other corner of the wedge.

   ```
   Specify other corner or [Cube Length]:
   ```

3. Click to specify the diagonally opposite corner of the wedge in the drawing area. The preview of the 3D solid wedge appears, see Figure 13.20 and you are prompted to specify its height. Note that the sloped side of the wedge is always opposite the first corner specified.

   ```
   Specify height or [2Point] <1.0000>:
   ```

4. Enter height of the wedge and then press ENTER. The 3D solid wedge of the specified height is created, see Figure 13.21.

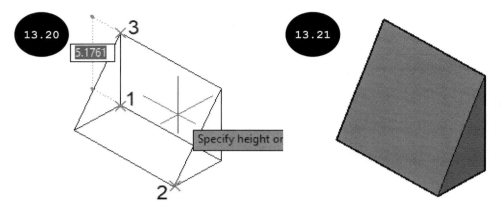

Creating a 3D Solid Torus

You can create a 3D solid torus by using the **Torus** tool, which is discussed next.

1. Invoke the **Primitive** flyout and then click on the **Torus** tool. You are prompted to specify the center point of the torus. Alternatively, you can enter **TOR** in the Command Line window and then press ENTER to activate this tool.

   `Specify center point or [3P 2P Ttr]:`

2. Click to specify the center point of the torus in the drawing area. The preview of a circle appears and you are prompted to specify its radius.

   `Specify radius or [Diameter] <4.0000>:`

3. Enter the radius value of the torus circle and then press ENTER. The preview of the torus appears and you are prompted to specify the tube radius of the torus.

   `Specify tube radius or [2Point Diameter]:`

4. Enter the tube radius of the torus and then press ENTER. The torus of specified tube radius is created, see Figure 13.22.

Creating 3D Models

In addition to creating predefined 3D solid primitives such as box, cylinder, cone, sphere, pyramid, and torus, you can create user-defined 3D features of a model by using the solid modeling tools such as **Extrude**, **Revolve**, **Sweep**, and **Loft**. In AutoCAD, to create a 3D solid model, you need to create all its feature one after another by using the solid modeling tools, see Figure 13.23. The first created feature of a model is known as the base or parent feature of the model. However, before you start creating the base or parent feature of a model, it is important to understand about the world coordinate system (WCS) and user coordinate system (UCS).

Working with World Coordinate System (WCS)

By default, when you start a new drawing file, the world coordinate system (WCS is provided at lower left corner of the screen, see Figure 13.24. The WCS allows you to create the 2D sketch of a feature on the fixed Top plane (XY plane) and add material along the Z axis only, see Figure 13.25. However, it is not possible to create all features of a 3D model on the default Top plane (XY plane) of the WCS. For example, you cannot create a feature such that its 2D sketch is created on Front plane and material is added along its normal direction by using the WCS, see Figure 13.26. Similarly, you cannot create a feature on the right side of the existing model by using the WCS, see Figure 13.27.

Figure 13.27

To overcome with this situations, you can create user coordinate system (UCS), as per your requirement, which is discussed next.

Working with User Coordinate System (UCS)

User coordinate system (UCS) is a movable coordinate system which allows you to change the position of the origin and the orientation of the X, Y, and Z axes to established the work plane (XY plane) as per your requirement. The tools to control the UCS are available in the **Coordinates** panel of the **Home** tab, see Figure 13.28 and are discussed next.

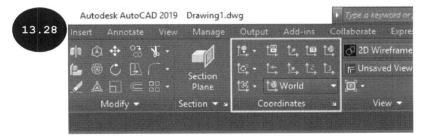

Figure 13.28

UCS

The **UCS** tool is used to create a new user coordinate system by specifying the UCS origin to the desired location. The method to create a new user coordinate system by using the **UCS** tool is discussed next.

1. Click on the **UCS** tool in the **Coordinates** panel of the **Home** tab, see Figure 13.29. The preview of the UCS is attached to the cursor and you are prompted to specify the origin of the UCS. Alternatively, you can enter the **UCS** in the Command Line window and then press ENTER to activate this tool.

Figure 13.29

2. Click to specify the origin of the UCS, see Figure 13.30. You can also enter the X and Y coordinates to specify the origin of the UCS. You are prompted to specify a point on X-axis.

3. Press the ENTER key. The UCS is created in the specified position without changing the orientation of the X, Y, and Z axes, see Figure 13.31. Now, you can create the object on the XY plane of the UCS.

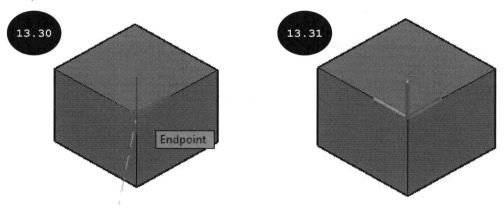

Note: After specifying the origin of the UCS, you can also specify two more points to define the orientation of the X and Y axes, respectively. The first point defines the X axis and the second point defines the Y axis of the UCS. The method to create a new UCS by specifying three points is discussed next.

3 Point

The **3 Point** tool is used to create a user coordinate system by specifying three points. The method to create a UCS by using this tool is discussed next.

1. Click on the **3 Point** tool in the **Coordinates** panel of the **Home** tab, see Figure 13.32. The preview of the UCS is attached to the cursor and you are prompted to specify a new origin point. Alternatively, you can enter the **UCS** in the Command Line window and then press ENTER to create a UCS by specifying three points.

2. Click to specify the origin of the UCS, see Figure 13.33. You can also enter the X and Y coordinates to specify the origin of the UCS. You are prompted to specify a point to define the positive X-axis of the UCS.

3. Click to specify a point to define the positive X-axis of the UCS, see Figure 13.34. The positive X axis of the UCS is defined and you are prompted to specify a point to define the positive Y-axis.

4. Click to specify a point to define the positive Y-axis of the UCS, see Figure 13.35. The UCS is created, see Figure 13.36. Now, you can create the object on the XY plane of the UCS.

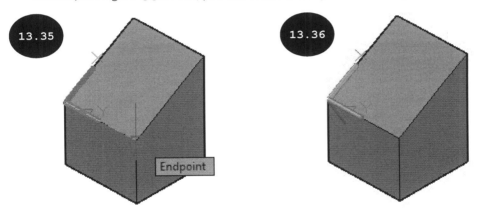

UCS, Previous

The **UCS, Previous** tool is used to restore the previous position of the user coordinate system. For doing so, click on the **UCS, Previous** tool, see Figure 13.37. The previous created UCS is restored. Alternatively, enter **UCS** in the Command Line window and then press ENTER. Next, click on the **Previous** option in the command prompt. You can undo/restore the last 10 UCS that are created in the current session of AutoCAD by using this tool.

Origin

The Origin tool is used to shift the user coordinate system to a new location by specify its origin in the desired location. For doing so, click on the **Origin** tool, see Figure 13.38 and then click to specify the position of the origin. The user coordinate system is created in the specified position without changing the orientation of its X, Y, and Z axes. Alternatively, you can use the **UCS** tool/command to create a new user coordinate system by specifying its origin, as discussed earlier.

Z-Axis Vector

The Z-Axis Vector tool is used to create a new user coordinate system by specifying its origin and the positive Z axis positions. For doing so, click on the **Z-Axis Vector** tool, see Figure 13.39 and then click to specify the origin of the UCS. Next, click to define the positive Z axis of the UCS, see Figure 13.40. Alternatively, enter the **UCS** in the Command Line window and then press ENTER. Next, click on the **ZAxis** option in the command prompt to create the UCS by specifying its origin and the positive Z axis positions.

X

The X tool is used to change the orientation of the existing UCS by rotating it around its X-axis. For doing so, click on the **X** tool in the **Coordinates** panel, see Figure 13.41. Next, specify the rotation angle of the UCS about the X-axis and then press ENTER. Alternatively, enter UCS in the Command Line window and then press ENTER. Next, click on the **X** option in the command prompt to activate this tool.

13.41

Y and Z
Similar to the X tool, the Y and Z tools are used to rotate the UCS about the Y-axis and Z-axis, respectively.

View
The View tool is used to align the XY plane (work plane) of the UCS parallel to the screen. For doing so, click on the View tool in the Coordinates panel, see Figure 13.42. The XY plane of the UCS becomes parallel to the screen. Alternatively, enter UCS in the Command Line window and then press ENTER. Next, click on the View option in the command prompt to activate this tool.

Object
The Object tool is used to create a new UCS aligned to an object. For doing so, click on the Object tool in the Coordinates panel, see Figure 13.43 and then move the cursor over the object. The preview of the UCS appears aligned to the object. Next, click to specify the origin of the UCS. The UCS is created such that its Z-axis is perpendicular to the face of the object selected. Alternatively, enter UCS in the Command Line window and then press ENTER. Next, click on the Object option in the command prompt to activate this tool.

13.42   13.43

Face
The Face tool is used to create a new UCS aligned to a face. For doing so, click on the Face tool in the Coordinates panel, see Figure 13.44 and then move the cursor over a Face. The preview of the UCS appears aligned to the face, see Figure 13.45. Next, click to specify the origin of the UCS. The UCS is created such that its XY plane is aligned to the selected face. Alternatively, enter UCS in the Command Line window and then press ENTER. Next, click on the Face option in the command prompt to activate this tool.

UCS, World

The **UCS, World** tool is used to position the user coordinate system to the default world coordinate system. For doing so, click on the **UCS, World** tool, see Figure 13.46. The user coordinate system is located to the default world coordinate system. Alternatively, enter UCS in the Command Line window and then press ENTER. Next, click on the **World** option in the command prompt to activate this tool.

Setting Work Plane to Predefined Orthographic View

In AutoCAD, you can also set the work plane (XY plane) of the UCS to predefined orthographic views such as Top, Front, Left, and Right by using the **Named UCS Combo Control** flyout of the **Coordinates** Panel, see Figure 13.47.

Setting the work plane (XY plane) to a predefined orthographic view is one of the easiest way to manage work plane for creating a 3D object. For example, to create an object on the front view, click on the **Front** tool in the **Named UCS Combo Control** flyout. The work plane (XY plane) of the UCS is set to the front view for creating an object, see Figure 13.48. In this figure, the work plane (XY plane) of the UCS is set to the front view for creating the object.

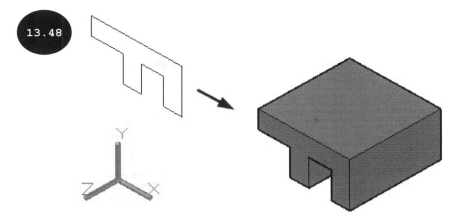

Similarly, you can set the work plane (XY plane) of the UCS to other orthographic views by click on the respective tool in this flyout.

Working with Dynamic UCS

Dynamic UCS is a temporary UCS that appears automatically when you move the cursor over a face of a 3D solid object. For example, to create a circle on a face of an existing object, activate the **Circle, Radius** tool and then move the cursor over the face of the object. The face of the object gets highlighted and the Dynamic UCS appears, see Figure 13.49 which allows you to create the circle on the highlighted face of the object. Note that the XY plane (work plane) of the Dynamic UCS aligns to the face of the existing object. To activate or deactivate the **Dynamic UCS** mode, click on the **Dynamics UCS** tool in the Status Bar, see Figure 13.50. Note that if the **Dynamics UCS** tool is not available in the Status Bar, then you need to customize to add it. For doing so, click on the **Customization** tool in the Status Bar and then click on the **Dynamics UCS** tool **in the Customization** menu that appears, see Figure 13.51.

514 Chapter 13 > Introducing 3D Basics and Creating 3D Models

You can also activate or deactivate the Dynamic UCS mode by using the UCSDETECT command or by pressing the F6 key.

Controlling the Display of the UCS

In AutoCAD, you can control the display of the UCS icon in the drawing area by using the **Show UCS Icon at Origin**, **Show UCS Icon**, and **Hide UCS Icon** tools of the **Coordinates** Panel, see Figure 13.52. Alternatively, you can also control the display of the UCS icon by using the UCSICON command.

The **Show UCS Icon at Origin** tool is used to display the UCS icon at the origin (0,0) in the drawing. The **Show UCS Icon** tool is used to display the UCS icon at the lower left corner of the drawing area. The **Hide UCS Icon** tool is used to hide the display of the UCS icon in the drawing area.

Creating an Extrude Feature

An extrude feature is created by adding material, normal to the work plane (XY). Note that the sketch of the extrude feature defines its geometry. Figure 13.53 shows different extrude features that are created from the respective sketches. In AutoCAD, you can create an extrude feature by adding material, to a closed sketch or a region, along the Z-axis using the **Extrude** tool. The method of creating an extrude feature is discussed next.

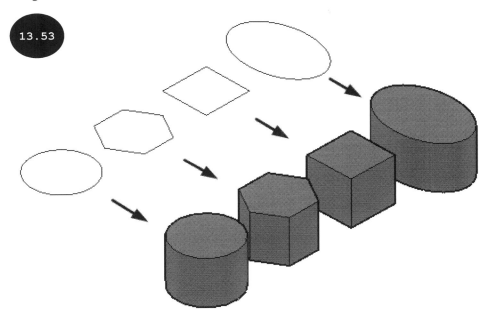

13.53

1. Create a closed sketch on the work plane (XY plane) by using the drawing tools available in the **Draw** panel of the **Home** tab, see Figure 13.54. In this figure, the closed sketch is created by using the **Polyline** tool. Note that before you create a sketch, you need to set the work plane (XY plane), as required by creating a new UCS.

13.54

> **Note:** If the closed sketch is created by using the **Line** tool, then first you need to convert it into a region by using the **Region** tool or REG command for creating a 3D solid extrude feature. You will learn about converting a closed sketch into a region later in this chapter.

516 Chapter 13 > Introducing 3D Basics and Creating 3D Models

2. Click on the **Extrude** tool in the **Modeling** panel of the **Home** tab, see Figure 13.55. You are prompted to select an object to extrude.

   ```
   Select objects to extrude or [Mode]:
   ```

3. Click on the closed sketch as the object to be extruded and then press ENTER. The preview of the extrude feature appears and you are prompted to specify the height of extrusion.

   ```
   Specify height of extrusion or [Direction Path Taper angle
   Expression] <4.0000>:
   ```

4. Move the cursor on either side of the work plane to define the direction of extrusion.

5. Enter height of extrusion and then press ENTER. The extrude feature is created by adding material of specified height along the Z-axis, see Figure 13.56.

13.55

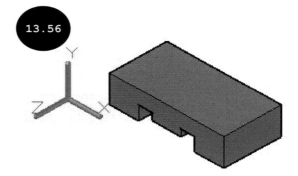

13.56

Note: You can also add tapering in the extrude feature, specify direction of extrusion other than Z-axis, or extrude along a path by using the **Taper angle**, **Direction**, and **Path** options, respectively that appear in the command prompt when you are prompted to specify height of extrusion. To add tapering in the extrude feature, click on the **Taper angle** option in the command prompt and then specify the taper angle. Next, press ENTER. The preview of the extrude feature with specified taper angle appears. Next, specify the height of extrusion and then press ENTER. The extrude feature having tapering in its all sides is created, see Figure 13.57.

To specify direction of extrusion other than the Z-axis, click on the **Direction** option in the command prompt and then specify two points to define the direction of extrusion. To extrude the feature along a path, click on the **Path** option in the command prompt and then select an entity as the path to create the extrude feature.

Converting a Closed Sketch into a Region

In AutoCAD, if a closed sketch is created by using the tools such **Line** and **Arc**, then you need to convert it into a region for creating a 3D solid feature. It is because, the entities of such sketch act as individual entities and cannot be used to create a solid feature. In AutoCAD, the individual entities or open sketch is used to create a surface feature. Figure 13.58 shows a closed sketch that is created by using the **Line** and **Arc** tools and Figure 13.59 shows the resultant surface feature created by extruding all its entities. The method to convert a sketch into a region is discussed next.

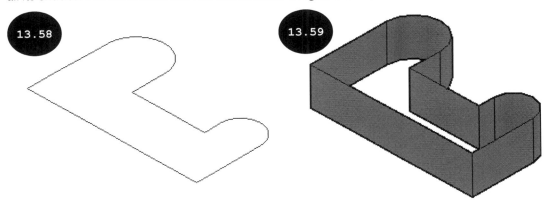

1. Click on the **Region** tool in the expanded **Draw** panel of the **Home** tab, see Figure 13.60. Alternatively, enter REG in the Command Line window and then press ENTER to activate this tool. You are prompted to select objects.

518   Chapter 13 > Introducing 3D Basics and Creating 3D Models

2. Select all entities of the closed sketch one after another by click the left mouse button. You can also draw a window around the entities to be selected.

3. After selecting the entities, press ENTER. The selected entities are converted into a region and act as a single object. Now, you can extrude the sketch to create a solid feature, see Figure 13.61.

13.61

Tip: In case of opened sketch, you can use the JOIN command to merge all the individual entities of the sketch and convert them into a single object.

Creating a Revolve Feature

A revolve feature is created by revolving the sketch around an axis of revolution. Note that the sketch to be revolved should be on either side of the axis of revolution, see Figure 13.62. You can define axis of revolution by specifying two points in the drawing area or by selecting a linear entity. You can also used the X or Y axis of the UCS as the axis of revolution. In AutoCAD, you can create a revolve feature by using the **Revolve** tool. The method to create a revolve feature is discussed next.

1. Click on the **Revolve** tool in the **Modeling** panel of the **Home** tab, see Figure 13.63. You are prompted to select objects to revolve. Alternatively, enter REV in the Command Line window and then press ENTER to activate this tool.

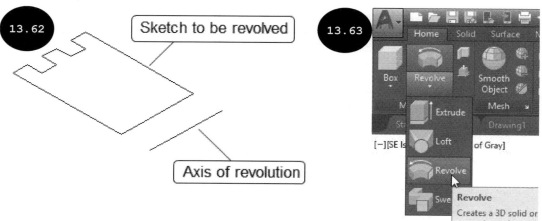

2. Select the sketch to be revolved and then press ENTER. You are prompted to specify start point of the axis or select an object as the axis to revolve the selected sketch.

   ```
   Specify axis start point or define axis by [Object X Y Z]
   <Object>:
   ```

3. Click to specify the start and end points in the drawing area to define the axis of revolution one after another and then press ENTER. The preview of the revolve feature appears and you are prompted to specify the angle of revolution. By default, the direction of rotation is defined by using the right-hand thumb rule, where the right hand thumb points toward the axis of rotation and the curled fingers define the positive direction of rotation.

   ```
   Specify angle of revolution or [STart angle Reverse EXpression]
   <360>:
   ```

   Note: To select an object as the axis of revolution, click on the **Object** option in the command prompt and then select an object as the axis of revolution. You can also revolve the sketch around the X, Y, or Z axis by using the **X**, **Y**, or **Z** option that appears in the command prompt.

4. Click on the **Reverse** option in the command prompt to reverse the direction of rotation, if needed.

5. Enter the angle of revolution and then press ENTER. The revolve feature is created by revolving the sketch around the axis of revolution, see Figure 13.64.

Creating a Sweep Feature

A sweep feature is created by sweeping a profile along a path. Figures 13.65 and 13.66 show a profile and a path as well as the resultant sweep feature created by sweeping the profile along the path. Note that the profile defines the cross-section of the sweep feature and the path defines the route followed by the profile for creating the feature. The profile and path can be opened or closed. However, if the profile is closed, the solid feature will be created, whereas if the profile is opened, then the surface feature will be created. Figure 13.65 shows a closed profile and an opened path. Figure 13.66 shows an opened profile and path. The method to create a sweep feature is discussed next.

1. Click on the **Sweep** tool in the **Modeling** panel of the **Home** tab, see Figure 13.67. You are prompted to select objects to sweep. Alternatively, enter SWEEP in the Command Line window and then press ENTER to activate this tool.

2. Select an object as the profile and then press ENTER. You are prompted to select a sweep path. Note that you can select single or multiple objects to sweep along the path. However, all the objects must be created on the same work plane.

> **Note:** You can also twist the profile along the path by specifying the twist angle using the **Twist** option that appears in the command prompt. You can also specify the base point for the sweep feature by using the **Base** option that appears in the command prompt. By default, the center point of the profile is used as the base point of the sweep feature. Moreover, by using the **Scale** option of the command prompt, you can scale the profile along the path.

3. Select a sweep path in the drawing area. The sweep feature is created, see Figure 13.68. Note that all entities or segments of the path mush act as a single object. In Figure 13.68, the path is created by using the **Polyline** tool. Also, profile and the path as well as the resultant sweep feature must not self-intersect.

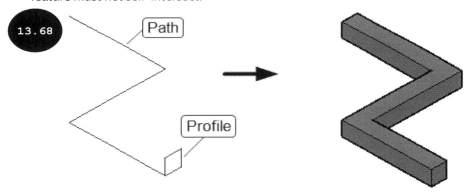

Creating a Loft Feature

A loft feature is created by lofting two or more than two profiles (sections) such that the cross-sectional shape of the loft feature transits from one profile to another. Figure 13.69 shows three profiles created on different work planes having offset distance between each other or at different elevations. Figure 13.70 shows the resultant loft feature created.

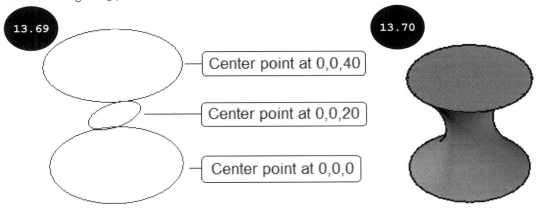

522   Chapter 13 > Introducing 3D Basics and Creating 3D Models

In AutoCAD, you can select all opened or all closed profiles to create a loft feature. Note that if all profiles are opened, then the surface loft feature will be created, whereas if all profiles are closed, then the solid loft feature will be created. The method to create a loft feature is discussed next.

1. Click on the **Loft** tool in the **Modeling** panel of the **Home** tab, see Figure 13.71. You are prompted to select cross sections in lofting order. Alternatively, enter LOFT in the Command Line window and then press ENTER to activate this tool.

2. Select all the profiles as the cross sections of the loft feature one by one in an order. The preview of the loft feature appears, see Figure 13.72. Next, press ENTER. You are prompted to select an option: **Guides**, **Path**, **Cross section only**, or **Settings** for creating the loft feature. The options are discussed next.

   ```
   Enter an option [Guides Path Cross section only Settings] <Cross
   section only>:
   ```

Guides: The **Guides** option allows you to create a loft feature with profiles and guide curves. Guide curves are used to guide the cross-sectional shape of the loft feature, see Figure 13.73. In this figure, two profiles and one guide curve is selected to guide the cross-section shape of the loft feature. You can select single or multiple guide curves for controlling the shape of the loft feature. For doing so, click on the **Guides** option and then select the guide curves.

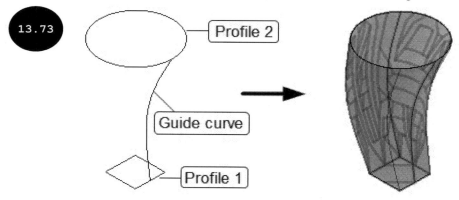

Path: The **Path** option is used to maintain the neutral axis of the loft feature and consistent transition between the profiles, see Figure 13.74. For doing so, click on the Path option and then select the path of the loft feature in the drawing area. Note that all entities or segments of the path mush act as a single object. In Figure 13.74, the entities/segments of the path are merged together by using the JOINT command. You can only select one path to create the loft feature.

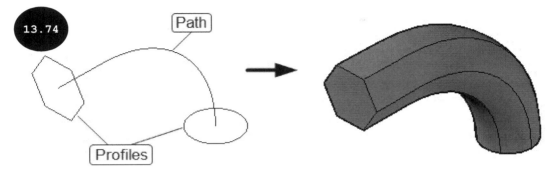

Cross section only: The **Cross section only** option is used to create a loft feature only with profiles. By default, this option is selected. As a result, to create a loft feature only with profiles, press the ENTER key.

Settings: The **Settings** option is used to specify settings such as start continuity and end continuity types for creating the loft feature. For doing so, click on the **Settings** option. The **Loft Settings** dialog box appears. The **Ruled** radio button of the dialog box is used to maintain the straight transition between the profiles of the loft feature, see Figure 13.75. The **Smooth Fit** radio button is used to maintain the smooth transition between the profiles, see Figure 13.76.

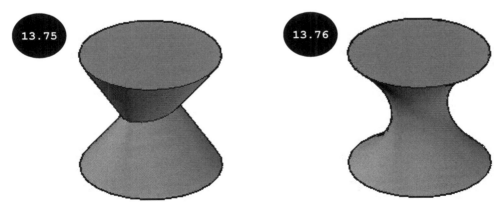

The **Normal to** radio button of the **Loft Settings** dialog box is used to create a loft feature, normal to the profiles/cross-sections. You can create a loft feature normal to all cross-sections, start cross-section, end cross-section, or start and end cross-sections by selecting the respective option in the **Normal to** drop-down list of the dialog box. The **Draft angle** radio button is used to specify the start and end draft angle and magnitude in the respective fields of the dialog box.

The **Close surface or solid** check box is used to create a closed loft feature such that the start and end profiles/cross-sections of the feature connect with each other, see Figures 13.77 and 13.78. Figure 13.77 shows the preview of a loft feature when the **Close surface or solid** check box is cleared and Figure 13.78 shows the preview of a loft feature when the **Close surface or solid** check box is selected. To create a closed loft feature, minimum three sections/profiles are required. Also, the total angle between the start and end sections should be more than 120 degrees.

3. Select the required option **Guides**, **Path**, **Cross section only**, or **Settings** to create the loft feature, as required.

4. Press the ENTER key to create the loft feature.

Working with Presspull Tool

The **Presspull** tool is one of the powerful tool for quickly and dynamically creating or modifying a solid model. This tool is used to create or edit a 3D solid model by adding or removing material depending upon whether you perform press or pull operation on a closed region of a sketch. If you pull a closed region, it adds material, see Figure 13.79 (a), whereas if you press a closed region of an existing 3D model, it removes material, see Figure 13.79 (b). The method to add or remove material by using the **Presspull** tool is discussed next.

a) Material added   b) Material removed

1. Click on the **Presspull** tool in the **Modeling** panel of the **Home** tab, see Figure 13.80. You can prompted to select an object or boundary area..

2. Select an object or a closed region (boundary area) of a sketch, see Figure 13.81. The preview of the feature appears and you are prompted to specify the height of extrusion.

3. Move the cursor in the required direction (press or pull). Next, enter the height of extrusion and the press ENTER. The material is added or removed to the selected region of the sketch, see Figure 13.82. In this figure, the material is added to the selected region of the sketch.

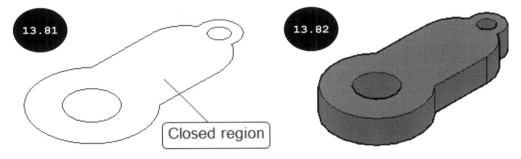

Note: You can select a closed sketch consists of lines, circles, arcs, and polylines. You can also select a region or a face of a 3D model to add or remove material by using the **Presspull** tool, see Figures 13.83 and 13.84. In Figure 13.83, the top face of the model is divided into two regions by creating a line and Figure 13.84 shows the model after removing the material by pressing a region of the top face using the **Presspull** tool.

Creating a 3D Wall-like Polysolid

In AutoCAD, you can create a 3D wall-like polysolid feature by using the **Polysolid** tool. The method to create a 3D wall-like polysolid feature is discussed next.

1. Click on the **Polysolid** tool in the **Modeling** panel of the **Home** tab, see Figure 13.85. You can prompted to specify the start point of the wall.

   ```
   Specify start point or [Object Height Width Justify] <Object>:
   ```

2. Click on the **Height** option in the command prompt and then type the height of the wall and then press ENTER.

3. Click on the **Width** option in the command prompt and then type the width of the wall and then press ENTER.

   Note: If you did not specify the height and width of the wall then the wall will be created with default height and width.

   After specifying the height and width of the wall, you can start creating the wall.

4. Click to specify the start point of the wall in the drawing area, see Figure 13.86. The preview of the wall with specified height and width appears and you are prompted to specify the next point.

5. Click to specify the second point in the drawing area, see Figure 13.86. A wall is created and you are prompted to specify the next point of the wall.

6. Similarly, click to specify other points in the drawing area one by one to create the wall and then press the ENTER key to finish the creation of wall.

13.85

13.86

Note: Instead of specifying points in the drawing area for creating a wall of specified height and width, you can select an object (a line, a polyline, an arc, or a circle) to create the wall. For doing so, click on the **Object** option in the command prompt when you are prompted to specify the start point of the wall. Next, select the object to create the wall.

Performing Boolean Operations

In AutoCAD, you can perform boolean operations such as combine, subtract, or intersect two or more than two solid features by using the **Solid, Union**, **Solid Subtract**, or **Solid, Intersect** tool, respectively. The tools to perform boolean operations are available in the **Solid Editing** panel of the **Home** tab. The methods to perform different boolean operations are discussed next.

Combining Solid Bodies

You can combine two or more than two solid features/bodies together and form a single body by using the **Solid, Union** tool and is discussed next.

1. Click on the **Solid, Union** tool in the **Solid Editing** panel of the **Home** tab, see Figure 13.87 to combine two or more than two solid features/bodies together. You are prompted to select objects. You can also activate this tool by using the UNION or UNI command.

2. Select two or more than two solid features/bodies in the drawing area one by one, see Figure 13.88. Next, press ENTER. The selected bodies get combined together and act as a single body, see Figure 13.89.

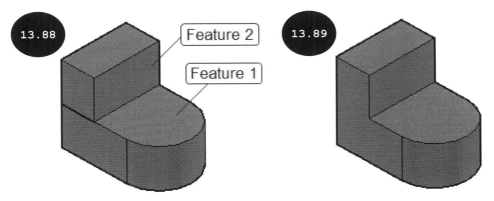

Subtracting Solid Bodies

You can subtract single or multiple bodies/feature from another body by using the **Solid, Subtract** tool and is discussed next.

1. Click on the **Solid, Subtract** tool, see Figure 13.90 or type SUBTRACT command and then press ENTER. You are prompted to select objects.

13.90

2. Select two or more than two solid features/bodies in the drawing area to subtract from, see Figure 13.91. Next, press ENTER. You are prompted to select objects as the tool bodies.

3. Select a body or bodies in the drawing area to subtract and then press ENTER. The first set of body or bodies gets subtracted from the second selected set of body or bodies, see Figure 13.92.

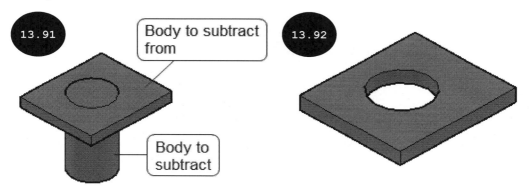

Intersecting Solid Bodies

You can create a composite solid body by only keeping the intersecting/common material between the existing bodies using the **Solid, Intersect** tool and is discussed next.

1. Click on the **Solid, Intersect** tool, see Figure 13.93 or type INTERSECT or IN command and then press ENTER. You are prompted to select objects.

2. Select bodies in the drawing area and then press ENTER. A new composite solid body is created by only keeping the intersecting/common material between the selected bodies, see Figures 13.94 and 13.95.

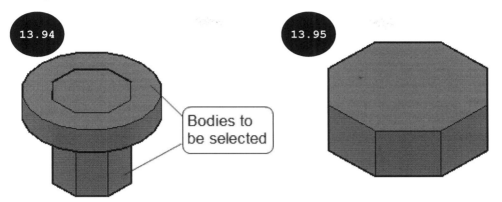

Checking Interference between Bodies

In AutoCAD, you can also check the Interference between two or more than two bodies by using the **Interfere** tool. For doing so, click on the **Interfere** tool in the **Solid Editing** panel of the **Home** tab, see Figure 13.96 or type the INTERFERE in the Command Line window and then press ENTER. You are prompted to select the first set of objects. Select the first set of bodies and then press ENTER. You are prompted to select second set of bodies. Select the second set of bodies and press ENTER. The **Interference Checking** dialog box appears which displays the results, see Figure 13.97. Also, the interference that is deducted between the selected sets of bodies gets highlighted in the graphics area. After reviewing the interference, click on the **Close** button in the dialog box to exit it.

Copying Edges of a Solid Feature

In AutoCAD, you can copy the edges of an existing 3D solid feature by using the **Copy Edges** tool. The copied edges can be used for modifying feature or creating a new 3D solid feature. The method of copy the edges of an existing 3D solid feature is discussed next.

1. Click on the **Copy Edges** tool in the **Solid Editing** panel of the **Home** tab, see Figure 13.98. You are prompted to select edges. Alternatively, enter SOLIDEDIT in the Command Line window and the press ENTER. Next, click on the **Edge** option to copy the edges.

2. Click on the edges to be copied one by one. The selected edges gets highlighted in the drawing area, see Figure 13.99. In this figure, only one edge of the existing 3D solid feature is selected.

3. After selecting the edges, press ENTER. You are prompted to specify a base point. Note that the base point acts as a reference point for copying the selected edges.

4. Click to specify a base point, see Figure 13.100. You are prompted to specify a second point of displacement.

5. Click to specify the second/displacement point in the drawing area, see Figure 13.100. You can also enter the displacement distance value and then press ENTER. You are prompted to select an option: **Copy**, **Color**, **Undo**, or **Exit**.

   ```
   Enter an edge editing option [Copy coLor Undo eXit] <eXit>:
   ```

6. Press ENTER to exit the tool. The selected edge gets copied in the specified location, see Figure 13.101. Now, you can add or remove material by using the **Presspull** tool, see Figure 13.102. In this figure, material is added by pulling a region of the top face of the model which is created by the copied edge.

Note: If you click on the **Copy** option, the **Copy Edges** tool remains activated and you are prompted to selected other set of edges to be copied. The **Color** option is used to color the selected edges of the existing model. The **Undo** option is used to undo the previously performed operation.

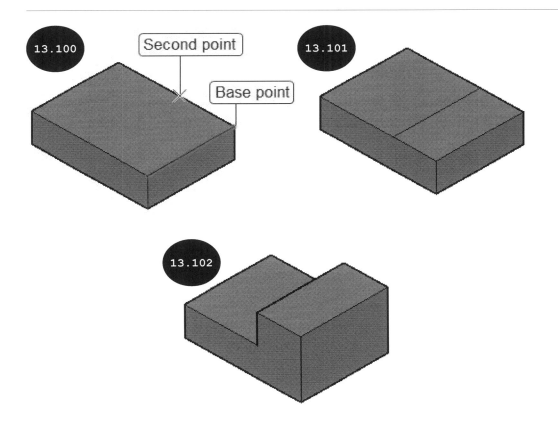

Performing Modifying Operations

In AutoCAD, you can perform various modifying operations such as move, rotate, scale, copy, array, mirror, and fillet by using the modifying tools available in the **Modify** panel of the **Home** tool, see Figure 13.103. The methods to perform various modifying operations are same as discussed earlier while creating 2D drawings.

13.103

Tutorial 1

Create the 3D model, as shown in Figure 13.104.

13.104

Section 1: Starting a new AutoCAD Drawing

1. Start AutoCAD and then click on the + sign next to the **Start** tab of the initial screen. The new drawing file with the default drawing template gets invoked.

Section 2: Defining Drawing Limits

1. Follow the command sequence given below for defining the limits of the drawing.

   ```
   Command: LIMITS (ENTER)
   Specify lower left corner or [ON/OFF]<0.0000,0.0000>: 0,0 (ENTER)
   Specify upper right corner <12.0000,9.0000>: 250,150 (ENTER)
   ```

Section 3: Selecting the Workspace

Now, you need to activate the 3D Modeling workspace for created the 3D model.

1. Click on the **Workspace Switching** button in the Status Bar. A flyout appears, see Figure 13.105.

2. Click on the **3D Modeling** option in the flyout to activate the 3D Modeling workspace.

Section 4: Creating the Base Feature of the 3D Model

Now, you need to create the base feature of the 3D model. The base feature of the model is an extrude feature.

1. Turn off the display of grids in the drawing area by click on the **Display drawing grid** button in the Status Bar.

2. Change the view orientation of the drawing to SE isometric by click on the **SE Isometric** tool in the **View** flyout of the **View** panel in the **Home** tab, see Figure 13.106.

534 Chapter 13 > Introducing 3D Basics and Creating 3D Models

3. Make sure that the Ortho mode is turned on. You can turn on or off the Ortho mode by clicking on the **Ortho Mode** button in the Status Bar or by pressing the F8 key.

4. Make sure that the Dynamic Input mode is activated. You can turn on or off the Dynamic Input mode by clicking on the **Dynamic Input** button in the Status Bar.

5. Draw a rectangle of length 72 units and width 145 units by using the **Rectangle** tool in the drawing area, see Figure 13.107.

   Now, you need to create a 3D solid feature by extruding the rectangle.

6. Click on the **Extrude** tool in the **Modeling** panel of the **Home** tab or type **EXT** and then press ENTER. The **Extrude** tool gets activated and you are prompted to select objects to extrude.

7. Select the rectangle in the drawing area and then press ENTER. The preview of the extrude feature appears and you are prompted to specify the height of extrusion.

8. Enter **25** units as the height of extrusion and then press ENTER. The extrude feature of 25 units height is created, see Figure 13.108.

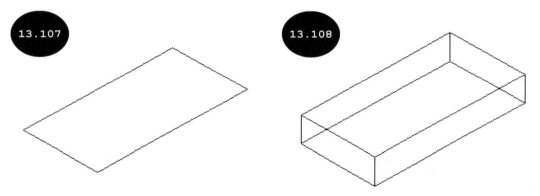

9. Change the visual style of the model to "shaded with edges" visual style by clicking on the **Shaded with edges** tool in the **Visual Style** flyout of the **View** panel in the **Home** tab, see Figure 13.109. Figure 13.110 shows the model in "shaded with edges" visual style.

Section 5: Creating the Second Feature

Now, you need to create the second feature of the model.

1. Click on the **Copy Edges** tool in the **Solid Editing** panel of the **Home** tab, see Figure 13.111. You are prompted to select edges to be copied.

2. Click on the front edge of the top planar face of the base feature. The edge gets selected, see Figure 13.112. Next, press ENTER. You are prompted to select a base point.

3. Click anywhere in the drawing area to specify the base point, see Figure 13.113. You are prompted to specify a second point of displacement.

4. Move the cursor horizontally along the positive Y-axis direction, see Figure 13.113.

5. Type **36** and then press ENTER. The selected edge is copied on the top planar face of the base feature at the offset distance of 36 units, see Figure 13.114. Next, press ESC to exit the tool.

Now, you can create the second feature by adding material.

6. Click on the **Presspull** tool in the **Modeling** panel, see Figure 13.115 or enter PRESSPULL in the Command Line window and then press ENTER. The **Presspull** tool gets activated and you are prompted to select object or bounded area.

7. Click on the front enclosed region of the top planar face of the base feature, see Figure 13.116. The preview of the second feature appears and you are prompted to specify the extrusion height.

8. Move the cursor vertically upward. Next, type 65 and then press ENTER. The second feature is created by adding material to the height of 65 units, see Figure 13.117.

Section 6: Creating the Third Feature

Now, you need to create the third feature of the model. The third feature of the model is created by removing the material.

1. Click on the **Copy Edges** tool in the **Solid Editing** panel of the **Home** tab. You are prompted to select edges to be copied.

2. Click on the front vertical edge of the model, see Figure 13.118 and then press ENTER. You are prompted to select a base point.

3. Click anywhere in the drawing area to specify the base point. You are prompted to specify a second point of displacement.

4. Move the cursor horizontally along the negative X-axis direction, see Figure 13.119. Next, type 36 and then press ENTER. The selected edge is copied on the front face of the model at the offset distance of 36 units, see Figure 13.120. Next, press ESC to exit the tool.

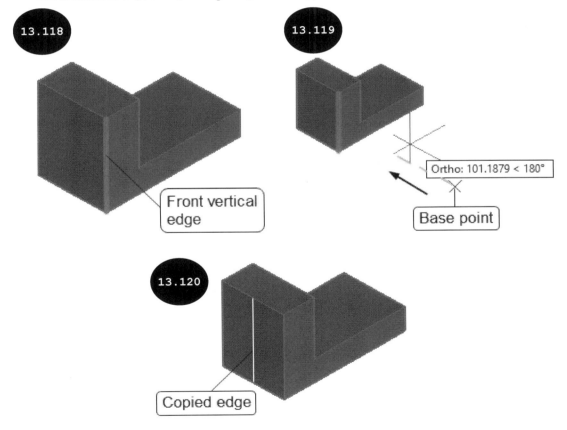

538 Chapter 13 > Introducing 3D Basics and Creating 3D Models

Now, you need to change the work plane (XY) to the Front view of the drawing.

5. Invoke the **Named UCS Combo Control** flyout in the **Coordinates** panel of the **Home** tab and then click on the **Front** tool to set the work plane (XY) to the Front view of the drawing, see Figure 13.121.

6. Click on the **Center, Radius** tool in the **Draw** panel of the Home tab and then draw a circle of radius 25 units whose center point is at the midpoint of the previously copied edge, see Figure 13.122.

After creating the circle, you can erase/delete the copied edge.

7. Type **E** and then press ENTER. The Erase command gets activated and you are prompted to select objects to be erased.

8. Select the copied edge by clicking the left mouse button and then press ENTER. The selected edge gets erased, see Figure 13.123.

Now, you can create the third feature by removing the material.

9. Click on the **Presspull** tool in the **Modeling** panel or enter PRESSPULL in the Command Line window and then press ENTER. The **Presspull** tool gets activated and you are prompted to select object or bounded area.

10. Click inside the previously drawing circle as the region to remove the material. The preview of the feature appears and you are prompted to specify the extrusion height.

11. Move the cursor along the negative Z-axis direction. Next, enter **12** as the height of extrusion and then press ENTER. The third feature is created by removing the material, see Figure 13.124.

Section 7: Creating the Fourth Feature

Now, you need to create the fourth feature of the model. The fourth feature of the model is created by removing the material.

1. Copy the top and bottom edges of the front planar face of the model to the distance of 30 units, respectively by using the **Cody Edges** tool, see Figure 13.125.

2. Invoke the **Presspull** tool and then press and hold the SHIFT key. Next, select two enclosed regions one by one by click in the left mouse button, see Figure 13.126.

3. Release the SHIFT key and then press ENTER. You are prompted to specify the height of extrusion.

4. Move the cursor toward back and then type 12. Next, press ENTER. The fourth feature is created by removing the material from the model, see Figure 13.127.

5. After creating the fourth feature, you can erase the copied edges by using the ERASE command.

13.127

Section 8: Creating the Fifth Feature

Now, you need to create the fifth feature of the model. The fifth feature of the model is created by removing the material.

1. Make sure that the work plane (XY) is set to the Front view.

2. Invoke the **Center, Radius** tool and then click to specify the center point of the circle when the cursor snaps to the center of the front semi-circular edge of the model, see Figure 13.128. You are prompted to specify the radius of the circle.

3. Type **12** and then press ENTER. The circle of radius 12 units is created, see Figure 13.129.

13.128   13.129

4. Remove the material by pressing the region inside the previously created circle using the **Presspull** tool to create a through hole, see Figure 13.130.

5. After creating the feature, you can erase the copied edge.

Figure 13.130

Section 9: Creating the Sixth Feature

Now, you need to create the sixth feature of the model.

1. Copy the edge of the top planar face of the base feature to the distance of 50 units by using the **Copy Edges** tool, see Figure 13.131.

2. Invoke the **Named UCS Combo Control** flyout in the **Coordinates** panel of the **Home** tab and then click on the **Top** tool to set the work plane (XY) to the Top view for creating the sketch on the top planar face of the base feature, see Figure 13.132.

Figure 13.131 Figure 13.132

3. Draw the sketch of the sixth feature by using the **Circle, Radius** and **Line** tools, see Figure 13.133. Note that the center point of the circle is at the midpoint of the copied edge.

Figure 13.133

4. Erase the copied edge by using the ERASE command and trim the unwanted entity of the sketch by using the **Trim** tool. Figure 13.134 shows the final sketch of the sixth feature.

5. Invoke the **Presspull** tool and then remove the material through all the model by selecting the enclosed region of the sketch. Figure 13.135 shows the model after creating the sixth feature by removing the material.

Section 10: Creating the Seventh Feature
1. Create the seventh feature by coping the edges of the model, see Figure 13.136 and then removing the material by using the **Presspull** tool to the depth of 50 units, see Figure 13.137. After creating the feature, erase the copied edges. Figure 13.137 shows the final model after creating all its feature.

Section 11: Saving the Model
1. Save the model with the name "Tutorial 1" in the *Chapter 13* folder. You need to create this folder inside the *AutoCAD* folder.

Hands-on Test Drive 1

Create the 3D model, as shown in Figure 13.138. The different views and dimensions are given in the same figure.

13.138

Hands-on Test Drive 2

Create the 3D model, as shown in Figure 13.139.

13.139

Hands-on Test Drive 3

Create the 3D model, as shown in Figure 13.140. The different views and dimensions are given in the same figure.

Summary

In this chapter, you have learned about creating 3D Models in the 3D Modeling workspace. You have learned how to invoke the 3D Modeling/3D Basics Workspace for creating 3D models. You have learned creating various 3D primitives such as box, cylinder, sphere, cone, and torus. You have also learned about World Coordinate System (WCS) and how to create User Coordinate System (UCS). You have also learned how to set the work plane to predefined orthographic view, work with Dynamic UCS, and control the display of UCS. Besides, you have learned how to create an extrude, revolve, sweep, loft, and 3D wall-like polysolid features of a 3D model. You have also learned how to perform various boolean operations, check interference between solid bodies, copy edges of a solid feature, and so on.

Questions

Answer the following questions:

- In AutoCAD, you can create 3D models in the _____ or _____ workspace.

- The tools in the _____ flyout of the **View** panel in the **Home** tab are used to control the visual style for the 3D model.

- The _____ is a movable coordinate system which allows you to change the position of the origin and the orientation of the X, Y, and Z axes to established the work plane (XY plane) as per your requirement.

- The _____ tool is used to create a user coordinate system by specifying three points.

- The _____ tool is used to restore the previous position of the user coordinate system.

- The tools in the _____ flyout of the **Coordinates** panel in the **Home** tab are used to set the work plane (XY) of the UCS to the predefined orthographic views such as Top, Front, Left, and Right.

- In AutoCAD, the _____ is a temporary UCS that appears automatically when you move the cursor over a face of a 3D solid object.

- The _____ tool is used to convert the individual entities of a closed sketch into a region for creating a 3D solid feature.

- The _____ tool is used to create a sweep feature.

- A _____ feature is created by lofting two or more than two profiles (sections) such that the cross-sectional shape of the loft feature transits from one profile to another.

- The _____ tool is used to create or edit a 3D solid model by adding or removing material depending upon whether you perform press or pull operation.

- The _____ tool is used to create a 3D wall-like polysolid feature.

- The _____ tool is used to check the interference between two or more than two bodies.

- The _____ tool is used to copy the edges of an existing 3D solid feature.

INDEX

Symbols
+VPORTS 446
2 Point Tool 82
2D Model Space 63
3 Point Tool 508
3 Point Tool 83
3D Modeling Workspace 496
3-Point Tool 86

A
Absolute Cartesian Coordinate System 66
Absolute Polar Coordinate System 69
Accessing the Model Space within a Viewport 448
Add Page Setup Dialog box 474
Add Plot Style Table Dialog box 467
Add Plotter Dialog box 464
Add-A-Plot Style Table Wizard 467
Add-A-Plotter Wizard 464
Adding Text by using the Multiline Text Tool 355
Adding Text by using the Single Line Tool 353
Adding Text/Notes 352
Adding, Renaming, and Deleting a Layout 439
Align Decimal Separators Radio button 299
Aligned Tool 306, 307
Aligned with Dimension Line 288
All Selection Method 218
Always Keep Text Between Ext Lines 290
Angular Tool 308
Annotation Scale of the Current View 38
Annotative Check box 277, 291
Application Menu 26
Applying Baseline Dimensions 317
Applying Continue Dimensions 319
Applying Dimensions 302
Applying Multiple Dimensions 320
Applying the Ordinate Dimension 315
Arc Length Tool 311
Arrow Size 282
Assigning Color to a Layer 125
Assigning Linetype to a Layer 125
Assigning Lineweight to a Layer 127
Assigning Objects to a Layer 133
Attach External Reference Dialog box 421
Autodesk App Store 29
Axis, End Tool 181

B
Baseline Spacing 278
Baseline Tool 317
BEDIT Command 413
Beside the Dimension Line 291
BLOCK AUTHORING PALETTES 415
Block Definition Dialog box 402
Block Editor 63
Block Editor Tool 413, 415
Both Text and Arrows 290
Box Tool 498

C

Canceling, Erasing and Restoring Objects 93
Cartesian Coordinate System 66
Center Tool 181
Center, Diameter Tool 81
Center, Radius Tool 80
Center, Start, Angle Tool 91
Center, Start, End Tool 91
Center, Start, Length Tool 92
Chamfer Tool 232, 233
Chamfering Drawing Entities 232
Changing the Background Color 46
Changing the Color Scheme 45
Changing the Dimension Text Justification and Angle 344
Changing the Oblique Angle of Extension Lines 343
Changing the Position of Dimension Text 346
Changing the Position of Extension Lines 347
Changing the Space between Dimension Line and Object 347
Checking Interference between Bodies 529
Circumscribed Polygon 174
Clean Screen 39
Clip Tool 449
Clipping a Viewport 449
Close Block Editor Tool 414
Close Surface or Solid Check box 524
Color-Dependent Plot Style Table 469
Combining Solid Bodies 527
Command Line Window 30
Cone Tool 501
Configuring a Plotter (Output Device) 463
Construction Line Tool 189, 190
Continue Tool 92, 319
Controlling Layers Properties for Viewports 451
Controlling the Display of Objects in a Viewport 451
Controlling the Display of the UCS 514
Convert to Block 404
Convert to Mtext Tool 358
Converting a Closed Sketch into a Region 517
Converting the Single line Text to the Multiline Text 358
Coordinate Systems 65
Copy Edges Tool 530
Copy Tool 238
Copying Drawing Objects 238
Copying Edges of a Solid Feature 530
Create Block Tool 402
Create New Dimension Style Dialog box 276
Create New Drawing Dialog box 40
Creating 3D Models 505
Creating 3D Primitives 497
Creating a 3D Solid Box 498
Creating a 3D Solid Cone 501
Creating a 3D Solid Cylinder 499
Creating a 3D Solid Pyramid 502
Creating a 3D Solid Sphere 501
Creating a 3D Solid Torus 504
Creating a 3D Solid Wedge 503
Creating a 3D Wall-like Polysolid 526
Creating a Block 402
Creating a Drawing 72
Creating a Loft Feature 521
Creating a New Layer 122
Creating a New Workspace 47
Creating a Plot Style 466
Creating a Polygonal Viewport 444
Creating a Rectangular Viewport 443
Creating a Revolve Feature 518
Creating a Sweep Feature 519
Creating a Viewport by using a Closed Object or Geometry 445
Creating a WBlock 410
Creating an Extrude Feature 515
Creating and Modifying a Text Style 352
Creating New Dimension Style 276
Creating Pre-Define Standard Viewports 446
Creating the Gradients 393
Creating the Hatches 390
Creating Viewports 442
Creating Viewports in the Model Space 454
Cross Polygon Selection Method 218
Cross Section Only Option 523

Cross Window Selection Method   216, 217
Customization Tool   39
Cylinder tool   499

D

DDEDIT Command   345, 357
Decimal Separator   293
Deleting a Layer   130
Deleting a Viewport   442
Diameter Tool   312
Different Components of a Layout   436
DIMALIGNED Command   306
DIMBASE Command   317
DIMBREAK Command   283
DIMCONT Command   319
DIMDIA Command   312
DIMEDIT Command   342
Dimension Style Manager Dialog
  box   274, 275, 276, 300
Dimension Style Tool   275
Dimension Tool   304
DIMJOGGED Command   313
DIMJOGLINE Command   314
DIMORD Command   316
DIMRAD Command   312
DIMTEDIT Command   344
Display Alternate Units Check box   295
Display Drawing Grid Button   62
Display Drawing Grid Tool   34
Donut Tool   188
Drafting Settings Dialog box   62, 63
Draw Dim Line Between Ext Lines   292
Draw Frame Around Text   287
Drawing a Circle   80
Drawing a Line   72
Drawing a Polygon   173
Drawing a Polyline   174
Drawing a Rectangle   163
Drawing a Rectangle by Specifying Area
  and One Side   165
Drawing a Rectangle by Specifying Diagonally
  Opposite Corners   164
Drawing a Rectangle by Specifying
  Dimensions   166
Drawing a Spline   183
Drawing an Arc   86
Drawing an Ellipse   180
Drawing an Elliptical Arc   182
Drawing Construction and Ray lines   189
Drawing Donuts   188
Drawing Points and Defining Point
  Style/Size   195
Dynamic Input   35
Dynamics UCS Button   513

E

Edit Block Definition Dialog box   413, 415
Editing a Block   413
Editing a Viewport   441
Editing Dimensions by using DDEDIT
  Command   345
Editing Dimensions by using DIMEDIT
  Command   342
Editing Dimensions by using Dimension
  Grips   346
Editing Dimensions by using DIMTEDIT
  Command   344
Editing Dimensions by using Editing
  Tools   349
Editing Dimensions by using PROPERTIES
  Palette   348
Editing Dimensions by using the Extend
  Tool   350
Editing Dimensions by using the Stretch
  Tool   351
Editing Dimensions by using the Trim
  Tool   349
Editing Objects by using Grips   373
Editing Objects by using PROPERTIES
  Palette   377
Editing the Dimension text/Value   345
Editing the Single Line and Multiline
  Text   357
Either Text or Arrows (Best Fit)   290
Elliptical Arc Tool   182
Equal X and Y Spacing   64
ERASE Command   93
ERASE Tool   93
Example Sheet Set   48
Existing Drawing Sheet Set   52
Extend Beyond Dim Lines   280
Extend Beyond Ticks   278

Extend Tool 221
Extending Drawing Entities 221
EXTERNAL REFERENCES Palette 420
External References Palette Tool 420
Extrude Tool 515

F

Face Tool 511
Fence Selection Method 219
Fill Color 286
Fillet Tool 230
Filleting Drawing Entities 229
Fixed Length Extension Lines 280
Fraction Format 293
Fraction Height Scale 286
Freezing a Layer 128
Freezing a Layer in New Viewports 131
Freezing the New Layer in All Viewports 131

G

Getting Started with AutoCAD 18
Getting Started with Paper Space/Layout 436
Gradient Tool 394
Grid On Check box 63
Grid Settings Option 62
Grid Spacing 64
Grid Style 63
Grid X Spacing 64
Grid Y Spacing 64
Guides Option 522

H

Hatch Tool 390
Help 30
Hide UCS Icon Tool 514

I

ID Point Tool 379
Identifying Coordinates of a Point 379
InfoCenter 29
Inscribed Polygon 173
INSERT Command 412
Insert Dialog box 407, 408
Insert Tool 407, 412
Inserting a Block in the Drawing 407
Inserting a WBlock in the Drawing 412
Installing AutoCAD 18
Interfere Tool 529
Interference Checking Dialog box 529
Intersecting Solid Bodies 528
Invoking a Selection Method within a Command 217
Invoking the 3D Modeling/3D Basics Workspace 496
Isolate Objects 39
Isometric Drafting 35

J

Jogged Linear Tool 314
Jogged Tool 313
Joining Two Viewports 455

L

Last Selection Method 219
LAYER PROPERTIES MANAGER 121, 122
Layer Properties Tool 121
Leading Check box 294
Lengthen Tool 243
Lengthening Drawing Objects 243
LIMITS 61
Line Tool 72
Linear Tool 304
Linetype 278
Linetype Ext Line 1 279
Linetype Ext Line 2 279
Lineweight 278
Lineweight Dialog box 127
Load Button 126
Load or Reload Linetypes Dialog box 126
Lock Tool 450, 451
Locking or Unlocking a Layer 129
Locking the Object Scale in a Viewport 450
Loft Settings Dialog box 523, 524
Loft Tool 522

M

Major Line Every 64
Making a Dynamic Block 415
Match Properties Tool 377
Matching Properties of an Object 377

Menu Bar   304
Mirror Tool   228
Mirroring Drawing Entities   228
Mirroring Objects by using Grips   376
Model or Paper Space   34
Modify Dimension Style Dialog box   301
Modifying Existing Dimension Style   300
Move Tool   237
Moving Drawing Objects   237
Moving Objects by using Grips   374
Multiline Text Tool   355
Multiple Points Tool   195
MVIEW Command   443

N
Named Plot Style Table   469
Navigating 2D Drawing   94
Navigation Bar   33
New Layer Button   122
New Tool   23, 40

O
Object Snap   36
Object Snap Button   117
Object Snap Settings Option   117
Object Snap Tracking   36
Object Snap Tracking Button   120
Object Snap Tracking Mode   119
Object Tool   511
Offset From Dim Line   288
Offset From Origin   280
Offset Tool   235
Offsetting Drawing Entities   235
Open Read-Only Option   54
Open Tool   53
Opening a Drawing File   53
Ordinate Tool   316
Origin Tool   510
Ortho Mode   35
Ortho Mode Button   109
Over Dimension Line, without Leader   291
Over the Dimension Line, with Leader   291
Override Button   301
Override Current Style Dialog box   301, 302
Overriding Dimension Style   301

P
Page Setup Dialog box   438
Page Setup Manager Dialog box   437, 438
Page Setup Manager Option   437
Page Setup Tool   437
Pan   98
Partial Open Option   54
Path Array Tool   227
Path Option   523
Performing Boolean Operations   527
Performing Modifying Operations   532
Place Text Manually   292
Plot Dialog box   473
Plot Style Table Settings Dialog box   471, 472
Plot Tool   473
Plotter Manager Tool   463
PLOTTERMANAGER   463
Plotting a Drawing   473
POINT Command   195
Point Style Dialog box   195, 196
Point Style Tool   195
Polar Array Tool   225
Polar Coordinate System   69
Polar Tracking   35
Polar Tracking Button   112
Polar Tracking Mode   112
Polygon Tool   173
Polyline Tool   174
Polyline with Halfwidth   179
Polyline with Line and Arc Segments   176
Polyline with Line Segments   175
Polyline with Width   178
Polysolid Tool   526
Precision   293
Prefix   293
Presspull Tool   524
PROPERTIES Palette   348, 377
Properties Tool   348, 377
Property Settings Dialog box   378
Pyramid Tool   502

Q
QDIM Command   320
Quick Access Toolbar   27
Quick Dimension Tool   320

R

Radius Tool 311, 312
Ray Tool 189, 194
Rectangle Array Tool 224
Rectangle at an Angle 167
Rectangle Tool 163, 164, 165, 166
Rectangle with Chamfer 168
Rectangle with Elevation 170
Rectangle with Fillets 169
Rectangle with Thickness 171
Rectangle with Width 172
Rectangular Tool 444
Region Tool 517
Relative Cartesian Coordinate System 68
Relative Polar Coordinate System 70
Restoring the Dimension Text to Original Position 343
Restoring Viewports 455
Restricting a Layer for Plotting 130
Revolve Tool 518
Ribbon 27
Rotate Tool 239
Rotating Drawing Objects 239
Rotating Objects by Using Grips 375
Rotating the Dimension Text 342
Round Off 293

S

Save Block Tool 414
Save Drawing As Dialog box 55
Save Tool 54
Saving a Drawing File 54
Scale Dimensions to Layout 291
Scale Tool 240
Scaling Drawing Objects 240
Scaling Objects by using Grips 376
Search 29
Select Color Dialog box 125
Select Linetype Dialog box 125, 126
Select Template Dialog box 23, 24
Set Current Button 124
Setting Drawing Limits 61
Setting the Current Layer 123
Setting Transparency of a Layer 130
Setting up a Default Plot Style 471
Setting up Drawing Units 57
Setting up the Sheet/Paper Size of a Layout 437
Setting Work Plane to Predefined Orthographic View 512
Shades of Gray Tool 499
Sheet Sets 48
Show Annotation Objects 38
Show UCS Icon at Origin Tool 514
Show UCS Icon Tool 514
Show/Hide Lineweight 38
Sign In 29
Sign In to Autodesk Account Tool 29
Single Line Tool 353
Snap Mode 34
Snap On Check box 64
Snap Spacing 64
Snap X Spacing 64
Snap Y Spacing 64
Solid, Intersect Tool 528
Solid, Subtract Tool 527
Solid, Union Tool 527
Specifying Grid and Snap Settings 62
Specifying the New Dimension Text/Value 342
Sphere Tool 501
Spline CV Tool 186
Spline Fit Tool 184
Start from Scratch Button 40
Start, Center, Angle Tool 88
Start, Center, End Tool 87
Start, Center, Length Tool 89
Start, End, Angle Tool 89
Start, End, Direction Tool 90
Start, End, Radius Tool 90
Starting a New Drawing File 23
Starting a New Drawing file by Using a Template 41
Starting a New Drawing file by Using a Wizard 41
Starting a New Drawing File by Using the Create New Drawing Dialog box 40
Starting a New Drawing file from Scratch 40
Status Bar 33
Stay Connected 29
Stretch Tool 242
Stretching Drawing Objects 242
Stretching Objects by Using Grips 374

STYLESMANAGER 467
Subtracting Solid Bodies 527
Suffix 293
Suppress 279
Suppress Arrows if they Don't Fit Inside
    Extension Lines 290
Sweep Tool 520
Switching Between Workspaces 47
Switching to the Model Space 453

T

Tan, Tan, Radius Tool 84
Tan, Tan, Tan Tool 85
Text Color 286
Text Height 286
Text Style 285
Text Style Dialog box 285, 352
Text Style Tool 352
Toggle Override Highlight 131
Tolerance Format 297
Torus Tool 504
Trailing Check box 294
Trim Tool 220
Trimming Drawing Entities 220
Turning a Layer On or Off 128
TXT2MTXT Command 358

U

UCS Tool 507
UCS, Previous Tool 509
UCS, World Tool 512
Understanding Coordinate Systems 65
Understanding Different Components of a
    Layout 436
Undo Command 93
Unlock Tool 450, 451
Use a Template Button 41
Use a Wizard Button 41
Use Overall Scale of 291
User Coordinate System (UCS) 507

V

View Tool 511
ViewCube 31
Viewport Color 452
Viewport Configuration 454
Viewport Freeze 452
Viewports Dialog box 446
Visual Styles 499
-VPORTS 443, 444

W

WBLOCK Command 410
Wedge Tool 503
Window Polygon Selection Method 218
Window Selection Method 216, 217
Working with Components of a
    Dimension 274
Working with Dynamic UCS 513
Working with External References (Xrefs) 419
Working with Layers 121
Working with Object Selection Methods 216
Working with Object Snap 117
Working with Object Snap Tracking 119
Working with Ortho Mode 109
Working with Polar Tracking 112
Working with Presspull Tool 524
Working with Sheet Sets 48
Working with the Array 223
Working with User Coordinate System
    (UCS) 507
Working with Various Components of a
    Drawing 26
Working with Viewports 440
Working with Workspaces 47
Working with World Coordinate
    System (WCS) 506
Workspace Switching 38
Workspace Switching Button 47, 496
World Coordinate System (WCS) 506
Write Block Dialog box 410
Write Block Tool 410

X

X Tool 510

Z

Z-Axis Vector Tool   510
Zoom   94
Zoom All   95
Zoom Extents   96
Zoom In   97
Zoom Out   97
Zoom Previous   96
Zoom Realtime   94
Zoom Window   96

Manufactured by Amazon.ca
Bolton, ON

11523692R00304